ITALY IN THE MODERN

Also Published by Bloomsbury

FLORENCE: CAPITAL OF THE KINGDOM OF ITALY, 1865–71 (2017)
Edited by Monika Poettinger and Piero Roggi

MODERN ITALY IN HISTORICAL PERSPECTIVE (2010)
by Nick Carter

ITALY IN THE MODERN WORLD

SOCIETY, CULTURE, AND IDENTITY

Linda Reeder

BLOOMSBURY ACADEMIC
LONDON • NEW YORK • OXFORD • NEW DELHI • SYDNEY

BLOOMSBURY ACADEMIC
Bloomsbury Publishing Plc
50 Bedford Square, London, WC1B 3DP, UK
1385 Broadway, New York, NY 10018, USA

BLOOMSBURY, BLOOMSBURY ACADEMIC and the Diana logo are trademarks
of Bloomsbury Publishing Plc

First published in Great Britain 2020

Cover design: Adriana Brioso
Cover image: Fly TWA Italy poster by Lacano (© David Pollack/Corbis via Getty Images)

A catalogue record for this book is available from the British Library.

A catalog record for this book is available from the Library of Congress.

ISBN: HB: 978-1-3500-0518-1
PB: 978-1-3500-0517-4
ePDF: 978-1-3500-0519-8
eBook: 978-1-3500-0520-4

Typeset by Deanta Global Publishing Services, Chennai, India
Printed and bound in Great Britain

To find out more about our authors and books visit www.bloomsbury.com
and sign up for our newsletters.

CONTENTS

Contents

ILLUSTRATIONS

Figures

Maps

Tables

PART ONE
ITALIANS AND THE MAKING
OF ITALY (c.1800-71)

Historians and the Risorgimento

The 150th anniversary of Italian unification in 2011 marked an occasion for reevaluating the meaning of the Risorgimento.[1] The term "Risorgimento," commonly translated as resurgence, generally encompasses the period between 1815 and 1861, when Italy emerged as a modern nation-state. Beyond its chronological and geographical meaning, the word has been inseparable from politics. The term first appeared in the late 1840s as a means to fuse the multitude of revolutionary and reformist movements into an inexorable force for Italian liberation. After unification, scholars, politicians, and critics used the term to attack, or defend, the legitimacy of the nation-state. In the last two decades, a new body of historical literature uncoupled the Risorgimento from debates about the success or failure of the liberal state. Rejecting the notion that the Risorgimento was a decisive break between one world and another, a wealth of new historical studies offers a more nuanced analysis of the social, cultural, and political processes that culminated in the creation of modern Italy.

Early Risorgimento histories mined the past for proof of Italy's national destiny and for patriotic heroes. Two decades of revolutionary turmoil and the election of a seemingly progressive pope inspired the first histories. In chronicles of the revolutions of 1820s and 1830s, and biographies of Italian patriots and martyrs, historians unearthed evidence of the inevitability of Italian independence.[2] After unification, these hagiographic and historic works took on a political cast. Scholars sympathetic to the moderates emphasized the astute political and diplomatic roles played by the Savoyard monarchy and Count Camillo Benso di Cavour in the process of unification. Those on the left highlighted the importance of the democratic revolutionary movements. By 1880, elements of the democratic histories had woven themselves into celebratory narratives privileging the role of moderate elites in the creation of a constitutional monarchy replete with unified Italy and a pantheon of founding fathers including Garibaldi, Mazzini, Cavour, and Vittorio Emanuele.

In the 1890s, historians challenged this optimistic vision. Surveying Italy at the end of the nineteenth century, historians wondered why the state seemed incapable of building a firm democratic base or claiming its place among the great powers of Europe. The central political tension of the Risorgimento—the struggle between regional authority and central state power—continued to plague the new state. In the first decades of the twentieth century, the idea of an unfinished or incomplete Risorgimento gained traction among moderates and Nationalists. The need to realize the dreams of the Risorgimento justified arguments for a stronger central state and imperial expansion.[3]

For much of the twentieth century, the historiography of the Risorgimento was held hostage by fascism. After 1945 two competing arguments emerged: a liberal vision arguing that the success of the Risorgimento and the liberal state proved fascism to be an aberration; a leftist interpretation claiming that the seeds of fascism were sown in the failure of the Risorgimento. Liberal historians embraced the ideas of the historian Benedetto Croce. Croce's central thesis held that the ideals of liberalism, unification, and modernization embedded in the Risorgimento were realized in the liberal state. Fascism was an anomaly, born solely from the chaos and horror of the First World War.[4] Throughout the 1950s and 1960s, most liberal historians followed Croce's path, examining the financial, political, and social difficulties faced by nineteenth-century Italian liberal elite. Some lauded Cavour for his daring embrace of reform and diplomacy, while others applauded the pragmatism and economic savvy of the moderates. Liberals insisted that the idea that the elite's failure to mobilize the peasantry proved the Risorgimento a failure was pure fantasy. Rosario Romeo, a leading liberal historian of the postwar era, argued that the prosperity of the liberal state depended on the exclusion of the peasantry. A few contended that Italy's protectionist policies weakened the state in ways that thwarted the development of liberal institutions. In either case, liberal historians generally agreed that the unification of Italy was an astounding achievement, despite the challenges posed by geographic disunity, reactionary governments, poor fiscal decisions, or economic backwardness.[5]

Meanwhile, Marxist historians insisted that fascism proved the Risorgimento a failure. The historical narrative of the left was based on the prison writings of Antonio Gramsci, a political theorist and founding member of Italy's Communist Party who spent over a decade in a Fascist prison. Gramsci's thoughts on the Risorgimento appeared in the posthumously published collection subsequently entitled *Prison Notebooks* in 1947. According to Gramsci, the Risorgimento was an incomplete, or "passive," revolution marked by political and institutional changes but not by structural transformations. The preunification social and political elites adapted to parliamentary rule and capitalism without altering existing social relations. In the decades following unification the liberal state remained weak, while social and geographic divisions widened, enabling fascism to take root.[6] In the following decades, Marxist historians looked to the first decades of the nineteenth century for evidence to support Gramsci's hypothesis, and to seek historical explanations for the failure of Risorgimento democrats to mobilize the peasantry, and realize a social revolution.[7] In the 1960s and 1970s, Marxist historians widened the chronological limits of the Risorgimento, expanding into the late eighteenth century, without substantially altering the terms of the debate. The publication of the first and third volumes of the *Storia d'Italia* by Einaudi were informed by Gramsci's theory of failure, reinforcing the image of Italian liberalism as conservative and limited in nature.

A notion of Italian exceptionalism emerged from both moderate and leftist historical interpretations. The Croce/Gramsci framework suggested that Italy alone of the European powers had failed to lay the foundations of a modern industrial nation, and embarked on its own unique path of development. Rejecting the liberal idealization of the founding fathers and the Marxist demonization of the Italian bourgeoisie, some historians conceived of the Risorgimento as a kind of historical accident. According to these scholars, unification was an unplanned process, a consequence of the bumbling responses of Cavour, and the moderate liberals to the threat of democratic revolution, the growing anti-monarchical sentiment, and the repressive restoration governments.[8] Although the works of Denis Mack Smith in particular proved controversial in Italy, the body of work opened up new avenues of research. By the 1970s, liberal historians acknowledged character flaws in their heroes, and Marxists recognized that the Risorgimento movement was not as elitist as some suggested.[9]

In the 1980s, a new generation of historians came of age within the academy transfiguring the history of the Risorgimento. Born after 1945, informed by the student movements and feminism, these scholars found arguments about Risorgimento victories or defeats irrelevant, and instead focused on understanding the social, economic, and political changes on their own terms. Mining new sources, appropriating new methodologies, and widening the range of historical subjects to include women, rural residents, workers, and elites, historians produced a wide range of works focusing on the how and the why Italian unification occurred. Scholars explored the multiple visions of resistance, liberation, renovation, and independence that spread through the Italian states. A united liberal Italy was just one of the many possible outcomes, not the driving force of the Risorgimento. These new works expanded the fields' chronological and geographic boundaries and challenged assumptions about the nature of the Restoration and the Risorgimento.[10]

In the new histories, the Italian Restoration appears less repressive, and more as a conservative force of change. Focusing on processes of state formation, these new studies describe a world trying to come to terms with the post-1789 realities. While acknowledging that Restoration rulers did, at times, attempt to turn the clock back to squash political dissent, their efforts were generally short lived and followed by careful reforms seeking to stave off revolution by creating more liberal governments.[11] Reconsideration of Restoration politics accompanied a reevaluation of Italian society. Scholars had long pointed to the absence of an Italian middling class, similar to the British industrial bourgeoisie, as one of the explanations for the Risorgimento's failure to realize a social revolution. By abandoning north European models of class formation that identified the middle classes with industry, urbanization, and manufacturing, scholars discovered a distinct Italian middling class, linked by land, kin networks, and culture. The Italian inclination to rely on land for wealth and status was not a sign of backwardness but a rational response to material conditions. The rehabilitation of the Restoration uncovered a more diverse and dynamic Italy, where local elites, often in conjunction with governments, engaged in local modernization programs.[12] These works deepened our understanding of the forces that shaped the Risorgimento, but did little to explain why an idea of creating an Italian nation took hold in the first place.

Intrigued by the question, a few historians began to trace the emergence of symbols and rhetoric of Italian rebirth shared by the reformers and revolutionaries. While historians

3

agreed there was little evidence of the existence of a coherent political Nationalist movement in the first decades of the nineteenth century, new works suggested that there was evidence of a national-patriotic cultural movement.[13] Analyzing early nineteenth-century novels, essays, and poetry, Alberto Banti found signs of an emerging national identity, anchored in a common past and culture. The cultural turn produced a wealth of new research on the nationalizing influence of cultural, scientific, literary, and intellectual associations. Considering the Risorgimento as a cultural revolution, spreading the idea of an Italian nation tied by blood, sentiment, and history suggests the existence of a much more expansive and fluid movement deeply embedded in a wider community. Without negating the importance of diplomacy, state building, secret societies, and political movements in the unification of Italy, these works help explain how diverse regional movements found common ground in a shared vision of an independent nation-state.[14]

The new approaches made visible women's involvement in the Risorgimento, and the constitutive role gender played shaping Nationalist visions. Cultural approaches widened the definition of the political to include household and family. The erosion of the boundaries between public and private spaces brought new attention to women's participation in the movement. Women hosted salons, published works promoting Nationalist ideas, joined patriotic societies, took to the streets during uprisings, and voted in plebiscites.[15] Beyond women's involvement in the Nationalist cause, scholars have explored the gendered nature of the Risorgimento project. At the center of the Cultural Revolution stood the conviction that independence and liberty could remake men and women. The Risorgimento was as much about transforming effeminate and decadent men into soldiers, citizens, and workers, and masculine women into mothers and wives, as it was about forging political boundaries.[16]

Tracing the cultural Risorgimento made apparent its transnational dimension. New research maintained mobility was integral to the creation of both an imagined and a physical Italy. Italian patriots were physically and intellectually linked to international communities. Donna Gabaccia's work on the Italian diaspora pointed to the emergence of an "Italy" among emigrant communities in the Americas and Europe long before the notion of a unified state gained traction. More recently, scholars have explored the metaphoric and material importance of exile. Symbolically, exile was central to the Risorgimento imagination, and materially, the foreign communities provided sanctuary, money, and support.[17]

While recognizing the significant ways the works of cultural revisionism has reshaped the geographic and social landscape of the Risorgimento, not all historians are willing to reject conflict as integral to the process of unification. Italy was born out of wars that had winners and losers. In 2008, Eva Cecchinato and Mario Isnenghi published the first volume of a multivolume work on the history of Italy. In the collection of essays on the Risorgimento, Isnenghi and Cecchinato suggest that the emergence of a national culture, and political movements that shared vision of an independent nation, also created divisions. Isnenghi and Cecchinato stress the cultural, political, social, gendered, and geographic divides that characterized the Risorgimento process. The sixty-odd essays focus on social actors, key places, and representation and memory that incorporate the experiences of both the "winners," the democratic and moderate patriots, and the "losers," the reactionary movements led by crown and church, into the foundation of Italy.[18]

The new framework encourages historians to consider the evolving positions of institutions, governments, and people in relation to various forms of Italian patriotism. This insight has led to a reevaluation of the role of the church. Long seen as an intractable force of opposition, revisionist histories suggest that the institution played a more complicated role. Acknowledging that after 1848, the pope stood as a formidable enemy of the state; the anticlericalism of Italian independence did not mean that Italians jettisoned their beliefs or practices. Popular religion was instrumental in shaping support for Italian unification, yet we have little understanding of how the religiosity of the Risorgimento informed relations between church and state in the liberal era.[19]

Current historical trajectories revised the geography of the Risorgimento. The reactionary bent of the Bourbon monarchy went largely unquestioned, and the notion that southern Italians played a central role in the struggles for independence and liberation was generally dismissed. Reassessments of the Restoration and Italian nationalism suggest that southern Italians—wealthy, poor, rural, and urban—were sympathetic to revolutionary change and receptive to the idea of an independent Italy, although many opposed a state dominated by Piedmont. Scholars have revisited the "war of the *brigantaggio*," the civil war that broke out in the aftermath of unification and long seen as the last gasp of ancien régime opposition. Returning to the archives and focusing on local events, scholars described how the wars of unification created local resistance, and how the brutality of the civil war sowed resentment toward the newly formed state. The deep social, cultural, and political divides between the South and North that mark the history of modern Italy were rooted in unification itself.[20]

The new histories of the Risorgimento reinvigorated the field, encouraging new methodological approaches, incorporating new sources, and erasing the notion that unification had created an ill-formed state, unable to develop in the same way as its European neighbors. By uncoupling the Risorgimento from the fate of the Liberal state and Mussolini's dictatorship, the new historiography enabled historians to understand the process as a complicated, multilayered project.

CHAPTER 1
ITALY IN 1800

"The Italians are much more outstanding for what they have been and by what they might be then what they are now," wrote Madame de Staël in her popular novel *Corinne* published in 1807.[1] Madame de Staël's depiction of a world in decline echoed a European wide consensus of the state of Italy and Italians. Northern European travelers who came to Italy seeking communion with the classical world and Renaissance masters were struck by the contrast between the magnificence of the past and the poverty of the present. While extolling the artistic glory, military prowess, and imperial reach of ancient Rome, Northern Europeans looked around with some dismay at a divided world. Each new border crossing, accompanying a new currency, language, and cuisine, belied the notion that the peninsula had ever been unified, or would be again. Describing contemporary life, foreigners lingered on what they saw as a superstitious and dissolute people. Italian critics echoed these descriptions of foreigners. However, while Europeans often attributed the decline to character and climate, Italians pointed to centuries of tyrannical rule as the cause of the ruin of its people.

The insistence on contrasting an older, unified civilization to the fragmented, insular worlds found across the peninsula obscured the political, cultural, and economic changes unsettling the old order. The participation of Italian intellectuals, artists, writers, and scientists in the European enlightenment project transformed the derogatory descriptions of Italians into demands for reform, linking the renewal of an Italian people to ideas of liberty, equality, and freedom. The transnational circulation of new ideas, people, and goods brought political reforms, economic change and altered social relation, and proved fertile ground for transforming ideas of a cultural Italy into a political movement as revolution swept across the peninsula.

Italy through the eyes of foreigners

In the years following the end of the Seven Years' War, wealthy British, French, and German men and women took to the roads in ever-growing numbers. In 1765, contemporaries estimated over 40,000 English travelers alone descended on the continent. For men, the Grand Tour marked their passage into adulthood. A profusion of popular travel books reinforced the idea that a continental tour, including the Forum, the Basilica of Florence, Tiziano's work in Venice, and Michelangelo's Sistine Chapel, was an essential component of a young nobleman's education. By standing in the midst of the ruined temple or in front of Raphael's *School of Athens* could a man understand the meaning of the art and philosophy he studied as a boy. When Goethe reached Rome in early November of 1786, he wrote back to Johann Gottfried and Caroline Herder:

> When you look at a phenomenon that is 2,000 years old and more, changed so profoundly and in so many ways by the vicissitudes of time, and yet still the same ground, the same hill, indeed, often the same column and wall, and among the people still traces of the old character; then you feel you are sharing the great decisions of destiny.[2]

The journey itself was central to this rite of passage. Crossing mountains in a bitter cold wind, enduring days of bone-crushing carriage rides covered in dust with little to eat or drink, facing down rapacious innkeepers and thieves transformed boys into men.[3] Although women traveled, they were far fewer in number. Women tourists were more likely defying cultural norms, rather than conforming to expectations.

Europeans came to the peninsula to commune with the ancient world, to revel in the genius of Michelangelo, and to discover the origins of the progressive and rational cultures of their own nations in the past greatness of ancient Rome and the Renaissance. They did not come to learn about new commercial ventures, technologies, scientific innovations, or political philosophies. As the German historian Johann Wilhelm von Archenholz commented, "Whilst other nations reap the fruits of knowledge, they [Italians] are but slowly vegetating."[4] The apparent stagnation, however, provided an opportunity to meditate on the causes of cultural and political decline. A shady seat in the Forum, surrounded by the ruins of the Roman Empire, and the dome of St. Peters provided the perfect place to meditate on the strengths of Republican rule and the dangers of unrestrained power.

Observers differed in their opinions of the underlying causes for Italy's fall from greatness. Protestant travelers often pointed to Catholicism as the root cause of the peninsula's apparent decline; others placed the blame on climate and custom. In 1748, Montesquieu published *The Spirit of the Laws*, a political treatise that sought to delineate the historical, cultural intellectual, and geographical boundaries of Europe, and to provide scientific and cultural explanations of European supremacy. The innate superiority of northern Europeans, their love of virtue, democratic ideals, and liberty, was, he argued, a consequence of climate. Temperature, Montesquieu argued, made "for very different characters. . . . In northern climate, you shall find peoples who have few vices, a sufficient number of virtues, and a lot of frankness and sincerity. Draw near the southern countries, and you will think you have left morality itself far behind." Montesquieu depicted a world where northerners were industrious, rational independent, and virtuous, and southerners were lazy, passionate, and emotional.[5]

Eighteenth-century Italian and foreign descriptions of the decline of the Italian lands had a gendered quality. After a visit to Venice in 1762, John Hinchcliffe wrote: "If states like men have their different ages in which they in a manner naturally flourish and decay, this of Italy surely is near its grave. Not only the blessing itself is gone, but the very idea of love and idea of Liberty, and a low sneaking *politique* is substituted in place of manly generous sentiments."[6]

The decline of Italian genius is evident, they argued, in the servile, dependent men. The figure of the *cicisbeo* came to symbolize the moral decay of the Italian peoples. According to the contemporary descriptions of the practice, shortly after marriage, a noble woman, often in conjunction with her husband, chose one or more male companions to keep her company. The *cicisbeo* joined his lady for morning coffee as she lounged in bed, discussing the latest fashion and scandals, accompanying her on her afternoon visits, and in the evening to the theater and opera. In the eyes of the northern visitors, the aristocratic practices of sociability transformed Italian men into women, and women into men.[7]

Contemporary art reinforced the image of a once great, now degenerate land. British, French, and Russian artists painted a world that reflected their northern imaginings, creating lush landscapes where one or two peasants lurked in the shadows of monumental ruins. Joseph Wright of Derby and John Constable, Katherine Read,

Figure 1 Pompeo Girolamo Batoni (1708–87), "Portrait of a Young Man," 1763. Buyenlarge/ Getty Images.

and J. M. W. Turner all completed their obligatory tours to return home to paint landscapes and portraits of a mythic Italy well into the nineteenth century. Italian artists responded to the aesthetics of this growing art market. Pompeo Batoni based in Rome catered to the tourists, developing a new portrait style, placing the subject in front of the Temple of Vesta Tivoli, a bust of Minerva or hazy landscapes of the Roman countryside. The Venetian artist Antonio Canaletto's paintings of quaint gondoliers or peasants living in the shadows of ruins became the Italy the next generation of travelers expected to see (Figure 1).

Critics noted that the only exception to this narrative of decline was music. During the course of the eighteenth century *Opera Seria*, or Neapolitan Opera, became fashionable throughout the courts of Europe. The new genre, born in reaction to the increasingly farcical, comic, and complicated productions of the seventeenth century, suggested that remnants of Italian artistic genius remained. Naples emerged as the center of musical innovation, where composers transformed moral, virtuous poems and stories into innovative, highly structured productions, incorporating new vocal stylizations and plots drawn from history rather than myth. The reopening of the magnificent San Carlo Theater in 1737 cemented Naples's reputation as a European musical center, and Italian librettists, composers, and performers marked the pinnacle of musical sophistication. Although Italy did not exist as a political entity, nor could Italian describe a people, the words conjured up a distinct physical and cultural world.[8]

The Italian Enlightenment

The unflattering images found in the Grand Tour travel books resonated with Italian elites. In the eyes of urban, educated Italians, the decadence described by Europeans was a consequence of foreign government, the tyranny of the Catholic Church, and an intransigent aristocracy.[9] Unlike foreigners, however, Italian critics saw in the ruins of ancient Rome seeds of regeneration. In the architectural, artistic, and intellectual rubble venerated by the tourists, Italian intellectuals saw proof of the existence of a national culture. Two centuries earlier Italian art and culture dominated most of Europe; Italian dress, manners, and cuisine set the standard throughout high society. The poems of Petrarch and Castiglione's etiquette book, *Il libro del cortegiano*, established Tuscan dialects as the Italian language, and attested to the beauty and power of Italian literature. While few Italians could imagine a unified political state, the idea that Italy existed as a cultural entity, sharing a common past, culture, and traditions, gained strength as the Enlightenment political and social critiques grew stronger.

It is commonplace to trace the spread of Enlightenment ideas from London, Paris, and Amsterdam outward to the margins of Europe, but the circulation of ideas between center and periphery was more complex, weaving through local, national, and international networks.[10] Italian intellectuals and critics were part of a cosmopolitan exchange of letters, scientific publications, and philosophical treatises. Northern European tourists may have been instrumental in creating the idea of a languishing, backward land, but they also brought the latest scientific and philosophical discoveries to the peninsula. Noble women of Milan, Venice, Turin, and Florence hosted salons bringing local and foreign scholars together to debate the merits of economic, administrative, and political reforms. Just as northern elite traveled south, Italian poets, writers, and scholars traveled north, taking their own grand tours through Paris, Munich, and London publishing their observations on foreign customs and life.

Enlightened intellectuals on the Italian peninsula (*illuministi*) shared the general conviction of European thinkers that the systematic application of reason and science could create a more prosperous, progressive, and equitable society based on natural rights. In the coffee shops of Milan and Naples, the *illuministi* joined in international discussions about the nature of good government. Local conditions ensured that critiques focused on the horrible consequences of tyrannical foreign rule and religious fanaticism on the health of the nation, and proposed pragmatic solutions emphasizing the need for reform and education. Italian political theorists put their hopes in an Enlightened ruler, a kind of "legal despot," capable of imposing the reforms necessary to enable law and the economy to function according to the rule of natural law, and thereby ensure prosperity for all.

In Naples, the discussion of the nature of good government dominated debate. The Spanish defeat of the Austrians in 1734 and the creation of an independent kingdom under the Bourbons accompanied expectations of reform among the first generation of Italian enlightenment intellectuals. Fueled by the works of the philosophers Giambattista Vico (*Scienza nuova*, 1725) and Paolo Doria (*Vita civile*, 1709), both reprinted in the 1740s, Neapolitan intellectuals examined the importance of natural law as the basis of legislation and civil codes. Antonio Genovesi worked to transform theory into reality.[11] In the north, Pietro and Alessando Verri, Pompeo Neri, Pietro Giannone, and Ludovico Muratori countered the notion that condition of the Italian states was a consequence of nature. In 1764, Pietro Verri founded the journal *Il Caffe*, publishing articles declaiming the damage done by centuries of oppressive rule by the Spanish and Bourbon monarchies and the insidious influence of the Catholic Church on liberty, reason, and freedom. *Illuministi* critiqued the legal and fiscal inequities found in the region's kingdoms large and small, and railed against censorship. The Italian Enlightenment was marked by its attack on the church. In the wake of the Reformation, the Catholic Church was increasingly associated with privilege, ignorance, censorship, and parasitic wealth. Italian intellectuals placed much of the blame of Italian decadence at the doorstep of the church, transforming the Vatican into an example of the worst form of government, and demanding the separation of temporal from spiritual power.

The celebrations of the peninsula's past genius accompanied fears that centuries of tyrannical rule may have made it impossible for the Italians to ever "awaken." Italian men in particular had become too slothful, vice-ridden, and womanly to claim their liberty or independence. The image of the dissolute, effeminate Italy rendered idle and indolent by centuries of bad government created through the back-and-forth exchanges of ideas, conversations between foreigners and Italians, framed imaginings of an Italy and Italians long before unification.[12]

Political reforms in the many Italies

Geography, war, and invasion shaped the Italy of 1800. Topography had an enormous influence on the political landscape. A long narrow mountainous land jutting deep into the Mediterranean, capped by the Alps to the north and nearly touching Africa to the south, offers the deceptive impression of a clearly defined, protected territory. Hannibal and his elephants, among others, proved the steep rock faces and expansive glaciers of the Alps to be more permeable than they appeared. Over 4,500 miles (7,600 kilometers) of coastline, easily accessible by fishing boats and warships alike, left the coasts equally vulnerable to invasion. Settlers, traders, and armies carved out paths through the mountains. Eighteenth-century armies and tourists joined an older procession of soldiers, pilgrims, and traders swarming up and down the Apennines and over the islands. The history of mobility accompanied one of isolation. In the southern reaches of the Apennines Mountain, villages were often cut off from neighboring towns by deep ravines and swift running rivers. Southern roads snaked along the coastline, rarely venturing into the mountainous interior. The local roads were often impassible for much of the year.[13] While the permeability of Italy's borders enabled foreign armies to move in and tied villages to the wider world, poor roads, steep mountains, and rushing rivers separated residents from their neighbors. New monarchs and rulers altered the political borders, but had little impact on the lives of most people, where town, parish, custom, and kin continued to define notions of identity and belonging.

Italian lands had long been a battlefield in the wars of others, divvied out as prizes to solidify dynastic or military alliances among European powers. For roughly 200 years, Spain dominated much of the peninsula, directly governing Milan, Sardinia, Naples, Sicily, and a sliver of Tuscany, and indirectly influencing the surrounding duchies and principalities. After the Treaty of Utrecht in 1713 ended the wars of Spanish succession, much of the north passed to Austria. The treaty of Aix-la-Chapelle (1748), ending the war of Austrian Succession, ushered in fifty years of peace. The treaty created a balance of power among twelve states, anchored by the three largest: the duchy of Milan, controlled by the Habsburg Empire; the Kingdom of Sardinia; and the Kingdom of Naples (including Sicily) linked to the Spanish Hapsburgs. Alongside the larger kingdoms stood the Papal States, the Republics of Venice, Genoa, and Lucca, the duchies of Parma and Modena, and the Grand Duchy of Tuscany (also dynastically linked to the Austrian Habsburgs). The papacy controlled the central region. The struggles between the Spanish, French, and Austrians on Italian lands were just one in a series of wars and invasions marking the history of the peninsula (Map 1).

In the aftermath of the wars, Italian sovereigns adopted the trappings of enlightened rule in their efforts to curtail the local aristocracy. During the wars, the nobility, constituting roughly 1 percent of the population, had expanded their control over the economic and political fortunes of the various states. By the 1770s the nobility and clergy of Lombardy controlled almost 70 percent of all agricultural land, and nearly half of the arable lands in the Kingdom of Naples. Apart from the Republic of Venice, property was exempt from land taxes. The poor shouldered the bulk of the tax burden.

Map 1 Italy in 1789.

To add insult to injury, feudal lords demanded tithes, regulated hunting and fishing, and enforced their own civil and criminal codes over the residents. As monarchs and rulers faced the rising costs associated with war, they challenged aristocratic privileges, seeking to secure control over their lands and tax revenues through reform. Although the intransigence of the nobility and clergy hindered the successes of these early reforms, the monarchs continued their efforts, looking to leading Italian enlightenment thinkers for assistance.[14] In the 1760s and 1770s, Pietro and Alessandro Verri, Antonio Genovesi and Pompeo Neri all accepted positions in government and led efforts for a new round of fiscal and legal reforms. Lombardy and Tuscany were the sites of the most successful collaborations between the *illuministi* and rulers. In Lombardy, the Tuscan Pompeo Neri completed the census necessary to reform the tax base, and introduced agricultural improvements. Economic reforms focused on eliminating guilds, restructuring levies, and opening markets.

Tuscany under Peter Leopold offers the best example of enlightened rule in Italy. When Leopold came to power in 1765, he worked with reformers to enact a series of radical changes, introducing tax reforms, embarking on ambitious public works projects, improving the roads, and dividing up ecclesiastical lands into smallholdings to increase agricultural production. Although the nobility blocked efforts to expand the number of peasant landholders, Leopold managed to enact a series of enlightened legal and medical reforms, including abolishing capital punishment and torture, in accordance with the legal principles articulated by Cesare Beccaria, in his classic work *Dei delitti e pene* (*On Crimes and Punishments*) published in 1764. Shunning the retributive justice of the Old Testament, Beccaria argued that punishments should be a rational response to the crime, and designed to dissuade people from committing crimes. Beccaria's more humane vision of justice accompanied a similar transformation regarding the insane. Leopold appointed Vincenzo Chiarugi head of Bonifazio, a new hospital for the mentally ill in Florence. Chiarugi banned the use of chains in the asylums, and demanded that all patients be treated with respect and care. Drawing on the works of Italian intellectuals, Leopold's reign became a model of enlightened despotism.

Reform efforts also spread south through the Kingdom of Naples, where the jurist Gaetano Filangeri and economist Domenico Grimaldi attacked feudalism, called for the elimination of guilds, embraced free trade measures, and supported the implementation of new agricultural methods. Filangeri, in particular, took aim at the clergy, arguing that they too should submit to the rule of law. A series of devastating earthquakes between February and March of 1783 shook Calabria, leaving thousands of people dead, destroying entire towns, redirecting rivers, leaving some villages without water. The destruction, combined with the consequent cholera epidemics, gave new urgency to the need for rational state action, and laws limiting the power of the barons.

Although many of the *illuministi* were soon disillusioned with the ability, or will, of the existing regimes to effect concrete change, their work and writings created a transregional network of politically engaged intellectuals. The movement of intellectuals through the various governments and intellectual circles spreads common critiques of tyranny, the clergy, mercantilism, and incorporated the calls for reform circulating throughout Europe on the eve of the French Revolution. By the last decades of the century, the hardening of relations between rulers and the nobility, the growing number of poor, and the fundamental failure of the political reforms created fertile grounds Italian revolutionary movements.

Economic and social change

Late eighteenth-century economic reforms, enacted to counter the general decline in industrial and commercial activities, transformed the markets and the nature of work. Between 1500 and 1700, Italian economies became more agrarian, and in the early seventeenth century fell into a severe recession. Critical sectors of the economies including luxury trades, ship building, and finance collapsed. Multiple factors led to the economic decline across the peninsula: the shift of world trade from the Mediterranean to the Atlantic, the growth of north European industrial markets, and the structural limitations that hindered trade between the Italian states (customs duties, different currencies, lack of infrastructure). In response to declining demand for silks, furs, leather goods, or gold, the nobility shifted their wealth from trade to land, further weakening manufacturing. By 1700, Italy went from being a principal to a subordinate player in the European economy. Its primary exports of olive oil, wheat, silk, and wine depended on the demands of northern European markets. By the end of the century, much of the peninsula's economies were more closely linked to European ports than neighboring markets: more wine left Palermo for London than for Naples.[15]

Governments responded to the economic decline in a variety of ways. In Naples, the Spanish Viceroy sold off lands to the nobility, replete with feudal privileges. The owners of the large estates, the *latifundia*, met the sharp decline in global wheat prices by expanding wheat production and enclosing more land. The result was widespread deterioration of the land and the impoverishment of the peasants. In Tuscany and Piedmont, landowners responded by diversifying production, shifting more land into rice and corn production. Cycles of crop rotation, including hemp and linen, not only improved the soil but also strengthened ties between agriculture and manufacturing sectors in the region. Regardless of whether they consolidated lands or diversified production, local economies shifted toward the lucrative markets in Europe and the Americas.

At the end of the eighteenth century over 80 percent of people across the peninsula worked the land in some capacity. Even in the more industrialized region surrounding Milan, over 40 percent of the people were engaged in agricultural production. People worked according to a variety of contracts, some sharecropped lands, others took tenancies, and still others worked the lands as serfs. Women comprised a significant portion of the labor force. In the northern regions, women worked in the silk industries, or earned wages spinning, winding, and weaving flax, hemp, and silk. Often alternating between fieldwork and the looms, women's work proved important to household incomes. Agrarian families teetered on the edge of disaster. Even with both men and women working, a family's income was rarely enough to provide adequate food or housing. Just one bad crop, hail storm, epidemic, earthquake, or flood could destroy entire communities. The famine years of 1763–64 were particularly traumatic, leaving thousands of starving refugees wandering the streets of Turin and Naples, or emigrating abroad.

As foreign demand for grain, silks, olive oil, and citrus grew in the second half of the century, the lives of working men and women grew even more precarious. In response to the heightened demand, landowners adopted new strategies. In the upper Po valley, landowners incorporated surrounding fields, putting many of the smaller independent peasant farmers out of business. Having lost their livelihoods, men and women took to the roads to look for work on other farms or in the cities. Southern landowners enclosed more land for private production, threatening the livelihood of people dependent on communal rights to access grazing, hunting, and gleaning. The changing economies heightened divisions between peasants and landowners. In general, government officials supported efforts to expand private property, commercial farming, and export markets, even if it meant rising unemployment, violence, vagrancy, and banditry. The final decades of the century witnessed increased transalpine migration into Germany, Austria, and Britain, as artisans and merchants looked for more lucrative markets.

Despite depictions of an Italy frozen in the past, the people and governments of the Italian states were responding to a fast changing world. Enlightenment critiques of traditional sources of authority and political legitimacy and its insistence on individual liberties informed political and economic reforms. The movements of Italian intellectuals, merchants, traders, and workers across the peninsula and Europe were instrumental in circulating new ideas, implementing reforms and strengthening links between Italian states and European capitals. Reforming impulses and critiques of church and crown unsettled social relations. Church and nobility resented efforts of Enlightened rulers to limit their privileges, while artisans, peasants, and workers grew angry as they lost access to guild protections, customary land use rights, and their livelihoods. On the eve of the French Revolution, Archenholz's "slowly vegetating" Italian men and women were actively remaking their world.

The French Revolution and Napoleonic armies

When Napoleon's armies poured down across the Alps and marched into Milan in May of 1796, thousands of people greeted the arrival of the revolutionary army with joy, but others looked on with trepidation. Since 1789, Italians had followed the events in France, reprinting the latest pamphlets from Paris, circulating the news from the National Convention and Parliament, and translating Robespierre's speeches. Supporters of the revolution, including intellectuals, students, members of the nobility, and professionals, gathered in social clubs and universities to debate the possibilities of bringing the revolution home. Some, like Filippo Buonarroti, abandoned their homes and joined the revolution in Paris, and others chose to stay and push for reforms or revolution at home. In cities and provincial towns small groups of nobility, clergy, professionals, and middling classes founded patriotic societies to plot the overthrow of the local political order. The ideological bent of the societies varied, ranging from liberal groups calling for constitutional reforms to more radical clubs demanding Republican rule. Despite the efforts of the governments to close the societies, membership grew between 1792 and 1796. The societies failed to instigate revolution or revolt, but did create new networks that brought revolutionary ideas into the cities and towns.[16]

Italian rulers watched the spread of revolutionary ideas with growing unease. Soon after revolution broke out in France, rulers including the pope, Vittorio Amedeo III, the king of Sardinia, and Ferdinand I, the king of Two Sicilies, strengthened internal security forces, increased censorship, and in some cases, banned public discussion of revolution. The Austrian Emperor, Francis II, deployed secret police in the Italian territories to ferret out French sympathizers. Even the enlightened Leopold grew fearful of the growing unrest in Tuscany and reinstituted the death penalty and tightened controls on trade. Their fears were fueled by the threat of peasant uprising and popular social unrest. The Italian states were not immune to the wave of popular protest spreading across Europe. In 1792 a group of Piedmont peasants petitioned Vittorio Amadeo III to abolish the annual rents demanded and to provide food. If the king refused their demands, they announced that there would be "no need for the French, there are enough of us to rise up against those infernal wolves of lords and stewards."[17]

Influenced by the stereotypes of the lazy, capricious Italian, incapable of self-government, French diplomats dismissed their enthusiasm and showed little interest in exporting the revolution southward. When war broke out in 1792, the French government moved to annex Savoy, claiming that the territory fell within the natural frontiers of France, but went no further. Only in 1795, when faced with growing domestic discontent with the cost of the war, did French officials consider invading Italy. Moving south secured resources for the troops and drew the coalition forces away from the German front, easing the burden on France. The French had no interest in collaborating with Italian revolutionary supporters. A French agent, Francois Cacault, cautioned his superiors, "One must be extremely mistrustful of the extreme petulance and dash of the youth of Italy, excited and carried away by ideas borrowed from our revolution. . . . If one trusts too much in them, this party of self-interested men will do nothing but spoil matters by pushing too hard."[18]

The Italian campaign began in late March of 1796. In a matter of weeks, Napoleon had defeated Piedmont armies and forced the Austrians into retreat. By January of 1797, Austrian forces withdrew from their Italian territories, and Pope Pius VI sued for peace. In October of 1797, Napoleon signed the Treaty of Campoformio, creating the Cisalpine and Ligurian Republics in the north. The speed of Napoleon's military victories, combined with French reluctance to ally with Italians, erased traces of Italian revolutionary activities from the historical record, replacing them with Napoleon's version of a downtrodden people liberated by the French. In his proclamation to the Cisalpine Republic on November 17, 1797, Napoleon announced: "We have given you liberty. Take care you preserve it. . . . Divided and bowed by ages of tyranny, you could not alone have achieved your independence."[19] Napoleon's gift of liberty to the Italians was marred by his willingness to give Austria the Venetian Republic in order to secure peace for France. The surrender of Venice left Italian patriots disillusioned and angry.[20]

French occupation initially kindled Italian Nationalist sentiment. Patriots proudly wore the revolutionary cockade and gathered around the Tree of Liberty. Four months after arriving in Milan, Napoleon opened an essay competition exploring what type of government would be "best suited to the happiness of Italy." The competition urged participants to "recall the ancient glories of Italy," as evidence of the existence of an Italian nation and a foundation for a new political order, based on liberty, equality, and prosperity. Most of the essayists looked to France for inspiration, envisioning an indivisible nation, a smaller number of authors argued that only a federation could bring peace and prosperity to a land so divided by custom, climate, law, and government. Melchiorre Gioia of Piacenza won the competition. In his essay, he argued that a republic, capable of guaranteeing individual liberties and equality under the law, could overcome Italy's long history of regional division and political fragmentation. Only in a republic could the "uneasy and fearful affections that divide the various Italian peoples be changed into sweet and generous affections no longer marked as Sicilians, Florentines, or Turinese but Italians and men."[21] The conviction that good government could transform Italians into an industrious, virtuous, and loyal people ran through most of the essays.

These theoretical imaginings of an independent Italy accompanied the establishment of new territories. In the Cispadane Republic (1796), Republican leaders called for elections, drew up a constitution, adopted the white, green, and red tricolor flag, and introduced a limited parliamentary government. They also formed a citizen army and evicted the church from the schools. Although the Cispadane Republic was short lived, replaced by Napoleon with the Cisalpine Republic in 1797, the Republican reforms endured. French administrators organized each Republic into departments, governed by a moderate constitution and a legislature elected by limited franchise. During the revolutionary period, Republican governments abolished feudal privileges, judicial torture, and guilds. Professions previously reserved for the clergy or nobility were opened to all.

Ultimately, however, the occupation inspired anti-French sentiment and anger. The French filled their coffers by plundering Italy. Napoleon sent gold, silver, horses, oxen, grain, paintings, and statues back to Paris. In May of 1796, Bonaparte announced to the people of Lombardy that since their liberty depended on the French army, they should provision the troops. He ordered Lombardy to provide twenty million francs to the French forces, "a slight impost for so fertile a country when all the advantages which will result from French occupation are considered."[22] The French ordered Modena to pay 7.5 million francs, Parma 2 million, and the Papal States 21 million lire worth in gold, silver, livestock, clothing, and foodstuffs. If the monies extracted were painful, it was the art that was perhaps the most galling. The paintings of Caravaggio, Michelangelo, and Botticelli, along with manuscripts from Leonardo da Vinci and works of Virgil, proof of Italy's cultural genius, were shipped to Paris.

Rather than unifying the Italian states, the occupation deepened regional rivalries and social divisions. Cities vied with one another to secure jobs and public contracts. In the countryside, people rose in revolt against taxes, military conscription, and grain requisitions. Attacks on the clergy proved particularly outrageous to deep-rooted popular Catholic sentiment, provoking uprisings in Tuscany and Romagna. The violence was even worse in the south. The French troops marched into the Kingdom of Naples at the end of 1798, and in December Ferdinand IV called on all subjects to rise in revolt.

In Naples, the *lazzaroni*, the urban poor, spilled into the street attacking the French troops. After fierce fighting, the French claimed an uneasy victory and announced the creation of the Republic of Naples. Throughout the countryside, people continued to violently resist the French occupiers. In February, Cardinal Fabrizio Ruffo raised an army of over 40,000 volunteers. When Ruffo's army marched into Naples in May of 1799, they indiscriminately slaughtered anyone they took to be a Republican sympathizer, leaving the beheaded bodies piled high in the streets. While the *Sanfedisti*, or the

"Army of the Holy Faith," are often credited with the defeat of the French in 1799, they proved a critical factor in only a few battles between locals and French forces. Local residents led most of the uprisings, but the violence and brutality of the *Sanfedesti* made them the public face of the resistance.[23]

The massacre in Naples signaled the beginning of the collapse of French rule in Italy. A coalition of Austrian and Russian forces had retaken Milan by April, and French troops were forced from Tuscany a few months later. Popular sentiment fell on the side of the coalition troops, and just a handful of patriots continued to see political unification as the peninsula's salvation. It appeared as though a century of reform culminating in revolution had trampled Italian patriotic sentiment. For patriots, the revolution seemed to confirm their fears that Italians lacked the character and moral fitness for liberty and self-government.

Napoleon returned in 1800, defeating the Austrians at the Battle of Marengo, and securing control over the Italian states with the Peace of Lunéville in 1801. The Cisalpine Republic was reconstituted and enlarged as the Italian Republic in 1802, with the addition of Veneto and Modena, the Romagna and the Marche. Although Napoleon initially maintained the fiction of Republican rule, appointing Italian patriot Francesco Melzi d'Eril as vice president, effective power remained in his hands as president. Napoleon blocked Melzi's attempts to carve out an autonomous state, implement a separate Italian legal code, and dictate foreign policy. In 1804 Napoleon abandoned the pretense of Italian liberty and ordered Melzi to offer him the crown of Italy. In May 1805, Napoleon was the crowned king of Italy in a spectacular ceremony in the Cathedral in Milan. Napoleon's dismissive attitude toward the Italians grew stronger on his return. A few months after the coronation, in July of 1805, he wrote to warn his Viceroy Eugène: "It is dangerous to think of Italians as children: there is evil in them. Never let them forget that I am the master to do as I wish."[24]

Within a few years, Napoleon's family governed most of the peninsula. In 1805, Napoleon renamed the Republic the Kingdom of Italy, and appointed his stepson Eugène de Beauharnais as the viceroy. Piedmont was directly annexed to France, while the republic of Lucca became a principality, ruled by Napoleon's sister Elisa. The Kingdom of Naples was conquered in 1805 and ruled first by Napoleon's brother Joseph, and then by his brother-in-law Joachim Murat. The Papal States were annexed to France in 1809, and the pope was sent to France. Only Sardinia and Sicily remained outside of Napoleon's power (Map 2).

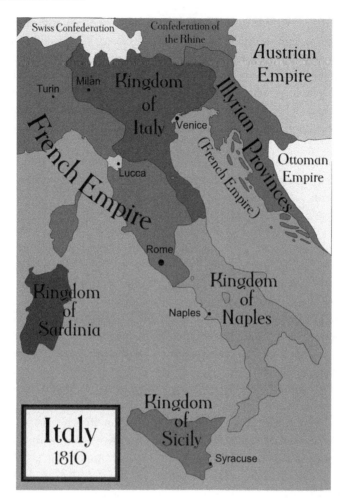

Map 2 Italy under Napoleon in 1810.

Despite the ways that Napoleonic rule fused the idea of an independent Italy to French arrogance, oppressive taxation, and vehement anti-Catholicism in the popular imagination, administrative reforms united the disparate states. Napoleonic governments replaced the multitude administrative systems and fiscal practices with uniform alternatives. Annexed territories, kingdoms, and principalities were divided into districts, which were in turn divided into communes, each with specific administrative and fiscal functions. Appointed councils, comprised of local landowners, merchants, and professionals, governed the communes. The expanding state bureaucracy swelled the ranks of the civil service. French officials introduced new legal codes throughout the regions, replacing the multiple legal codes and jurisdictional authorities with a single code applicable to the wealthy and poor alike. The state expropriated land usurped from previous monarchs by the nobility, and further diminished the power of the nobility by enacting a series of fiscal reforms, including a uniform land tax. Stripped of patriotic calls for liberty and independence, the centralization of government and the dissolution of traditional authority succeeded in unifying Italian territories in ways that the eighteenth-century reformers had only dreamed of.

Napoleonic rule widened old social divisions, and created new ones, between those who supported the new order and those who resisted. Urban professionals and landowners able to take advantage of the sale of ecclesiastical and feudal lands welcomed the land reforms. Many among the elite found good positions as civil servants in the growing bureaucracy. If governments were able to dampen the deep-rooted hostility to French rule among the middle and upper classes, they were less successful in gaining the cooperation of the rural residents, urban workers, and the poor. In 1809 and 1810 insurgents in the north set fire to the houses of the wealthy merchants and sacked the town halls, destroying the tax rolls. In Naples, discontent, fueled by popular faith and anger at the new fiscal regime turned into guerilla warfare, as the British and exiled Bourbons backed the peasants with money and guns. Over 20,000 French soldiers were killed in Calabria and Abruzzi. The most famous of the mercenary leaders was *Fra Diavolo*, who first fought with Cardinal Ruffo, and then returned to lead an army of his own against the French. The French responded by burning entire villages in retribution. The divisions between those who flourished under the regime and embraced the new forms of civic nationalism and those who despised the French, and their godless ways, became embedded in Italian Nationalist visions.

CHAPTER 2
RESTORATION, REVOLUTION, AND THE RISORGIMENTO (1815–47)

When Napoleon surrendered to the coalition forces in 1815, few Italians shed tears. Years of heavy taxation, growing civil strife, and rising prices undermined support for the French throughout the peninsula. Napoleon's defeat reignited dreams of Italian liberation among a few patriots, although the Congress of Vienna quickly squashed them. The Congress proved once again that European interests outweighed those of Italians in determining the geographical and political shape of the region. The new regimes proved fragile, struggling to find stability in world marked by social unrest, economic change, and political polarization. Despite Europe's efforts to keep Italy divided and weak, the first decades of the nineteenth century witnessed the emergence of an Italian cultural nationalism that took on political meaning during the revolutions of the 1820s and 1830s. Efforts to crush the multitude of ideologically disparate Italian patriotic movements that emerged in the wake of the French defeat failed. Italian Nationalists continued their work in exile. A global network of Italian patriots promoted dreams of an Italian nation at home and abroad, and by the 1840s their visions morphed into genuine political movements.

Restoration

The representatives of the great powers meeting in Vienna were well aware of the enormity of the task they faced: redrawing European borders in such a way as to secure peace and create stable legitimate states. Metternich, Castlereagh, Talleyrand, and even Alexander I recognized that restoration meant restoring order, not returning the old order back to power. Ensuring peace in Europe, navigating continental rivalries, and balancing territorial interests required an expansive understanding of what constituted legitimate rule. The Congress was ostensibly committed to the return of displaced monarchs to power, unless the restoration contradicted the interests of the balance of power in the new Europe. The territorial redistribution, combined with the implementation of the Congress System, succeeded in preventing the outbreak of major continental wars for a century; however, by ignoring growing Nationalist sentiment, it also fueled revolutionary movements.[1]

Italy had no standing at the Congress, and the Italian lands were divvied up into eight states, with Austria overseeing the whole. In Piedmont, Vittorio Emanuele I returned to a kingdom that now included the former Republic of Genoa. The Austrians controlled Lombardy-Venetia; Consalvi, the Vatican representative in Vienna managed to return the pope to power. In Tuscany, Grand Duke Ferdinando III came home to rule a duchy that now include the isle of Elba and the Duchy of Lucca. In the South, European leaders placed Ferdinando IV as Ferdinando I, ruler of the Kingdom of the Two Sicilies. Parma, Modena, and the Republic of San Marino managed to remain independent, closely tied to Austria. Members of the Habsburg family ruled the duchies of Modena, Parma, and Tuscany, while the pope and Ferdinand I signed agreements authorizing the Austrian military access to their lands. Only the Kingdom of Sardinia managed to keep some semblance of autonomy, serving as a buffer between France and Austria. In disposing of Italian lands, the diplomats in Vienna were far more concerned with Europe's balance of power than peninsular politics (Map 3).

Italian restoration governments implemented a variety of strategies to centralize state power in the aftermath of the revolution. Some tried to return to crown and nobility all ancien régime privileges and powers, while others adopted a version of Metternich's idea of amalgamation. Recognizing the threat to postwar stability posed by both reactionaries and revolutionaries, Metternich argued that the best way to secure the emperor's power was through the adaptation of modern centralized administrative practices, introduced by the French. In essence, the idea was to shore up the monarchy with an efficient modern bureaucracy.

But, as monarchs throughout Europe discovered, regardless of the policies implemented, efforts to secure monarchical power in the post-Napoleonic world proved destabilizing, angering the nobility, the church, the emerging middling classes, or the poor.[2]

King Vittorio Emanuele I of Sardinia and Duke Francis IV of Modena both returned to power determined to erase every trace of the French. When Vittorio Emanuele moved back to Turin, he rode through the streets in powdered pigtails sporting a tricorn hat, the height of fashion in the 1760s. His first official act was to annul all French legislation and replace it with the Royal Constitutions of 1770, reinstating feudal rights and privileges, with the exception of serfdom. The crown revoked guarantees of fair and open trials, restored patriarchal and ecclesiastical judicial prerogatives, reopened guilds and trade corporations, and reinstated custom duties restricting internal and external trade. The church returned as an ally of the monarchy, reasserting control over schools and private life. Vittorio Emanuele's inflexibility riled members of the aristocracy, bureaucrats, and officers who saw little hope for stability in the crown's refusal to countenance even the most limited reform.

The pope proved slightly more willing than the Savoyard monarch to consider reforms. Immediately on returning to Rome in 1814, Pope Pio VII reasserted papal power, reopening ecclesiastical orders, reviving the Jesuits and the Inquisition, and revoking religious toleration, but he also recognized the utility of embracing limited change. Under the influence of Cardinal Consalvi, the secretary of state, the papacy pursued its own version of "amalgamation." In July of 1816, the pope issued a *motu proprio* promising

Map 3 Italy in 1827.

to reorganize the temporal rule of the church in recognition of the demands of modern times, paving the way for an administrative and judicial reorganization modeled on the French system. The motu proprio confirmed the sale of ecclesiastical lands, opened some minor government positions to laymen, abolished torture, espoused equality under the law, suppressed some feudal rights and customs, although it kept the baronies remained intact. Papal attempts to create a more unified and efficient state proved bitter to the *zelanti*, the most reactionary of the Cardinals and liberals alike.

Emperor Francis I and King Ferdinand I were elected to build on the French reforms, creating hybrid "administrative monarchies," repealing what they considered the most radical French reforms, but keeping economic and legal changes that strengthened executive power. In Lombardy-Venetia, Francis I replaced the Napoleonic civil code, with the Austrian legal code, but kept most of the other administrative reforms in place. Francis encouraged a limited integration of local elite into government. Local nobility was given some say over the distribution of new taxes, the approval of local budgets and nominees for local office. The sons of the Italian nobility could hold minor governmental posts, but were barred from high offices. Emperor Francis relied heavily on schooling and the church to ensure social and political stability. Under Austrian rule, elementary education was made compulsory, in an effort to forge quiescent, if not loving subjects. Francis also sought to mend relations with the church, reversing Napoleon's 1810 decree dissolving monasteries and convents. In the Bourbon south, the need for security and stability also tempered the desire for retribution. The King Ferdinand I, abolished the constitution, restored the church to power, but did not reinstate feudalism or repeal administrative reforms. The king retained most of the military officials and civil servants who had been appointed during the Napoleonic era, and recognized the land purchases and titles acquired under Murat. Overriding the fierce opposition of the prince of Canosa, minister of police, the crown granted full amnesty to those who supported the French.

Despite the efforts of amalgamation to quell reactionary and revolutionary discontent, resentment continued to grow. In the northern territories, onerous conscription laws requiring residents to send their sons to serve in the imperial army for eight years fueled anger at Austrian rule. Merchants resented the restrictive trade laws and customs barriers that cut them off from their established markets in France and Piedmont. Austria's religious toleration laws irritated the church, particularly those stipulations requiring a priest to perform marriages that violated canon law. Even those who worked for the Austrian administration grew disgruntled as they discovered their opportunities for advancement limited by linguistic and cultural prejudice. Grumblings about Austrian authoritarianism were met with heightened censorship and an expanded spy network, intensifying anti-Austrian sentiment.

In the Bourbon south, the abrogation of the constitution and the extension of direct rule over Sicily extended the French reforms to the island. The abolition of feudalism, including entails and traditional usage rights, appealed to a small cadre of Sicilian liberals, but infuriated the aristocracy and the peasants. The imposition of military conscription on the island fueled resistance and draft evasion across the island. The Sicilian nobility, in particular, resented the demotion of Palermo from a capital to a provincial city, with its attendant loss of power and influence. While the administrative monarchies provided more flexible frameworks for post-Napoleonic governments committed to strengthening monarchical power, they did little to resolve the deeper social tensions that accompanied the conflicting interests of crown, nobility, middling classes, and peasants. Neither reaction nor reform succeeded in establishing stability.

Cultural nationalism

Discontent provoked by the restoration governments did not lead to a cohesive political vision for Italy, but did find voice in a growing cultural nationalism calling for Italian liberation. Historian Alberto Banti dated the emergence of a "Risorgimento canon," beginning under Napoleonic rule and continuing through the Restoration. Sifting through memoirs, autobiographies, diaries, and letters of Italian patriots, Banti, identified a collection of common texts that inspired Nationalist sentiment in a generation of Italian men and women, who came of age during the restoration. Banti argues that these texts written between 1801 and 1849 constructed the idea of Italian nation linked by love, blood, and a shared history, capable of voluntarily coming together to pledge allegiance to an imagined independent Italian state.[3]

The earliest texts in this canon appeared between 1798 and 1280, included the works of Ugo Foscolo, Giovanni Berchet, Silvio Pellico, Vincenzo Cuoco, Giacomo Leopardi, and Vincenzo Alfieri. The novels, poems, and histories crystallized a vision of an Italy defined by a common past, but now crushed by foreign occupation. In the poem *Dei Sepulcri*, published in 1807, inspired by Napoleon's order forbidding the erection of tombs or inscriptions within the city center, Ugo Foscolo reflected on the power of tombs to link the living to the dead through bonds of history and affection. A few years later, Foscolo published his popular novel *Ultime Lettere di Jacopo Ortis* (1814). A story of a young Venetian patriot forced into exile in the wake of the Campoformio agreement, who falls in love with a woman pledged to another. Mourning for his country and his love he wanders through the countryside, stopping to wonder at the power and glory in the ancient ruins, but ultimately fails to find solace in a world where every vista is spoiled by foreign occupation.

The warnings against foreign occupation and imported promises of liberty, woven through Foscolo's writings, echoed in the histories and fiction of Vincenzo Cuoco. Born into a well-to-do provincial family in the Molise, Cuoco left for Naples to study law in 1779, but soon turned his attention to his twin passions: history and philosophy. Cuoco, a strong supporter of the short-lived Neapolitan republic, was forced into exile when the Bourbons returned to power in 1799. In *Saggio sulla rivoluzione di Napoli del 1799* (*Historical Essay on the Neapolitan Revolution of 1799*), published in 1801, he argued that the critical failure of the 1799 revolution was the inability of its leaders to rally the support of the masses. Cuoco contended that a nation's liberation depended on the awakening of its own consciousness, and awareness of a shared history and culture. He expanded on these themes in his philosophical novel *Platone in Italia* (Plato in Italy) published in 1806. Written as series of exchanges between the young Cleobolo and his mentor, Plato, traveling through Magna Grecia, the novel makes a case for the existence of a great Italian nation brought down by moral decay and invasion. During the journey, Ponzio, a member of the flourishing Sannitis (or Sabelli) people now subject to Roman rule, explains to Cleobolo:

> I believe our wise men who say, with certainty, that in ancient times Italy flourished, its laws, agriculture, armies and commerce. When this was I cannot tell you: although you will easily find others who can say better than me. All I can tell you is this, that in those times all Italians formed one people, the Etruscans.[4]

By reminding his readers that there was once a proud, strong, and prosperous Italian nation, Cuoco implied that it could rise again.

Although Banti's canon includes only works by men, women also published biographies and critical essays countering the European narratives lamenting the immorality of Italian women. Ginevra Canonici Fachini published a compilation of short biographies of Italian women artists and intellectuals in response to Lady Morgan's contention that Italian women were immoral, poorly educated, and lacking in maternal affection.[5] In this wider body of work by women and men, a vision of Italy as an organic nation, bound by history, sentiment, culture, and geography, fractured and weakened by centuries of foreign rule, but capable of regeneration took root and expanded during the restoration.

In Lombardy-Venetia and Tuscany, this cultural revival appeared shortly after the Napoleon's defeat. In an effort to co-opt the voices of dissent, Austrian authorities funded a local literary journal, entitled *Biblioteca italiana*, initially recruiting Ugo Foscolo as editor, although he refused the position when told that he had to swear allegiance to the emperor. The inaugural issue, published in 1816, opened with an article by Madame de Staël, innocuously entitled *Letteratura ed arti liberali: Sulla maniera e la utilità delle traduzioni* ("Literature and Liberal Arts: On the Manner and Use of Translations"). The essay criticized the propensity of Italian writers to imitate ancient Roman writers rather than create anything original. She lamented that when a country's writers could only copy the images and styles of past masters, unable to create innovative works, its literature becomes sterile and insignificant. She urged Italian poets and playwrights to leave behind their ancient myths, and generate works capable of revitalizing the soul of the Italian nation.[6] Despite the struggles between the editor Giuseppe Acerbi to publish the best works and Austrian censors determined to muffle implicit critiques of the regime, *la Biblioteca* reached over 700 subscribers.[7]

In 1818, frustrated with the limitation imposed by Austrian censors, leading political, literary, and scientific figures, including the politician Count Frederico Confalonieri, the poet Giovanni Berchet, and the economist Count Giuseppe Pécchio, founded *Il Conciliatore*, publishing articles on history, literature, economic modernization, political theory, and geography. The review became the voice of Italian romanticism and liberalism, and within a year Austrian censors suspended its publication. *Il Conciliatore* was not the only literary review in circulation. During the restoration hundreds of literary and scientific reviews encouraged a wider educated elite to engage in civic debate in cities and provincial towns.

Cultural debates were not confined to the pages of literary magazines; restoration culture accompanied the expansion of civic consciousness in the public sphere. Wealthy urban women opened their private homes, inviting authors, scholars, and scientists to speak. Bianca Milesi, born into a Milanese merchant family in 1790, typified the women of the salons. After completing her schooling, and her requisite grand tour of Tuscany, Switzerland, Hungary, and Germany, she returned home to Milan where she became a central figure among the liberal anti-Austrian intellectual community. A talented artist and prolific writer, Milesi opened a salon in 1818, hosting talks by the historian Simonde de Sismondi, and Confalonieri among others. The thinly veiled political critiques swirling through salons, cafes, the opera houses, theaters, and university hall inspired direct action.[8]

The works of Foscolo, Cuoco, and others that enabled patriots to envision themselves as members of an Italian community had a deeply political dimension. The national community conjured through the tragedy of young *Jacopo Ortis* were rooted in Republican political visions formed in the French Revolution. The culture tropes and imagery shaped the multiplicity of moderate, democratic, and even conservative liberal political designs that waxed and waned in the first decades of the nineteenth century.[9]

The revival of conspiratorial societies made evident the political power of the cultural Risogimento. First formed during the Restoration, the clubs attracted reactionary conservatives, moderates, and revolutionaries. Conservative members of the Christian Amity in Piedmont and the *Calderai* in Calabria positioned themselves as defenders of the faith in the face of Napoleon's anticlericalism to call for popular resistance. In Romagna, local liberal elites formed the *Guelphi*, promoting the idea of constitutional monarchies united in a loose federation to form an independent Italian state. Disillusioned Jacobins joined the *Filadelfia* and *Adelfi* societies in the north, and the *Carboneria* in the south. The *Carboneria* was the largest and the most ideologically diverse. Despite their political differences, all societies decried tyranny, extolled the military virtue of Italians, adopted secret initiation rituals, and distributed diplomas, identification cards, and tokens to members. Movements of exile and return ensured that many of the societies took on a transnational dimension, linking chapters in Italy, France, Great Britain, and Spain.[10]

After 1815, the societies expanded, finding eager recruits among the soldiers, students, educated elite, craftsman, clergy, and women disgruntled with reaction and reform. In the north, the *Adelfia* grew under the leadership of the Jacobin, Filippo Buonarroti becoming a loose knit federation of various sects, drawn from a broad cross section of society, including nobility, middling classes, army officers, united in their hatred of the Austrians. Artists, writers, and cultural critics also joined the societies: nearly all of the editors of *Il Conciliatore* were members of the local *Carboneria*. Women played an active role in the expansion the political societies. In Ferrara, women comprised 20 percent of the members of the *Circolo Unione*, the center of liberal opposition. Ginevra Canonici Fachini, a member of the *Circolo*, served five years in prison for *carbonari* association. In March 1821, Bianca Milesi and Matilde Viscontini founded *la società delle giardiniere* (the Garden Society), the woman's auxiliary to the *Carboneria* in Milan. Women's clubs organized meetings, passed messages between the groups, recruited new members, and tended to those imprisoned. By 1821, Francis I ordered the secret police to put the Milanese association under surveillance, and in 1822, arrested Bianca and her cousin, Maria Frecavalli, for subversive activities. In the southern regions, the disaffected soldiers, civil servants, and professionals bolstered the rolls of the local *carbonaria*. By 1820, King Ferdinand's advisers warned that the sect boasted over 50,000 members, although likely a gross exaggeration, it was clear that the movement had spread wide. Despite their growing numbers, the societies posed no real threat to the regimes, as proven by the revolutions of 1820. They did, however, create a resistance network capable of tapping into a more generalized discontent, keeping the vision of an independent Italy alive.

Revolutions of 1820

In January of 1820 a mutiny among Spanish troops in Cadiz forced the Spanish king to restore the constitution of 1812 transforming simmering resentment against the restoration into revolution, and inspiring Italian patriots to rise in revolt. On July 1, 1820, junior officers and members of the *Carboneria* marched through the streets of Nola, a small town outside of Naples, demanding that Ferdinando I grant the Spanish Constitution. The rebellion spread quickly. Four days later, Field Marshal Guglielmo Pepe, a former general under Murat, and his 10,000 soldiers joined the rebels. Within days, the militants forced Ferdinando I to capitulate, and to extend the Spanish Constitution across his kingdom. In Palermo, disgruntled aristocrats seized the opportunity to declare independence and reinstate the Sicilian constitution. The Palermo revolution garnered little support from the island's provincial nobility, uninterested in substituting the Bourbon monarch for Palermo princes, or from Neapolitan revolutionaries, unwilling to dissolve the kingdom. Sicilian separatism was one of the many divisions that threatened the national parliament when it was opened in October of 1821. The short-lived revolutionary alliance among those who resented the loss of corporate privileges and the liberal ambitions of the *carbonari* collapsed in the face of a recalcitrant monarch. In February 1821, Austrian troops crossed into the Bourbon Kingdom, and a month later restored Ferdinando I to power.[11]

As the Austrian troops marched south toward Naples, revolution broke out in Piedmont. In the face of the Spanish and Neapolitan uprisings, Vittorio Emanuele I's refusal to consider any reform angered moderates and radicals alike. By the end of the year, the *carbonari* sects joined a number of young aristocratic officers, who backed a constitutional monarchy, to plot the king's overthrow. Done with the intransigent, curmudgeonly Vittorio Emanuele, a younger generation of officers pinned their hopes on his distant cousin, Carlo Alberto, who appeared more amenable to constitutional rule. The rebellious officers envisaged a conservative, paternalistic Kingdom of Italy that would include a newly liberated Lombardy. The insurrection spread across Piedmont and into Savoy; however, what little popular support it enjoyed quickly dissipated when Vittorio Emanuele I abdicated in favor of his son Carlo Felice, and appointed Carlo

Alberto as temporary regent. Carlo Alberto agreed to grant the Spanish Constitution, subject to Carlo Felice's approval, but refused to mount a military expedition to liberate Lombardy. In March, Carlo Alberto abandoned Turin, and joined King Carlo Felice in Modena, where they awaited Austrian assistance. The insurrectionary army was defeated by the Austrians at the Battle of Novara in 1821.

Both monarchs returned to power furious and eager for revenge. In the southern kingdom, most of the members of the provisional government fled into exile. Ferdinand purged revolutionary collaborators from office, and forbid them from practicing their professions. Officers linked to the *Carboneria*, or appointed under the French, were dismissed or imprisoned. The king imposed harsh censorship laws and limited freedom of association. Likewise, in Piedmont, Lombardy, and Venetia sectarian activities were crushed, and members of the *carbonari* arrested. In Lombardy-Venetia, the Austrians sentenced nearly half of the prisoners on trial to death, although they later commuted most of the sentences to life imprisonment in the notorious Spielberg prison, or exile. In Piedmont, where the conspirators were commonly linked by blood or friendship to the ruling aristocracy, those involved in the insurrection were encouraged to leave in advance of their sentencing, and the majority of death sentences were delivered *in abstentia*. Revolutionary repercussions rippled through the Papal States, strengthening the *zelanti* (zealots) faction within papal politics. In 1823, the reactionary wing of the church emerged victorious, electing the ill and elderly Cardinal Della Genga as Pope Leo XII. Months after becoming pope, Leo XII issued an encyclical, *Ubi Primum*, condemning all forms of religious toleration, ordered Jews back to the ghettos, returned the Jesuits to control universities and schools, increased police surveillance, and legalized torture.

The failed uprisings marked a critical turning point in the making of modern Italy. The revolutions offered a number of important lessons that informed later Nationalist strategies: that there existed the possibility of building a moderate conservative alliance in Piedmont; that the Bourbon Kingdom rested on a rickety foundation, riven by deep social and geographic divisions; that Italian states remained dependent on Austria. The revolutions also transformed the cause of Italian freedom into a transnational concern.

Exile and revolution

Although merchants, missionaries, explorers, intellectuals, and artists from the Italian states traveled across the world for centuries, the restoration created a new kind of "diasporic nationalism," among emigrants and exiles.[12] The thousands of Italians forced into exile from Piedmont, Lombardy-Venetia, and the Kingdom of the Two Sicilies in the aftermath of the revolutions made their way northward, to Florence, Modena, or left the Italian peninsula altogether, moving to Cadiz, Paris, London, New York, or Buenos Aires. By 1821 the French police identified over 250 Italian exiles living in Paris. Over the course of the next two decades a third of early Italian Nationalists traveled to northern Europe or the Americas.[13] The exiles joined older enclaves of merchants, artisans, and workers from the Italian states. Over the years, these emigrant communities, comprised of Genoese, Neapolitans, Venetians, Florentines, and Sicilians, embodied a particular idea of Italy as a cultural and geographic space in the foreign imagination. With the arrival of the exiles the idea of the existence of a distinctive cultural "Italy," generated by older transnational commercial circuits, and strengthened by the grand tourists, took on a deeper political significance.

For exiles, these varied communities, some home to wealthy merchants, others to chimney sweeps, organ grinders and cobblers, speaking a multitude of different languages, fostered an expansive notion of what constituted Italy and Italian. Patriots from Lombardy, Piedmont, and Naples shared their stories of resistance, finding common ground in sacrifice and struggle. The erosion of regional divides accompanied the recognition of cross-class alliances. Initially, exiled patriots generally viewed the masses as inherently reactionary, blaming peasants and workers for the revolutionary failures. The collapse of the 1820 Spanish revolution deepened these pessimistic assumptions about the revolutionary potential of the people. For those who moved through the emigrant communities in London and Paris, however, exile fostered a more democratic vision of the Italian nation based on shared cultural, traditional, linguistic, and culinary traditions. Shared narratives of exile and longing for a faraway homeland reinforced the sense of belonging to a larger imaginary community transcending social, geographic, and political divisions.[14]

The exiles proved instrumental in securing the sympathy of a wider European public. Émigrés spent their time promoting their cause, publishing widely, giving speeches, and making contacts with sympathetic and wealthy Europeans. Writers produced a growing body of literature—memoirs, novels, poetry, histories, and political treatises—testifying to the legitimacy and inevitably of Italian liberation, promoting multiple visions of what a free Italy would look like. Italians in exile acclaimed Gioachino Rossini's *Guglielmo Tell* (*William Tell*), the story of intrepid Swiss men who defeat the Austrian forces and declare Switzerland free when it opened in Paris in 1829. The British aristocracy expressed their sympathy for the exiles by hiring them as Italian tutors, or offering material support to write. An 1830s English translation of Silvio Pellico's memoir, *Le mie prigioni* (*My Prisons*), became a best seller. Pellico's denunciation of Austrian behavior, and his own pious suffering, tugged at British heartstrings, and helped transform Austria into the enemy of Italian independence. Journalists and critics fascinated by the growing community of politically and intellectually engaged Italians increased their coverage of contemporary politics and living conditions on the peninsula, writing articles condemning Austrian, Papal, and Bourbon abuses of power.[15]

Exile linked the cultural-political visions of Italian patriots to a wider global revolutionary movement. The 1820 refugees joined those who had gone into exile in 1815 and had formed ties with the European wide liberal movement prior to the outbreak of revolutions. The first wave of émigrés, including Buonarotti in Paris, held fast to the dream of a Jacobin inspired radical Republican revolution, and tied the success of Italian liberation to freedom for all peoples. The idea that fighting for the liberation of one group meant fighting for the freedom of all justified Italian, French, or British participation in the Spanish and Greek revolution. By the 1820s even some moderates recognized that their struggle was linked to those of other peoples; Santorre di Santarosa, who led the Piedmont military uprising, went into exile in England, and died fighting for Greek independence in 1825. The theoretical and physical ties between Italian émigrés and global liberation movements strengthened the idea of an Italy as a national entity, even if no one could agree on its territorial, demographic, or political form, among emigrants and the liberal Europeans.

Although the revolutions of 1831 had little impact on the peninsula, they expanded diasporic nationalism. When the July Revolution broke out in Paris, forcing King Charles X to abdicate in favor of the more liberal Louis Philippe, leaders of the *Carboneria* in Modena seized their opportunity. Believing they had the backing of Francis IV, the duke of Modena, and Louis Philippe in France, the liberal exiles in Modena began to plot insurrections in Parma, Bologna, and Modena. The duke and the king of France soon abandoned the conspirators, wary of revolution and the threat of Austrian invasion, while Italian exiles watched the insurrectionary waves with growing excitement. Many began packing their bags to return and making plans to return to join the struggle, only to find that Louis Philippe closed the borders. With no real support, the revolts of February 1831 proved short lived. By the end of April, Austrian troops restored the pope and Maria Louise, duchess of Parma, and Duke Francis IV to power. Once again in the aftermath of the revolution, thousands of conspirators joined their compatriots in exile, adding their voices to the call for Italian independence.

At home and abroad, the revolutions of 1831 made clear that after two decades of plotting and planning, moderate and democratic liberals were incapable of leading a revolution. The failure of the secret societies to overcome ideological divisions, or their local interests, doomed them to failure. Patriots at home and abroad became aware that in order to realize their dreams of Italian independence, they needed to link territorial unification to cultural nationalism. This realization, in many ways, marked the beginning of the Risorgimento, culminating in the creation of the Kingdom of Italy in 1861.

The Risorgimento

In 1831, the twenty-six-year-old lawyer, Giuseppe Mazzini, stood trial in Genoa on charges of treason stemming from his participation in the revolutions of 1830. Born into a moderately well-to-do Genoese family in 1805, that showed little sympathy for Italian Nationalist visions, Mazzini had been drawn to the movement through friends and teachers. Steeped in the poetry of Foscolo, Leopardi, the writings of Dante, Petrarch, Vico, Herder, and Goethe, Mazzini embraced the dream of a free and united Italy, a nation bound by culture and history suffering under oppressive tyrannical rule. At university, Mazzini joined the student literary society, believing that literature could bring about the moral and political renewal of the Italian people.[16] In 1829, he became a member of the local *carbonaria*, participating in the 1830 revolutions in Liguria and Tuscany. Betrayed by a coconspirator, Mazzini was arrested and sentenced to exile.

During his time in prison, and his first year of exile in Marseilles, Mazzini reflected on the lessons from the failed revolutions of 1820 and 1830 and began to sketch out a new plan of action. Declaring the *Carboneria* dead, he argued that Italian independence depended on an open, united coordinated action and popular support. Patriots, he insisted, had to embark on a massive popular educational campaign. The people could not be bought with offerings of material compensation, but they could learn to love the nation. Mazzini's own political ideology was complicated, incorporating a vision of democratic, cosmopolitan nation-states linked together in a kind of transnational brotherhood, a model of the liberal state anchored in the patriarchal hierarchy of the family, and a conviction that sex and wealth determined duties toward God and country.

In 1831, Mazzini decided to put his ideas into practice, founding *Giovine Italia* (Young Italy). Adopting the motto *Dio e Popolo* ("God and the People"), Mazzini laid out the goals of the new organization: a unified republic composed of a free and equal brotherhood, aware of belonging to a common nation. The means to achieve this goal are education and insurrection. Mazzini embraced an expansive definition of a republic as government by the people. If a king proved willing to serve the will of the people, a monarchy would be acceptable, but not necessary. Mazzini's good looks and oratorical skills proved persuasive among men and women alike, and membership grew rapidly. His rhetorical power rested on his appeals to sentiment and love, comparing the bond of citizen to nation to the organic tie between mother and child: a bond forged from love and faith. Familial and patriotic love stood at the heart of *Giovine Italia*'s politics transforming intimate ties of friendship, kinship, collegiality, and geography into a larger national community (Figure 2).

Young Italy flourished at home and abroad. Its rally cry of "Italy, one, free and independent" took hold from London to Naples among the educated elite and workers. Supporters of Young Italy tended to be urban, educated, and steeped in the Risorgimento canon. Followers passed pamphlets and publications outlining the movement's goals and principles, generally printed France and Great Britain, from hand to hand until they appeared in the drawing rooms and taverns throughout the Italian states. The Italian émigré communities and wealthy patrons in France, Switzerland, Germany, England, and the Americas proved a rich recruiting ground for the new movement and a lucrative source of funding. Young Italy struggled to recruit workers and peasants at home, but was more successful in crossing class boundaries abroad. Mazzini wrote impassioned articles coming to the defense of Italian laborers denigrated by the British press. The 1839 Chartist movement deepened Mazzini's interest in working-class politics. A year later, he opened schools for Italian artisans and workers, offering lessons in reading, writing, arithmetic, Italian, and English and lectures on the recent history of Italy and the movements for unification.

Young Italy proved more effective in promoting Italian nationalism than in plotting revolution. Early efforts to spark a national revolt ended in failure. Their plans to instigate a revolt in 1833 among Piedmont army recruits were discovered by customs officials hidden in a trunk addressed to Mazzini's mother. The conspirators were arrested. A year later, a planned uprising in Genoa, led by the merchant marine captain Giuseppe

Primo incontro tra Mazzini e Garibaldi a Marsiglia, nel 1833.

Figure 2 Giuseppe Garibaldi first meets Giuseppe Mazzini in Marseille, France, 1833. Keystone-France/Gamma-Keystone/Getty Images.

Garibaldi, was uncovered before it began. Carlo Alberto, crowned king after the death of his cousin Carlo Felice in 1831, immediately exiled or executed all those involved, and outlawed Young Italy. After 1834, Mazzini's efforts to incite revolution at home waned, although he continued to capitalize on the protests that broke out across the peninsula. Mazzini publicized local demonstrations sparked by food shortages, unemployment, and cholera epidemics, as evidence of a simmering Italian nationalism. Young Italy became the model for new Nationalist movements in Germany, Poland, and Ireland. By the 1840s, Mazzini became the symbol of national revolution, and Metternich declared him the "most dangerous man in Europe."

Mazzini's publicity campaign proved extraordinarily successful. Based on the coverage of Italian uprisings in the foreign press, the peninsula appeared to teeter on the brink of full-scale revolution. Press accounts of the uprisings in Calabria convinced the brothers Attilio and Emilio Bandiera, both ardent Mazzinians, living in exile in Corfu, that the Bourbon south was ripe for revolution. Despite Mazzini's efforts to dissuade the brothers, they were determined to organize an armed insurrection, insisting that "Italy will never live until Italians learn to die."[17] On June 16, 1844, the brothers and a small band of patriots landed on a beach near the town of Crotone, just north of Catanzaro. Instead of the bands of eager and armed insurgents they expected to greet them on the beaches, the motley crew of foreigners found wary peasants heading to work in the fields. The small band of rebels decided to retreat, but fearing that they would be arrested in Crotone, they decided to cross over the mountains to the western coastline. The next day, they were taken into custody by local residents. A few were shot and killed, some managed to escape, and nine were sent to prison to await trial. All nine of those who stood trial were found guilty and executed.

Their bravery and commitment to the cause even in the face of death became the stuff of legend. Stories circulated of how as the men walked barefoot through the dusty roads toward the firing squad, they sang the chorus from Marcadante's opera *Donna Caritea*: "Who dies for the fatherland/has lived long enough . . . far better to perish/in the prime of life/than languish for years/under a tyrant's yoke."[18] The Mazzinian press turned the Bandiera brothers into heroes, extolling their bravery, self-sacrifice, and love of nations in poems, pamphlets, and eulogies. Proof positive that Italian men would die for their country. As Emanuele Celesia wrote shortly after the ill-fated Bandiera expedition,

> Grown under the invasive stink of Austrian tyranny, they wanted to purge the shame of the imposed foreign ruler . . . to transform, like Spartacus their iron chains into swords of the free citizen. But our destiny was not yet ripe, and hey fell with the name of Italy on their lips. They went happily to meet their deaths, bearing witness to the people that Italians know how to die.[19] (Figure 3)

The military exploits of Italian patriots in South America offered further evidence of Italian valor. Exiled from his home in Nice in 1835, Giuseppe Garibaldi made his way to Brazil. Within a year he organized volunteer legions of Italian emigrants to fight for Brazilian and Uruguayan independence. In 1846, Garibaldi's volunteers defeated the Argentinean forces at the battle of Salto in defense of Montevideo. Captivated by the adventures of Garibaldi and the Italian Legion, Mazzini transformed these soldiers-for-hire into moral crusaders for freedom and democracy. Garibaldi, the "hero of the two worlds," epitomized the selfless soldier, fighting for freedom, not for money, promotion, or land. In their red shirts, carrying the Italian Legion flag, into battle, Garibaldi and his soldiers embodied a virtuous and brave resurgent Italy.

By the mid-1840s, as the possibility of Mazzini's democratic Italian revolution becoming a reality faded, the idea of a moderate independent Italy gained traction. In 1843 a Piedmontese priest, Vincenzo Gioberti, published a widely popular book entitled *Del Primato Morale e Civile degli Italiani* (*On the Moral and Civil Primacy of the Italians*), suggesting that existing Italian states form a confederation, with the pope as president. Gioberti's conservative vision rested on the Nationalist cultural narratives. Pointing to the past preeminence of Italians in science, arts, music, philosophy, literature, and history as proof of their place as moral and civil leaders, Gioberti argued that Italy's recent decline stemmed from political fragmentation. Unification under the leadership of the pope would enable Italians to return to their rightful place in the world. Gioberti's neo-guelphism made the idea of a united Italy palpable to conservative Catholic and monarchical communities. In 1844, Cesare Balbo offered a secular alternative to a papal

Figure 3 Camillo Costa, execution by firing squad of the Bandiera brothers in Cosenza. DEA/L. VISCONTI/De Agostini/Getty Images.

confederation in *Delle speranze d'Italia* (*On the Hopes of Italy*), dedicated to Gioberti. Balbo envisioned an Italy created by incorporating Lombardy-Venetia into Piedmont, and whose national mission was to protect and glorify the papacy. Balbo's argument for Piedmont leadership, if not his vision of Italy as papal protector, took hold among the nobility and elite, sparking discussion of what an Italy under the Savoy crown would look like.

By 1847, Metternich's assertion that Italy was a "mere geographic expression" was in some ways more wish than reality. While it was true that Italian states were fragmented, diplomatically impotent, socially and politically divided, and largely dependent on Austria, the idea of an Italian nation had taken hold among the cultural elites in Italy, and the wider European imagination. By 1845, even Carlo Alberto and the new pope, Pio IX, began to reflect on the wisdom of the proposals of Balbo and Gioberti, and consider what a unified Italy would look like. While few imagined a kingdom stretching from Sicily to the Alps, the idea of a unified Italy no longer seemed so impossible.

CHAPTER 3
MAKING ITALY (1848–60)

In the summer of 1847, Ferdinand II toured Sicily seeking to calm his starving and discontented subjects by doling out food and words of comfort. As the king's carriage wound through the crowded narrow streets of Palermo, a bystander tossed a pamphlet to his lap. The leaflet, *Protesta del popolo delle due Sicilie* (*The People's Protest in the Two Sicilies*), warned its readers that decades of corruption and wickedness on the part of the court, clergy, and military, combined with mass arrests, arbitrary executions, onerous taxes, and military obligations, had left the people filled with anger and hatred. Recent royal indifference in the face of poor harvests and cholera epidemics, fueling rumors that the government was intentionally starving the people and poisoning the wells turned the simmering rage into rebellion.[1] Furious, the king ordered the arrest of the unknown author, and arbitrarily imprisoned all publishers in Palermo.

A few months later, anger turned into open resistance. On September 1, the people of Messina rose in revolt only to be gunned down by Bourbon soldiers. Calls for revolution grew louder: posters denouncing the monarchy appeared in the streets, shouts of "Viva Italia" echoed through the theaters of Naples and Palermo. On January 10, 1848, residents of Palermo and its environs awoke to posters plastered all along the streets calling on Sicilians to rebel, proclaiming:

> The time for useless prayers has passed. Protests, supplications and peaceful demonstrations are useless. Ferdinand has scorned them all. And are we, a free people weakened by chains and misery, once again going to delay the reclamation of our rights? To arms sons of Sicily![2]

On the morning of January 12, the people of Palermo took to the streets, and soon forced the Bourbons to retreat. By the end of the month, the Sicilian parliament convened a provisional government declaring its independence from the Bourbon crown, and reinstated the constitution of 1812. From Sicily, the revolutions spread to the mainland.[3]

The uprising in Palermo marked the end of the democratic revolutions and the first of the wars of Italian Risorgimento. The revolutions of 1848, originating in similar impulses to the earlier revolutionary waves—local famines, unemployment, loss of land, military conscription, and state repression—spread wider, lasted longer, and had very different consequences. Although 1848 may have proved Republican patriots to be incapable of instigating revolution, the uprisings attested to the endurance and power of their visions. If statesmen wanted stability and security, they had to address democratic demands. In Piedmont, the revolutions of 1848 convinced Vittorio Emanuele to accept limited constitutional rule rather. In the following years, Piedmont implemented a series of progressive economic and liberal reforms, offered sanctuary to political exiles, and implicitly endorsed the Nationalist cause. By embracing Italian unity, the Piedmont government transformed the revolutionary struggle into a liberal state-making project.

Winds of change

On June 1, 1846, the papacy announced the death of Pope Gregory XVI. Two weeks later the cardinals elected Giovanni Maria Mastai-Ferretti, the bishop of Imola, as Pope Pio IX. The new pope appeared an innocuous choice, best known for his conciliatory nature and ability to stay out of politics. Shortly after his election, he extended amnesty to all political prisoners. Pardoning political prisoners was not an unusual act of grace for a newly minted pope, but in the political climate of 1846, the amnesty took on deeper political significance: the release of thousands of political prisoners, including revolutionaries, appeared as a sign of the pope's liberal sympathies. Could Pio IX be the savior envisioned by the neo-Guelphs? By autumn, it seemed that the pope had indeed sided with the liberals. Within the first months in office he opened an inquiry into the judicial system, loosened censorship laws, creating a representative consultative assembly, and authorized a rail system linking Papal States to neighboring lands. A year later, the famous anticlerical Garibaldi offered the support of his Italian Legion in the event the pope took up the Italian cause.

The first years of the new pope's reign were unsettled. Bad harvests in 1845 and 1846 were followed by even worse crop failures in 1847, causing severe localized famines, pervasive food shortages, and prices to rise. Faced with starvation and the threat of disease, thousands of peasants made their way to the cities, adding to an already overburdened urban infrastructure. Worsening conditions fueled anger at an indifferent, or worse, complicit, government. The situation was exacerbated by natural disasters. In August of 1847 an earthquake shook Tuscany, leaving thousands homeless. Riots and demonstrations broke out across the peninsula, and the liberal elite redoubled their calls for economic and political reform. In the fall of 1847, Carlo Alberto in Piedmont and Archduke Leopold II in Tuscany joined with the pope in creating a custom's league that eliminated tariffs between the states. A liberal wind seemed to blow across the peninsula, relaxing censorship, lowering tariffs, and increasing free trade.

The reforms fed a growing political enthusiasm. In cities and towns people gathered in cafes and salons to discuss the latest events. The general public readily read Nationalist sentiment into lectures, poetry readings, and theatrical performances. In Milan and Venice, patriots transformed banquets, the funeral of Federico Confalonieri and the visit of Richard Cobden, a staunch opponent of the British Corn Laws, into calls for autonomy, tax reforms, and freedom of the press.

Opera, in particular, became a site of Nationalist demonstrations. In the charged atmosphere of the 1840s even innocuous lines took on a political cast as audiences responded with wild applause. When Verdi's Nabucco premiered at La Scala in 1842, the audience read the story of Italians into the tale of the suffering of the Jews under Nebuchadrezzar's tyranny. In its first year, Nabucco was performed over sixty times. When audiences heard the chorus sing the line *oh mia Patria si bella e perduta* ("Oh my Country, so beautiful and lost"), in *Va, pensiero* ("Chorus of the Hebrew Slaves"), they rose to their feet and demanded an encore (Figure 4).

Older works were reinterpreted with a political slant. The chorus of Mercadente's *Donna Caritea* became fused with the heroism of the Bandiera brothers. Lyrics in Bellini's work referencing freedom, or the call of war, were heard as cries for Italian independence, eliciting shouts of "Viva Italia," or "Viva Pio IX." Neither Verdi, Bellini, nor Mercadente set out to write political operas, constrained by heavy-handed censors, and the need to make a living. Regardless, their words became rallying cries for radicals and moderates alike. By the fall of 1847, the Austrian authorities had made it a crime to shout "Viva Pio IX," or "Viva Italia."[4]

By 1847, the spontaneous demonstrations against foreign rule turned into calls for organized resistance. In late December, a group of young Milanese nobles announced a boycott of tobacco and the state lottery to begin on January 1, 1848, to protest the oppressive tax system. The taxes on tobacco alone generated millions of lire in revenue for the Austrian government. Within the first days of the boycott, tobacco and lottery sales declined precipitously. Austrian soldiers, puffing on their cigarettes and pipes, taunted and attacked the protesters with their swords and bayonets, killing five people and wounding over sixty.[5] Austrian authorities responded to the growing popular rage by stationing more troops in the region.

Figure 4 Italian patriots writing "Viva Verdi" on a wall. Bettmann/Getty Images.

Rumors of revolution, the return of the secret societies, public demonstrations, and the growing popularity of tricolor cockades and flags renewed fears of another Jacobin terror. Liberals urged monarchs to take control of the movement, publishing impassioned editorials making the case for liberal nationalism, and reminding readers of the dangers of democratic revolution. The emperors and kings refused to listen.

Revolutions of 1848

Two weeks after the *Palermitani* rose in revolt, the people of Naples took to the streets. By the end of the month, Ferdinand II's subjects had forced the king to grant a constitution. Other monarchs took heed. On February 17, Leopold of Tuscany readily approved a constitution, granting full rights to all subjects regardless of religion, and guaranteeing freedom of the press. On March 4, Carlo Alberto offered the people of Piedmont a *statuto* (statute), establishing a representative government, guaranteeing civil and political rights, and freedom of the press. It extended limited suffrage to propertied subjects, enabling approximately 2 percent of the people to vote in parliamentary elections. The *statuto* was not a constitution, but a gift from the king to his subjects, which could be revoked at any time.

By the time Carlo Alberto promulgated the *statuto*, revolutions had broken out in Paris, Berlin, Frankfurt, and Vienna. On March 13, the Austrians had forced Metternich into exile, and on March 18, the people of Milan and Venice rose in revolt. For five days the men and women of Milan, workers, aristocrats, artisans, students, and even a few clergy mounted barricades and took up arms to oust the 12,000 Austrian troops stationed in the city. According to eyewitness accounts, men and women poured into the streets, armed with rifles, sticks, or shovels: "Mothers urged their ill-prepared sons to combat, threating to close the door in their faces if they returned before the defeat of the enemy; wives armed with spades stood at the side of their husbands; sisters provided arms to their brothers."[6] Two days later, the countryside had joined the revolt, cutting Austrian supply lines. Running low on food and ammunition, combined with rumors of an impending Piedmont invasion, the Austrian Commander Radetzky ordered his troops to retreat to fortresses near Verona and Mantua. In Venezia, Daniele Manin, the Republican leader of the Venetian independence movement, immediately proclaimed a Republic. In Milan, insurgents vacillated between defending the Republic and joining with Piedmont to create a unified kingdom. In April, Mazzini arrived in Milan to strengthen the Republican case, but in the end, moderate fears of democrats proved stronger than their dislike of a Piedmont king.

Meanwhile, in Turin, calls for the king to go to war in the name of Italy grew louder. Carlo Alberto mobilized his troops, and on March 23 declared war on Austria. The next day, the Royal Sardinian army, marching under its new flag—the Italian tricolor with the Savoyard arms in the center—crossed Lombardy. The military standard made clear the king's willingness to embrace Italian unity, if it served the interests of the Savoyard monarchy. The arrival of the Piedmontese meant the end of the democratic revolution.

In May, overriding the protests of the democrats, the provisional government called for plebiscites: 84 percent of voters approved annexation. Furious, Milanese Republicans protested the replacement of one monarch for another. Through the early summer, Carlo Alberto led his troops across the northern states, holding similar plebiscites in Parma, Modena, and the Venetian mainland. Even Venice eventually agreed to annexation in exchange for military support against the Austrians.

Italian patriots greeted Piedmont's declaration of war on Austria with unbridled enthusiasm. Volunteers rushed to join the army, and to be a part of the first conventional war for national unity. Students left their classrooms, forming voluntary battalions. Garibaldi returned from South America to lead a volunteer force against the Austrians in the foothills of the Alps. Throughout the Italian states the people pressured rulers to send troops in support of the Piedmont army. Even the pope initially sent a small contingent, although he quickly recanted and ordered his soldiers home. The pope's denunciation of Carlo Alberto, combined with his refusal to declare war on Austria, transformed the struggle for Italian independence into an anticlerical movement. Thousands of volunteers returned home after the pope's declaration, unwilling to participate in a war the church opposed. In May, Ferdinand II recalled troops after staging a coup d'état, dissolving the Neapolitan parliament, and sparking a new wave of revolutions at home. Having lost the support of other Italian rulers, and distrustful of the remaining volunteers, Carlo Alberto made little headway against Austrian troops.

By mid-summer, Austria gained the upper hand when arms and men finally made it over the Brenner Pass from Vienna. On July 25, at the Battle of Custoza, Radetzky defeated Carlo Alberto's forces. By early August, Austrian troops retook Milan. Carlo Alberto signed an armistice and returned to Turin where he tried to secure the annexed land through diplomatic channels. When it became clear that his efforts would fail, Carlo Alberto led his troops back into battle, hoping to incite another wave of insurrections. By this time, support for Piedmont had vanished, and the people of Lombardy stayed home. On March 23, 1849, Austria decisively defeated the Piedmont army at the Battle of Novara. Carlo Alberto abdicated in favor of his eldest son, Vittorio Emanuele II, and went into exile in Portugal. Only Venice, under the leadership of Manin, held out for another year.

As Radetzky led the Austrian advance in the summer of 1848, Ferdinando worked to subdue the revolutions sweeping through the Kingdom of the Two Sicilies. By the end of the summer, he had quashed revolts in the mainland provinces, and turned his attention to the island. Sicilians had rejected Ferdinando's offer of autonomy and set up a provisional government, hostile to both Italian unity and the Bourbons. In September, Ferdinando opened fire on the island. The fierce bombardment of Messina nearly destroyed the city, and earned the monarch the nickname *Re Bomba*. In May 1849, the Bourbons retook Palermo. Martial law was imposed across the island, and thousands of people were summarily executed.

Surveying the situation in August, Mazzini declared that "the royal war is finished, the war of the people begins," and over the course of the next few months the democrats took control of the revolutions.[7] In Venice, support for Manin's Republic remained strong, despite the food shortages. In November of 1848, the people of Tuscany installed a radical government and, when Grand Duke Leopold fled, proclaimed a republic. In Rome, radicals seized power when the pope fled to Gaeta after the assassination of Pellegrino Rossi, the head of the provisional government. Safe in his southern fortress, under the protection of Ferdinand II, the pope sent out an appeal to Catholic kings to come to his aid. Meanwhile, on February 9, 1849, the democratically elected constituent assembly of Rome announced the formation of the Roman Republic.

Radicals flocked to Rome, seeing in the Republic the birth of a new Italian nation. Garibaldi became the military commander in chief, while Mazzini, one of the three triumvirs of the new Republic, emerged as the de facto leader of Rome. The leaders of the Roman Republic moved quickly to establish the new state, introducing universal manhood suffrage, guaranteeing freedom of the press, abolishing the inquisition, ending the death penalty, repealing government monopolies on salt and tobacco, and reforming the tax system. They also limited church power, ending clerical control of education and expropriating select church properties, but in general did little to incite further Catholic hostility, well aware of the symbolic importance of Rome in the wider world.[8]

Austria, Spain, Naples, and France heeded the papal cry for help. French war ships appeared in the port of Civitavecchia at the end of April, and General Oudinot immediately marched his troops toward Rome. In the meantime, the Bourbon army began marching north. Garibaldi marshaled his forces, comprised of ex-papal guards and volunteers. On the morning of April 30, Garibaldi's forces, comprised of ex-papal guards and volunteers, defeated the French troops, and a few days later forced the Bourbon army to retreat. Garibaldi's army managed to hold out for two months. But, on June 20, Oudinot coordinated a surprise attack on Rome, capturing the hills near Villa Corsini. After a full day of fighting, and heavy casualties, Garibaldi ordered a retreat. From his perch in the hills, Oudinot laid siege, bombing the city day and night. Over 5,000 volunteers, including women, children, and the elderly, defended Rome for a month.

By the end of June defeat was inevitable. Garibaldi announced to his followers that they had three options: surrender, fight, or retreat. On July 3, the French retook Rome. Mazzini returned to exile in London. Garibaldi, his wife Anita, pregnant with their third child, and 4,000 volunteers headed toward Venice. Garibaldi's retreat from Rome became the stuff of legend.[9] Traveling at night, over difficult terrain, many of the volunteers fell ill, or quit. By the time they reached San Marino their numbers were so depleted, Garibaldi disbanded the volunteers. Many who continued on through Austrian territories were captured and killed. Garibaldi, Anita, and a few others managed to escape over the Apennine Mountains. During the journey Anita fell ill and died. Garibaldi buried her in a shallow grave near Ravenna. Over 4,000 Italians were killed or wounded in the defense of Rome. By the end of the summer the revolutions ended; the Tuscan Republic collapsed in April. In August, the Republic of Venice finally surrendered; starving and dying of cholera, Venetians could not withstand Austrian bombardments (Figure 5).

Figure 5 Giuseppe Garibaldi carrying Anita through marshes of Comacchio, August 1849, Oil on Canvas. DEA/G. CIGOLINI/De Agostini/Getty Images.

The revolutions of 1848 revealed the limits of Italian cultural nationalism. The ideas of national unity circulating in novels, poems, and operas had not really taken root. Despite being ushered in on cries of "Viva Italia," the revolutions of 1848 remained essentially local revolts against Austrian, Bourbon, or Papal rule. Venetians fought for their own Republic and Sicilians for a separate state. For the most part, rural residents had little interest in a unified state, and even those committed to a Nationalist cause were divided over what a united Italy would look like. Although the revolutions failed to create Italy, the harsh reprisals that followed convinced many that there could be no political stability in the peninsula absent an independent state. Between 1849 and 1859, sympathy for the Nationalist cause grew among foreigners and Italians alike, preparing the way for a moderate-liberal path toward unification.

Revolutionary consequences: New strategies

As in the past, Italian rulers returned to power seeking vengeance; however, unlike in the 1820s or 1830s, efforts to restore absolute rule found little support among European powers and generated sympathy for Italian patriots. Radetzky, Pio IX, and Ferdinand II immediately abrogated constitutional reforms, cracked down on dissent, increased police surveillance, and heightened censorship laws. In Lombardy-Veneto, Radetzky's harsh punishments of accused traitors—billing mothers for the cost of their son's executions, tossing the bodies into unconsecrated ground, imposing life sentences for minor infractions, seizing the property of exiled patriots—increased sympathy for the Italian cause and anti-Austrian sentiment among a wider European public.

The pope's insistence on wielding worldly authority in the most repressive manner possible severely undercut the standing of the church. In 1858, the case of Edgardo Mortara became a cause célèbre, and left more Europeans than ever convinced that the temporal rule of the pope was anachronistic in a liberal age. In the spring of 1858, papal troops kidnapped six-year-old Edgardo Mortara, from his Jewish family in Bologna. A maid testified that she had secretly baptized Edgardo when he had fallen ill as an infant, and papal law forbade Jews from raising Catholic children. Exiled Italian Nationalists made sure the heart-wrenching story of a child torn from his family reached the press. Throughout Western Europe and the Americas people called for the pope to return the child. The Vatican mounted its own public relations campaign, spinning Edgardo's kidnapping into a tale of liberation and salvation, lambasting all protesters as godless liberals.[10] In the climate of the 1850s, the kidnapping of Edgardo exemplified the abuses inherent in the illiberal papal state. Support for the pope's temporal powers melted away. Even Napoleon III, whose troops provided pontifical protection, grew disgusted.

Italian exiles promoted these stories of brutality alongside testimonies of the courage of a new generation of Italian revolutionaries. Emigrants in London, Paris, New York, and Buenos Aires produced a wide range of articles, pamphlets, memoirs, novels, and poetry commemorating the heroics of Giuseppe Garibaldi, and the bravery of the peoples of Milan, Venice, Rome, and Palermo. Publishing houses translated patriot prison memoirs into English and French to reach a wider audience. The post-1848 narratives of courage and sacrifice strengthened a sense of national belonging among emigrant Italians and bolstered support for an independent Italy in Europe and the Americas.

Heightened support for Italian nationalism abroad accompanied deeper commitments to the cause at home. Even though the revolutions of 1848 failed to convert the majority of peasants or the elite to the Nationalist cause, they mobilized more people than previous uprisings. Thousands of men and women in the cities, provincial towns, and countryside mounted the barricades, marched to war, volunteered to nurse the wounded, and voted in the plebiscites. The short-lived Republics and expansion of constitutional democracy politicized a wide swath of people, including property-owning elite, peasants, and women. By the mid-1850s, a wealth of memoirs, published in Turin, London, Paris, and New York, emphasized the geographic and social reach of the revolutions: "*le Cinque giornate di Como,*" *Le cinque giornate di Milan, Con Garibaldi alle porte di Roma*, document collections recounting the heroics of the people of Palermo and Naples, attested to the vital role peasants, lawyers, students, doctors, shopkeepers, and artisans played in the struggle for Italy. The accounts marveled at the mothers who pushed their sons out the door to join the fighting, the peasants who hid revolutionaries from the Bourbon soldiers, the women who nursed the sick, the men and women took to the barricades. These stories of everyday heroics attested to the widespread popular support for unification.

Explicit models of patriotic femininity emerged in the aftermath of 1848. In the midst of the revolutions the patriotic press lauded Italian women: "As long as there is danger, as long as the nation needs them, as long as the unfortunate need consolation and relief, we will always find Italian women at the vanguard, ready to . . . make all the necessary sacrifices circumstances demand."[11] Caterina Franceschi Ferruci published a poetic call to arms in the name of Italian mothers and wives. Shortly after, Mazzini published a treatise urging women to educate their sons to love their country and hate the tyrants. Postrevolutionary accounts of the Roman Republic emphasized the role played by women. The revolutions of 1848 proved that Italy was not a land of ruins, but a nation inhabited by brave men and virtuous women, committed to the creation of an independent Italy.[12]

The growing acceptance of Italian nationalism helped turn Piedmont's constitutional monarchy into a leader of Italian unity. Although Pio IX's rejection of his liberal past put an end to Gioberti's federalist visions, the revolutions had legitimized moderate Nationalist ambition making the idea of a Piedmont-led unification effort more acceptable. Even Gioberti admitted that Piedmont had proven capable of leading the fight for Italian unification in his last work, *On the Civil Renewal of Italy*. Although democrats professed little faith in the new king, a large, squat man, rough in his ways with a great love for hunting and woman, and very little for the constitution, his willingness to keep the *statuto*, extend relatively liberal free speech protections, and welcome tens of thousands of radicals and democrats exiled from the other states, made Piedmont appear the best hope for their political aspirations. Under the canny leadership of Count Camillo Benso di Cavour, Piedmont prepared the way for the creation of a liberal Italian state by energizing moderates, wooing Republicans, and allying with European powers.

Born into an old noble Piedmont family, Cavour had grown up in a relatively liberal atmosphere. As a young man, Cavour embarked on his grand tour, studying political theory and economics in Paris and London. Taken with the ideas of Jeremy Bentham, he returned to Turin eager to put theories touting the social and political benefits of modernization and liberalism into practice, becoming a champion of agrarian reform. He increased production on his family's estates by introducing new machinery, shifting crop rotations, and implementing new animal breeding methods. The events of 1848 drew him to the city where he became active in politics. As coeditor of the newspaper *Il Risorgimento*, with Cesare Balbo, he promoted a moderate Nationalist vision, linking territorial unity with economic prosperity.

Cavour was elected to Parliament shortly after the passage of the *statuto*. His first legislative proposals focused on the expansion of individual and economic liberties, and the separation of church and state. He supported the Siccardi laws, passed in 1850 abolishing the privileges of the Catholic Church, providing the basis for a union, or *connubio*, between the radicals and moderates. As the minister of agriculture and commerce, and then minister of finance, he signed a variety of commercial treaties lowering tariffs, cutting postal costs, and raising land taxes. In 1852, Cavour replaced Massimo D'Azeglio as prime minister, and continued his efforts to modernize from above. For the next seven years, Piedmont invested in transportation and communication networks, expanding railroads, shipping, and roads. Cavour proved a brilliant political strategist, able to create a broad-based coalition of conservative liberals, radical democrats, and moderate members of Parliament to support his plans for economic modernization and state expansion.

Cavour's vision of the Italian state consisted of expanding the borders of the Piedmont constitutional monarchy to included Veneto, Lombardy, Modena, and Parma, stopping at the edge of the Papal States. He had no intention of leading a democratic revolution, but envisioned an Italy formed through annexation with Piedmont. Cavour had little interest in bringing the Bourbon Kingdom into Italy. Like many in the north, he considered southerners to be cut from a different cloth. Cavour remained unconvinced by the Sicilian Republican Giuseppe La Farina's arguments that the stories of southern corruption, violence, and poverty were exaggerated, and the problems that did exist were the fault of Bourbon bad government. The prime minister had even less interest in undermining the pope's temporal authority, sparking a conservative backlash at home, and incurring the wrath of the European Catholic states.

Cavour was well aware that he would need to secure the backing of Great Britain, Prussia and, most importantly, France, in his bid to unite Italy. Napoleon III's ascension to power in 1852 paved the way for an alliance between Piedmont and France. Napoleon III saw himself as his uncle's heir, a national liberator, and an enemy of Austrian tyranny, but like Cavour, he distrusted democracy. The outbreak of the Crimean war in 1853 offered the first occasion for Cavour to move Piedmont onto the European stage and solidify an alliance with France. In 1855, Piedmont sent in an expeditionary force to fight alongside the British and French. The 18,000 Sardinian soldiers proved instrumental in ending the siege of Sebastopol. Sardinia's participation succeeded in securing Cavour a place at the peace negotiations in Paris in 1856. Although he failed in gaining any territorial concessions at the peace conference, he was successful in formally introducing the subject of the "Italian question" into diplomatic discussions. Cavour returned home having gained the goodwill of the French and British.

Republicans aided Cavour in uniting democrats and moderates behind his vision of a unified Italian state. Democrats emerged from 1848 deeply divided. Mazzini's refusal to hear criticisms in the face of failed revolutions led many supporters to distance themselves from Young Italy. A series of disastrous insurrectionary expeditions further tarnished Mazzini's reputation. An attempt to incite an uprising in Milan in 1853 left sixteen revolutionaries dead; a year later, a bid to start an insurrection in Modena ended in failure, as did an effort to instigate a revolt in Palermo in 1856. Carlo Pisacane's expedition to Sapri, south of Naples, proved the most damaging. Pisacane and a small band of followers landed on the beaches near Sapri on June 28, 1857. Instead of sparking a revolution, the insurgents were rounded up and executed; nearly one hundred men were killed by Bourbon soldiers and peasants. Although poets immortalized Pisacane's exploits, the Sapri expedition proved the final straw for the Republican movement. Mazzini remained the face of Italian nationalism in Great Britain, but in Paris and Genoa, democrats joined rival organizations. Cavour capitalized on Mazzini's decline.

At the Paris Peace conference, Cavour met with Italian exiles to recruit them to the Savoyard cause. A month after Pisacane's expedition, democrats Daniele Manin, Giorgio Pallavicino, and Giuseppe La Farina formed the *Società Nazionale Italiana* (Italian National Society) to promote an alliance between Republicans and Piedmont. By December, even Garibaldi had joined the society, committing to back the Kingdom of Sardinia. The new society ensured that Italian nationalism would be linked to political stability instead of revolution, making it far more palatable to conservatives. Having secured the backing of the major European powers and the support of radical leaders, Cavour was ready to take advantage of the first chance to oust the Austrians from north Italian lands.

Italy unified

Cavour's opportunity came through an unexpected avenue. On January 14, 1858, Felice Orsini, an Italian émigré and disillusioned Mazzinian, launched three hand grenades at Napoleon III and his wife; the attack left eight dead and many more wounded. Orsini used his trial to plead for Italy's liberation, writing a direct appeal to Napoleon III. Orsini's plea did not stay his execution, but it did not fall on deaf ears. Napoleon III ordered the letter be published in France and Piedmont, helping to make a martyr of Orsini.[13] The French Emperor agreed with Orsini's assessment that political stability in Europe depended on resolving the Italian question, and used the assassination attempt as an opportunity to form an alliance with Cavour.

In July of 1858, Cavour and Napoleon III met secretly in the northeastern French town of Plombières to divvy up the Italian states and fix the terms of the alliance. Under the Plombières agreement, Piedmont would directly annex Lombardy-Venetia, and rule over a Kingdom of upper Italy comprised of the duchies of Modena-Reggio, Parma, and Romagna, and the Marche. A ruler would be appointed over a second kingdom consisting of the duchy of Tuscany and the vestiges of the Papal States, with the exception of Rome and the surrounding territories, which would remain under direct Papal rule. The new kingdoms would form a loose federation under the presidency of the pope. In the south, Lucien Murat, the son of Joachim Murat who ruled Naples under Napoleon I, would replace Ferdinand. Napoleon III insisted that Piedmont cede the provinces of Nice and Savoy to France, a clause that had to remain secret to avoid popular protests. Nice, the birthplace of Garibaldi, held a special place in the hearts of Italian Nationalists. In January of 1859, Cavour signed the secret treaty committing France to come to Piedmont's aid in a war against Austrian aggression. Now all Cavour had to do was incite Austria to attack Piedmont.

In the first months of 1859 Piedmont prepared for war. Cavour intensified his anti-Austrian propaganda campaign, and began an extensive rearmament campaign. He called on the *Società Nazionale Italiana* to organize volunteers, and appointed Garibaldi as commander of one regiment. Desperate to provoke a war with Austria, Cavour even tried to incite a revolt in Modena, despite his fears of popular insurrection. Perhaps to his relief, the uprising never materialized. The growing threat of war worried European powers, who began to plan a peace conference to settle the French and Austrian dispute. Just when it seemed Cavour's plan had failed, Austria issued an ultimatum, demanding that Piedmont demobilize or they would invade.

The second war of the Risorgimento began when Austrian troops crossed the Ticino River into Piedmont on April 29, 1859. Heavy rains and overflowing rivers slowed the Austrian advance, enabling nearly 200,000 French troops to cross over the border by train in time to join the Piedmontese army, some 60,000 strong, and a volunteer army of over 20,000 soldiers. The French and Sardinian troops defeated Austrian armies at the Battle of Magenta on June 4, 1859. Three weeks later they repeated their victory at the brutal Battle of Solferino, which lasted from six o'clock in the morning until seven o'clock at night. As the summer sun finally sank behind the hills, over 30,000 men lay dead and wounded. The retreating Austrian forces enabled pro-Piedmont governments to come to power, but apart from the central states, there was little genuine popular enthusiasm for the new regime.

By August, Napoleon III's commitment to the war waned. The Austrian forces had not suffered a decisive defeat, and domestic support for the war began to fade. The prolonged war, combined with rumors that Prussia contemplated coming to the aid of Austria, prompted the emperor to open peace negotiations. On July 11 Napoleon III and Emperor Franz Joseph met alone in Villafranca. Excluding Piedmont from discussion, the two rulers agreed to reconstitute the Italian lands as a confederation, including a Kingdom of Sardinia expanded to include Lombardy, and Austria. Napoleon agreed to abandon his claim on Savoy and Nice, but insisted that Piedmont bear the full costs of the war. The terms were presented to Vittorio Emanuele who had no choice but to sign. Livid, Cavour resigned.

The treaty of Villafranca reignited Nationalist sentiment across Italy. In Turin and Milan, people spilled into the streets denouncing the peace. Although people of Lombardy and Veneto had little love for Piedmont, they were even more infuriated with Napoleon III's treachery, and willingly supported Cavour. In the south, patriots voiced their support for Piedmont's efforts. Francesco Crispi, a young Sicilian, and ardent supporter of Mazzini, returned to Sicily to hold a bomb-building workshop for Nationalists prepared for insurrection. In central Italy, elected representatives of the provisional governments demanded annexation to Piedmont. Throughout the fall, the central states remained in the hands of Piedmont. Neither Austria nor France was willing to go to war to enforce the terms of the treaty and restore the rulers to power.

In January of 1860, Cavour returned as the prime minister, and renegotiated a final settlement with Napoleon III. The emperor agreed to acquiesce to Piedmont's annexation of the central states, if approved by the majority of the people, in exchange for Nice and Savoy. On March 11, 1860, polls opened in Modena, Florence, and Parma. Thousands of people walked down streets lined with the Italian flag to the polls. All voting was done by public ballot, and landowners and clergy escorted peasants to the polls. When the final votes were tallied, the yes votes far outnumbered the no votes: Liguria reported 38,026 votes in favor of annexation, 333 opposed; in Firenze, 101,386 people from 30 communes voted yes, and 2,809 voted against annexation. The plebiscites satisfied the liberal need for the appearance of popular support. The annexation of the central states to Piedmont inspired Nationalist demonstrations in the surrounding lands.

Garibaldi and I Mille

As Italians in the central regions went to the polls, patriots in the Bourbon south prepared for war. Throughout the spring, Republicans mounted a publicity campaign denouncing Bourbon rule. Rosolino Pilo, a member of the Sicilian aristocracy and devoted *Mazzinian*, landed near Messina with suitcase full of hand grenades in early April to recruit new members and stockpile weapons. The handsome and charismatic Sicilian traveled west toward Palermo, stopping in small villages to announce the imminent arrival of Garibaldi. By the end of April, he had recruited over a thousand volunteers, know as I Mille (the thousand). After local police quashed an attempted revolt in Palermo in early April, the remaining rebels gathered in Carini, on the outskirts of the city. Over the course of the next few weeks, thousands of patriots from Sicily and the mainland joined them and readied for war.

Back in Genova, Crispi and fellow patriots begged Garibaldi to mount a Sicilian expedition; Garibaldi refused to commit. His allegiance to the house of Savoy had been sorely tested when they ceded his hometown to the French. In May, Garibaldi finally agreed. Early in the morning of May 6, two small steamers, The *Lombardo* and the *Piemonte*, with slightly more than 1,000 volunteers, including two women, set sail for Sicily under the banner of Italy and Vittorio Emanuele.[14] Garibaldi's pragmatic embrace of Cavour's plan to unify Italy left the prime minister in quandary. The vision of the "hero of two worlds," as the head of a Republican army, liberating Palermo, Naples, and even Rome, without the backing of Piedmont, was too much for the conservative minister to bear. Cavour offered his tacit approval, while doing everything in his power to ensure that the expedition would fail. It did not.

On May 11, 1860, Garibaldi's red-shirted band of volunteers landed at Marsala, on the western edge of the island, and began to move eastward across the island. Four days later, the volunteers defeated the Bourbon troops in battle on the outskirts of Calatifimi. Although far from a decisive military triumph, the battle proved a moral victory. News of Bourbon losses encouraged local residents to join Garibaldi, and the volunteer army swelled. On May 27, Garibaldi's men reached Palermo and, after three days of fierce street fight, forced the Bourbons to retreat. By July, Garibaldi's army had driven the Bourbons off the island, and by the end of August, the expeditionary force had landed in Calabria. The *Garibaldini* met with little opposition as they marched up the Calabrian coast. On September 4, King Francesco II, who had taken the crown on the death of his father a year earlier, abdicated and fled north to the fortress of Gaeta. The people of Naples greeted Garibaldi amid wild celebration. In four months, Garibaldi had ousted the Bourbons, and now he turned his sights on Rome (Figure 6).

Fearing a war with France, and the loss of the southern lands, Cavour took action. In September, Vittorio Emanuele II led Piedmont troops across Umbria and the Marche, in an effort to block Garibaldi's path to Rome. Meanwhile nearly 25,000 Garibaldini marched north from Naples. On October 1, 1860, they met the Neapolitan army, 50,000 strong, on the banks of the Volturno River. After two days of fighting, Garibaldi emerged victorious, but had lost precious time. Unable to reach Rome before the arrival of the Sardinian army, Garibaldi chose to return to Naples. On October 13, Garibaldi agreed to hold plebiscites throughout the former Bourbon Kingdom, a political victory for Cavour, and a defeat for the radicals. On October 21, all adult men across southern Italy and Sicily went to the polls to vote yes or no for an "Italy one and indivisible, with Vittorio Emanuele, constitutional king." Like the earlier plebiscites, these elections were held in public, and the results were unsurprising: 1,734,117 votes in favor, 10,979 opposed.

Three weeks after the elections, Garibaldi rode out to Teano to meet Vittorio Emanuele, and with a handshake officially transferred the former Kingdom of the Two Sicilies to the Piedmont crown. On October 24, 1860, a single, independent Italian kingdom was born. After more than sixty years of struggle, exile, and sacrifice, Italian patriots established a unified Italy, although in a manner few envisioned and even fewer desired. When Vittorio

Figure 6 I Mille. Garibaldi lands in Sicily, in Marsala on May 11, 1860. Color lithograph by Baroffio, Italy approx. 1860. Fototeca Gilardi/Getty Images.

Emanuele II opened the first Italian parliament in 1861 as the king of Italy, his kingdom was a fractured land. Incomplete territorial unification undermined the legitimacy of the new Italian state, keeping the Risorgimento alive. Civil war in the southern regions and Nationalist wars in the Veneto and Rome challenged the foundational myths of the Risorgimento as a united popular movement (Map 4).

Map 4 Kingdom of Italy, 1861. Veneto remained under Austrian rule, and Lazio remained under Papal rule. The arrow line delineates the route of Garibaldi and I Mille.

A fragile union

After unification, the Italian government pursued a policy of occupation rather than integration in the southern regions. Repression began under Garibaldi's dictatorship. Garibaldi had secured local support by promises of land to all volunteers and the repeal of the hated grist tax. However, the liberators also had to woo the property owners, if they hoped to ensure stability and elicit the necessary support for unification. By June, Garibaldi issued a series of orders placating the elites: introducing compulsory military service, making theft, looting and murdering capital offenses, and declaring all offenses against public order to be punishable by summary trial and execution. Popular support for the liberators began to evaporate.

On the night of August 1, 1860, residents of the small town of Bronte, on the slopes of Mount Etna, rose up against the local government. Marching through the streets, shouting "*Viva l'Italia*," the rioters looted stores and offices, setting fire to the communal archives, dragging landowners out of their beds, killing them, and throwing their bodies on to bonfires. Reports filtering out described how the local militia stood paralyzed in the face of the insurgents. On August 6, General Nino Bixio, Garibaldi's trusted companion, a man known for his fierce loyalty and great cruelty, brought 400 soldiers to Bronte. Bixio immediately imposed martial law, arrested Nicolo Lombardo, leader of the "Communists," and four others, held a summary trial, and publicly executed them a few days later. Over 200 people were arrested, rounded up, and sent to prison. Bronte was not an isolated incident, but one of the many instances where residents challenged those local elite who used their access to political power for personal gain. In the aftermath of the violence and trials, many southern Italians wondered if the new king was really any different than the old one.[15]

The imposition of onerous fiscal and physical obligations, the failure of the state to enact any real social or economic reforms, and the refusal of the Catholic Church to recognize the legitimacy of the Italian state, deepened resentment against the new state, fueling armed resistance. In Sicily, the introduction of conscription sparked a deep and abiding anger. Sicilians who had been exempt from Bourbon military service were now called to serve for five years, thousands refused. By 1863 an estimated 20,000 draft evaders roamed the island. Ideologically diverse alliances formed, comprised of decommissioned soldiers (many who had fought alongside Garibaldi) peasants, and Bourbon supporters stood united in their hatred of the new authorities. Throughout Campania, Puglia, Calabria, and Sicily, bands of outlaws roamed the hills preying on soldiers, travelers, and government officials. In an effort to quash the resistance, the government imposed martial law across southern Italy, suspended freedom of the press and prohibited assemblies. In 1863 Parliament passed the Pica laws, mandating that all criminal cases involving anyone accused of brigandage be tried in military courts, possibly sentenced to forced labor or death. Turin justified these measures by pointing to the rampant criminality in the old Bourbon lands.

Between 1860 and 1865 a civil war raged south of Rome. Although official records place the number of dead at approximately 5,000 people, unofficial estimates run as high as 100,000. Virtually no town was untouched by the violence. Politicians dismissed the unrest as a counterrevolutionary plot. This narrative of a few disgruntled royalists and clergy funding local outlaws in order to bring down the state became the official history. Members of the Italian parliament meeting in Turin refused to consider that the war reflected a deeper discontent with the new political order. Although the civil war ostensibly quieted by the end of the 1860s, the memory of the brutality of the government troops lived on. For northerners and southern Italians, the civil war cemented the idea of the existence of a distinct North and South Italy.

If the incorporation of the South proved a problem for the new government, so did its failure to liberate Veneto and Rome. Garibaldi returned to his farm in Caprera in November of 1860 and soon began raising money and volunteers to liberate the *terra irredenta* (unredeemed land), still in the hands of the Austrians and the church. In 1862, inspired by the words of Garibaldi, Francesco Nullo led a small group of volunteers across the Alps to start an insurrection. Worried about international repercussions, the Italian government arrested the patriots near the Austrian border. The arrests sparked riots and demonstrations in nearby Brescia, ending only when the police fired on the crowd. In June of 1862, Garibaldi traveled through the South to raise an army of volunteers to liberate Rome. Prime Minister Rattazzi grew nervous as he watched Garibaldi's army grow larger as it moved across Sicily and the mainland. Ratazzi ordered his generals to stop Garibaldi's advance through Calabria. On August 29, 1862, the two armies met in the mountains of Aspromonte. Italian troops opened fire, wounding Garibaldi in the foot. The army arrested hundreds of soldiers. The shooting of Garibaldi's foot at Aspromonte became evidence of the failure of the Italian state to act in the interests of the people. Public outcry forced the dismissal of Rattazzi (Figure 7).

Figure 7 Giuseppe Garibaldi wounded at Aspromonte. Stefano Bianchetti/Corbis/Getty Images.

Acutely aware of the pressing need to resolve the territorial questions, La Marmora's government leaped at the chance of allying with Prussia in its war against Austria in 1866. The Austro-Prussian war offered the new state the opportunity to prove to the world that Italy could mount an effective military campaign. The Italian military proved unprepared and ill-equipped, and suffered a humiliating defeat at the Battle of Custoza. The Italian navy fared no better, defeated by a smaller Austrian fleet at the Battle of Lissa. Only Garibaldi, who had been reluctantly given command of a small poorly outfitted brigade and sent to the Alps in order to placate his supporters, gained significant ground against the Austrians. Prussia, not Italy, defeated the Austrians. Austria relinquished Veneto to the French, who then gave it to Italy. The acquisition of Venice through diplomatic channels did little to bolster faith in the state or resolve the northeastern territorial disputes. Italy had not won the land, but received it from the victors, and Trieste and surrounding lands remained outside the nation.

Throughout the 1860s Rome also remained a problem. The city possessed a symbolic importance in Risorgimento mythology. For patriots, Italian unification depended equally on the dissolution of the Papal State and the expulsion of the Austrians. Both Mazzini and Garibaldi insisted that the Eternal City was the spiritual center of a unified Italy. The newly formed government thought otherwise, and readily abandoned Rome in order to ensure peace. In 1864, the government signed the September Convention with France, agreeing to recognize and guarantee Papal rule in Rome. Parliament also announced it would move the capital from Turin to Florence, apparently acquiescing to international pressure that Rome would not become the capital of a united Italy. In exchange, France would withdraw its troops. The treaty was enormously unpopular among Democrats and Radicals, who refused to renounce Rome and immediately began to make plans to liberate the city.

When Rattazzi returned as prime minister in April of 1867, he hatched a convoluted plan to use Garibaldi's obsession with Rome to boost the monarch's standing at home. The government would secretly supply Garibaldi with money and weapons, and send him across the pontifical border to instigate a rebellion, which would enable the king to send in the troops without angering European powers. Despite concerns among his friends and advisers that the plan was a trap, Garibaldi spent the spring of 1867 raising money and volunteers for the expedition. Garibaldi's call to arms was so successful that Napoleon III insisted Rattazzi squash the campaign. To placate the French, the prime minister placed Garibaldi under house arrest in Caprera; a few weeks later he escaped and rejoined his volunteers in Tuscany. At the end of October, Garibaldi and his army of 3,000 volunteers crossed into Papal lands. Furious with the Italians, Napoleon III sent troops to Rome. On November 3, Garibaldi's forces were defeated by the French at the Battle of Mentana. The military defeat turned into a public relations nightmare for the government. Not only had they failed to make good on the promises of the Risorgimento, but they had acted in an underhanded and weak manner. Italy finally claimed Rome in 1871, when French troops were forced to return home during the Franco-Prussian war.

The wars of the Risorgimento succeeded in creating an independent but not unified Italy. The new state was founded in an atmosphere of distrust, fear, and division. The ongoing wars deepened the divisions: the contempt of the north toward the south, conservative fears of democracy, the competing interests of peasants, artisans, and landowners. Mazzini's vision of an Italian state forged from a free citizenry, freely choosing to subordinate familial, local, or personal interests to the needs of a nation, was never more than a dream.

CHAPTER 4
SETTING UP HOUSE (1860–76)

In December of 1864 in the wake of the signing of the September Convention, Francesco De Sanctis published a short article, entitled *Turin unificatrice* ("Turin the Unifier"). Reflecting on the significance of the move to Florence, De Sanctis drew attention to the limits of the Savoyard monarchy's unifying capabilities. The incomplete territorial unification, combined with the ongoing civil war, suggested the Piedmont lacked the financial, military, and political resources to truly unite Italy and Italians: Turin, the revolutionary capital could not be the nation's capital. De Sanctis, a Neapolitan literary scholar and patriot, imprisoned and exiled by the Bourbons, understood that the proclamation of the Kingdom of Italy was the beginning of unification, not the end.

> With the first revolution, we chased out the principal enemies of Italy, and proclaimed national unity. But it was still unity in the abstract. And while it was a matter of shouting: *Viva Italia Una*! (Long Live One Italy) we all shouted. But when it came time to translate the idea into fact, oh then began the protests. Each part of Italy had its laws, its customs, it traditions and its pride. To unify the country, one had to remove special interests, offend vanity, stomp prejudices and traditions.[1]

In recognizing the necessity of moving the capital to Florence, De Sanctis expressed his hope that a strong centralized government would unify a divided Italy, and forge an authentic Italian people. In certain respects, De Sanctis's hopes were realized. In its first decade, the Italian state was remarkably successful in unifying the territory, accommodating itself to a foreign enemy, the church, within its borders, and incorporating the historical divisions into regional networks. The administrative, institutional, and political successes of the new state could not erase the deep cultural and social divides. The institutional and administrative efforts to build a strong central state created geographic and gendered divisions that challenged De Sanctis's visions of national unity.

Church and state

When the newly elected members of Parliament met in January of 1861, they immediately turned their attention to the problem of the church. Politicians on both the left and right recognized that the church posed an immediate threat to the new state. In 1861, a furious pope refused to recognize the legitimacy of the Italian state, or its claim over the former Papal States. He had instructed all "good Catholics" to refuse to pledge allegiance to the government, excommunicating those who did, including Vittorio Emanuele II. The pope called on foreign powers to protect his temporal powers by diplomacy or war. Papal intransigence signified more than just the last of the ancien régime powers to be evicted in the name of national unity. Unlike the Bourbons or the Habsburgs, whose presence mobilized Italian patriotic sentiment, the hostility of the church in a Catholic land made the consolidation of political power within Italy more difficult.[2]

For conservative Italian Nationalists, the church had long stood as an ally, a bulwark against radical Republicans, but the statesmen were also committed to the principals of liberalism, including religious toleration. As a consequence, the state took an ambivalent position vis-à-vis the church. One the one hand the first article of the *Statuto Albertino*, now the constitution of Italy, asserted that the "Roman Catholic religion is the only religion of the state"; on the other, Article 24 of the Constitution asserted the equality of all citizens under the law, offering legal protection to people of all faiths. Efforts to balance the needs of liberal unification and assuage Catholic fears failed. Cavour's attempt to temper the announcement that Rome was the natural, historic, and cultural capital of the new state, by guaranteeing "a free Church in a free state," provoked outrage in the Vatican. The pope closed churches to all patriotic celebrations, and refused to allow *Te Deum* masses to consecrate the new state. Conservative Nationalists had lost an important political ally. The conciliatory overtures to the pope angered radicals and democrats in Parliament, who saw the efforts as antithetical to the struggle for liberation. Garibaldi and his colleagues had never hidden their hatred for the church, condemning bishops, priests, clerics, and friars as traitors and tyrants. Throughout the 1860s, the hostility of the church polarized popular political sentiment between a loyal Catholic contingent and an increasingly infuriated anticlerical faction. The pope and Garibaldi were equally capable of creating powerful opposition movements.

Prussia's victories over Austria and French, signaled the death knell of papal hopes that the armies of the Catholic states would once again swoop down the peninsula and restore the pope to his lands. As the possibility of reclaiming territorial sovereignty faded, the pope focused his anger on liberalism and the Italian state. In December of 1864, the Pius IX issued the encyclical *Quanta Cura* and the notorious *Syllabus of Errors Condemning Current Errors*, denouncing the expulsion of religion from civil society, and listing what the church considered to be the common errors of modern thought, including free speech, freedom of the press, religious toleration, and rationalism. The pope continued to wage war against the Italian state. In 1868, the pope issued the *non-expedit* decree, officially prohibiting Catholics from participating in parliamentary elections, and sanctioning the motto "neither elector nor elected."

Faced with papal obstinacy the government vacillated between curtailing church privileges and policies of appeasement. The question of civil marriage made evident the ambivalent position of the new state. The passage of the civil code was critical to imposing legal unity and an important step in establishing state legitimacy, and yet it took the new state for five years. At the heart of the difficulty lay the struggle between church and state over the family. Liberal politicians held that marriage was the first form of voluntary association, a contract that formed the basis of all civil and political rights in a nation-state, and so had to be regulated by the state. The church contended that marriage was a sacrament, not a contract, and it could not be broken. The passage of the civil code, legalizing civil marriage, and invalidating those performed by a priest alone, marked a victory of the state over church. While civil marriage was a hallmark of all liberal states, Italy's marriage law prohibiting the possibility of divorce was unique. By choosing to define marriage as an unbreakable civil contract, essentially incorporating church doctrine into civil law, the statesmen avoided directly challenging Catholic ideas of the sanctity of marriage, and offending the Catholic majority.[3]

The pope's declaration of papal infallibility in the summer of 1870 fueled anti-Catholic sentiment and isolated the church at home and abroad. European leaders sympathetic to the pope's temporal claims viewed the declaration with concern. Papal infallibility undermined secular authority, and led many to question the patriotism of Catholic citizens. However, perhaps, even more significantly, issuing such an absolutist doctrine at the end of the nineteenth century once again marked the church as an enemy of progress. Within a matter of days, Austria broke its treaty with the Vatican, and over the next few years Germany and Switzerland enacted harsh anticlerical laws.

Italy's acquisition of Rome in 1870 ushered in a cease-fire in the church/state struggles. When Italian troops marched into Rome, the pope proclaimed himself a "prisoner of the Vatican," and refused to even turn over the keys of the Quirinal Palace, Vittorio Emanuele's official residence. In November, the pope issued an encyclical rejecting the occupation of the Papal States, pledging to resist until the bitter end. Pio IX's pronouncements were more performative than political. Even under mounting pressure by French Catholics, the French government, the pope's last hope, refused to invade. By the time Italy transferred its capital to Rome in 1871, Pio IX had given up on European rulers coming to his aid, putting his faith in God and the people.

The pope's diplomatic isolation ended the threat of military invasion, enabling the government to reach a tentative accord with Catholics, if not the church. Vittorio Emanuele II had little interest in moving to Rome, a city he considered too provincial and too religious, but Parliament was acutely aware that if the government did not move to Rome it risked inciting the anticlerical left to revolt. Overriding papal and monarchical opposition, Parliament voted to move the capital from Florence to Rome in January of 1871. In order to stave off concerns from European powers that the pope would become a subject of Italy, and therefore Catholics everywhere would become Italian citizens, as well as to placate domestic Catholic concerns regarding the welfare of the pope, Parliament passed the Law of Guarantees. The new law defined the pope as an independent sovereign power, entitled to keep armed guards and full diplomatic privileges. The state relinquished its right to appoint bishops, a source of contention throughout the 1860s, and no longer required high clergy to swear loyalty to the king. In effect, the Law of Guarantees created a state within a state, providing the pope space to rail against liberal Italy. The pope continued to vent his fury over the expropriation of church properties, the closing of monasteries and convents, and the revocation of the long-standing exemption of Catholic seminarians and clergy from military conscription; however, when Vittorio Emanuele II lay on his death bed in January of 1878, Pio IX lifted the order of excommunication and allowed him last rites

The unacknowledged easing of tensions between church and state created a new, potentially, divisive force: a growing Catholic lay movement. Despite the anticlerical rhetoric woven through the Risorgimento, the majority of the new Italians continued to identify as practicing Catholics. The church sought to use its influence to combat the perceived dangers of secularism, modernity, and socialism. After 1872 there was an explosion of a Catholic popular publications, including newspapers, and journals written for wealthy landowners, professionals, women, and the working-poor. The Catholic press mounted a widespread attack on Italy in particular and liberalism in general. When Pope Pius IX died in 1878, one month after Vittorio Emanuele II, there were over one hundred periodicals and nearly twenty daily newspapers aligned with the Catholic Church. While Leo XIII did not rescind the *non-expedit* decree, he did encourage Catholics to take an active role in local government, promoted mutual-aid societies, opened rural banks and cooperatives, and set up the *Opera dei Congressi* to coordinate social initiatives on a national scale. The church was ultimately successful in transforming spiritual power into political influence in Italy, but it did pay a price.

Contentious relations between church and state undermined the institutional power of both the government and the Vatican. Those on the left saw the conciliatory actions of the state as evidence that the monarchy had betrayed the Risorgimento, while the Catholic faithful never fully accepted the right of the state to rule. Moreover, the struggle heightened distrust between the state and nation. Liberal Italy remained predominately Catholic, leaving many politicians and statesmen doubting the loyalty of the people, and reluctant to expand democratic participation. Papal opposition to Italy weakened the hold of the Vatican over those Italians who identified as ardent patriots and devout believers. Popular adoration of Garibaldi translated into a hatred of local clergy and the Jesuits, but also spurred a rise in popular religiosity. New cults devoted to the Madonna and local saints throughout Italy, and especially in the South. Local religious practices, incorporating new rituals and sacred objects, attracted large numbers of women. The struggle accelerated the general nineteenth-century trend of the feminization of formal and informal religious practices, and the declining political influence of parish priests.[4]

Piedmont in a unified Italy

While patriots held tight to their faith in the regenerative nature of unification, no one knew how exactly unification would transform Italians into an energetic and virtuous nation. The democratic left insisted that a strong dynamic Italy depended on its ability to fuse the country's diverse cultures, languages, and traditions together into something new. Those who embraced Cavour's vision of Italy insisted that only a strong central state could create a healthy nation. In the decade after unification, it became clear that Cavour's vision of imposing a nation-state had won. Unification proceeded by expanding the laws of Piedmont across the land. The "piedmontization" of Italy, begun as a short-term solution to quell southern unrest and incomplete territorial unification, became policy within a few years after unification.[5]

The unilateral imposition of Piedmont currency, legal codes, and educational systems generated anger at Piedmont arrogance and distrust of the new Parliament. Vittorio Emanuele II's insistence on speaking French rather than Italian, and his disparagement of the southern regions, exemplified the refusal, or incapacity, of the elite to renounce local allegiances. It did not help matters that Vittorio Emanuele refused to mark the new kingdom with a new title. By insisting on keeping his numerical designation and being crowned Vittorio Emanuele II, he reinforced the notion that the Kingdom of Italy was merely an expanded version of the Kingdom of Sardinia. The monarchy did nothing to alleviate fears that the king saw Italy as something he had conquered with the grace of God: his power, in no way dependent on the people.

The new Kingdom of Italy was a constitutional monarchy, where legislative authority resided in an elected body; however, Parliament proved incapable, or unwilling, to counter the centralizing and authoritarian inclination of the crown. Italians had little experience and few positive associations with representative government, and few saw the institution as a safeguard for democracy: people had fought and died for a free country, not for representation. Only in Sicily did historical memory credit Parliament as a defender of the people. The monarchy had no reason to voluntarily cede its authority to Parliament. Not even the patriots put much faith in the institution, unsure how an elected body could do anything but mirror the defects and failures of the electors. The weakness of Parliament as a representative institution was made manifest in the first elections in 1861, carried out under the terms of the 1848 Piedmont election law stipulating that only literate men over the age of twenty-five, paying a minimum of forty lire a year in direct taxes, could vote. Of the 418,695 (1.9 percent of the population) men eligible just 239,760 (1 percent) voted. In some districts, a few dozen men were enough to send their chosen candidate to Parliament. The laws created a parliament designed to protect the interests of a few, not the wishes of the majority.

In the course of the 1860s, members of Parliament adopted a program of political and administrative centralization, rejecting the autonomous and decentralized proposals of Minghetti and Farini that devolved power on the regions. In 1865, the government introduced a prefecture system, following the Napoleonic model. The government appointed prefects to each city, and sent subprefects to provincial towns. The majority of prefects came from the Piedmont, Lombardy, or Tuscany, reinforcing the sense of occupation in the southern regions. The prefects supervised elections, controlled public order, censored the local press, oversaw town councils, and ensured local administrations followed national law. Prefects served as the eyes and ears of the state, reporting signs of discontent or lawlessness. The Italian state imposed compulsory primary education, taxes, and military obligations. By 1865 a new civil code and commercial code further strengthened state authority over regional. Resistance to centralizing fiscal, judicial and administrative power coalesced around the question of the death penalty. Tuscany refused to accept the Piedmont penal code reinstituting the death penalty within its court system. Until 1889, with the passage of a unified penal code (banning the death penalty), the Italian criminal system was marked with regional variations.

The process of centralization provided the illusion of unity by consolidating power within the national government, but did little to strengthen representative institutions. Italian statesmen viewed national political parties with suspicion, serving to foster self-interest rather than a national spirit. Elected representatives, they believed, should govern for the good of the whole, not in the interests of a party. As a result, Italian politicians remained divided by the political inclinations manifest during the wars of the Risorgimento, rather than by ideology or political theory. *La Destra* (the Historic Right) constituted the political heirs of Cavour, and remained the parliamentary majority until 1876. Many of them, including Rattazzi (twice prime minister) Lanza, and Sella, were born in Piedmont; others including Ricasoli, Minghetti, and Farini came from Tuscany or Emilia-Romagna. The political vision of these northern men was marked by an adherence to moderate social conservatism, laissez faire economics, limited suffrage, and a draconian fiscal policy marked by heavy taxation designed to strengthen and support the constitutional monarch. *La Sinistra* (the Historic Left), on the other hand, considered themselves the heirs of Garibaldi, who reluctantly accepted the necessity of a constitutional monarchy, but refused to forget the democratic origins of the Risorgimento. A smaller contingent of parliamentarians, comprising the radical or extreme left, continued to identify with Mazzini, and clung to the dream of a Republican Italy. The loose political allegiances that made up each bloc dissolved in the face of regional or personal interests.

The first years of Italian parliamentary life were marked by a practice of political compromise between members of opposing sides. These temporary alliances formed around specific legislative issues became formalized when the Historic Left came to power in 1876. Through a series of moderate initiatives, the Historic Left distanced themselves from an increasingly radical left, and forged voting alliances with members of the Historic Right. This political maneuver of creating shifting coalitions referred to as *trasformismo*, formally implemented under Depretis, created a parliamentary system that was stable and flexible, but also open to corruption and bribery. Obligated to a small number of male, property-owning electors, and able to vote according to their self-interest, individual deputies tended to legislate for personal gain or local interest. There was little incentive for politicians to create structured political parties anchored in political constituencies, when members of Parliament could utilize the system to secure access to government contracts and monies in exchange for their votes, enriching themselves, their families, and their friends.

By 1876, the Italian state had contained the threat posed by the church, created a state bureaucracy imposing a more or less uniform system of rights and obligations, but had failed to strengthen a sense of national belonging. Administrative, legal, and economic reforms enriched a few, but for the vast majority of Italians, the state meant high taxes, military conscription, continued censorship, and a growing bureaucracy that complicated both personal and professional transactions. The establishment of parliamentary rule did not strengthen the legitimacy of the liberal monarchy among many Italians. In the decades following unification divisions between governed and government grew wider. The 1866 revolt in Palermo and the uprisings in the northern regions in 1869 both ultimately quelled by military intervention revealed the depths of popular anger and the strength of regional loyalties. A decade after unification, efforts to centralize the state seemed to have reinforced the regional and social divides the founding fathers hoped to erase.

Regionalism and the creation of the "South"

One of the first tasks undertaken by the new government was to undertake a survey of Italy. A General Statistics Division within the Ministry of Agriculture and Industry was established in October of 1861, and the first census was taken two months later. The statistical and cartographic mapping project served to symbolically lay claim over all the land and its resources, and would, hopefully, prove the basis for the creation of rational administrative boundaries and provide a solid foundation to the new state. Statisticians believed that their science could clear up debates over the best way to divvy up the new lands and forge an Italian nation. But, as historian Silvana Patriarca observed, while these scientists excelled at counting and mapping, their science failed to provide an objective description of the nation. Instead, statistical overviews reinscribed long-standing regional divisions and stereotypes into Italian politics and society.[6]

The first Italian census incorporated the contradictory impulses between regional autonomy and centralized authority. Statisticians accepted territorial demarcations that closely conformed to preunification states, incorporating the historical regional borders into the new state. The 59 provinces (*province*) were subdivided into 193 districts (*circondari*) and 7,721 towns (*comuni*) varying in size from a few hundred residents to over a million. The provinces, reinforcing historical political boundaries, rather than geographical or topographical borders, were demographically and environmentally unbalanced. To compensate for the uneven administrative divides, Pietro Maestri, the director of the Office of Statistics, created a new unit, the region (*compartimento*) that had no legal standing, but served, in theory, to carve the country up into proportional units. Maesti intended for the *compartimenti* to undermine provincial loyalties and promote national integration, but in reality, they served to reinforce the underlying historical regional divisions.[7]

The region or province was no more natural a unit of identity than the earlier duchies or kingdoms, and did little to mitigate existing rivalries. The natural focus of identity for most Italians was the city, village, or parish, defined by kin, community, history, and culture. Birthplace anchored each individual into a particular world, with its own dialect, culture, and customs. Urban residents marked the borders of their world by city walls, rural residents by the sound of the church bell. *Campanilismo* defined one's place in the world, where all those born within the sound of the church bells (*le campane*) constituted *paesani* (fellow countrymen) and those outside, *stranieri* (foreigners).[8] Rural residents looked on nearby urban centers with suspicion, resenting the financial demands that the cities had had long imposed on the countryside. The administrative boundaries did nothing to improve urban/rural relations, and the designation of provincial capitals unleashed deep-seated rivalries between cities. Perugia's urban neighbors outright refused to recognize its status as a regional capital. Rather than uniting Italians, the new internal boundaries incorporated geographic and cultural divisions strengthening existing regional loyalties.[9] Administrative efforts to build a strong centralized state ended by creating a system where regional power stood as a challenge to state authority.

After unification, critics and writers set out to describe the variety of the new lands, emphasizing the ways that food, music, dress, and dialect sharply delineated the borders of the new regions. The publication of regional cookbooks, local histories, dictionaries of local dialects, and ethnographic studies of proverbs and local customs reinforced the image of a culturally divided land. The focus on cultural and historical divisions erased earlier divisions between the aristocracy and poor, urban and rural. Culinary markers, in particular, strengthened broader geographic divides: northerners were identified as polenta eaters, while southerners were linked to pizza and macaroni.[10] These first administrative divisions undertaken to unify the territory proved instrumental in shaping the linguistic, cultural, and culinary divisions that mark Italy today.

Statesmen were as concerned with mapping the population as they were the territory. The founding fathers were deeply concerned with the health and fitness of the people given that the military and economic power of a nineteenth-century nation-state rested on the size and strength of its population. In the first census, statisticians counted twenty-two million residents, tracking the number of centenarians, births, deaths, weddings, those who could read or write, those engaged in work, and young men eligible for military service. The statisticians happily reported that Italy's military force compared favorably with other European powers, even surpassing that of Great Britain.[11]

The analyses of the numbers revealed implicit regional biases. Examining the markedly different rates of military participation (67 percent in the northern regions versus 12 percent in some southern regions) statisticians concluded that southern men were disloyal. Maestri, born in Milan, attributed the higher numbers in the North to the longer history of military service, and the lower numbers in the South to the recent imposition of the draft and the unwillingness of the state to enlist "elements which in the moment appear to nurture an antinational spirit."[12] High rates of illiteracy in the southern regions appeared to mark residents as backward and less able to participate fully in political and civil life. The interpretative frameworks placed on these statistics obscured the ability of politicians to see the common structural causes of statistical differences. For instance, rather than analyzing conditions common to all sharecroppers, statisticians chose to impose a regional analytic frame comparing sharecropping in the Tuscany to conditions in Sicily.

The statistical picture that emerged from the census supported the idea of an Italy divided between a backward poverty-ridden South and a vibrant, progressive North. Statistical sciences seemed to affirm the deep-rooted belief that the southern regions constituted a separate world, alien to the Italy of the Roman Empire, Renaissance, and the Risorgimento. Initially, the higher crime rates, lower literacy levels, and endemic poverty noted in the first census were attributed to the Bourbons. In 1866, shortly after the Palermo uprising, Giuseppe Ciotti published an essay, arguing that the events of September were the result of the Bourbon legacies of ignorance, corruption, and superstition, and not a protest against the liberal state. A decade later, Ciotti's position was no longer tenable. Pointing to the higher rates of homicide and draft dodging, critics and statesmen concluded that the problem resided in the people not the government. By the 1870s brigands were no longer seen as mercenaries in the pay of the Bourbons or pope, but part of criminal culture, defined by the camorra and mafia.[13] A decade after unification, the South emerged as the Achilles heel of the new state.

The idea of constitutionally criminal South as a threat to the political order took hold among the elite in the 1870s. In the 1874 elections held in Sicily, forty out of the forty-eight electoral districts elected opposition members to Parliament, and the island seemed poised to bring the left to power. In a last-ditch effort to stay in control, members of the Historic Right raised the specter of the mafia, accusing the left of threatening the country's unity and integrity by relying on southern criminals, murderers, and extortionists for votes. Parliament immediately introduced a series of repressive laws, expanding the power of local government to arrest suspected mafia members and their political patrons, holding them in prison for up to five years without a trial. The law targeted southern politicians and landowners alike. Sicilian politicians, led by Crispi on the left, accused their colleagues of denigrating the South.

The political debates led to the first parliamentary inquiries into the mafia. Statesmen traveled through the island, collecting testimony describing mafia control of the citrus industry, its involvement in the revolts of 1860 and 1866, and denying its very existence. Across the island, local elites explained to the statesmen that, in Sicily, mafia was a term of respect, symbolizing a man of action and honor. The contradictory images found their way into a parliamentary report that concluded that the mafia was "an instinctive, brutal, biased form of solidarity between those individuals and lower social groups who prefer to live off of violence rather than hard work. It unites them against the state, the law and regular bodies."[14] In the eyes of the northern politicians, the statistical divisions between North and South could be explained by culture and criminality.

The notion of the South as a separate world gained currency as critics and journalists published their thoughts on the "Southern Question." In 1875, the historian and politician Pasquale Villari published a series of letters in *L'Opinione*, an influential journal of the Historic Right, describing the living conditions in the South. Villari, a Neapolitan political exile who had lived in Florence for over twenty years, had grown disillusioned with the government's inability to enact real social or economic change. Villari focused his political critique on his homeland, seeing the South as representative of all the people the political elite had overlooked. In his essays, Villari described the squalid conditions of the slums of Naples, the violence, poverty, dirt, the presence of the camorra and mafia. Villari's essays had an immediate effect, prompting journalists to examine the social conditions of the South, and politicians to commission a government inquires and reports.[15] Stories of the misery of the South fixed the image of a wretched and backward South in the collective imagination. In highlighting the "southern question" to a wide readership, Villari attempted to instill a sense of moral obligation among northerners for southerners, but much of the literature only served to heighten the sense that the problems of the South were qualitatively different than the North [16]

Villari's work inspired two young politicians, Leopold Franchetti and Sidney Sonnino, to journey through Sicily. In 1876, they published their groundbreaking report on the administrative and political conditions of Sicily; the politicians concluded that fifteen years after unification the state had failed to affect any sort of moral authority in the region.[17] In their report, detailing the endemic corruption across the island, Franchetti and Sonnino provided a systemic analysis of the workings of the mafia, concluding that the mafia was embedded in the history and culture of the island. According to Franchetti and Sonnino, the only way to root out the illness was through repressive legislation that removed Sicilians from all positions of authority. The two politicians failed to consider that the mafia had emerged as a power broker between the state and local government with unification. The administrative reforms of the 1860s that created new spaces for corruption, and funneled money and resources through government officials, enabled local elites to consolidate their relations with the government.[18] By 1876 efforts to unify the kingdom through political centralization and statistical mapping had created two Italies: a North and a South.

Gender and the making of Italy

Gender, like geography, was central to the creation of new social hierarchies. The success of the new state rested on its ability to create a citizenry composed of patriotic men, willing and able to rush to the defense of the country, and loving, virtuous, hardworking wives and mothers. For decades patriots had pointed to the gender disorder visible under the oppressive tyrannical rule of the Bourbons and Austrians, insisting that independence would transform these weak and enervated men into providers and protectors, and turn selfish women into loving wives and mothers. The last wars of the Risorgimento appeared to prove the patriots correct. By unification, an image of the ideal patriotic man and woman had taken concrete form in art and story. *I Garibaldini* volunteers willing to take up arms and sacrifice their lives for their country and family proved the virility, strength, and honor of all Italian men.[19] The visual expression of women's patriotism took the form of the emotional sacrifice of sending a son or lover off to war, and the torment of waiting for him to return. Gone was the figure of the female revolutionary who took to the barricades or donned men's clothes to join the fight. Instead, the ideal patriotic women sewed the flags and tended the wounded. The wars of the Risorgimento had shown Italians were capable of becoming patriots, but it was left to the nation-state to transform the people into good husbands and loving wives and mothers, capable of reproducing a healthy citizenry (Figure 8).

Statesmen recognized that territorial unification alone did not create a strong national body. In 1867, Massimo D'Azeglio published *I miei ricordi* (*My Recollections*). Reflecting on the success of the Risorgimento in fashioning the Kingdom of Italy, chasing away

Figure 8 Women repairing the tricolor flag, Girolamo Induno. DEA/G. CIGOLINI/De Agostini/
Getty Images.

foreign armies, and uniting the distinct regions under one political roof, he warned
readers that they had failed to secure the future of the new state. He wrote: "The most
dangerous enemies of Italy are not the Austrians, but the Italians." To succeed, Italy
urgently needed Italians "gifted with a noble and strong character," and "each day," he
lamented, "we move in the opposite direction: unfortunately, Italy has been made, but
Italians have not."[20] While the passage of the civil code in 1866, guaranteeing equality
and individuals freedom, was an important step in the making of new Italians, the
construction of the national body required a deeper social reordering, a full-scale
remaking of men and women.

In publishing his recollections, D'Azeglio hoped that his life story could provide a
model for future citizens. D'Azeglio considered his father, Marchese Cesare D'Azeglio,
and his mother, Cristina Morozzo di Bianzè, the ideals of a virtuous, honest, and
industrious citizenry. Although a member of the Piedmont aristocracy, Cesare instilled
in his son the belief that individual virtue, not birthright, made a man.[21] His father's life,
from his choice of a wife based on love, rather than self-interest, to his willingness to
sacrifice all he held dear in the interests of his king, to his resolute and ethical character,
illustrated the corrupt nature of the Old Regime and the best of the patriotic generation.
His mother, a woman of piety, grace, and culture instilled in her children a deep sense
of civic duty, self-sacrifice, and generosity. Other memoirs reinforced D'Azeglio's vision,
emphasizing the importance of a loving marriage in the making of an altruistic, self-
sacrificing man.[22] Most of the personal narratives echoed the gender assumption

underlying treatises on male citizenship rights and obligations, emphasizing that the social good and political rights rested on a male citizenry capable of self-sacrifice and understanding of their individual and collective duties. A good citizen was measured by his standing as a husband, father, and worker.[23]

Ideas of liberal manliness seeped into administrative and legislative debates. In discussions over state centralization or regional devolution, statesmen voiced their concerns that the men of the provinces were incapable of shouldering the obligations attendant on self-governance. The new visions of manliness were visible in discussion of civil marriages, where the image of the unmarried cleric as a danger to social order loomed large. In 1862, Ferdinando Petrucelli della Gattina, a member of Parliament on the radical left, introduced a proposal for a civil marriage bill that would ensure that all Italians, including priests, had the right to marry. In his opening remarks to the Chamber of Deputies, he described how forced celibacy leaves clergy with little choice other than to succumb to "monstrous vices, take a concubine, or threaten the honor of other families."[24] In the struggles between church and state, the heterosexual married man became the marker of a loyal male citizen.

The construction of the ideal woman proved less political but no less important to the statesmen. Both conservatives and radicals embraced Mazzini's description of the angel in the house. In *Doveri dell'uomo*, Mazzini gave scant attention to the duties of women to God or nation, instead mentioning them solely in relation to the family; seeing mother, daughter, or sister as the "angel" who renders all of a man's duties less arduous. The invisibility of women in liberal political theory rested on the refusal to consider women as worthy of rights, and therefore freed from many, although not all, obligations and duties. There was no outpouring of works on the making of a good wife or mother to accompany the writings on the making of the good husband. Women were the custodians of national morality and character, assigned to their mission by nature and God, not active participants in the making of the nation.

As debates around the civil code grew, some women challenged the passive role of women in the new state. In 1864 the women's rights activist, Anna Maria Mozzoni, published *La donna e i suoi rapport sociali* (Woman and her social relations), in response to the revision of the civil code. Mozzini directed her words to members of Parliament engaged in revising the legal code, arguing that only through the full inclusion of women into the national body could the liberal state succeed in its moral and social mission. In her work, she urged Parliament to ensure women's right to access education, to own property, to suffrage, and to claim equal standing within the family as necessary in shoring up the moral foundation of the new nation. Mozzoni insisted that educating women was a priority, for only when women could think for themselves could they fulfill their domestic and political roles.[25]

Sympathetic to Mazzini's Republican vision, Mozzoni embraced the idea of women as being the moral force within the family and nation. Unlike Mazzini, however, Mozzini held that only educated women, able to participate in the nation's economic and civic life, could exert a beneficial influence on society. The angel of the family exists where woman "is esteemed and cultured; only when education and respect have made her conscious of that which natures requires from her, an awareness that can only come through much study."[26] Grounding her arguments in natural law, Mozzoni rejected the liberal idea that a man's morality depended on a woman's love. Instead she claimed that when men recognized the full autonomy of women, and could voluntarily curb their physical strength and passions, they would deserve women's love. Until the time when both men and women could enter marriage as equals, the institution remained corrupt, rendering women passive and men dependent. Mozzoni's call for marital equality fell on deaf ears. The civil code passed in 1865 assured women's exclusion from political life.

Women continued to struggle for inclusion in the national body. Gualberta Alaide Beccari, the daughter of a Republican nationalist, founded *La donna*, a woman's journal featuring the writings of Mozzoni among others. Beccari insisted on the necessity of recognizing the role of women in the cultural renewal of the nation. The journal published articles on equal pay, prostitution, divorce, and the political rights of women. Mozzoni continued to advocate for women's education, and in 1881 founded the league for the Promotion of the Interests of Women in Milan, one of the most influential equal rights women's organizations.

In the decades following unification statesmen laid the foundation of the new state. The political solutions, administrative reforms, and social reconfigurations served to secure the new state, but in the process, created new geographic and gendered hierarchies. The exclusion of women and workers from full political participation, the privileging of property over work or birth, the marginalization of the south, shaped the society, economy, and culture of the liberal state.

PART TWO
THE LIBERAL STATE (1860–1914)

Historians and the liberal state

Until recently the history of liberal Italy has been read as a dismal failure. As Nick Carter wrote, it is a story of "unfulfilled dreams of national resurgence, of chances missed and wrong turns taken, of decadence, division and deviancy, of vanity, vice and violence."[1] The rise of fascism cast a pall over the nineteenth-century state, attesting to the failure of its institutions to survive. Moderate historians looked to exonerate liberal Italy from any responsibility for fascism. In their histories, the 1860s and 1870s marked a period of institutional, geographic, and social consolidation, where a moderate-liberal political class comprised of the Historic Right and Historic Left overcame debt, a backward economy, and the remains of repressive governments, followed by a time of steady democratization and industrial growth. These historians maintained that even if liberal politicians were not perfect, they did their best.[2] On the left, Marxist historians viewed the liberal state as the breeding ground of fascism. Leftist historians pointed to the weakness of party politics, the practice of *trasformismo* (trading votes and coopting politicians), political corruption, institutional weaknesses, the growing economic inequality between North and South, and repressive measures taken to quell social and political unrest, as proof that Italy had veered from the "normal" path of modernization.[3] In both cases, the question of the state's responsibility for fascism stood at the center of historical studies.

The revisionist movement of the 1980s reframed the historiography of the liberal state. Instead of fixating on the question of the state's culpability in the rise of fascism, historians explored processes of state building, nation formation, and industrialization. The new work deepened our understanding of the international, gendered, and class dimensions of the processes of state formation. Through local, national, and transnational studies historians repositioned the nation's history within a broader European and global framework. Most historians no longer see Italy's processes of democratization and modernization as evidence that it moved along an aberrant path leading toward fascism. Scholars now stress the particular circumstances—church intransigence, North/South divide, social relations, material conditions—that shaped Italy's political and economic formation. Combined the work has led to a reconsideration of politics, society, the economy, regionalism, and the integral role internal and transnational migrations played in shaping modern Italy.

Recent scholarship has altered understandings of the nature of Italian liberalism. For decades scholars pointed to the lack of civil voluntary associations, the limited franchise and legislative initiatives as evidence of the state's authoritarian nature.

New works have challenged this assumption, suggesting instead that the construction of state institutions was a response to the material and social constraints that accompanied territorial unification. Given the country's geographic diversity, the sporadic presence of local self-government, and the limited size of civil society, it was difficult to imagine the spontaneous emergence of a functioning participatory democracy in the 1860s. The leaders of the Historic Right believed that the centralization of state power and administrative unification could safeguard the new state, serving to slowly introduce liberal ideals. In this version, slow expansion of suffrage was not a reflection of the state's reluctance to embrace liberalism, but a consequence of the difficulties in widening democratic participation without unleashing attacks by its opponents, particularly a hostile church. Centralization, as a strategy of building a liberal nation-state, met with limited success. Rather than forging alliances between citizens and the state, the process of state building created spaces for local elites to undermine state authority. The necessity of imposing liberalism, what Raffaele Romanelli termed an "impossible command," helps explain the difficulties the government faced in creating a strong unified political foundation.[4]

Reconsiderations of the formation of the liberal state have led to reevaluations of nation formation. Scholars have often argued that united Italy was a state that had failed to make a nation of Italians, as evidenced by the pronounced lack of patriotism, civic participation, and the marked opposition of Catholics, Socialists, and conservatives. New cultural and social histories have taken more nuanced approaches to the question of national allegiance, distinguishing between a sense of being Italian (*Italianità*) and love of country. Scholars have pointed out that in the last decades of the nineteenth century, Italians were not really any more disunited than the French or Germans. Despite the deep divisions that marked the Italian states, the majority of residents shared a common religion and ethnicity. Social and cultural historians have focused on how the liberal state successfully forged a sense of national belonging through military service, education, national holidays, art, literature, and monuments. Historians of migration have shown how the experiences of leaving deepened notions of national identity.[5] Yet, despite evidence of the attachment of Italians to an imagined Italy, the gulf between the people and the state seemed to widen over the course of the nineteenth century. Perhaps the problem was not a failure to "make Italians," but an inability to bind the nation to the state.

The new scholarship revitalized work on the Italian middle classes. Historians often rendered the bourgeoisie as nonexistent or ineffective because of their penchant for land investment and political fragmentation. While it is true that there were few liberal industrialists, recent scholarship suggests that the landowners, entrepreneurs, industrialists, and professionals who comprised the middling classes embraced new technologies and industries in accordance with liberal ideals. The Italian proclivity for land investment was not unique to Italy; across Europe the emerging middle classes continued to invest in land. In Italy, where manufacturing lagged behind its northern neighbors, there was even more reason to concentrate their investments in land, and landowners proved adept at embracing capitalism. Historians no longer consider agricultural investment evidence of a risk adverse bourgeoisie. The political fragmentation of the middle classes also now appears less backward or anomalous. The diversity of ideological positions (some embracing free market principles, while others lobbied for state intervention) reflected the range of economic interests. Professional standing, wealth, and geography also informed individual political beliefs. The middling classes tended to be parochial, organizing cultural, professional, and educational societies at a local level. Much as in the rest of Europe, the defining characteristic of the middle classes was a sense of a common culture, rooted in family, civic life, a deep sense of patriotism, that distinguished them from the aristocracy and workers.[6]

In light of the reassessment of the middling classes, scholars have called for a reconsideration of the history of labor movements and working-class histories.[7] For decades, the accepted argument held that the working class took form in the 1880s, forged in the factories, and then joined the Socialists, anarchists, or the trade-union movements. The history of labor movements, marked by late industrialization, large agricultural labor force, particular forms of worker unrest and collective action, seemed to prove Italy's anomalous "backward" economic development. New social histories challenged the notion that working-class consciousness emerged only with the development of industrial capital. These studies stretch the chronological and geographical scope of labor histories, tracing the creation of working-class cultures back to the Risorgimento, emphasizing the local and regional boundaries of worker communities. In these accounts, mobility plays a central role in the construction of a wage labor force, as underemployed agricultural workers moved to the cities for seasonal employment, and urban workers returned to the fields for the harvest. The creation of the working class was a multicentric process, both urban and rural. These new approaches to working-class history recognize the importance of understanding labor militancy, or lack thereof, in both local and transnational contexts.[8] Like the work on the middle classes, the new working-class studies critique notions of Italian exceptionalism and failure, and offer a more nuanced story of a how various collective responses to changing economic conditions shaped social relations and class consciousness.

Historians of women further revised our understandings of nineteenth-century society and politics. Works in women's history focused on women's political activities, paid work, and domestic life. Recognizing women as historical subjects highlighted the illiberal nature of the liberal state where legal reforms appeared to relegate women to the intimate worlds of family and domesticity. Insisting on the historical significance of private life, historians showed how women carved out new political and social spaces, transforming maternity and domesticity into bases for demanding legal rights.[9] Their work explored the contradictions between the social ideals of a liberal state (equality and liberty) that rested on gendered notions of family hierarchies and the subordination of women. Studies of the expansion of the state showed how efforts to create a nation (the expansion of primary education, for example) undermined the gender norms that supported the state.[10] Close analysis of census records revealed that despite the declining number of women in the wage work force, women continued to work in agriculture and textile industries. Initial assumptions of the marginalization of women have given way to new studies stressing women's agency and mobility, making visible the interdependent relationship between public and private spheres.[11]

By the 1990s, scholars moved from telling the stories of women as citizens, mothers, or workers to exploring women's subjectivity and embracing gender and sexuality as categories of analyses. Current works focus on the constitutive role gender played in processes of state formation and the construction of national identities at home and abroad. Studies exploring the influence of science and medicine in the constructing and justifying social norms have deepened our understanding of how gender and sexual constructs were naturalized in law and society. Historians of sexuality have carved out new research trajectories, expanding earlier studies of prostitution, examining the underlying medical, legal, and cultural discourses regulating sex and bodies, and exploring how codes defining sexual relations informed cultural and social changes. Far from being marginal to the political and economic development of the state, gender and sexuality were integral in the making of Italy and Italians.[12]

The reassessment of the politics and society of the liberal state cast new light on the economy. Until recently, historians on the left and right based their economic analyses on the existence of a "backward" economy. Marxist historians argued that the absence of an agrarian revolution during the Risorgimento was at the root of Italy's inability to industrialize. Liberal historians insisted that poor investment strategies, parliamentary crises, a risk adverse bourgeoisie, and rural labor struggles stunted the "industrial revolution."[13] Current works reject the notion of a "backwar" economy, and that its industrial revolution was late or limited. By taking a longer view of economic growth, tracing the changing conditions from the early nineteenth century to the end of the Giolittian period, the economy emerges steadier and stronger. Post-unification crises no longer appear linked to unification, but as part of an ongoing process of changing industrial and agricultural practices. Although the stewards of the liberal state did not always make the right choices, historians contend that for the most part economic policies encouraged, rather than inhibited growth.[14]

The historical reappraisal of the liberal economy contributed to radically revising understandings of the economic development of the South, and the southern *latifondo*, the large estates considered the clearest example of the failure of modernization. New studies suggested that southern landowners were not as "backward" as historians had assumed. Instead, the *latifundia* were entwined with the global export market economy. Combined these histories have questioned the essentialist assumptions that characterized debate about the deep economic North/South divide. Following unification, the South, like the North, was an economically diverse region, attempting to navigate changing domestic and foreign markets.[15]

Studies of the southern economy are part of a broader new history of the South. Beginning in the late nineteenth century the South emerged as a "problem," for the liberal state. In the historiographical frame of success/failure, the South appeared as evidence of the failure of the liberal state to create a cohesive nation, part of the general failure in its mission to make Italians. In their efforts to explain why the South failed to thrive, some historians blamed the Bourbons, some the liberal state, and others the people. Regardless of where they placed blame, scholars saw the South as marginal to the central narratives of Italian history.[16] In the 1990s, historians reframed the story, placing the South at the center of Italy's history. The South was not a "problem" that the state had inherited or had failed to address, but emerged as part of the processes of unification and state formation.[17] The liberal state played a central role in identifying the South with lawlessness and inferiority. Rejecting the notion that the mafia was a product of southern culture, scholars argue that the state enabled the organized crime to flourish and embed itself in the economy and government.[18] Recent works explore how positivist theories of race and social Darwinism naturalized the marginalization of southern Italians within the national body, and justified repressive rule.[19] Alongside studies of the political and cultural construction of the South stand social histories exploring the diverse ways that southern Italians responded to the material conditions and the cultural constraints. The history of South Italians no longer appears as a story of passive acquiescence or exile.[20]

One of the most significant consequences of the recent historiographical trends has been to reposition migration at the center of the history of liberal Italy. The back-and-forth movements of people between regions, nations, cities, and countryside have become central to histories of urbanization, industrialization, social relations, and politics. Historians had long recognized that seasonal circuits of migration defined relations between rural villages and cities, while the emigration of over thirteen million Italians between 1880 and 1915 shaped Italy's place in the world. Yet, for the most part scholars tended to focus on the impact of transnational migration on the receiving societies, exploring questions of assimilation and ethnicity in the new lands. In the 1990s, historians began to think about the significance of mobility on the history of Italy. Scholars began to pay more attention to the sending communities, tracing the roles of the women who remained behind in the decision-making process underlying migration, the impact of remittances on the local economies, and the ways transnational migrations reconfigured relations with the state at home and abroad.[21] These studies revealed the complicated ways internal and transnational migration altered the nature of family economies, gender roles, economic development, shaping notions of national identity, Italy's foreign politics, and its imperial ambitions.[22]

New historical approaches, methodologies, and subjects undermined the notion that liberal Italy had taken a wrong turn. Although these histories run the risk of being overly optimistic in their analyses of social, political, and economic change, the recognition that there is no one story of success or failure as enriched the field. These new works have made the history of liberal Italy relevant to a much wider audience. No longer a footnote to general trends in nineteenth-century European history, the history of Italy provides an important case study of how gender, race, and mobility proved critical in the creation of European nation-states, social hierarchies, and national identities.

CHAPTER 5
WORK AND FAMILY

Caterina Chiapasco was born in the village of Monesiglio near the French border in 1882. Her family owned a small parcel of land and two cows. As she remembered later in life, "There were those who were worse off and those who were better off than us." Chestnuts and polenta comprised the bulk of the family's diet, meat and bread appeared only rarely. Her family lived off their land, the wages they earned working in the local silk industry, and the money they made working in the fields and factories in France. As a child, Caterina went to work in the mills, despite the passage of the first child labor law in 1886, stipulating that no child under the age of nine was allowed to work in industries, quarries or mines. When the inspectors appeared at the door, the children hid. Caterina worked a twelve-hour day, earning one lire for every sixteen hours of work. When work was scarce, Caterina and her siblings walked over the mountains to France to work the fields. Like others born in the first decades after unification, she grew up in a world defined by work, travel, hunger, and scarcity.[1] While her daily life echoed the rhythms of her parents and grandparents, Caterina came of age in a rapidly changing world. By the end of the century, economic growth transformed how and where Italians worked and lived. Industrialization and urbanization strengthened the geographic and social hierarchies underpinning the new state, altered class relations, and reshaped the family.

Agriculture and industry

In the nineteenth century, the vast majority of people worked in agriculture. In 1861, 70 percent of the labor force worked the land, 18 percent found work in industries, the remaining 12 percent worked in commerce, transportation, banking, service, and public administration. Forty years later, over 60 percent of the workforce still earned their living off the land.[2] Statistical continuity obscured changes occurring in the workforce. Between 1861 and 1911, northern Italians left agriculture and moved into industry, and the proportion of women in the paid workforce fell.

In the Italian and European imagination Italy constituted a veritable "garden of Europe," a lush, fertile land, but, the reality, as Senator Jacini reminded his readers in the final report of the detailed agricultural inquiry commissioned by Parliament in the 1880s, was far different. Nearly a third of the land was mountainous, and difficult, if not impossible to farm, while the malarial lowlands were equally inhospitable. In most villages, residents worked long days to eke out a meager living. Although there were pockets of prosperity, along the Po valley and in the fertile plains of Lombardy, where the land produced an income of over 2,000 lire per hectare (Tables 1 and 2), in many places

Table 1 Percentage of workforce (over age 15) by gender and industry 1861–1911

Year	Men			Women			Men and Women		
	Ag	*Industry*	*Other Activities*	*Ag*	*Industry*	*Other Activities*	*Ag*	*Industry*	*Other Activities*
1861	71.9	13.2	15.0	66.5	25.3	8.3	69.7	18.1	12.2
1871	69.0	15.2	15.8	65.2	25.3	9.5	67.5	19.1	13.3
1881	66.8	17.1	16.1	63.0	25.6	11.4	65.4	20.2	14.4
1901	62.1	21.2	16.7	60.9	24.5	14.7	61.7	22.3	16.0
1911	58.2	23.5	18.3	58.8	24.2	17.0	58.4	23.7	17.9

Source: Istat, Statistiche Storiche, Popolazione, Tavola 10.3—Popolazione attiva in condizione professionale per sesso e settore di attività economica ai Censimenti 1861–2011 (a) (in migliaia e composizioni percentuali).

Table 2 Percentage of men and women working by industrial sector 1861-1911

Year	Agriculture		Industry		Other Activities	
	Men	Women	Men	Women	Men	Women
1861	61	39	43	57	73	27
1871	62	38	48	52	72	28
1881	65	35	54	46	71	29
1901	68	32	65	35	71	29
1911	70	30	70	0	72	28

Source: Istat, Statistiche Storiche, Popolazione, Tavola 10.3—Popolazione attiva in condizione professionale per sesso e settore di attività economica ai Censimenti 1861–2011 (a) (in migliaia e composizioni percentuali).

the yield was closer to 5 lire. According to Jacini, the unwillingness of landowners to adopt modern methods was to blame for low productivity. Owners preferred to extend production into mediocre lands, requiring vast amounts of fertilizer and irrigation rather than improve their existing holdings. Unable to produce enough wheat to satisfy domestic demand, Italy had import grain from Russia and Turkey.[3]

The northern regions boasted the most abundant harvests. The Po valley stretching across the peninsula from Piedmont to the Adriatic Sea constituted some of the most fertile lands in the nation. The well-irrigated fields grew corn, wheat, rice, hemp, flax, and forage. The yield per hectare was nearly double the national average. Landowners implemented a complex system of crop rotation alternating between wheat and maize. Two-thirds of the cattle and half of the pigs in the country were bred in Piedmont, Lombardy, Veneto, and Emilia. Vineyards, fruit, olives, and flowers grew throughout the foothills. The size of the farms varied greatly. In the rice-growing region of Vercelli, some farms reached over 100 hectares; in Piedmont the average farm was significantly smaller. In the 1880s and 1890s, landowners in the north and central regions began to shift production toward the export market, planting their fields with tobacco and beets. Sugar beet production increased sharply, from 100 tons in 1880 to over 50,000 tons by the late 1890s. Although the region accounted for only 21 percent of arable land, it produced 42 percent of goods sold at market.[4]

Northern artisanal or cottage industries grew to meet world market demands for wool, silk, and cotton. Manufacturing was closely linked to the agrarian economy and depended on export markets. The mills and industries that opened in the course of the 1880s and 1890s were usually located in the countryside, where employers could recruit labor from nearby rural communities. In the 1880s, silk comprised the largest export, accounting for one-third of the value of all exports. Italy stood second only to China in the production of raw silk. The industry relied on peasant workers to raise the silk worms and manufacture the silk, and all stages of production were located in northern rural regions. The rural character of the early industrial sector was a consequence of the entrepreneurial strategies adopted by business owners. Acknowledging the relatively small domestic market for their goods, and their dependency on the notoriously unstable export markets, manufacturers sought to open their workshops where they could take advantage of a cheap, flexible, and skilled labor force.

After unification, northern rural workers relied on both agriculture and industry to make a living. The vast majority of peasant owners reported in the census resided in the mountains and foothills of Piedmont, Lombardy, Veneto, and Liguria. Landholdings were often too small and scattered to support a family; so many peasant landowners also sharecropped lands. The contracts varied widely. Some landlords provided secure multiyear contracts, others charged tenants annual rent in kind or cash. By the 1880s rural residents increasingly sought wage work in agriculture and local mills, sometimes traveling further afield to find seasonal employment. The rice fields in the province of Novara employed over 100,000 men and women in 1871, many traveling from their homes to work the harvest before returning home. Increasingly rural residents also worked in local industries for part of the year.

In the North, the number of people employed in agriculture declined after unification, while the number of those working in industry rose. In Piedmont, the agricultural laborers fell by 17 percent between 1861 and 1901, and in Lombardy by 15 percent. Many found work in local industries. The number of Piedmontese employed in industry rose by 11 percent.[5] The gradual shift to wage work accompanied the disappearance of women from the workforce. In the last decades of the century, the percentage of women classified as "without profession" or as housewives increased, as the percentage of women engaged in industry and agriculture declined. Women continued to work in the fields, to spin, weave, and sew for the family, and in food production, but since their labor was often uncompensated by wages it no longer counted as work.[6]

Mezzadria, or sharecropping dominated the central regions. By 1900, over half of all workers engaged in agriculture in Tuscany worked under sharecropping contracts. The most common contracts required tenants to pay half their crops in rent, although the details of contracts varied according to custom and the quality of the land. The *mezzadria* system lent itself to labor-intensive cultivation of specialized crops such as grapes or olives where all family members worked in the fields. It was a uniquely stable system, anchored in the extended family. The system was also resistant to modernization. Tenants rarely earned enough profit in a season to purchase new machinery or embark on capital intensive land improvement projects, and the property owners had no incentive to invest money that would secure only a partial return. Although most residents sharecropped the land, a few owned small plots of land, while others worked as day laborers. Tuscany, Emilia-Romagna, and Umbria all witnessed a decline in the number of agrarian workers and a slight increase in industrial worker over the last decades of the nineteenth century, although not nearly as marked as in the northern provinces.

The southern provinces and Sicily were characterized by extensive grain production in the interior, and smaller more intensive citrus orchards and olive groves on the coast. The *Latifunda*, vast wheat estates stretching for miles across Calabria and western Sicily, were first introduced by the Romans, and consolidated under centuries of feudalism. Property ownership remained in the hands of a few; in 1871 only 2 percent of Sicilians owned property compared to 15 percent in Piedmont.[7] In the course of the 1800s, local nobility generally turned management of their landholdings over to middle men who contracted with peasants to plant the wheat and herd the sheep. Rural residents worked the land under onerous sharecropping contracts or for daily wages. Although the sharecropping contracts varied from estate to estate, in general, the terms of the agreement left the worker with little profit at the end of the harvest. Workers who could not afford to sharecrop worked as wageworkers earning around one lire a day.

Residents, living in the densely populated agro-towns, perched high above the wheat fields often owned small plots of land near the outskirts of town, sufficient to produce vegetables for the family but not for market. Access to pasturage, wood, and foraging had been severely curtailed with the abolition of feudalism and the loss of traditional rights to common lands. If the interior of southern Italy was golden yellow, the coastal regions were a deep green. Around the bay of Naples and the *Conca D'Ora* in Palermo, landowners tended citrus and olive groves and sold their produce on a growing export market. By the 1870s it was estimated that Sicily's lemon groves accounted for some of the most profitable agricultural land in Europe. Despite the dismissal of southern agricultural as backward, landowners in Calabria and Sicily had adapted to the demands of the modern market. Between the 1860s and 1890s, many Calabrian *latifundisti* had implemented a series of changes in response to market demands including planting new crops, introducing new methods, and shifting to a more mobile and flexible labor force. The cumulative effects of the changes left the *latifundia* more dependent on the global market and vulnerable to the government economic policies.

Post-unification land reforms, determined to break up the large estates and create a class of small-property owners, similar to the northern land-tenure system, disrupted the southern economy. In the first decades of unification large swaths of southern lands were put on market, by 1865 over 250,000 hectares had been auctioned off. Yet, despite their stated ambitions, the sales bolstered the fortunes of a small new class of non-noble landowners who reconstituted the large estates through later sales or coercion.[8] Rather than enlarging the number of small-property owners, the reforms expanded the pool of landless agricultural wageworkers. As in the North, the shift from sharecropping to wage work accompanied the disappearance of southern women from the wage labor force.[9]

Across the South, unification ushered in a period of industrial decline. The creation of a national market placed southern industry at a distinct competitive disadvantage in respect to both Lombard and Piedmont products and foreign imports. Foreign capital that seeded post-unification development in the north failed to make its way to the south. Shipbuilding and textile manufacturing virtually disappeared in the South. Southern economic development reinforced the northern image of the South as a backward, violent land, filled with recalcitrant landowners and stoic, illiterate peasants. Discounting the material difficulties that faced southern agriculture, including the lack of roads, scarcity of banks, frequent earthquakes and droughts, politicians and economists pointed to the moral failures of the residents to account for the continued poor yields and poverty.

State policies increased the growing economic disparity between northern and southern regions. Until the 1880s, politicians adhered to the principles of free trade, abolishing import tariffs, dismantling trade restrictions, eliminating price controls, and privatizing land. Support of a free market accompanied the expansion of transportation and communication networks, including railroads. In 1859, the railroads only covered 2,000 kilometers, by 1865, the network had doubled in size, and by 1876 it had quadrupled. Foreign capital fueled the early railroad constructions. French and German firms provided the rails and railway cars, providing little room for domestic industries to profit from the rail works. After 1876, the government abandoned austerity measures and began to play a more active role in economic development, gradually taking over the largest railroad networks in a public/private partnership. The northern regions connected remote rural communities to major cities and foreign markets. In the South, few roads or railroads crossed the mountains, leaving many of the communities as isolated as they were in the 1850s. The opening of markets, combined with improved transportation, enabled northern property owners and industrialists to expand domestic markets and maintain existing trade relations with European neighbors. The south benefited little from the new economic regime.

Burned by heavy debts incurred by the wars of unification, the government's little monies left for investments deepened social and geographic divisions. Immediately after 1861, politicians geared fiscal policy toward balancing the budget through taxes and land sales, but well into the 1870s, expenditures continued to outpace revenue. The implementation of a uniform tax code provided the largest source of revenue, and did away with some preunification disparities, but the code was profoundly regressive. The grist tax in particular weighed heavy on consumers and the poor (Maps 5 and 6).

Food and taxes comprised the bulk of a family's budget leaving little or nothing to purchase goods produced by local artisans or tradesmen. Government investments in schools, military barracks, and roads benefited the North more than the South. The state used the profits gained from the sale of church and demesne lands in the south to fund public works in the north. The years following unification accompanied a significant transfer of wealth from the South to the North.

State policies helped protect the economy from the worst of the global recession of the 1870s. The decision to implement the *Corso Forzosa* (forced circulation) and replace all gold and gold backed currency with inconvertible paper currency in 1866 was undertaken in the hopes to rein in the ballooning national debt, and acted as a form of protectionism. The depreciation of the lire made exports cheaper in foreign markets and foreign goods more expensive. As the nation's finances improved, the government gradually moved back to the gold standard. The return to the gold standard accompanied calls for government protection. At the end of the 1870s, agricultural exports suffered from the low agricultural prices, and the availability of cheap American grain and Asian rice and silks. In 1878, the Cairoli government agreed to impose tariffs on wool, cotton, juke, and silk imports, protecting the most developed northern industries from low priced competition, while leaving others vulnerable to the vagaries of global markets.

By the mid-1880s Italy too felt the effects of the global collapse of agricultural prices. Political support for the implementation of protectionist measures grew stronger, bolstered by a civic demand and government investments. A united front of northern

Map 5 Italian railroads, 1861.

industrialists, landowners, worker's associations, and mutual-aid societies presented a formidable political force. The economic crisis in the 1880s affected northern agriculturalists and industrialists the worst. By 1885, it appeared as though the country's most dynamic economies were on the verge of collapse; when profits kept falling there was little incentive to modernize equipment or reinvest money into production. The threat of unemployment encouraged workers to add their voices to the protectionist chorus. Increased government investments in steel and iron convinced many lawmakers to readily abandon their free market beliefs. As part of an effort to expand the navy, the state had invested in the Terni steel mill that had just opened in 1886. Between 1885 and

Map 6 Italian railroads, 1870.

1889 annual steel production increased from approximately 3,000 tons to 157,000 tons.[10] In an effort to respond to the threat of falling prices the government passed new tariffs.

The general tariff approved by Parliament imposed levies on imported sugar, coffee, and doubled duties on imported wheat. While these tariffs may have pleased landowners, consumers suffered as prices for bread, coffee, and pasta rose. The government imposed the highest tolls on manufactured goods, especially steel and textiles, providing protection for government industries and the northern textile manufacturers. The law was idiosyncratic in many ways, shaped by political patronage and backroom deals. Levies on cotton yarn were much higher than cloth, reflecting particular interests, ultimately nullifying the purpose of protection. The tariffs left the nascent machinery factories completely unprotected. The combination of rising costs and a shrinking consumer market forced many industries to close and foreign investors to leave.

The effect of the implementation of protectionist tariffs on the economy is difficult to calculate. In the short term, iron and steel production rose, and the cotton industry flourished. However, the tariffs could not compensate for the global decline in prices and falling domestic demand. A trade war with France from 1889 to 1891 further complicated the economic picture. The trade war, cutting exports to France by half, profoundly affected wine and silk industries. In the South, the protectionist measures undercut the markets for fruit, olive oil, and wines. The tariff war coincided with the collapse of the speculative construction boom that triggered a severe banking crisis. By the 1890s, signs of recovery appeared in the North. Government measures to reorganize the banking industry, and the founding of the Bank of Italy in 1892, provided a firmer footing for credit. Access to capital encouraged industrial growth in the north, including automobile factories and electric plants. The new industries concentrated in an industrial triangle linking Milan, Genoa, and Turin.

There was no silver lining in the South. As global wheat prices declined after 1873, southern landowners shifted more land over to citrus, olives, and wine, although they continued to plant wheat profiting from the increased aggregate demand that offset lower prices. In this way, southern landowners were able to weather the worst of the recession until the 1880s. The passage of the protectionist measures had an immediate and damaging impact on the southern economy. The tariffs imposed under Depretis in 1887 caused a severe agricultural crisis in the south, marked by rising unemployment and lower wages. Government intervention transformed the southern economy into a colonial market for northern goods.

Surveying the history of the economy after 1861, it is evident that a combination of free market measures, the creation of a common market, increased capital investments, and the passage of select protectionist measures strengthened the economy. The steps taken during the period of crisis positioned industry to thrive between 1890 and the First World War. The economic development of Italy was uneven. Prosperity in the North accompanied economic decline in the South. The economic transformations also brought more people into urban centers, changing the workforce, sharpening class divisions and changed family life.

Mobility and urbanization

The years between 1860 and 1900 were marked by increased mobility. The expansion of railroads, the growth of cities, combined with a growing wage labor force, encouraged Italians to seek work beyond the boundaries of their hometowns. Political unification merged older migratory circuits with new ones. Preunification migration was largely rural in character, confined to the mountains and countryside, holding fast to the rhythms of the agricultural calendar, sowing, harvesting, and gleaning. Villages often specialized in particular kinds of work or trades. Tuscan workers traveled to Lazio to prune the olive trees, while the Abruzzesi worked the fields. Chimney sweeps traveled out from the Val d'Aosta, stone masons left Biella. Migration strengthened ties between the city and countryside. Struggling urban artisans and laborers worked the harvests, while peasants willingly took temporary jobs in construction when work was scarce in the fields. By eliminating internal border, unification expanded these circuits.[11]

Demographic growth helped fuel increased mobility. Throughout the nineteenth century the population grew steadily, accelerating after unification: between 1861 and 1911 the population rose from twenty-two million (excluding Veneto and Rome) to thirty-five million. Like elsewhere in Europe, demographic growth was a consequence of declining mortality rates. Mortality rates fell below 30 per 1.000 in the 1880s, and below 20 per 1,000 in the 1900s. Improved food supplies, housing, sanitation, and the end of the periodic epidemics accounted for the longer life spans. Between 1863 and 1900 the median age at death for men rose from forty-nine to sixty-two years of age, and for women from fifty to sixty-three years of age. As mortality rates dropped, particularly the numbers of infant deaths, birth rates held steady, above 30 per 1,000 well into the twentieth century.

Post 1861 economic and political transformations encouraged people to seek their fortunes further afield. The rising number of agricultural workers wageworkers created a more mobile labor force that readily alternated between manufacturing and agricultural work. The rice fields of Vercelli, Mortara, Novara, and Pavia attracted thousands of workers from the villages in the Apennines, the Alps, and throughout the plains. Workers flocked to Cremona, Mantua, and Brescia to harvest mulberries, corn, and oats, or to tend silkworms. Work varied by season. From June to July migrants harvested fields of wheat or corn, or weeded the rice fields. In September, when the grapes ripened, workers moved to the vineyards. In Sicily, the grape harvest in Acireale brought in 10,000 migrant workers. Between 1861 and 1890, these agricultural migratory paths expanded as more land was brought into production; however, the basic system changed little: the rice paddies and wheat fields of the Padana valley, the Maremma, and Agro, the fertile regions of Puglia and Sicily attracted migrants during the summer and fall when work at home was scarce.[12]

Conditions for migrant works varied depending on gender and skill. Although most migrants were men, women dominated specific networks. Over 45,000 migrants, mostly men, came to work the fields in Lazio in June and July, living in temporary housing of mud and straw. Despite the risk of malaria and the poor living conditions, workers returned each year to work for the relatively higher wages (1.5–2 lire a day in 1879). Work was gender specific. Women gleaned, weeded, and raised silkworms. Recruiters from the rice fields in Piedmont traveled to far flung villages in Lombardy, Reggio Emilia, and the nearby villages in the foothills of the Alps offering contracts for summer work. The average pay varied between .80 and 1.25 lire a day. Migrant women comprised nearly half of the labor force hired to weed the rice fields in Vercelli and Novara during the summer months. These young women, many unmarried, lived in rough huts where clean water was scarce, and in the hot summer months even the well water turned undrinkable as human waste and animal carcasses seeped into the land. Recruiters provided meals for migrant workers often consisting of watery soups and polentas made from cornmeal, beans, and bacon. Most of the workers were young, unmarried men and women.[13]

The last decades of the nineteenth century accompanied rapid urbanization promoting new migrations from rural to urban centers. Between 1860 and 1900 the urban population of the major cities, including Turin, Milan, Rome, Naples, and Palermo grew rapidly. The population of Milan rose 62 percent, from 199,009 residents to 321,839, between 1871 and 1881 alone. The population of Rome nearly doubled between 1871 and 1901. In the South, Bari and Catania saw the sharpest rise in population, although the population of both Naples and Palermo increased by 10 percent and 25 percent, respectively. Immigrants from the surrounding countryside and far flung regions fueled urban growth. In 1881, 53 percent of Romans were born outside the city limits, the majority coming from Tuscany, Piedmont, and Campania. By 1911, 42 percent of the population of Milan had been born in the city, and only 38 percent of the population of Turin claimed birthright.[14] The cities welcomed the new residents. After unification, local politicians tore down the old walls encircling the cities, providing jobs for residents and encouraging the construction of new housing developments.

Urban expansion redefined relations between the poor and wealthy. On the outskirts of the major cities new residential and commercial neighborhoods sprung up. Housing for the wealthier residents, elegant apartment buildings and villas surrounded by gardens, displaced the small landowners, farmers, and poor who traditionally worked and lived in the shadows of the walls. Lawyers, doctors, and wealthy merchants moved their families to the quieter suburbs. Working-class neighborhoods sprouted on the edges of the cities. In 1877, developers broke ground on a new Roman residential district outside Porta San Lorenzo, between the train station and the cemetery, for families of unskilled construction workers, railroad employees, and tram drivers. Although the facades of the new apartment buildings in San Lorenzo modeled the designs of those built for the middling classes and shopkeepers, the apartments themselves were designed to house the largest number of people and ensure the highest possible rent per square foot. Each apartment building was built around a small central courtyard in order to maximize the amount of living space. The separate worlds of the wealthy, bourgeoisie, and workers were linked by expanding public transportation networks. The first tramline was opened in Milan in 1876, and by the early 1890s, electric lines replaced horses.[15]

Urbanization was fueled by the growth of state bureaucracy, commerce, finance, and the construction trades, not factory work. Working men and women left the fields to take jobs in construction, the rail yards, restaurants, shops, and garment industries. According to a 1908 study of Milan, over 70 percent of the men who worked in trattoria, hotels, and cafes were born elsewhere. As the size of family landholdings diminished, or families lost their farms altogether, parents sent young girls to work in domestic service in the cities. The families of doctors, lawyers, and civil servants required maids, cooks, and nannies. According to critics, the working urban poor were reluctant to enter domestic service; only 12 percent of domestic service workers in Milan were born in the city. New arrivals comprised 58 percent of industrial workers, and 70 percent of those engaged in commerce. City residents preferred wet nurses and nursemaids from rural regions. Women skilled in needlework earned money by taking in piecework. Every day the new arrivals poured in to the working-class neighborhoods, spilling out of the newly built apartments. Middle-class migrants—young professionals, doctors, and lawyers—poured into the cities between the 1870s and 1890s, ensuring continued demand for new housing, and providing a robust consumer market for local artisans and tradesmen. The expansion of public sector jobs, civil service, transportation, and communications attracted educated young men from the provinces. Over 70 percent of Milanese men employed in public administration, and 60 percent of those employed in private administration, were born outside the city. Wealthy urban elite were the least likely to move.[16]

The growth of the cities strengthened ties with the surrounding countryside. Each morning artists, musicians, merchants, and farmers came to the city by train or on foot to sell their wares or seek city services. Rural women offered their services as nursemaids at the foundling hospitals. In exchange for taking a child home to nurse, the public charities paid each woman a small stipend.[17] In the 1880s and 1890s large public hospitals and asylums were opened in the cities, serving the surrounding regions. Alongside those seeking services, military recruits required to serve far from their hometowns, comprised a significant portion of temporary urban migrants.

Urban elites surveyed their burgeoning cities with trepidation. Journalists, academics, lawyers, and doctors fed fears that the new immigrants brought crime and disease, and called for increased policing and surveillance. In a study of the police and the "dangerous social classes," Giovanni Bolis, a lawyer wrote, "As a wave runs to the sea, so to the large cities flow all those perverse and roving people who shun work and disdain the slender salary of a laborer."[18] Vagabonds and prostitutes appeared the most threatening to the bourgeoisie, and critics called for stricter laws regulating loitering, solicitation, and prostitution. The economic crisis heightened middle-class fears. The collapse of the construction industry revealed the fragility of the urban economies. As urban unemployment rose in the 1890s, residents tried to pay rent by bringing borders into their already overcrowded apartments, overburdening the sewage and water systems. Poorly constructed to begin with, the new apartment buildings quickly fell into disrepair.[19] By the 1890s, some critics focused on the miserable living conditions of the slums and tenements and called for urban renewal projects. They held that the squalid housing, filthy water, and overcrowding were the sources of prostitution, crime, and disease, not the perversity of the poor.[20]

Mobility played a critical role in the growth of the economy. Territorial and market unification enabled the growing pool of wageworkers to travel in ever widening circles through the countryside and cities, often settling in the growing cities. The combination of state centralization, industrialization, urbanization, and migration altered the form and function of families.

Family

Throughout the century, the family served as the primary economic and social unit, providing food, shelter, and social networks. Family forms and household compositions varied across the country. Local economies played a major role in shaping family forms. Nuclear families predominated among wageworkers and the wealthy. In Sicily, as in Piedmont, families who depended on wage income were comprised of husbands, wives, and children. Among the aristocracy and wealthy landowning elite, the nuclear family ensured that land and wealth could be passed on to the eldest sons. Multiple family households linked by blood and marriage prevailed in regions where families owned small farms or held tenancies, and required labor. Among sharecroppers of Umbria and Tuscany the household served as the center of production, as well as the space of consumption and reproduction. Nuclear families and multiple family households anchored individuals to the wider community, determining status and place within the larger collectivity. Births and marriages tied each person to a specific village, town, or city, and to a wider social community. Villagers carried with them stories of a family's trials or their good fortune. Trades and talents were assigned at birth as sons and daughters grew with the expectation that they would continue the family business. Although families are inherently conservative institutions, they are subject to change. The creation of the liberal nation-state, economic changes, and mobility eroded divisions between that public and private life, altered domestic relations and geographically stretched the boundaries of family.[21]

The passage of the 1865 civil code (*Codice Pisanelli*) reinforced the primacy of the nuclear family in law. The new legal norms regarding marriage and inheritance affected people differently depending on class and gender, but across the board the laws strengthened the economic and juridical power of fathers and husbands. The civil code placed new conditions on the acquisition and dispensation of familial property. At marriage, the code abolished the obligation of fathers to dower daughters, long a common impediment to marriage. Although the wealthy and middle classes continued to provide dowries, particularly in the South where the custom was deeply entrenched, a dowry was no longer legally required. The elimination of the dowry was, in some ways, emancipatory for women, who were now free to marry after the age of twenty-one regardless of parental approval; however, in other ways the new law impoverished elite women by shifting wealth to men. A few of the preunification legal codes allowed women to retain control of their dowries after marriage. In Sicily, Sardinia, and Puglia, dowries were often comprised of land, and served as a form of anticipated inheritance. Under the new code, women were forced to relinquish control over their property to their husbands. Inheritance law in general privileged the nuclear family and patriarchal power. The new code stipulated that where there was no will, estates had to be divided among all legitimate children regardless of age or sex, favoring legal blood ties over extended kin networks.

The liberal state reaffirmed the judicial power of husband and father within the family. Marital authority was conferred on the husband, obligating a wife to obtain formal permission before engaging in commerce or exercising direct control over property or money. Until 1919, a woman could not take out a mortgage, loan, give money to charities, or even open a bank account without her husband's permission. A husband's legal authority over a wife's business transactions was not unique to Italy. Great Britain and France had similar legal provisions. However, the Austrian legal code never imposed restrictions on a woman's right to engage in public transactions, and the women of Veneto and Lombardy found themselves forced to seek permission from their husbands only after 1865. Fathers also wielded greater power over children. *Patria potesta,* or parental authority was ostensibly granted to both father and mother, but was primarily held by the father. Husbands had the right to dictate terms of a child's education and allowances that were binding even after death. Fathers alone had the right to give permission for a minor child to marry. A widow's ability to raise her children was limited by the presence of an appointed male guardian, or the local *consiglio di famiglia* (family council), a government committee designed to protect the interests of orphan children, the mentally ill or physically handicapped. The reinforcement of patriarchal power accompanied a general expansion of state into private life.[22]

The first national education law passed in 1861. The Casati Law, introduced in 1859 in Piedmont, was extended across Italy immediately after unification. Primarily concerned with restructuring higher education, the law required all incorporated town to provide two years' free education to all boys and girls between the ages of six and eight. Faced with deep debts, the state did not fund the schools, leaving city councils responsible for finding the monies to rent space and hire teachers. Government inquiries and investigations soon proved what many suspected: northern cities with more established schools generally conformed to the law and reported increased enrollments and high literacy rates. By 1900, over 80 percent of resident in the North could read. In the absence of established schools, southern towns found it difficult to open classrooms, hire teachers, or convince residents of the importance of education without government assistance. In the South, illiteracy rates roughly 70 percent of residents could not read or write, and attendance sparse.[23] When the left came to power in 1876, they passed the Coppino law, making primary education compulsory, but did little else to improve the quality of education, to provide buildings or to mandate attendance.

Parliamentary attitudes toward education were decidedly ambivalent. On the one hand, government officials and politicians recognized the need for a minimally educated citizenry, schooled in civic duties. However, government officials were wary of the dangers of education. One Sicilian inspector wrote in his annual report to the Ministry of Public Education:

The teachers' duty is to make the child understand the world in which he lives . . . and teach him to love it with all of its privileges and defects, with its satisfactions and disillusions, and so to create an individual full of fire, of energy and activity, understanding of his duties and rights, productive for himself and for others, ready and willing to fulfill his role on earth.[24]

The inspector echoed Coppino's insistence that the goal of primary education was to create contented citizens.[25]

Gender-specific classroom lessons placed the family in service of the state. Young boys were told that their duties were to work, pay taxes, and serve in the military. Lessons for girls emphasized nutrition, health, hygiene, and the importance of sacrifice. In *Casa Mia, Patria Mia*, a popular textbook for third-grade girls, a lesson entitled *Madri di eroi* ("Mothers of Heroes") outlined the civic duties of women in relation to the state. One morning a classroom receives a postcard of a statue depicting a woman holding a flag surrounded by her five sons entitled *La Famiglia Cairoli* (the Cairoli Family). As the teacher passed the postcard among her students, she recounted the story of Adelaide Cairoli.

> As I have told you many times, the nation lived through sad times; Italy was enslaved and divided. Patriots sought to free her. Adelaide Cairoli had nothing but her five sons, who had grown strong and good around her; but when the people began to rise, when the war against the oppressors was declared, Adelaide did not hesitate for one moment and said to her sons: "I am a woman and I cannot fight; you are men and can: go: the country needs you."[26]

The teacher concluded telling the girls, "Adelaide Cairoli who lived a simple and good life, ardently loved two equally great things: her country and her house." To drive home this lesson, Fabiani urged students to "remember, good, prudent, hardworking women make a happy home; and happy homes make a happy state." The fate of a family was inextricably connected to the fate of the nation. If the legal codes reinforced a father's authority within the family, compulsory education diminished the scope of their authority. The function of the family was to generate a healthy nation for the state, not private wealth or power.

By the 1880s, the ideal family promoted in law and culture took the shape of a nuclear family based on conjugal love and complementary roles. The new legal code in theory ensured that families grew from loving unions, bolstered the position of husband as provider, producer, and protector, and defined women as mothers and wives, legitimizing their exclusion from politics and the workforce. In the eyes of the state, the primary purpose of the family was to create loyal, ethical citizens, yet in the nineteenth century, the family remained an economic and social unit. Increased mobility made extended family ties even more important. Working-class and middle-class families remained tightly linked by kin and blood networks. Families of shopkeepers, civil servants, those engaged in trade and commerce mobilized kin networks to find work for their sons and husbands for their daughters. Mobility and wage work reshaped domestic relations within working-class families. The increased dependence on wages transformed married women into household managers. While her husband and children worked in the workshops and fields, a woman became the de facto head of household, managing money and lands.

The social and economic development of liberal Italy bolstered the foundations of the state and strengthened the geographic and social divisions. Economic development reinforced the idea of a backward, problematic South, and gender norms that identified men as providers and protectors and women as mothers and wives. Yet, at the same time, markets fostered new kinds of mobilities reshaping family forms and expanding social networks in ways that challenged regional divisions.

CHAPTER 6
ITALIANS ON THE MOVE

In early September of 1905 Salvatore A. and a dozen other young men from Sutera boarded the train for Palermo bound for the coal fields near Birmingham, Alabama. This was not the first time Salvatore had traveled across the Atlantic. He first left shortly after he and Giuseppa S. married in 1903. Now, three years later, leaving his wife pregnant with their second child, he set sail to rejoin his brother in Alabama. The story of Giuseppa and Salvatore was common in Sutera, a small hill town huddled at the base Monte San Paolino in the province of Caltanisetta. The men who left and the women who remained behind saw emigration as a means to better their lives back home, not an opportunity to settle in new lands. Although the decision to migrate was anchored in familial ambitions, transoceanic migration had a profound impact on Italy and Italians. Transnational migration created a back-and-forth exchange of people, money, ideas, and goods that linked Italians living in hill towns and villages to the nation and the wider world in new ways. The millions of Italians who traveled abroad between 1880 and 1922 affected local and national economies, redefined social relations, and altered notions of national belonging.[1]

Emigrants

Between 1870 and 1922 over sixteen million people from the North and South left their homes to work abroad. Although the resident population grew by nine million people between 1870 and 1910, nearly twice that number emigrated to Europe, the Americas, Asia, and Australia. By the First World War, Italy secured its reputation as a principle exporter of workers throughout the world at a time when people everywhere were on the move. In the first decades after unification northern Italians comprised the largest contingent of transnational migrant workers. After unification, men and women from Piedmont, Lombardy, and Veneto continued to travel over the mountains into France, Switzerland, and Austria to work in the fields and factories. Over 80 percent of those who migrated before 1880 came from the northern provinces, and the vast majority went to Europe. While these circuits were not new, unification expanded regional migratory patterns to include transnational destinations. In the 1880s, artisans and stoneworkers from the northern villages expanded their regional migrations through Italy and Europe into the Americas: the stoneworkers from Biella continued to work in France and Italy as they extended their range into Peru, Argentina, Bolivia, and into the United States. The central regions reported much lower rates of migration in the 1870s and 1880s. Only in the 1890s did people living in Tuscany, Marche, Umbria, and Lazio begin to look beyond Italy's borders for work, and even then, the regions reported significantly lower rates of migration. By the 1890s emigration rates from the southern regions of Campania, Calabria, Basilicata, and Sicily surpassed those in the North. By the first decade of the twentieth century 70 percent of emigrants came from the South.[2]

Gender, class, and region marked emigration patterns. The typical migrant was male, between twenty and forty years of age. Although artisans, merchants, and factory workers worked abroad, the vast majority of migrant men worked as manual laborers in agriculture or construction. Peasants comprised half of all migrants until the late 1890s, when landless wage workers from the South started to outnumber them. Most of the men left their wives and children behind. Until the First World War, male migrants outnumbered women by roughly three to one. The presence of female migrants was higher in certain regions: in Piedmont and Liguria, where women had long worked the fields of France, rates of female migration were exceptionally high, reaching over 20 percent to 25 percent in the 1890s. The women who left their homes were generally young and unmarried seeking work in the fields and factories across the Alps. In Lombardy and Veneto, women tended to stay home, while their men went off in search of work. In the South, initial emigration was heavily male, followed by a sharp increase in the number of women and children joining their husbands or fathers overseas. By the first decade of the twentieth-century women comprised nearly 30 percent of emigrants from Campania, and 25 percent of Sicilian migrants. Available work opportunities at home and abroad, combined with the distance and the duration of the trips, shaped these distinctive patterns.[3]

Those who left between 1880 and 1920 rarely left forever. In his 1907 study of Sicilian agricultural conditions, Professor Giovanni Lorenzoni wrote that most Sicilian migrants "did not intend to permanently establish themselves overseas, but they wanted to return home. They did everything possible in order to return after three or four years, as soon as they managed to save a respectable amount of money."[4] Although the government did not keep count of those who returned, estimates suggest that close to 60 percent of migrants eventually returned home. Again, region mattered. In Veneto and Friuli, where transnational migration closely followed the well-worn paths of seasonal migration, over 80 percent of emigrants returned. However, even in Sicily, where the vast majority of migrants traveled to the Americas, over half returned home. Salvatore's story of multiple migrations was not uncommon. Many men spent two or three years in America, returning for a year or two, and then re-emigrated, before settling in one place or another.

Repatriation rates testify to the importance of place in understanding migration. Unified Italy did not erase the power of birth place in shaping individual lives. The nineteenth-century diaspora was anchored in villages and towns. Although far from home, village networks continued to operate stretching over the ocean. Migrants traveled to the ports and across the ocean accompanied by family and friends from their home town. The back-and-forth movements of letters and people kept everyone apprised of news at home and abroad. Migrants replicated the village in the new world. Emigrants from Sambuca Sicily made their homes on Elizabeth Street in New York

City. A block east, on Mulberry Street, *campanilismo* continued to define the contours of community as migrants replicated the traditional boundaries of the village in new world neighborhoods.

Kin networks informed the experience of migration from the moment a person left home until he or she settled in the new land. Despite the statistics suggesting that most emigrants traveled alone, defined by the state as unaccompanied by parent or spouse, ship manifests show these unaccompanied men traveled in the company of brothers, uncles, in-laws, or cousins, along with others from their hometowns. When new arrivals disembarked in New York or Buenos Aires, uncles or brothers usually waited on the other side of the customs barrier to take them to their new homes and introduce them to their new bosses. The same networks that bound individuals, families, and household together at home shaped the social webs underpinning transnational emigrant groups. Surely some men and women fled overseas driven by dreams of adventure or escape, but for most, the entire process of transatlantic migration, including the initial decision to leave, organizing the journey, and finding work and housing in a new land, was a family enterprise.

Those who chose to leave for Americas or Europe saw their decision as part of a broader family strategy to better their lives back home. With the money earned overseas, family members who remained behind paid off debts built larger two-story houses, financed small businesses, and purchased land. Emigration as a family enterprise required the participation of all its members, those who left and those who stayed. In the South, both men and women mobilized their social networks to assess the viability of emigration. Men drew on contacts from work and their friendships at home. Working in the fields or strolling through the piazza on a Sunday afternoon proved excellent opportunities to exchange news about working conditions overseas. Information about employment and wages spread quickly fueled by government reports passed on by the clerks in City Hall, returning migrants, and the rare letter. When a family received news from an emigrant, they would often read it out loud in the main square. Women turned to their own friends and family to find out more about life on the other side of the ocean. Combined, these networks provided the information necessary to make the decision to either stay or go.[5]

The participation of family members in facilitating transoceanic migration created new kinds of tension. Government officials traveling through the South often depicted the women who remained behind as abandoned by their husbands or sons. In 1905, as Angelo Mosso, a young professor from Turin, traveled through Sicily, he described a heart-wrenching scene at an isolated railroad station, where hundreds of emigrants climbed on board, heading for the ports. As the train pulled out women ran alongside crying and shouting, pleading with their husbands not to forget them. Newspapers featured stories of new brides, jilted by husbands who married them to secure money for passage.[6] In other cases, the women who remained behind pressured reluctant husbands to leave. In Milocca, a Sicilian village, Charlotte Gower Chapman told the story of Zia Maricchia whose neighbors said had "driven her husband to emigrate to America by her un-wifely behavior. She had among other things refused to eat of the same dish with him, and insisted on having her own drinking glass at meals."[7] Yet the variety of ways in which men and women drew on collective resources to send family members overseas suggests that more often than not both those who left and those who stayed were deeply invested in the success of the venture.

Few people who contemplated migration believed it would be easy. In 1907 Professor Giovanni Lorenzoni reported to Parliament,

> The life of an emigrant is not rosy. From the moment he leaves his village accompanied by his wife, screaming and crying all the way to the train station or the docks where he holds her tightly to his chest one last time, to the voyage, to his arrival, to the long days toiling in different climates under brutal overseers, he sees the difficulties, the dangers, and travails growing in his life.[8]

Rural Sicilians told the story of how when Columbus returned from the Americas, he reported that he had found "flowers without fragrance, foods without flavor, and women without love."[9] The only reason to leave home was the chance of finding steady work that paid better than working the fields at home. Those who chose to seek their fortune in the Americas knew that their new lives would be hard, that work would be scarce at times, and that there would be moments of intense homesickness. Most people recognized the risks associated with transoceanic migration, and the vast majority chose to stay home. The decision to leave was never made lightly.

Conditions at home and abroad factored into a family's decision to emigrate or not. The economic crisis of the 1880s and 1890s that brought rising unemployment and falling wages spurred many to consider working overseas. Conscription also proved a powerful incentive for young men between the ages of eighteen and twenty-two to join their brothers, fathers, and uncles overseas. Emigrate offered a means to defer service, if not avoid it altogether. The decision to leave was also fueled by the failure of local labor organizations to improve working conditions. The founding of the Socialist Party in 1892 spurred the formation of local peasant leagues. Agricultural workers from the Po valley down to Sicily organized local collectives to demand better contracts, working conditions, and wages. Throughout the 1890s riots bread; riots and political protests broke out in Milan, Roma, and Turin. In the South, strikes and protests escalated into riots and spread across the countryside and cities.

By 1893 the Sicilian *fasci*, a combination of a mutual-aid society providing financial assistance to its members and a workers' collective committed to political and economic change, had spread from the cities into the countryside. The first *fasci* (from the root *fascio,* meaning bundle, and signifying strength in unity) appeared among urban artisan groups, but by 1893 they had taken root among the peasantry. Most members of the *fasci* identified as Socialist, although their ideological loyalties ranged from committed anarchists to liberals. In the early 1890s, leaders of the *fasci* ran for local councils, led strikes, and negotiated with land owners for better contracts. As the movement grew it became more violent, and the local gentry became more fearful. Prime Minister Giolitti, who had little love for the southern landowners or the peasants, refused to send troops to the island to quell the protests or address the demands for land redistribution. Government attitudes shifted in December 1893, when Francesco Crispi replaced Giolitti, forced to resign in the wake of the Banca Romana scandal. Crispi feared that without immediate and effective government action the Sicilian protests could bring down the state. In January of 1894 Crispi declared martial law across the island, and sent down 40,000 troops to quell the protests. By February, military tribunals had sentenced over 1,000 people to exile, banned public meetings, and reintroduced censorship. By January of 1894 the *fasci* and all workers' associations were dissolved.[10]

As hopes of realizing land reform at home faded, traveling to the Americas was becoming easier and cheaper. The expansion of the railroad and postal system made it easier to make the necessary arrangements, even from remote villages in Calabria or Sicily. The replacement of sailing vessels with steamships made travel to the Americas cheaper and faster. By 1900, a ticket from Naples to New York cost roughly twenty-eight dollars and took just a few weeks. The telegraph and postal service enabled local government officials to keep abreast of government reports on emigrant conditions, wages, and work opportunities.[11]

Once the decision to leave was made, the entire family participated in organizing the voyage. In 1905, a family needed roughly 200 lire to send 1 person overseas. For a southern day laborer, this constituted nearly 70 percent of an agricultural day laborer's salary. Some families took out high-interest loans to pay for passage. The business of migration expanded moneylending opportunities within small rural towns, where few had access to bank loans. Often, women who remained behind willingly loaned out the remittances they received from family working abroad to those eager to emigrate. Women also raised money by pawning the linens that comprised a woman's trousseau. Labor recruiters, often returning migrants, offered prepaid passage or loans to those willing to work in for a specific mining company or planation. These *padroni* (bosses) were instrumental in the creation of late nineteenth-century global-labor networks, and many grew enormous wealth off the commissions charged for their services. The monopoly of the *padroni* faded as more people emigrated and sources of information expanded.[12] Migrants drew on kin resources in ways that stretched families across the ocean. Distance did not break the ties that bound migrants to family, village, or nation.

Transnational Italy

Transnational migration created complex networks linking families across time and space. In some communities, cyclical return migration ensured close physical ties with home. Emigrants from Piedmont living in France often returned home for Christmas, Easter, or local feast days. In Sicily, where emigrants traveled to the Americas or North Africa, remittances, goods, and letters kept emigrants tied in to the family circle, even when they were physically gone for years. Differing labor recruitment strategies, work, and living conditions carved out distinct, if overlapping, internal and transnational migratory circuits.

In Veneto, Lombardy, Piedmont, and Friuli transalpine and transatlantic migratory routes created two distinct kinds of transnational ties between villages and emigrant communities. Each year families watched as young women and men left for France, Switzerland, and Austria to work in the fields, the glassworks, the silk mills, the construction trades, or go into domestic service as wet nurses or maids. This post-unification generation of transalpine migrants traveled in the footsteps of their parents and grandparents, proving that the new national borders remained permeable. Their means of travel had changed. Most left by train rather than walking over the mountain passes. New modes of transportation translated into new destinations, those who left in the 1880s and 1890s often traveled farther in one season. Over the decades these transalpine circuits enlarged the boundaries of village and family incorporating faraway spaces into the local community. As emigrants settled in the French cities, opening stores or restaurants, they became outposts of the village. When new migrants arrived from the village, they exchanged letters and packages from home for shelter and food. The vast majority of transalpine migrants were young and single, and usually returned home at the end of the harvest season, or for brief visits each year. The shorter distances meant that families remained physically linked during the year. Mobility embedded itself in the rhythms of family and village life. In Piedmont, marriages were commonly celebrated in the winter months, when seasonal agricultural workers were home.[13]

Alongside transalpine circuits flowed transoceanic pathways. Throughout the century musicians, artisans, engineers, merchants, architects, stonemasons, and seamen traveled established outposts in Brazil, Argentina, and New York. In the 1870s, agricultural workers took advantage of improved transportation networks and left for the Americas. Veneto provided the highest proportion of emigrants to Brazil between 1878 and 1894. In 1888, the year Brazil abolished slavery, they accounted for 70 percent of migrants to Brazil. By 1905, South Italians from Campania had overtaken their northern compatriots. The decision to seek work in Brazil was not a fluke. Brazilian labor recruiters targeted Italians in the 1870s. A combination of factors, including the decline of the slave trade and the expansion of the coffee industry into the province of São Paolo, encouraged Brazilian plantation owners looked to the North for labor. Recruiters appeared in villages offering contracts that included prepaid passage for entire families. In exchange migrants worked the plantations, clearing land, planting, and harvesting the coffee. After paying back the cost of the trip, the sharecroppers would receive a share of the crops. There was little back-and-forth movement between the emigrants and home, at least in the first six years, as families worked to pay off their passage. In Brazil, newcomers settled in small isolated communities maintaining symbolic rather than physical ties with their homes. As communities grew, they named them after their villages back home: Nova Veneza, Nova Padova, and Nova Treviso. They transplanted social clubs, churches, foods, and festivals, but life on the plantations was hard. Falling coffee prices meant rising debt for many families; cholera and malaria were endemic to the region, and many fell ill.[14]

By the late 1880s, fewer northern Italians chose to emigrate to Brazil. Word filtered back that many of the emigrants had fallen in debt. By the late 1880s horrific stories of migrants living in conditions of abject poverty, ill and unable to return filtered home.

In 1902, the government passed the Prinetti decree that banned all subsidized passage to Brazil.[15] By 1905, emigrants from Brazil outnumbered the immigrants: for every 100 emigrants who left Italy for Brazil between 1902 and 1925, 101 returned. Just as entire families left, entire families returned home. Although some individuals and families left the plantations for São Paolo or Rio de Janiero, most chose to return home. The case of Italians in Brazil counters the general assumption that the emigration of women and children signifies a permanent move.

Migration to Argentina and the United States followed a different trajectory. Although Italians were among the first Europeans to arrive in the United States and Argentina, their presence grew significantly after the 1870s. Until the 1890s, Argentina was the preferred destination for Italians. Nearly two million merchants, peasants, and artisans predominantly from Piedmont, Lombardy, Veneto, and Sicily made their way to Argentina between 1876 and 1913. In the United States, massive immigration from Italy began in the 1890s; over 75 percent of Italians who came to the United States did so between 1900 and 1915. In the absence of state-sponsored migration program, Argentina and the United States sent out circular advertising opportunities, and migrants utilized informal personal networks at home and abroad to finance their trips and find work. Unlike in Brazil, the Italians who first arrived in the United States and Argentina were predominately men traveling alone. Over the years the number of women migrants grew, testifying to a family's decision to settle in overseas. By the early twentieth century, the number of women in Buenos Aires was equal to that of men.

In Argentina and the United States residential patterns, social networks, return rates, and letters created transnational families and villages. A combination of regional and village networks shaped settlement patterns in both worlds in ways that replicated the divisions back home. Within the Boca neighborhood of Buenos Aires, residents from the small Adriatic village of Sirolo-Numana lived in three distinct neighborhoods, just a few square blocks wide. In New York City, scholars identified similar village-based clusters. Sicilians from Sambuca settled on Elizabeth Street; Neapolitans lived a few blocks over on Mulberry. The residents quickly replicated their villages, opening social circles, mutual-aid societies, and churches dedicated to the patron saint of the village. Local dialects echoed through the streets, and local foods, breads, pastas, and vegetables appeared in the grocery stores. These new world communities became part of village life. News from the Americas filtered back in letters and reports from returning migrants. Migrants traveled back-and-forth between the two communities on a regular basis, each journey strengthening the transatlantic ties. Italian language newspapers helped keep migrants abreast of news from home[16] (Figure 9).

The emerging Little Italies shaped transnational relations in multiple ways. These communities linked families across oceans and continents, sending news back home about their lives and conditions abroad, encouraging kin to either migrate or stay home, and providing material assistance to recent arrivals. They connected the disparate village communities scattered throughout Canada, North America, and South America. If each village served as a nodal point, linking disparate migrations throughout the Americas and Europe together, so did the emigrant enclaves. The opportunities offered within the

Figure 9 Mulberry Street, New York Street scene showing pedestrians, shoppers, and merchants with their vendor carts and stalls, circa 1900. PhotoQuest/Getty Images.

emigrant communities often transformed the initial intentions of migrants, encouraging them to purchase homes or invest in businesses abroad, in short, to settle permanently in the new worlds. Although over 50 percent of Italians who emigrated to North America returned, the rates were much lower in urban areas with older and more settled emigrant communities. Whereas, among migrants who came later, after 1905, and were recruited to work in the coalmines of Alabama or Pennsylvania, far from the centers of emigrant life, return rates were significantly higher. Living in boarding houses in company towns in Pratt City, Alabama offered little inducement to stay, and over three-fourths of the emigrants returned. As Italians moved across oceans and borders between 1870 and 1914, they wove an intricate web linking their hometowns to major metropolises, and to rural regions across the world. In the process, the experience transformed society and the economy.

Consequences of migration

Politicians and critics first reacted to the rising number of migrants with a combination of indifference, mixed with a tinge of fear, but over time, began to consider emigration as a force for good. In the early 1870s, as the demographic, social, and economic map of the new state began to emerge, politicians feared that rising rates of emigration would have a deleterious effect on the newly formed nation. Politicians assumed that the loss of citizens would weaken the workforce and the military. Yet, they were equally reluctant to prohibit emigration, seeing the right to move as central to the liberal project. In the end, the government left emigration virtually unrestricted. In 1887, Crispi introduced a bill stipulating that "emigration shall be free save for such duties as the laws impose upon citizens," in an attempt to ensure that all citizens kept all civic obligations. As the rates of emigration grew, politicians grew wary, fearing that any attempt to impose restrictions would lead to unemployment and social unrest would rise. In the 1890s, as worker protests and riots became more violent, emigration appeared as a safety valve. Invoking naturalistic imagery, statesmen compared emigration to the flows of water and air, which if contained could cause greater harm. Even the church held migration as inevitable. Bishop Bonomelli wrote: "Emigration is demanded by Nature and by the Author of Nature. To proceed to limit or to suppress it would be both stupid and wrong."[17] By 1900, as migratory circuits became more entrenched and remittances and markets for Italian goods grew, some officials began to see mass migration as a boon.

Opposition to emigration came from a number of different places. Those who favored emigration feared the effects of unrestricted mass migration and argued for greater government oversight. Stories of naïve emigrants, easy prey of disreputable ticket agents, corrupt port officials, and con men on both sides of the Atlantic, left destitute or dead spoke to the hazards of transoceanic migration. Senator Tommaso Tittoni wrote that "these great currents of our workers who go abroad resemble the currents of birds and fishes; the fishes are pursed by sharks seeking to devour them, the birds by falcons and other birds of prey seeking to ravish them, the emigrants are accompanied by a troop of exploiters eager to pounce and despoil them."[18] The strongest opposition toward migration came from the large landowners in the South who feared the loss of cheap labor. As workers from Campania, Calabria, and Sicily climbed on to steamships, the landowners lamented the loss of workers and rising wages, and urged the government to restrict emigration. Other critics and statesmen insisted that the government should step in and regulate, if not curtail emigration, decrying the social and moral dangers attendant on the exodus of young men. Critics pointed to rising rates of adultery, prostitution, illegitimate births, abortions, and infanticide, as evidence of the ways emigration weakened family ties. Critics argued that the women abandoned by their living husbands, the so called *vedove bianche* (white widows) had no alternative but to seek protection from other men, or turn to prostitution to survive. Unregulated emigration, they argued, led to the breakdown of families, increased crime and vice. Physician warned that returnees were also compromised, often coming home suffering from tuberculosis and alcoholism. Even though the conservative arguments rarely held up under close scrutiny, they took hold in the popular imagination.

Fears of the real and perceived dangers posed by mass migration led to the passage of the 1901 Emigration Law. The law set up an independent emigration commissariat reporting directly to the foreign minister. By removing emigration from the jurisdiction of the interior ministry, the new law expanded the responsibilities of the state. Until 1901, the state's only obligation was to curtail fraud and guard against human trafficking.

The creation of an independent commissariat required the state to oversee the welfare of the emigrants from the time they left their homes until they returned, or renounced their citizenship. The law outlawed all independent emigration agencies, guaranteed refund for passage if an emigrant missed his or her boat due to illness or travel delays. The commissariat set up dormitories for emigrants near the ports to ensure their safety, and organized charities and hospitals abroad. The law also gave the foreign ministry the right to temporarily suspend emigration to a particular destination if the state believed that the life, liberty, or property of emigrants was endangered. A separate law, passed the same year, set up a secure money transfer system through the Banco di Napoli, to ensure that the money emigrants made in the Americas would make its way safely back to Italy. By 1902, the government had come to see emigrants as assets, and sought ways to secure their allegiance and wealth to the nation.[19]

The experience of migration reconfigured notions of national belonging among those who left and those who stayed behind. Although some migrants cut all ties with Italy, for many, departure strengthened ties to their hometowns and to the nation. The affective and physical ties linking rural southern Italians to the wider world were circumscribed by the social and physical boundaries of the village. Birth certificates testified to their family circle and social networks, baptismal certificates placed them in the wider Christian community. In this world where church, family, and village defined belonging, the nation-state held little meaning. For South Italians, in particular, the Italian state had so far only meant paying taxes and military service. While not erasing the power of village in defining an individual's place in the world, the experience of migration brought the nation-state into rural worlds in more tangible ways, deepening notions of national belonging and complicating local identities. As soon as an emigrant landed in the new world, their sense of identity began to shift. In the eyes of American officials and non-Italian residents, regional and local distinctions disappeared, language, gestures, dress, and customs marked migrants from Piedmont or Sicily as Italians. Within the Little Italies, regional identities became more pronounced serving to distinguish the Neapolitan neighborhoods from the Sicilian or Calabrian. Within each neighborhood local allegiances still prevailed.

Disasters back home made visible this new sense of national allegiance. When disaster struck, emigrants sent money or returned home to help rebuild. Emigrants sent millions of lire in the aftermath of the earthquake that rattled Calabria in 1905, and sent more when Mount Vesuvius erupted in the spring of 1906. In the early hours of December 28, 1908, an earthquake struck Messina, all but leveling the town. The shaking lasted for nearly a minute, killing tens of thousands of people in an instant. As people climbed out of the rubble into a fine cold rain, they could hear the sounds of the wounded and dying buried under the debris. Surrounding towns also suffered, but Messina was nearest the epicenter. When the dust settled only 50,000 out of 150,000 Messinians were still alive. Overseas Italians from the North and South rushed to raise money. In Argentina, fundraising efforts by Italian social clubs and the local press reportedly netted over two million lire[20] (Figure 10).

Figure 10 Calabro-Sicilian earthquake, Messina, Roma Square. Ruins of RR Carabinieri Barracks. A postcard of a series published by the Red Cross to subscribe for the earthquake victims. Fototeca Gilardi/Getty Images.

The *Americani*, as residents referred to returnees, came home with a different understanding of themselves as workers and citizens. Politicians, critics, and scholars routinely noted how male migrants returned home with a stronger sense of personal authority and autonomy. Mayors, landlords, and government officials commonly complained of residents who returned home rude, arrogant, and acting above their station. Migrants refused to defer to authority. As one municipal secretary complained to Antonio Mangano, a journalist from the United States, "Residents used to appear in his office hat in hand, with great fear hardly daring to look at them. Now when they request a document they do not even take their hats off and they look the secretary directly in the eye."[21] Mangano concluded from this exchange that the returned emigrants were "intellectually awakened, . . . and that he will not, as a rule, be willing to put his neck under the yoke again and be content with his former life."[22] Observers noted that migrants returned with a stronger civic consciousness. In 1910 Luigi Rossi described how migration fostered a new understanding among migrants of the importance of participating in national elections as "the best way of defending their own interests."[23] Ultimately Lorenzoni concluded this new sense of personal dignity enabled migrants "to truly become men."[24]

Those who remained behind also carved out new relations with the state as a consequence of transnational migrations. Although Giuseppa S. never left Sutera, the departure of her husband repositioned her within the national body. With Salvatore overseas, Giuseppa turned to local and national agencies to negotiate family business. Women called on local government officials and utilized the growing consulate networks to protect the family's interests. They relied on the state to assist them in both personal and financial needs, facilitating overseas communications with their husbands or sons, navigating the complexity of transatlantic banking. If for some reason promised money never arrived, women marshaled all resources to track the missing funds, even dictating letters to the minister of foreign affairs and the police. Women filed complaints against steamship companies, taking them to court if necessary. Greater mobilities transformed local governments into conduits between rural residents and the state. Overseas migration also encouraged those who remained behind to go to school. Although the state had been fairly ineffective in legislating school attendance and increasing literacy, the demands of transnational separation brought rural residents into the classroom. In Sutera, attendance in the evening classes rose by 40 percent once men began to migrate. Family members increasingly relied on written correspondence and translation services that had to be paid for in cash and kind. Privacy concerns encouraged families to make sure at least one member could read and write. Social ambitions also encouraged families to learn to read. If personal pragmatic concerns initially motivated women to go to school, once in the classroom they learned the common history and language of the nation, and the obligations of citizenship. Although Sicilian women did not have the vote, and few left the household to work for wages, emigration brought them into the nation as active participants.[25]

If emigration altered relations between rural residents and the state, it also transformed the local economy and family dynamics. Remittances and exposure to new ideas combined to redefine village hierarchies and familial relations. The money emigrants sent home had an enormous impact on rural communities. In 1907, emigrants from Veneto sent nearly fifty million lire back home. Emigrants from Piedmont sent twenty-nine million and Sicilians sent nearly twenty-three million to family member. District officials reported huge influxes of cash into local banks and post office savings accounts. Families used the money to pay off debts and invest in real estate and land. Emigrant savings bolstered the local consumer economy. Families with access to money from overseas bought better food, incorporating pasta and meat into the weekly diet. The new houses also had to be furnished, and the residents clothed in styles that befitted their improved position. Goods followed people across the globe, carving out new trade networks between Italy, the United States, Australia, Brazil, and Argentina. Exports in foodstuffs took on a new importance, as pastas, olive oils, and cheeses were sent across the ocean to meet emigrant consumer demands. These "migrant marketplaces" not only were central in the construction of ethnic identities in the new worlds but also tied emigrants to their homelands.[26] Global migration created new trade networks. Emigration accelerated the transformation of peasants into industrial wage workers and consumers.

Transnational migration reconfigured familial relations. Although scholars long argued that migration acts as a conservative force on communities, luring away the most ambitious and hardworking, and slowing the demographic transition to low fertility that marked modern nation-states, closer analysis suggests that migration was a force of change. It was true that South Italy continued to report high birth rates well into the twentieth century; it was, at least in part, a consequence of emigration. Both these who left and those who remained risked much on the hope that emigration would provide the means of upward mobility, and proof of their success was visible in a large family. Children symbolized wealth and prosperity, and families of emigrants continued to have as many children as possible. Only when cultural norms shifted associating fecundity with poverty did migrant families shift their reproductive strategies, and wives of migrants sharply curtailed their child bearing years. Migration accelerated changing familial dynamics, often undermining patriarchal authority and encouraging the greater independence among sons and daughter.[27]

The fifteen million Italians who left to work overseas between 1880 and 1915 reconfigured the contours of the state and nation, transforming domestic and national social and political relations. Statesmen reconceived their vision of Italy to include the rapidly growing communities abroad transnational migration reconfigured intimate relations between men and women, strengthening the position of women as financial managers at a moment when wage-earning opportunities for rural Italian women were diminishing. Men returned home with new understandings of what it meant to be a husband, father, and citizen. The act of leaving fostered a closer identification with the nation. Deep-rooted local identities did not disappear, but coexisted alongside new notions of what it meant to be Italian.

CHAPTER 7
IMPERIAL AMBITIONS AND
DOMESTIC REFORMS

On March 3, 1896, Italians awoke to the news of disaster in Africa. Three days earlier the army had launched an attack against Emperor Menelik's forces at Adwa. After a day of fierce and bloody fighting, the army was forced to retreat, leaving nearly 5,000 dead. By the end of the battle the Italian dead and missing numbered over 14,000, and another 4,000 men were taken prisoner. Over 5,000 Eritreans were killed, wounded, or captured. Emperor Menelik's decisive victory brought an end to the war, and to Italy's quest to be an imperial power. At home, anticolonial protests began even before the full scope of the disaster was made clear, and by March 4 the demonstrations turned into full-scale riots in Turin, Rome, and Naples. The protesters demanded the resignation of Crispi and the complete withdrawal of soldiers from Africa. Government troops opened fire on the crowd. The protesters urged soldiers to desert or flee abroad to avoid conscription. In Milan, women's organization called on all mothers to refuse to send their sons to fight in the African wars. Calls for the dismissal of the prime minister grew louder, and liberals and conservatives feared the government and crown would be overthrown by the left. Within a week Crispi resigned and Marquis di Rudini took over as the prime minister. Francesco Crispi's foreign policy and political career were left in tatters. In October, Rudini signed the Treaty of Addis Ababa recognizing the independence of Ethiopia and bringing an end to first Italo-Ethiopian war.

The loss at Adwa had wide-ranging political and social implications. The defeat called into question Italy's status as a great power and accelerated a sharp shift in foreign and domestic policies. The soldiers left dead in Africa joined those killed in the previous defeats of Custoza and Lissa in 1866, to bear witness to Italy's military incompetence. In the wake of the first Italo-Ethiopian war, politicians embraced a new kind of imperialism; a "greater Italy" stitched together from the nation's diasporic communities, an empire built on trade and cultural nationalism. The attention on emigrants as agents of empire accompanied a shift in domestic politics. Foreign policy fiascos fueled social discontent and undermined faith in the government. As the century drew to a close, radical labor movements grew stronger, culminating in the assassination of King Umberto in 1900. Under Giolitti, the government abandoned strategies of labor suppression and adopted those of co-option and conciliation in its effort to bring social stability and political order.

Foreign policy in an age of empire

Until 1870, there had been little disagreement among politicians regarding foreign policy. Still largely shaped by unification, foreign ministers focused on territorial acquisition and securing Italy's standing among world powers. Until 1870, foreign policy goals remained unchanged, the eviction of Austria from Italian lands and ending Papal rule in Rome. Italy's alliances were also clear: Austria and the pope were enemies, while Britain, France, and, after 1866, Prussia were friends. Diplomatic projects rested on the assumptions that Italy itself was a great power, that Italy enjoyed a natural alliance with Great Britain and France (despite its defense of the pope) based on shared cultural and political ties, and that the other European powers approved of the nation's ambitions. The governments of the Historic Right and Left allocated large portions of the budget to build up armaments suitable for a European power, and continued Cavour's diplomacy based on national self-interest, alternating its allegiance between France and Germany. Although Crispi, and later Mussolini, berated what they considered a cowardly and shifty foreign policy, liberal Italy's diplomatic strategy worked. The liberal state secured Rome and Veneto, and remained a sought-after partner among the great powers.[1]

In the 1870s, deteriorating relations with France, combined with the rising fortunes of Germany, fractured the unanimity among politicians surrounding foreign policy. French defeat in the Franco-Prussian and the establishment of a Republican government made France a less than desirable ally. An alliance with Germany, and by extension Austria, seemed more useful in a world where Italy could no longer play Germany against Austria, or France against Germany. In 1873, King Vittorio Emanuele paid an official visit to Berlin and Vienna. Despite Austrian control of Trieste and Trentino, the crown and some statesmen believed that it was time to call a truce to the long-standing enmity between the two countries. The conciliatory move did not sit well with those who saw any alliance with Austria as a betrayal of the Risorgimento. Growing Nationalist voices demanded that the government focus diplomatic efforts on the liberation of all *terra irredenta*, and pursue a militant foreign policy that would force Europe to recognize Italy as a great power.

European imperial projects troubled these long-held assumptions underlying nineteenth-century foreign policy. Rising tensions with France over North Africa put to rest the idea of some kind of natural alliance and the notion that European powers unequivocally supported Italy's territorial ambitions. Throughout the Risorgimento, France made clear its support for Italy was contingent on its own domestic and international situation. But it was Tunisia that confirmed that France was no friend. For centuries, Sicilian fishermen and traders had maintained close trading ties with their southern neighbor. Over the course of the nineteenth century, Tunis had emerged as an important commercial center for Italians, French, and Greeks interested in trading across the Ottoman Empire and sub-Saharan Africa. Focused on the *terra irredenta*, statesmen showed little interest in claiming any sort of formal imperial control over the land.

In 1864, Italy turned down an offer to form a joint protectorate with France, preferring economic colonization over costly colonial wars. A decade later, as European powers encroached on a disintegrating Ottoman Empire, they offered to support the creation of an Italian protectorate in Tunisia, as a kind of advance compensation if their own territorial ambitions proved successful. Italy, again, refused the offer. In the meantime, France moved to secure colonial rule over Algeria and expanded formal control over Tunisia and Morocco in 1878. By the time Prime Minister Benedetto Cairoli realized that the French government would no longer recognize Italian interests in North Africa, it was too late. Since Italy had shown no interest in claiming control over the country, Great Britain and Germany reconciled themselves to French colonial expansion, and had no reason to negotiate with Italy.[2]

The 1878 Congress of Berlin widened foreign policy divisions among Italian statesmen. Prime Minister Cairoli traveled to Berlin intent on keeping Italy out of the scramble for Africa. Italy, he maintained, was committed to support the right to self-determination for all, and would not dirty its hands in empire building. While Cairoli's position attests to a certain integrity, it did not serve the country's interests. While Britain left Berlin with Cyprus, Austria with control over Bosnia-Herzegovina, and France with the backing of its North African claims, Italian diplomats came home with nothing, not even Trieste or Trentino. *Irredentisti* voices grew louder, insisting that Italy must secure its natural borders regardless of European support. The growing opposition forced Cairoli to resign in 1881 when France signed the Treaty of Bardo with Bey Muhammad as-Sadiq authorizing the French military occupation of Tunisia. When Agostino Depretis returned as prime minster, he reluctantly signed a secret defensive alliance with Germany and Austria against French aggression in May of 1882. By joining the Triple Alliance, the prime minister ended Italy's diplomatic neutrality, and eliminated the pope's last hope to regain temporal power. As word of the agreement leaked out, some Italians hoped that an alliance with Austria would open up new possibilities for acquiring Trieste and Trentino in exchange for Austrian control over other Balkan lands; others, including, Depretis's Foreign Minister Stanislao Mancini saw it as an opportunity to pursue a more aggressive imperial policy.[3]

Despite Italy's apparent reluctance to become a colonial power, its flag did fly over a small strip of land along the coast of the Red Sea. Throughout the century, merchants, explorers, industrialists, and missionaries established schools, towns, and businesses in Tunisia, Lebanon, Libya, Syria, and along the coast of the Red Sea. As early as 1830, missionaries had established an outpost at Massawa, and over the decades made inroads into Ethiopia. The expansion of private industry and missionary work heightened popular interest in colonial expansion. The opening of the Suez Canal in 1869 created the possibility of new ventures in the east, and that same year the Genoese shipping company, Rubattino, bought property along the coast of the bay of Assab to open a refueling station to service ships passing between the Mediterranean and the Indies. The Khedivate of Egypt protested the concession of land by a minor sultan and sent a military expedition to reclaim the land. The army arrived to defend Italian business interests and forced Egypt to withdraw. In 1881, Italy took formal control of the colony.[4]

The loss of Tunisia to the French emboldened colonialists, who believed that formal imperialism could resolve the emigration problem, fulfill the nation's civilizing mission, and ensure that Italy would never be trapped within the Mediterranean. Overriding the objections of those who argued that colonial projects were too costly for the cash-strapped nation, and that military resources needed to focus on the reclamation of Italian lands, Italy entered the scramble for Africa. Wary of the cost of colonial wars, Foreign Minister Mancini refused an invitation to join with the British and mount a military intervention in Egypt in the summer of 1882, but willingly expanded Italian influence along the coast of the Red Sea. In 1885, the military moved into Massawa, with the tacit support of the British. In January of 1887, Ethiopian forces moved against the troops at Massawa killing over 400 soldiers. The defeat at Dogali reignited debates over colonialism, and forced Depretis to tender his resignation, although he was quickly reappointed.

Dogali became a touchstone for supporters of colonial expansion who converted the defeat into a call for vindication and remembrance. In June of 1887 Crispi presided over a dedication of Egyptian obelisk to the fallen soldiers in the front of the Rome railway station. The plaza itself was renamed the *Piazza dei Cinquecento* in memory of the fallen soldiers. The defeat at Dogali brought Crispi back to power, first as minister of the interior under Depretis, and then four months later, on the death of Depretis, as prime minister. Rather than relinquishing his position as minister of the interior, he made himself minister of the foreign affairs as well, consolidating control over the most powerful branches of government. Crispi had been a vehement critic of Italy's passive foreign policy and a vocal proponent of war. Once in power, he embraced an aggressive foreign policy to resolve the nation's economic, political, and social difficulties. Focusing on the threat of French dominance in the Mediterranean, Crispi turned to Germany to try to provoke a war with France. Failing to convince Bismarck to go to war, Crispi sought to incite the French by celebrating the dedication of a statute honoring Giordano Bruno in the middle of the *Campo dei Fiori* in Rome. Crispi hoped that the public celebration of the sixteenth-century heretic would bring French troops rushing to the defense of a furious pope. Despite his best efforts, neither the French nor Germans took the bait, and war was averted.

When Crispi's European war failed to materialize, he turned his attention to Africa, appealing to Parliament to increase funding for Italian colonies. According to Crispi's vision, formal empire would redirect emigration to the colonies and keep emigrants under Italy's jurisdiction; state-sponsored colonial emigration had the potential to resolve the problems between landowners and agricultural workers by creating a large class of small-property owners. By 1889, Italian control in Africa extended over Asmara and into Eastern Somalia. A year later Crispi merged Assab, Massawa, and Asmara to form Eritrea, and proclaimed a protectorate over Ethiopia based on the infamous Treaty of Uccialli, signed on May 2, 1889, between Italy and Emperor Menelik.[5]

Crispi modeled Italian colonialism off the British, where settler colonies provided the material foundation for the establishment of formal empire. The government promoted private and public settlement initiatives. In 1890, Parliament gave Leopoldo Franchetti permission to open an experimental agricultural community resettling a dozen Italian families to Eritrea as property owners. Franchetti instituted a complex regulatory system for the expropriation and distribution of land among the settlers. Even when Crispi was forced out of office in 1891, colonial expansion continued. Oreste Baratieri, the military governor of Eritrea, promoted Italian missionary settlements to counter French influence in the region, a moment of rare church and state collaboration. Under the auspices of the church, Baratieri hoped to expand Catholic agricultural settlements, and in 1896, the industrialist Alessandro Rossi privately sponsored a settlement of 130 Catholic emigrants in Cheren, inland from Massawa in 1896. The idea of establishing colonies in East Africa resonated with southern Italians, and critics who viewed the exodus of emigrants as a threat to the nation-state. Radical and Republicans opposed imperialism.[6]

Devious diplomacy and the expansion of colonial settlements prompted Ethiopian and Eritrean chieftains to unite with Emperor Menelik against the Italians. Emperor Menelik, a signatory on the Treaty of Ucciali, was incensed when he discovered that the Italian version of the treaty had altered Article XVII, stating that the emperor of Ethiopia *could* turn to Italy for assistance regarding correspondence with European powers, to read that the emperor *must* turn to Italy, effectively turning Menelik's Ethiopian empire into a colony. Menelik denounced the treaty in 1893. Meanwhile, Franchetti's expropriation of land had so angered local chieftains that they agreed to join Menelik in war. General Baratieri embraced the possibility of war, firmly believing that Italy would emerge victorious. When full-scale war broke out in 1895, Baratieri was woefully underprepared. Despite intelligence reports insisting that Menelik could not assemble more than 40,000 men, the Italians faced an African army of well over 200,000 soldiers. At the Battle of Amba Alagi in December, Menelik's army defeated the Italians and massacred 2,000 Eritreans serving in the Italian military (*ascari*). When the news of the defeat reached Italy, northern Republicans and radicals renewed their anti-war demonstrations, while in the streets of Palermo, supporters of the war rallied to the cause.[7]

Throughout January of 1896 Menelik's troops kept advancing. Crispi urged General Baratieri to mount an offensive to avenge the deaths at Amba Alagi, inundating him with telegraphs berating his valor and courage. Baratieri's troops were exhausted and demoralized. His supply lines, stretched deep into the interior, were vulnerable to raids by Menelik's troops. Baratieri's own generals were fast losing faith in his command. Yet, each day fresh troops arrived eager for war. Caught between those urging him to advance, a weary army, and skeptical generals, Baratieri was on the edge of an emotional and physical breakdown. In mid-February, Crispi dismissed Baratieri as military commander, but before his successor arrived, Baratieri decided to launch one last offensive. At the end of February, Italian scouts reported that large sections of Menelik's troops appeared to have left on foraging expeditions in the surrounding countryside. On the night of February 29, 1896, Baratieri ordered an attack. Mobilizing 17,000 of his men in three columns, he sent them out through uncharted territory toward the heights of Adwa. The three columns separated, whether General Albertone pushed ahead intentionally contrary to orders or got lost is unclear, but at daybreak he found himself and his troops nearly four miles away from the main column. The Ethiopian soldiers quickly cut through the lines, overrunning the Italian artillery. The Italian army collapsed. Two generals died, and Albertone was captured. Thousands of Italian and Ethiopian soldiers were killed and wounded. Baratieri survived. The defeat in Adwa brought Italian colonialism to a screeching halt and ended Crispi's political career.

Crispi's successor as prime minister, Marchese Rudini, had long been a staunch critic of Italy's African enterprises. The colonies, he believed, held only the possibility of failure, and should be abandoned. However, in the age of empire, a complete withdrawal from Africa proved impossible, unless Italy wanted to forgo any claim to world power. Rudini opted to create a smaller Eritrea, preserving Italy as an imperial power, at least in name, appointing a civilian governor, who immediately banned all immigration to the territory. The Treaty of Addis Ababa, signed on October 26, 1896, embittered those Nationalists who had urged the king to continue the war. The treaty stood as evidence of liberal Italy's inherent weakness, becoming a Nationalist touchstone well into the twentieth century.

An emigrant empire

In the wake of Adwa, overseas Italians took on a new role among those reluctant to let go of a dream of a "greater Italy." Adwa discredited Crispi's aggressive foreign policy, colonial ambitions, and alliance with Germany, but not his main goal: securing Italy's reputation as a world power. A new vision of colonialism emerged, one based on free trade and emigration. Looking away from Europe and Africa, Italian foreign policy refocused on Italians abroad. People, not land, comprised the economic, social, and cultural resources of a "greater Italy." The response of the emigrant communities in the aftermath of Adwa highlighted the patriotic and economic possibilities that could be harnessed. Italian emigrants had closely followed events in Africa. When news of the massacre filtered back to New York and Buenos Aires, emigrants raised monies for the families of the wounded and dead. Italians living in Peru raised over 40,000 lire, and New York Italians donated over 50,000 lire. Checks poured in from Germany, Australia, Russia, France, and Spain. In June, three months after Adwa, the radical deputy Edoardo Pantano called on Parliament to abandon the artificial emigration schemes doomed to failure, and focus on securing the allegiance and wealth of the Italians abroad to the nation.[8]

Although Rudini fully supported the shift from formal to informal empire, he was unable to make much progress. During his two years in office he faced growing popular discontent, and was dismissed in the wake of bread riots in Milan. The new prime minister, General Luigi Pelloux, had little sympathy for his predecessor's foreign policy, and returned Italy to the path of formal empire. Shut out of Africa, Pelloux looked to the east where European powers were staking out claims along China's coast in the wake of Japan's victory in the first Sino-Japanese war. Pelloux sent an expedition to occupy the bay of San-Mun, just south of Shangai and the surrounding province. By the time the Italians arrived, China had decided to end European concessions sending the delegation home empty handed.

The fiasco in China, combined with continued social unrest threatened Pelloux's government. In an effort to reassert his authority, Pelloux introduced a set of exceptional measures restricting freedom of the press and freedom of assembly in the spring of 1899. The bills incensed the left. Throughout the summer Radicals and Socialists mounted a filibuster against the proposals. Pelloux tried to circumvent Parliament altogether and proclaimed the measures law by edict. A few months later the high court ruled the laws unconstitutional. Pelloux's efforts to return to Parliament to win passage of the laws alienated the center-left as well as the radicals. Having lost all parliamentary support, Pelloux was forced to call new elections. The June elections of 1900 brought the left back into power, and Pelloux resigned. Refusing to reach out to the leaders of the opposition, King Umberto asked the colorless Senator Saracco from Piedmont to form a new government.

Six weeks after the elections, Gaetano Bresci, an anarchist shoemaker recently returned from New Jersey, shot and killed King Umberto in Monza on the outskirts of Milan. Although Umberto's penchant for intervening in politics, especially his enthusiasm for an alliance with Austria, had weakened the prestige and popularity of the crown, his death united Italians in mourning. Conservative efforts to use authoritarian measures to suppress social unrest had clearly failed. Umberto's successor, Vittorio Emanuele III was a quiet king with sober tastes and a love of privacy. He exhibited little respect for Parliament, but unlike his father, was not inclined to interfere. In February of 1901, Saracco lost support of the conservatives, and his government collapsed. Vittorio Emanuele III appointed the liberal Giuseppe Zanardelli as prime minister. When Zanardelli withdrew for reasons of health in 1903, the king appointed Giolitti as prime minister, ushering in a decade or prosperity and stability.

The governments of Zanardelli and Giolitti succeeded where Rudini had failed. Influenced by a work of a young professor of economics at the University of Turin, Luigi Einaudi, Giolitti's government sought to carve out an empire comprised of oversea communities. In the spring of 1899, Luigi Einaudi published a short work, entitled *Principe mercante: studio sulla espansione colonial italiana* (*Merchant Prince: A Study of Italian Colonial Expansion*). Einuadi chose to tell the story of the merchant prince through the life of the Argentinian emigrant Enrico Dell'Acqua, who amassed a fortune by selling Italian goods to emigrants in Argentina and Brazil. Dell'Acqua's textile exportation to the Americas won him honors at the Exhibition of Italians Abroad at the 1898 *National Exposition in Turin*. According to Einaudi, Dell'Acqua was a modern version of the medieval merchant princes of Genoa and Venice. He argued that these "captains of industry" were "destined to transform the current little Italy in to a future 'greater Italy.'"[9] Transnational emigration was the authentic form of Italian colonialism, and as proven by Adwa, the only one that could succeed.

Intellectuals and politicians embraced the idea of an emigrant empire and began taking measures to make it a reality. The 1901 Emigration Law emerged as the centerpiece of Italy's new foreign policy. Placing emigration in the hands of the foreign ministry was the first step in the making of an emigrant empire. Regulations focusing on the safety of the emigrants in domestic ports and foreign lands were instrumental in outlining the new borders of a greater Italy that was anchored to a mobile citizen body crossing political borders. The diplomatic corps and the commissariat constructed the administrative and judicial structures of the informal empire. By counting who left, who returned, how much money migrants sent home, the number of Italian schools abroad, and Italian language publications, the Commissariat of Emigration provided statistical evidence of the empire's costs and benefits. The consulates promoted Italian exports, supported cultural associations and mutual-aid societies, and ensured that reservists and draft-age men could be called into service when needed. The new initiatives reinforced notions of national belonging among Italy's transnational families.

Two events underscored the importance of providing diplomatic protection for emigrants. On October 15, 1890, David Hennessy, the police superintendent of New Orleans, was shot on his way home from work. The gunmen were never found, but according to a bystander, Hennessy's dying words indicted Italians. Nineteen Italians were accused of murder, but none found guilty. After the trial ended, nine of the defendants returned to jail to await trial on separate charges. In March, an announcement appeared in the New Orleans morning newspapers calling all "good citizens," to meet and "remedy the failure of justice." Six thousand citizens showed up, broke into the jail, and lynched the prisoners. All told, eleven Italians were killed, and Italy briefly broke diplomatic relations with the United States. In the face of rising anti-Italian and nativist sentiment the consulate emerged as an important resource for Italians abroad. A few years later a second incident in France underscored the danger of unprotected emigration. In the summer of 1893 a French salt company began hiring for the sea-salt harvest. Faced with rising unemployment more French applied than ever before. The company, however, had already recruited workers from Piedmont. Angered by the company's recruitment policies and the Italians who worked while they remained unemployed, French day laborers took to the streets. Marching down the main street of Aigues-Mortes, singing the Marseillaise, the French workers attacked the Italians, leaving at least nine dead. The news of the riot sparked anti-French riots in Italy. The incidents in New Orleans and Aigues-Mortes emphasized the need for the government to provide emigrants legal services and resources, and by doing so, promote the benefits of Italian citizenship to its citizens living abroad.

The fusion of colonial ambitions with emigration brought the church and state together in new ways. Although the pope continued to maintain his position as "prisoner of the Vatican," bishops, clerics, and government officials began to open new avenues of communication and cooperation within emigrant communities. After Adwa and the fall of Crispi, the government began to fund Catholic schools, charity organizations, and hospitals abroad in its efforts to reach out to overseas Italians. In 1887, Giovanni Battista Scalabrini, the bishop of Piacenza, founded the Pius Society of Missionaries of St. Charles Borromeo, whose mission was to serve and protect emigrants. Within a few years, the order established over one hundred missions in the Americas, offering church services, schools, and charity. The Scalabrini missions operated under the motto—religione e patria ("religion and country"). The Scalabrini brothers, who shared a common language and culture, helped the emigrants navigate through foreign lands, while at the same time strengthening ties to the homeland. In 1900, Bishop Geremia Bonomelli founded a missionary organization for the assistance of Italian workers in

Europe and the Mediterranean. The Opera Bonomelli established churches and schools to promote the Italian language and culture. Like Scalabrini, Bonomelli believed that religious faith and patriotism could coexist. Giolitti encouraged cooperation between secular and religious institutions and expanded funding to all institutions. At home, liberals and conservatives welcomed the efforts of the church to incorporate emigrants into the national body as committed Catholics, and to weaken attachments to socialism or anarchism.[10]

Secular institutions were as important as the church in the post-Adwa imperial project. The Italian Geographic Society, the Italian Chambers of Commerce abroad, and, perhaps most importantly, the Dante Alighieri Societies promoted a vision of a shared Italian identity essential to the construction of a "greater Italy." The Dante Alighieri Society, founded in 1889 to promote the language of Dante and Italian culture among Italians living outside the nation's borders, originally focused on those still living under Austrian rule. The *irredentisti* continued to insist that Italy's foreign policy priority had to remain the reclamation of Italian lands, even as Crispi and the king sought to end the territorial disputes, and carve out an African empire. In 1896, when the Neapolitan, Pasquale Villari, took over the presidency, he expanded the scope to include emigrants in Africa, Europe, and the Americas, insisting that these communities also constituted "unredeemed lands?"[11] By the eve of the First World War, state-subsidized Dante societies had spread throughout the Italian global community, providing Italian language classes and Italian language lending libraries to migrants everywhere.

New directions in foreign policy forced the government to reconsider the terms of citizenship. For an emigrant empire to succeed, overseas Italians had to retain their original citizenship, yet many emigrants chose to take the citizenship of their new homelands. Italians living abroad recognized that real material advantages—access to land, jobs, and commercial opportunities—came with naturalization. According to the 1865 civil code, Italians who pledged allegiance to another country lost their citizenship. If Parliament did not take steps, naturalization could lead to a population hemorrhage. The law was amended in 1889, specifying that only voluntary naturalization would result in the loss of citizenship, to account for emigrants in Brazil, who automatically, and often unknowingly, became Brazilian citizens after independence. In the context of an emigrant empire the legal status of emigrants took on a new urgency. Politicians struggled with the question of how to secure allegiance among emigrants, who for pragmatic purposes sought naturalization abroad.

Italy, like other European nations, considered dual citizenship a legal abomination, believing that no one person could pledge loyalty to two nations. In 1912, the government passed a new citizenship law seeking to resolve the problem by essentially suspending the citizenship of a naturalized emigrant. Emigrants who chose to naturalize would lose their Italian citizenship but reclaim their rights as citizens once they had returned home for two years. Repatriation would not require special permission from the government. Specifically addressing the question of the "merchant princes," those emigrants who moved from Argentina to Brazil, and then on to the United States or Canada, the law stipulated that if the ex-Italian did not change his citizenship again, the emigrant could reclaim his Italian papers after living two years in the second country. The children of emigrants born in nations where citizenship was determined based on birthplace (*jus soli*) challenged Italian resistance to dual citizenship. If the father was not naturalized the government registered the child as a citizen based on blood (*jus sanguinis*), with all attendant obligations and rights, regardless of the fact that the receiving nation also staked claims on the newborn. While the new laws expanded the number of ex-citizens eligible to return as Italians, they also reinforced precarious position of women as citizens. According to the 1865 legal code privileging, *jus sanguinis* above *jus soli*, citizenship could only be transferred from father to children. A woman's citizenship followed from her father or her husband. Under the 1912 law, wives of emigrants who took Argentinian or Brazilian citizenship would also became naturalized citizens of those countries, even if they were not living abroad. Politicians and legal scholars argued that the unity of the family must prevail over a woman's interest. In choosing to create an emigrant empire, Italy carved out original foreign policy path informed by Risorgimento ideals, nationalism, and mobility.[12]

Protest and reform

Efforts to include emigrants into the national body accompanied attempts to strengthen the nation at home. Between 1901 and 1914, Giolitti convinced that Italy's fate rested on the government's ability to bring the working classes and agricultural workers into the national body ushered in a host of social and economic reforms. The ministries of Crispi and Pelloux made evident that the authoritarian, repressive measures the government had relied on since 1861 did not bring stability or prosperity. Giolitti, conservative by inclination, chose a path of collaboration. His efforts to increase spending for public works, pass worker protection legislation, and expand the suffrage were not intended to bring real political or social change, but rather to appease the opposition. He was a pragmatic and opportunist liberal.

By the 1890s, anarchists appeared as the most significant threat to the Italian political order. The Italian section of the International Workingmen's Association (IWA), founded in 1869, led by Errico Malatesta, stood committed to social revolution and the abolition of government. Malatesta was born into a well-to-do southern landowning family in 1853. While still a teenager, Malatesta embraced Mazzini's Republican vision. Inspired by the Paris Commune and the fiery speeches of Bakunin, he joined the IWA in Naples and rose up the ranks. The anarchists' vision of unity and fraternity, echoing the ideals of the Risorgimento, took hold among disillusioned Mazzinian Republicans. Bakunin's conviction that Italy's urban and rural proletarian was ripe for social revolution, countered the position of Marx and Engels who insisted that without an industrial proletariat there could be no revolution. Contrary to Marx, Bakunin held that true revolutionary potential lived in the millions of artisans, agricultural workers, and industrial laborers, the unorganized and unpolitical "lumpenproletariat." A transnational network of Italian anarchists including Malatesta, Carlo Cafiero, and Andrea Costa looked to transform popular discontent into social revolution.

In the summer of 1874 bread riots broke out in Tuscany, Emilia, and Romagna. Women raided bakeries and mills, furious at the rising price of bread and falling employment. Efforts of Lanza's government to quell the riots proved futile, and anarchists saw an opportunity to launch the revolution. In Imola, radicals mobilized 150 followers to march on Bologna, while Malatesta and Cafiero tried to rouse the peasants in the southern regions. Their efforts met with little success. The police broke up the protests, and the leaders of the movement were imprisoned or escaped into exile. Released from prison, Cafiero and Malatesta tried again to spark revolution in the South with the same dismal results. Cafiero and Costa were arrested, and Malatesta fled into exile, moving through Egypt, France, and Switzerland before finding refuge in London. After their release from prison, Costa and Cafiero went into exile. In Italy, the movement grew increasingly violent, culminating in Giovanni Passanante's attempted assassination of King Umberto in the fall of 1878, and a bombing in Florence that killed two people. Their campaign of violence succeeded in ousting Prime Minister Cairoli from office, but failed to spark a revolution. Heightened repression drove the leaders of the movement into exile in Europe or the Americas.

Weakened and divided, the anarchist movement fractured in the 1880s. A small group of Socialists argued for a more moderate, "evolutionary" path to revolution. A growing number of agricultural cooperatives and mutual-aid societies recruited workers. In 1873, there were roughly 1,500 mutual-aid societies, and by 1885 there nearly 5,000 with close to a million members. The societies were politically diverse, some conservative, others Republican or radical, and still others embraced Catholic principles. Socialist organizers joined those mutual-aid societies most sympathetic to their politics, in an effort to shift their program to increasing worker solidarities, rather than charity and mutual-aid programs. In 1885, these embryonic labor unions joined together into the *Partito Operaio Italiano* (Italian Workers' Party—POI). Other leagues and associations, less enamored with socialism came together under the umbrella of regional Chambers of Labor, designed to coordinate the efforts of individual unions. Trade organizations grew rapidly over the course of the 1890s. In 1906, the Socialist unions merged with those in the Chambers of Labor to form the General Confederation of Labor (CGL) and become a powerful political force.

The Socialist Party took on new life in 1879, when Andrea Costa returned from exile in Switzerland and announced his conversion from anarchism to "legalitarian" socialism. Although Costa never renounced revolution, he argued that the events of 1874 and 1877 proved that direct action was a failed strategy in Italy. Costa founded the Revolutionary Socialist Party of Romagna, which became the *Partito Socialista Rivoluzionario Italiano* (PSRI) in 1884, promoting a platform of education and activism designed to sow the seeds for later revolution. Costa held that reformist measures and political engagement were acceptable means of achieving revolutionary aims, and in 1882 was elected to Parliament. Filippo Turati, a sympathetic Milanese lawyer, founded a new Socialist journal, which became *Critica Sociale*, providing a coherent theoretical frame for Italian socialism.

Turati extended his ambition to political organizing, seeing a need for a legal and reformist Socialist democratic party similar to Germany's. In 1889, he founded the Milanese Socialist league, inviting workers and intellectuals, but not anarchists, to join. In August 1892 Turati and his partner Anna Kuliscioff, a Russian anarchist who became involved with the Italian movement after meeting Costa in Paris in 1877, organized the first congress of a new worker's party in Genoa. Hundreds of delegates arrived representing close to 324 workers' associations from the Sicily, the Po valley, Tuscany, and Romagna. Members of the *Partito Operaio Italiano*, the PSRI, and the *Lega Socialista Milanese* were all in attendance. The majority of delegates supported Turati's vision of a democratic Socialist Party and voted to approve the creation of the *Partito Socialista Italiano* (PSI). Anarchists walked out of the meeting vowing to form a separate party. Costa's attempts to mediate between the two sides failed. The acrimonious split divided the left, leaving many delegates reluctant to join either group. Costa's party joined the PSI a year later. Crispi's repressive laws targeting the political opposition forced the party underground, while in hiding the leaders centralized the organization of the party, ultimately making it stronger. By 1900 it had well over 30,000 members, 32 deputies in Parliament, and its own newspaper, *Avanti*. The PSI had become a national political force, advocating for parliamentary reforms, not revolution.[13]

The growth of the Socialist movement was linked to transnational workers movements. Costa, Malatesta, and others found support among friends in the Italian communities in Switzerland, Great Britain, France, and the America. Diasporic networks enabled political exiles to create a global movement. Malatesta continued his organizing efforts among Italians abroad, founding the first anarchist trade union in Argentina. In the United States, Italian language anarchist newspapers circulated among the emigrants, playing a critical role in forging a transnational Italian left. Articles bewailing the failure of the state to protect workers in Brazil appeared in papers in London, New York, and Paris. The increased repression during the 1890s brought some emigrants back home. Gaetano Bresci, supported by the local Italian language anarchist newspaper in Paterson, traveled to Monza to kill the king in revenge for the deaths of the Milan demonstrators in 1898. The networks carved out by anarchists and Socialists formed the basis for transnational antifascist movements in the 1920s and 1930s.[14]

When Giolitti came to power, he reached out to Socialist deputies to secure support for a number of labor initiatives. In 1902, he passed protectionist legislating mandating an eleven-hour workday for women and prohibiting employment of children under twelve. In 1907, he set a six-day work week, and a year later set limits on night work. The left supported the creation of state-sponsored maternity program relying on contributions from the state, employers, and workers. His attempts to expand the 1898 national insurance fund for health and old age were more difficult to realize. Mutual-aid societies resisted government encroachment into their programs. Over all though, between 1901 and 1913, wages rose, and living standards marginally improved. Perhaps Giolitti's most important act was to withdraw the government from labor disputes, a move that resulted in a sharp rise in strikes between 1901 and 1913. Absent state intervention, workers forced owners to make a number of labor concessions. Disgruntled landlords and factory owners railed against the government. Giolitti's efforts to win the confidence of workers and peasants proved moderately successful. Although he failed to bring the Socialists into the government, and under Turati the left continued to organize mass demonstrations protesting state violence, Giolitti's pragmatic politics, combined with his willingness to use force to quell strikes if necessary, succeeded in maintaining the conservative core of Parliament. Even the passage of universal manhood suffrage in 1912, enabling all men over thirty to vote, did little to change the social or political composition of Parliament.[15]

Giolitti did not need to make the same overtures to the church as he did to the left. The rise of anarchism and socialism had diminished the threat posed by the church. Maintaining its official position of intransigence in relation to liberal state, the church official recognized that international socialism posed a greater danger than liberalism. As Socialist organizations grew, the church countered with its own mutual-aid associations, cooperatives, banks, journals, and newspapers, coordinated under the auspices of the *Opera dei Congressi*. The church sponsored cultural productions, including theater, cinema, and sporting events to spread its moral, spiritual, and political messages. The conservative moderates who held sway over the lay Catholic movements lobbied for some kind of reconciliation with the state. Faced with the electoral successes of the left, the church lifted the *non-expedit*, edict in 1904, and by 1909 actively encouraged Catholics to vote for liberals in parliamentary elections. Despite the need to stem the tide of socialism, the pope remained opposed to formal reconciliation with the state, and took steps to curtail the independence of the lay Catholic associations. In 1905, the pope abolished the independent congresses, reconstituting them as part of Catholic Action, an umbrella organization under the control of the Bishops and the Vatican. Giolitti had no interest in reaching out to the grassroots Catholic associations or the Vatican, although he did encourage Catholics to vote. Giolitti held that the church and state should move in "parallel lines," with each bolstering the other as needed to serve its own ends.

After nearly two decades of social unrest, banking scandals, authoritarian illiberal policies, mass emigration, and military defeats, liberal Italy seemed to have landed on relatively secure shores. The constitutional crisis of the 1890s had been resolved, and the threat of revolution ended. The foreign policy shift from formal to informal empire turned Italy and its "merchant princes" into a world power, reconfiguring the boundaries of the national body to include overseas Italians. The shift in foreign policy paved the way for Giolitti to quiet old political rivalries and sources of social tension. But he did not successfully co-opt everyone. Furious with imperial defeats and the failure to wrest Trieste and Trentino from the Austrians, new Nationalist voices emerged, challenging the authority and vitality of the liberal state. Alongside political resistance new cultural movements challenged social and political stability.

CHAPTER 8
SCIENCE AND ART

In 1906, Giuseppe Prezzolini and Giovanni Papini published a collection of polemical essays entitled *La colture italiana* (*Italian Culture*), launching an attack on the cultural establishment. In the introductory essay, they described how almost fifty years after unification the "Italian spirit has not yet reconquered the boldness that, until the end of the Renaissance, made it the equal of the Greek." Under the guidance of the "children of the liberators," the Italian soul

> has become narrow, cautious, timid, afraid, cowardly—a lover of compromises, hypocrisies, of things half said, of the honeyed tongue, the garbled expression, enemy of things openly stated, of risky ventures, of new ideas, of nonconformity, of insults, of violence. Italians may enjoy political liberty but they still live in an atmosphere of moral servitude.[1]

According to Papini and Prezzolini, rather than revitalize the Italian people, the liberal state had weakened the nation.

Papini and Prezzolini's critique was part of a wider challenge to liberal culture. In the decades after unification, positivism had taken hold and shaping cultural production. Writers and artists insisted that observation, reason, and logic could reveal fundamental truths about the human condition in general, and Italians in particular. While many embraced the notion that art and science could provide empirical evidence capable of revealing the natural laws governing society, politics, and the physical world a small number of artists and writers resisted the dismissal of sentiment. In the last decades of the nineteenth century the opposition to positivist philosophical and social theories grew louder, strengthened by the growth of a mass-based popular culture. Urbanization, industrialization, rising standards of living, and increased literacy extended spaces of cultural production and consumption, fracturing the cultural foundation of the liberal state. On the eve of war, multiple cultural movements offered competing visions of Italy and Italians.

The scapigliatura and post-unification rebellion

Nearly as soon as Italy was born, writers and artists began to lament the failure of the Risorgimento to revitalize the nation. The growing disaffection with the founding fathers sparked a cultural rebellion. In the 1860s a loose collection of self-professed bohemians emerged in Milan and Turin. The *scapigliatura*, the unkempt and wild, took their name from Cletto Arrighi's novel *La scapigliatura e il 6 febbraio,* published in 1862, a fictional account of a failed Mazzinian revolt against Austrian rule in 1853. In the introduction, Arrighi defined the *scapigliatura* as a distinct class of disaffected, rebellious youth. If Arrighi's novel provided the name, Emilio Praga's poem, *Preludio,* made clear their collective rejection of the previous generation: "We are the children of sick fathers/eagles shedding their feathers/we flit around silent, awed, starved/on the agony of the spirit. . . . Chaste poet adored by Italy/ Old man absorbed in sacred visions/you may die . . . the time of the antichrist is now/Christ dies again."[2]

Ugo Tarchetti and Arrigo Boito, Emilio Prago and Cleto Arrighi stood at the center of *scapigliatura* movement, leading the fight against a Risorgimento they saw as culminating in repressive government, the tyranny of bourgeois morality, and the crass materialism of the cultural marketplace. Scorning classical aesthetic ideals and themes of rebirth, the young artists focused their work on death, decay, and horror. Influenced by Baudelaire and Poe, they conjured up the supernatural, celebrated the pathological, and exalted the ugly. Employing new styles, mixing dialect with Italian, and distorting conventional narrative structures, they challenged the boundaries between fantasy and reality. If capitalism and liberalism had destroyed "Art" and "Nature," then all an artist could do was focus on the world they lived in, to represent aspects of contemporary reality and accept, if not glorify, the power of science to uncover truth. Alongside the fiction and poetry, the *scapigliatura* journals took on social questions, focusing their works on the plight of the impoverished and marginalized, denouncing political corruption and scandal.

A similar rebellion occurred in the fine arts. Members of the *Macchiaioli* rejected post-unification celebratory paintings acclaimed in the museums and galleries, lamenting how little the Italy created in the 1860s, resembled the one they had imagined, and fought for in the 1850s. The artists refused commissions to paint the heroism of the founding fathers, to solidify the myth of the Risorgimento, choosing instead to paint the intimate scenes of domesticity and daily life. At the Café Michelangelo in Florence, the Macchiaioli debated new theories of composition and form. Like the French Impressionists, they tried to uncover emotional truth through the use of spots of color (*macchia di colore*), and playing with light and dark. The works of the key figures of the movement—Raffaello Sernesi, Giovanni Costa, and Giovanni Fattori—explored many of the same themes of passion, pain, poverty, and sentiment as the *scapigliatura*.[3]

The Hegelians and the positivists

The combination of romantic idealism and pragmatic realism visible in the cultural movements in the 1860s echoed in the two philosophical schools that shaped post-unification culture. Naples was the center of Italian idealism. Francesco De Sanctis, Camillo De Meis, Bernardo, and Silvio Spaventa, all born around 1820, came of age during the Risorgimento, their ideas shaped by war, exile, and the ideals of liberty and independence. De Sanctis, a supporter of Mazzini's Republican cause, participated in the 1848 revolution in Naples. In the aftermath of the uprising, the Bourbon government sentenced him to two years in prison, where he read widely in French and German philosophy, translating Hegal's logic into Italian. Released from prison in 1853, he was sent to exile in the United States, but fled instead to Turin, where he joined Bernardo Spaventa and Camillo De Meis.[4]

After unification, the Hegelians regrouped in Naples, promoting a secular idealism in their writings and teachings that seeped into literary and historical criticism. Central to their philosophy stood the assertion that things were knowable through the mind alone. Truth was born from ideas, not from the physical properties of material objects, and is manifest through form. For De Sanctis, a literary critic, this meant that the meaning or truth of literature lay in the art itself. Art, literary and figurative, was a consequence of the fusion between ideas, historical events, and social conditions in the mind of an artist. Critics had to delve into the lives of the writer, to understand how the artist transformed the stuff of politics and daily life into high art in a literary text.

Italian idealism had political implications. Corrupt politics debased culture, and cultural disintegration lead to immoral politics. The duty of educated men was the identification and articulation of a series of ideas capable of guiding the development of society and state. Recognizing the critical role of intellectuals in securing the new state, De Sanctis, De Meis, and Spaventa took active political roles. In 1861, De Sanctis was elected to Parliament and appointed minister of education serving for a year, returning in 1878 after the left came to power. As a deputy and minister of education, De Sanctis held that education was critical to the making of the nation. A close study of the lives and works of Dante, Vico, and Leopardi would unite Italians, transcend the emerging regional division by promoting a common understanding of the historic greatness of Italy. Silvio Spaventa, who served in the Ministry of the Interior, and was instrumental in designing the repressive policies of the 1860s used in the civil war, drew on Hegel's discussion of the ethical state to justify a strong, "legal" Italy.

In 1870s, positivism took hold among a new generation of scholars, challenging Hegalian idealism. In 1865, Villari gave an inaugural address amounting to the first "manifesto," of Italian positivism. Published in 1866, *La filosofia positive e il metodo storico* (positive philosophy and the Historical Method) called for the recognition of history as a science arguing that for Italian culture to flourish, intellectuals had to put aside their search for the "spirit" of a nation and focus on lived experience. He argued that the application of the scientific method to the study of society and politics could reveal the fundamental laws that govern society and politics. Rejecting the idea that culture guided a society, positivists held that culture was a product of social and physical phenomena (biology, physics, religion, etc.) that evolved according to the dictates of discoverable and natural laws. Relying on quantitative methods, proponents of positivism held that their studies paved the way to a more just society. Positivism offered a new interpretative framework across a wide range of disciplines, including law, history, literature, philosophy, psychiatry, anthropology, and psychology. In 1870, Roberto Ardigo gathered the multiple positivist intellectual strands weaving through the various disciplines into a more expansive unified system. In *la psicologia come scienza positiva* (*Psychology as a Positive Science*), Ardigo laid out the fundamental principles of a scientific philosophy: all truth is based on fact, facts are discernable through observation and analysis, and thoughts are shaped by the senses. Ardigo's articulation of positivism as a system strengthened the movement, creating closer alliances between a wide range of social sciences.[5] Although contemptuous of Hegelians, Italian positivists made similar claims for their science as Hegelians had for their philosophy, namely that empirical study of law, literature, history, politics, society, pedagogy, mental, and physical illnesses would secure the health of the state and nation.

Science and society

Like Hegelians, the leaders of Italian positivism entered political life, bringing their science into discussions of penal reforms, educational policy, and labor legislation. Positivists weighed in on the health of the individual and the nation, publishing tracts laying out the scientific evidence for best parenting practices and health and hygiene regimes. Social scientists and physicians sought to influence public policy as members of Parliament and in their journals. Analysis of research on diseases, insanity, fertility, mortality, and urban development sought to uncover the basic principles that could be used to shape society and politics in ways that could strengthen family, civil society, and the nation.

Echoing liberal political theorists, positivists considered the family the foundation of a well-ordered state, but they argued civic education alone could not ensure the physical and moral health of families. A wide range of studies collecting data on marriage ages, fertility patterns, mortality rates of married versus single and their relation to physical and mental diseases provided scientific evidence for the primacy of the nuclear family. Collectively these studies drawing on biology, psychology, and anthropology provided scientific justification for the gender norms underpinning the liberal state. The numerous empirical psychiatric and sociological studies on the nature of the female psyche and body, they claimed, proved women's physical and mental health was linked to maternity and domesticity, and that women were constitutionally unfit to bear the full burdens of citizenship. Italian psychiatry emphasized the importance of family in making moral citizens. Positivists pointed to statistical research on mortality, madness, and fertility, as evidence that marriage was equally critical to the construction of the male citizen. The inability of a man to thrive in marriage, they argued, suggested the existence of some kind of psychopathology.[6]

Concerns about the health of the family accompanied growing unease about the well-being of civil society, evidenced in the urban crime statistics. In 1876, Cesare Lombroso, a psychiatrist and professor of legal medicine at the University of Turin published a short work entitled L'uomo criminale ("Criminal Man").[7] The treatise argued that all criminals possessed atavistic abnormalities visible in their physiology and psychology that differentiated them from healthy citizens. In essence, these "born criminals," a term coined later by Enrico Ferri a lawyer and positivist sociologist, could be identified by their misshapen skulls, abnormal height, large chins, jug ears, darker skin color, and insensitivity to pain. Their personalities marked by cruelty, laziness, and a lack of remorse. Physical or mental traits, not a person's actions, defined a murderer or thief. Criminality, Lombroso contended, was an innate characteristic, a consequence of "evolutionary remnants" inherited from earlier stage in human development. In most people, these traits withered and died over generations, but in certain cases, the anomaly was passed on, making those who carried these characteristics dangerous to themselves and others. Building on a mass of statistical data and clinical studies of criminals held in insane asylums, Lombroso sought to scientifically prove that crime was a medical, not a judicial, concern.

Lombroso's work challenged the dominant legal theory based on free will. Criminal law held that all people had the ability to choose to abide by the law or not, and that punishment should be proportional to the severity of the crime. Lombroso's medical model of crime rejected the notion of free will, arguing that criminality was determined by biological, psychological, and social factors. Crime, much like a disease, required clinical examination and treatment. Punishment should not fit the crime, but the danger posed by the criminal. A woman arrested for petty thievery, but displaying the traits of a born prostitute, should be more severely punished. Lombroso and his followers weighed in on the ongoing debates surrounding the reform of the penal code. Pointing to the growing statistical body of evidence, categorizing and analyzing the physical characteristics of criminals, they argued that "born criminals" were immune to rehabilitative justice, and instead should be segregated from general society. They should not be locked away in traditional jails, breeding grounds for organized crime. Well-run prisons that provided prisoners with psychiatric services and work regimes could transform the "occasional" criminals, those who exhibited no evidence of a degenerative condition, into productive citizens, but did nothing for those possessing inherited atavistic traits.

In Lombroso's penal system, most "born criminals" would be sentenced to live out their lives in isolated institution. The worst offenders, *mafiosi* in particular, he insisted, should be sentenced to death. These prisons for "incorrigibles" would protect society, and eliminate a prison culture that glorified crime and undermined all rehabilitation efforts. The arguments of criminal anthropologists failed to have much impact on the legal system. The 1889 penal reform retained classical legal theories of free will and punishment as fundamental principles. However, the positivist school of criminology informed a wide range of social policies at both regional and national levels. Positivists managed to insert the idea of the "socially dangerous person" into the legal code, setting a precedent for the state to act to protect social order.

Positivists had an enormous impact on relations between North and South. When Villari first introduced the "Southern Question" into public debate, he intended to use his evidence of the conditions in the slums of Naples to argue for educational, economic, and social reform. Lombroso and his followers shifted the tenor of the debate, by offering "evidence," that the people of the South were something "other" than those of the North. In *L'uomo criminale* Lombroso introduced the idea that race was a critical component in understanding criminality. Racial stock accounted for the transmission of atavistic traits, and why they were clumped in certain regions. Race, he asserted, explained the existence of the Camorra and Mafia in the south: Palermitani were descendants of the Bedouins, who like the gypsies, he claimed, constituted a "race of organized criminals." Lombroso continued to call for better schooling and roads, but at the same time, insisted that southern Italians constituted a separate race.[8]

Psychologist Giuseppe Sergi pushed the racialization of the South even further. Dismissing skin color as a marker of race, Sergi insisted that only cranial morphology was a reliable marker of human taxonomy. Based on these cranial measurements, he posited the existence of a separate Mediterranean race that originated in Africa and spread through western Europe. Over time, EuroAfricans, became three races: African, Mediterranean, and Nordic, with differing skin colors and psychological variations, although retaining identical cranial forms. According to Sergi's theory, the Mediterranean race dominated in the south, whereas EuroAsians, a mixture of Aryan and Etruscan peoples, populated the North. Sergi hypothesized that the once great Mediterranean race responsible for the civilizations of Egypt, Greece, and Rome had degenerated, and was left behind as society and culture evolved. Over time, the individualism and creativity that made Rome great proved a liability in the more advanced political systems that relied on collectivity. The Aryans (the EuroAsiatics) who invaded Europe from the east thrived in the new European civilization. According to Sergi, the Mediterranean origins of Sicilians and Calabrians explained their extreme individualism, and accounted for the arrested social and cultural development of southern Italy in general.

At the end of the nineteenth century the anthropologist and statistician Alfredo Niceforo weighed in on the question of the South in two influential works: *Italia Barbera* (Barbarous Italy) and *Italiani del nord e Italiani del sud* (Italians of the north and Italians of the south). Drawing on a wealth of statistics regarding birth rates, marriage patterns, crime statistics, craniometric data, and physical characteristics presented in orderly charts and graphs, he claimed to have proved the existence of two separate races. By all measures, Niceforo claimed, northern Italians, descended from Aryan stock, exhibited a strong collective consciousness and social organization, as evidenced by their institutions and self-discipline, whereas southern Italians were individualists. Over all southern Italians, he asserted, were a *popolo donna* ("female people"), weak and dissolute, as opposed to the northern *popolo uomini* ("male people"). In Niceforo's telling, race explained the endemic poverty, disease, immorality, violence, crime, so carefully described by the *meridionalisti*, not ineffective legislation. The mafia and camorra were distilled versions of all degenerate traits of the southern people, not the consequence of a relationship forged between locals and the state in the aftermath of the civil war. These racial theories transformed the mafia into a pathological condition coursing through the blood of all southerners.[9]

Positivist racial theories elicited vehement opposition. A significant group of social scientists refused to accept the biological origins of poverty, crime, and vice, instead arguing that environmental factors (housing, hygiene, education, etc.) accounted for social disparities. Napoleone Colajanni was a vociferous critic of positivist racial theories, critiquing Lombroso's "science," and what he saw as his indiscriminate collection of facts and facile interpretations. Colajanni contended that people were not "born criminals," but were made so by poverty, living conditions and education. Filippo Turati also took issue with the biological determinists. Their critiques did little to shift the hardening ideas of the South as a distinct and separate world, inhabited by a violent, individualistic, law-breaking people, but they did contribute to undermining positivism. By the beginning of the twentieth century, new methodologies, theories, and research weakened the hold of positivism on science and culture.[10]

Positivism in literature and arts

The heated epistemological debates seeped into literature and the arts. Informed by French naturalism and positivism, the *veristi* (realism), including Luigi Capuana, Giuseppe Verga, and Frederico De Roberto, claimed that fiction could serve as a powerful weapon understanding contemporary social problems. If novelists could closely observe the daily lives of ordinary people, they could show how passion, superstitions, violence, hunger shape individual and collective destinies. In his first novel, *Giacinta*, Capuana examined how the physical shock of rape could create a psychologically mutilated woman, unable to love. In 1881, Verga published the first part of an ambitious series entitled *Ciclo dei vinti* (the cycle of the vanquished), exploring the struggle of human evolution and progress, completing two of the projected five volumes. *I Malavoglia*, the first work in the series, looked at the impact of economic ambition, while the second novel, *Maestro don Gesualdo*, examined social desires. In his work, there are no winners or losers, only the stories of people left on the wayside, victims of the disinterested and merciless march of progress; familial or individual misfortune were products of heredity, circumstances, and personality.[11]

The collective body of work of the *veristi* reinforced regional divisions. Luigi Capuana, Giuseppe Verga, and Frederico De Roberto were born in southern towns, although they had spent a good part of their lives in the literary centers of Milan and Florence. In some respects, their lives exemplified the geographic contradictions underpinning unification: increased mobility and circulation of people and ideas and the construction of seemingly static distinct regional spaces. The collected works of Verga and Capuana reified notions of the "backward" South, a world inhabited by a people who spoke a different language and lived according to a different set of rules. Matilde Serao's stories described the poverty and fatalism of Naples. In a similar fashion, Grazia Deledda's novels, set in Sardinia, depicted a primitive world steeped in tradition and custom. Further north, realism described emerging class struggles, the psychological emptiness of contemporary society, and the moral cowardice of the newly rich. Anna Zuccari Neera, one of the most prolific and profitable authors of the late nineteenth century, detailed the emotional barrenness of the worlds of bourgeois women.[12]

Veristi portrayals of the psychological, material, and cultural struggles faced by men and women invigorated Italian opera. In the decades following unification, opera fell into decline. Italian composers seemed to have lost their inspiration with unification. Verdi continued to write, but his production slowed: between 1845 and 1865, Verdi produced over sixteen operas, and in the following three decades, he completed only four. Theater managers continued to recycle the old works of Verdi, Donizetti, and Rossini. In the absence of groundbreaking Italian compositions, impresarios booked the works of Massenet, Bizet, and Wagner.

In May of 1890, Pietro Mascagni's *Cavalleria Rusticana* was opened at the Costanzi opera house in Rome. The unknown composer had drawn little publicity, and the house was just half full. Within the first few minutes, the audience realized that they were hearing something completely new, and burst into applause. At the end of the evening, the audience called the composer and singers out for over sixty curtain calls. Written for a competition, the Livorno born Mascagni reworked Verga's play, the *Cavalleria Rusticana*, into an opera. Originally a short story, *Cavalleria Rusticana* is a harsh depiction of love, passion, and death in a Sicilian village. Verga revised it for the theater to try to make money. The operatic version introduced distinct innovations. Unlike Verdi's epics, Mascagni's debut piece described one simple story, drawing the audience in by its dramatic intensity. Echoing the language of the *veristi,* the librettists chose to write in the language of the streets, but unlike the popular, but critically derided, operettas, *Cavalleria* adhered to the conventions of formal opera. Within months, managers began booking the new opera, and within a year, it had appeared in over forty cities and abroad.[13]

The predominance of positivist assumptions in science, fiction, and opera generated its own opposition. In the 1890s, a small contingent of writers, including Gabriele D'Annunzio, Antonio Fogazzaro, and Giovanni Pascoli, published stylistically diverse works, challenging positivist claims of objectivity and progress. Influenced by French decadents and symbolists, who sought to free art from the materialist demands of the market, they instead celebrated the irrational: sex, violence, death, pleasure, indolence, decay, and vulgarity. The work of Italian decadentism owed as much to the rebellion of the *scapigliaturi* as it did to Nietzsche's philosophy. D'Annunzio embodied the rebellious bohemian, whose life and work flouted convention and challenged bourgeois norms. Critics, including Giosuè Carducci, attacked D'Annunzio's poetry collection, *Intermezzo di Rime* (1883) celebrating sex, violence, and revenge. D'Annunzio's reworking of the story of Francesca da Rimini, from Dante's inferno, transformed a story of tragedy into a tale of blood and lust. D'Annunzio's adulterous affairs, duels, seduction, and drugs brought attacks from the establishment, but did little to dim the popularity of his work. In contrast to D'Annunzio's sex and violence, the poetry of Pascoli linked the intimate world of family, childhood, and home to sadness, loss, and the inevitability of death. Pascoli explored the unconscious, emotional world writing from a child-like self-centered perspective, and playing with subjectivity, symbolism, and poetic structure. Critics commonly derided Pascoli's work as infantile and simplistic.

In his short essay, *Arte e coscienza d'oggi* (contemporary Art and Conscience), Luigi Pirandello expressed the growing frustration with material explanations of human existence, and the inability of the symbolists or decadent poets to do better. Truth is elusive; all a writer can hope for is to describe a feeling to trace the constantly changing emotions born from the rational and the irrational. Instinct and reason drive human actions, not the laws of biology or psychology. In Pirandello's short stories and novels there is no essential self to uncover, characters shift in relation to every other character. Underlying much of Pirandello's work is a sadness for the absurdity of the human condition, where the instinctual seems to delight in subverting any rational attempt to find happiness. In different ways, D'Annunzio, Pascoli, and Pirandello challenged cultural norms.

The spread of photography in the last decades of the century further disrupted positivist and idealist narratives about art and knowledge. By the 1880s, photography had made its way into private and public life. By the 1860s, national magazines such as *Illustrazione Italiana* and *L'illustrazione popolare* relied on photographs to boost sales. Postcards (along with the expansion of the postal service) made it possible to see faraway places as they were. In a nation where literacy hovered around 40 percent in 1870, photography played a central role in shaping public opinion.

Positivists initially welcomed the new technology. The inherent objectivity of the photograph provided a formidable tool in the quest to uncover truth, and scientific experts called for its use in the court system. Photographs of criminals, the insane and the degenerates, provided new kinds of evidence to support spurious biological theories about race and disease. Verga, Capuana, and De Roberto all enthusiastically embraced photography. Capuana began taking pictures in the late 1860s and introduced Giuseppe Verga to the art. Verga took over 400 images of city and countryside, mothers with babes in arms, children playing in the streets, people at work, his friends and colleagues.

Photography raised thorny theoretical questions: Given the prevalence of the photograph, what was the role of the author? *Veristi*'s claim that narrative could objectively describe the world seemed ludicrous when compared to photography and film. One the other hand, a single photograph also highlighted things that were not there: Who stood outside the frame? What had happened the moment before the photo was taken? Photographs seemed to reinforce the growing sense that what humans observed was not always true or real. The mechanistic quality of photography forced a rethinking of the relationship between human and machine. In 1916, Pirandello published a short story entitled *Si gira!* (Shoot!), describing a world where machines had grown powerful off of the bodies and souls of humans. The hero of the story is the camera operator aware of that the picture is more than what it appears. Photography was not merely reflective of material reality; it altered people's perceptions of the world.

The same year Pirandello published *Arte e Coscienza*, Benedetto Croce launched a direct attack on positivists. In a short essay entitled *"La storia ridotta sotto il concetto generale d'arte,"* he rejected the notion that history was an art, not a science. Croce argued that historical change was contingent on individuals and events; it did not operate according to general laws. In 1903, Croce together with Giovanni Gentile published the first issue of the journal *La critica,* fiercely critical of positivism. Croce's work expanded the aesthetic and intellectual world, encouraging writers and authors to reject the constraints of *verismo*. Croce's criticism linking contemporary culture to past geniuses defended De Sanctis and Carducci's visions of a modern Italy. However, unlike the speculative idealism of the Hegelians, Croce and Gentile called for a kind of "militant idealism," meaning that their culture should be deployed to enact specific kinds of political change.[14]

Changing cultural landscape

The emergence of new cultural movements took place in a changing market. Rising literacy rates, higher wages, and more leisure time brought more people into the market as cultural consumers. Urbanization, industrialization, and new technologies opened new spaces for cultural production and consumption. An increasing literate public, an expanding print market, and new forms of cultural production challenged the ability of a small elite, ensconced in universities or institutes, to define "Italian culture."

In the decades following unification the size and shape of the consumer market changed. Between 1861 and 1911 literacy rates grew from 25 percent to 60 percent. Editors and printers responded to the new reading public offering a wide selection of journal, books, and newspapers. Between 1863 and 1886 the number of publications rose from 4,243 titles to a high of over 9,000 titles. The emergence of a more literate industrial work force, a larger commercial class, school teachers, civil servants, and professionals fueled the demand for scholarly texts, technical manuals as well as novels, poetry, and histories.

Mass consumer culture reinforced geographic disparities. Publications circulated within restricted geographic and social boundaries. Print media tended to be marketed where it was produced, rarely reaching rural communities. Cultural consumers congregated in the cities and provincial towns where residents had, on average, more disposable income. A similar pattern marked the distribution of newspapers. In 1900 only the *Corriere della Sera* could claim a national circulation. Newspapers advocating particular political ideologies or representing church interests profited by carving out strong local markets. Rather than working to create an "imagined nation," newspapers reinforced the notion of multiple Italies. By the 1920s a pattern of uneven cultural dispersion defined the Italian market.[15]

If publishing deepened regional divides, the expansion of print culture also highlighted the permeability of national borders. Within Italy the expanding reading public showed a strong appetite for French and British fiction, including the works of Victor Hugo and Daniel Defoe. In 1905, the publishing house Barbini reported that foreign authors comprised over half of their best-selling books. Authors found markets overseas; publishing houses in Milan, Rome, and Florence sold thousands of books overseas. By the end of the century emigrant communities, assisted by the expansion of the Dante Alighieri Societies, imported thousands of volumes a year. The contradictory local and transnational impulses characterizing the market for books and newspapers created alternating spaces of abundancy and scarcity of print culture within the global Italian community.

Women entered the market as both cultural consumers and producers. Newspapers targeted urban women readers, serializing popular novels, short stories, and humorous articles. Editors commissioned columns on fashion, health and hygiene, and mothering to attract a wider female readership. Women came into the market as agents of change. While the literary critics focused their analysis on the poetry of Carducci, the criticism of De Sanctis, the novels of Verga and Capuana, it was the works of a new generation of female authors that captured the hearts of the people. The stories of unhappy wives, rebellious daughters, illicit loves, and the tedium of domesticity challenged literary stereotypes of women as angels and whores. The best-selling novels of Neera described the emotional dilemmas of women caught between duty and passion. Grazie Deledda's descriptions of village life in Sardinia gained international fame, winning the Nobel Prize in 1926. The imagined worlds of much of women's fiction subverted those of the *veristi*, encouraging readers to empathize with their protagonists. Sibilla Aleramo was one of the few who overtly challenged gender norms. In her controversial autobiographical novel, *Una donna* (A Woman, 1906), she tells a story of a woman who abandons her child to escape an abusive marriage. Male critics assuaged their fears of the popularity of female authors by dismissing their work as imitative and only of interest to frivolous readers. The disdain of literary critics did not diminish sales. Collectively the works of women authors contested the limits of female identity and unsettled existing literary traditions and forms.[16]

Traditional cultural notions were further challenged by new forms of leisure activities: sport, film, and music. Cycling, automobile racing, and soccer became popular sports in Italy attracting participants and fans from across social classes. In the late nineteenth century, organized leisure activities gained mass appeal. In Italy, cycling, originally an aristocratic pursuit, became a Sunday activity as the cost of bicycles declined, and workers had more free time. British expatriates introduced soccer and cricket to Italy. While cricket failed to catch on, soccer did. In 1910, over 6,000 people came to see Italy defeat France in its first international competition. Soon local workingmen's associations, Catholic sports clubs, and political parties organized local teams and leagues. A growing sports culture expanded local and regional social networks and created new markets for cultural goods.[17]

In the evenings, men and women found entertainment at the popular *Teatro di Varietà*, or *Caffè Concerto*, similar to Vaudeville Theater in the United States. Beginning in the 1890s, these café-theater hybrids sprang up in nearly every major city. *The Eden* in Milan, the *Romano* in Turin, the *Alhambra* in Florence, the *Salone Margherita* in Naples, and *L'Orfeo* in Rome featured acrobats, popular singers, novelty acts, and skits. The audience comprised of the urban working class reveled in stories and songs drawn from the streets. The acts drew from popular and high culture, incorporating folk songs and dance, alongside parodies of critically acclaimed operas and theater. Social satires mocked the wealthy and powerful. Patrons were drawn to new cultural space that allowed them to linger over coffee and a cigar, visit with friends, and enjoy the show.

The rise of the *Caffè Concerto* highlighted the role of Naples in the making of modern Italian culture at home and abroad. Neapolitan ballads of love, longing, and betrayal entered into mainstream culture, appearing on stages in Florence, Venice, and Milan. The variety acts showcasing the songs of Naples were popular among emigrant communities. Italian acts made sizable profits traveling between Naples, New York, and Buenos Aires, performing folk songs and skits and strengthening emotional ties between emigrants and Italy. Italians at home and abroad saw profit in the marketing of books, movies, and songs that tugged on the nostalgic visions of a faraway home. By the First

World War, Neapolitan ballads, like macaroni and the mandolin, became inextricably linked to the idea of Italy in the minds of Italians and foreigners alike. The invention of the phonograph and the mass production of records further cemented the standing of the Neapolitan ballad. Born in the streets of Naples and popularized in the music halls, *O sole mio* and *ti voglio ben assai* became as identified with Italy as the arias from *Aida* or *Cavalleria Rusticana*. In American theaters, Enrico Caruso chose the songs of Naples to sing at encores, fusing images of Naples and the south with the gondolas and cupolas that had long signified the meaning of Italian. The emergence of a transnational Italian culture challenged the hegemony of elite culture, but it was the advent of film that most radically reshaped Italian cultural life[18] (Figure 11).

First introduced in the 1890s, films moved into larger theaters, often serving as opening acts in the *Teatro di Varietà*. Recognizing the profit potential of film,

Figure 11 Italy, 1899, a fusion of Venice, Naples, and New York. Color lithograph sheet music cover image of "Frangesa Neapolitan Two-Step" by Edward George, New York, 1899. Sheridan Libraries/Levy/Gado/Getty Images.

impresarios soon opened theaters dedicated to film. Within a decade nearly every city and provincial capital boasted a cinema. Unable to compete with the new venues, the variety theaters that had first embraced the possibilities of film were closed. In order to meet demand, production companies sprung up in Turin, Milan, Rome, and Naples, spitting out documentaries and grand historic epics, celebrating the greatness of ancient Rome (*Gli ultimi giorni di pompei*, 1908; *Quo Vadis*, 1913; *Cabiria*,1914), historical figures (*Beatrice Cenci*, 1909; *Lucrezia Borgia*, 1910), and the Risorgimento (*La presa di Roma*, 1905). Even the church recognized the potential power of film. Despite official pronouncements against the new art form, the church constructed an extensive network of parish movie houses and entered into production of feature-length films reflecting Catholic values. The advent of film challenged elite notions of culture in multiple ways. Cinemas threatened the existence of theatrical companies and the livelihood of stage actors and playwrights. Perhaps even more unnerving to the critics and elite was the power of film to generate and disseminate new historical narratives.[19]

By the beginning of the twentieth century, it is possible to conceive of the cultural geography of Italy as multiple overlapping local, national, and transnational circuits. Increased mobility, political discord, industrialization, and urbanization brought forth new sources of cultural production and carved out multiple consumer markets. The intellectual rebellion inspired and led by Croce, combined with the emergence of a mass popular culture, laid the ground work for a modernist movement.

Italian modernists

The turn-of-the-century cultural landscape proved fertile to a small group of artists inspired by the decadentism of D'Annunzio and the idealism of Croce, determined to carve out a new avant-garde movement. This new generation of poets, writers, and journalists, born between 1876 and 1882, rejected the notion that Italian culture was born in the past, but instead welcomed the chaotic, fragmented possibilities of the modern. In February 1909, Filippo Marinetti published *Il manifesto del futurismo* in newspapers across the country. The manifesto, denouncing Italy's obsession with its past and its fixation on liberal ideals, embraced the energy, speed, violence, and destruction of the industrial age. Italy, the futurists claimed, had become a museum, a cemetery, a place fit only for the dying or invalid. The futurists called for the destruction of the old in order to "free our country from the stinking canker of its professors, archeologists, tourist guides and antiquaries."[20] The poets, journalists, and artists celebrated the speed and power of the automobile, the glory of struggle, and the cleansing power of war.

The glorification of war, the equation of cowardice with the liberal institutions, and the disdain for social conventions resonated with a new generation of Nationalist intellectuals. Led by Giovanni Papini and Giuseppe Prezzolini the movement called for a spiritual and martial cultural revolution. First in the journal, *Leonardo* in 1903, and then in *la Voce* (1908), Nationalists decried the moral turpitude and squalor of contemporary life. Like the Futurists who saw Rome as a dead city, Nationalists saw Rome as the source of pollution and corruption. "Rome is the central leech of Italy . . . the fundamental cause of all our economic, moral and intellectual backwardness. Fish begin to stink from their heads: Italy from Rome."[21] Like the futurists, the Nationalists saw the nation's salvation in the revitalization of the nation, impossible under the tepid, pragmatic materialism of Giolitti. Only the purifying power of war could transform Italians into a strong, moral, and virtuous people.

On the eve of the First World War, the cultural world of liberal Italy was a messy place. Positivist commitment to the progressive possibilities of science and technology continued to shape academic and scientific life while facing a growing backlash. The celebration of the irrational, the unconscious as agents of historical change and human development energized new artistic forms and vision, and gave rise to an aggressive nationalism. Common to all the cultural movements, however, lurked the conviction that culture was critical to the making of Italy and Italians. The combination of an economic downturn, growing skepticism regarding Giolitti's ability to govern, and rising Nationalist movements made war seem inevitable.

PART THREE
WAR AND FASCISM (1914–48)

Historians, war, and fascism, 1914–48

Recent debates over the significance of war, the nature of Italian Fascism, and the impact of occupation and resistance have unsettled the historical narratives that long explained Italy's transition to a Republic. The general lines of the story told of how fascism emerged out the horrors of the First World War, and while many Italians initially supported Mussolini's Nationalist rhetoric, only a minority enthusiastically supported the dictatorship. Italians redeemed themselves during the Second World War, occupation, and resistance, proving themselves *brava gente* ("good people"), and providing an antifascist foundation for the new Republic. Although historians disagreed over the causes and consequences of particular events the basic narrative remained untouched. New works have produced a more complicated story. In these studies, the Great War, long relegated to the margins of Italian history, took on greater social, political, and emotional import. Analyses of fascism suggest the regime was both more and less violent than generally assumed, and have called into question the postwar idea of Italians as inherently *brava gente.* By drawing on a wealth of new sources and considering the power of memory and national myths to shape historical understandings, a picture of an Italy at once more ugly, generous, and resilient has emerged.

Reappraisals of the Risorgimento and the liberal state first encouraged scholars to take a new look at the Great War. For decades, the Italian war experience in 1915 had been relegated to the margins of both Italian and European history. Caught up in the debates about the origins of fascism, Marxist historians saw the war as evidence of the fragility of the state born out of an incomplete revolution. They argued that the exclusion of workers and peasants from the national body left Italy unable to face the exigencies of total war. Liberal historians considered the war as evidence of the success of liberalism, contending that in 1918, the state could finally claim to have realized the territorial ambitions of unification. In the wider literature on the European war, Italy fared little better, dismissed as an insignificant front in the military histories, and largely ignored in the new social and cultural histories.[1] Once historians uncoupled the war from the Gramscian/Croce debates, scholars reconsidered the political, social, and economic significance of the war on its own terms. In these new histories fascism emerged as one of a number of possible political outcomes of the war. Military historians challenged stereotypes of incompetence and defeat, calling attention to the bravery of the troops, the difficulties of waging mountain war, and the organizational weaknesses that plagued the command. Social historians explored how the war deepened class divides, transformed gender norms, and weakened political institutions, emphasizing underlying continuities between the liberal state and the Fascist regime. Combined the reassessment of Italy in war highlighted the diversity of individual and collective experiences that were shaped by the past and informed the postwar world.[2]

Influenced by the rise of social history, the stories of soldiers and civilians culled from letters, diaries, and memoirs played a critical role in writing the new history of the war. First person accounts testified to the brutality of war, and harsh military discipline, but also revealed an underlying patriotism and willingness to serve. Most Italians expressed little desire to go to war, but few opposed it. Conscripts did not enthusiastically rush to the colors, and desertion rates were higher than in other European armies, but the majority of conscripts stayed and fought. Histories of the war have shown how the experience of war—the miserable conditions and violence—eroded regional, linguistic, and cultural divides. These works provided a more complex understanding of the diverse ways the war strengthened national ties and called into question the legitimacy of the state. Social histories reexamined the nature of wartime work, including women's participation, and revealed that like soldiers, workers were not forced into war work. The studies explored the ways war deepened social divides, reconfigured regional divides, and acted as a contradictory force of polarization, unity, and modernization.[3]

The transformative power of the war is visible in the works exploring civilian experiences. Studies focusing on rural women and working women suggest that the war drew women into the nation in new ways. In the factories and rural villages women raised their voices to demand compensation for the loss of their men and better benefits for all families. In the industrial cities of Milan and Turin the war created new kinds of wage work and political opportunities for women. Scholars traced the variety of ways bourgeoisie women engaged in voluntary action through local women's associations or the Red Cross, organizing soup kitchens, providing material aid to refugees. Wartime experiences politicized women in diverse ways, some joined pacifist movements, others moved toward the Nationalist right, while others became members of the Socialist and Communist Parties.[4] Historians have explored the impact of war on children, suggesting that the ideological mobilization of children through schools, and the physical effect of the war, shaped the politics of a generation that came of age with fascism.[5] In the last few years, scholars have recognized the importance of mobility in shaping individual and collective experiences of war. Refugees and returning migrants unsettled social and political relations in the postwar period.[6]

The richness of work on the Great War revised histories of Italian Fascism. Until recently historians of fascism focused on its origin and its development. On the left, scholars argued that the Fascist state, born out of the Risorgimento's "passive revolution," was the defender of capitalist interests against the proletariat. Liberal historians, holding fast to the idea of fascism as an abomination, eschewed any sort of class analysis, insisting that the study of the state itself held little explanatory power. Few historians considered fascism as an ideological movement worthy of study, instead, defining the movement by what it opposed. As a consequence, scholars were left grappling with a number of central questions: Was the state authoritarian or totalitarian? Was Mussolini an effective dictator? What was the relationship between Italians and the state? What role did violence play in the regime? Was Fascist Italy a racial state?[7]

The nature of the Fascist state and the effectiveness of Mussolini remain a contested issue. Was the state revolutionary, with its own ideology, or was it merely a reactionary movement against modernity? For many the answers to these questions hinged on their evaluation of Mussolini. Those who considered Mussolini as little more than a buffoon, inclined to grandiose, theatrical performances with no vision, downplayed the importance of Italian Fascism. In 1974, Renzo De Felice challenged historians to take Mussolini seriously. Dismissing those who dismissed Mussolini, De Felice argued that he was a pragmatic, astute politician, who by the 1930s had embarked on a social revolution. Italian Fascism, De Felice insisted, differed from German National Socialism, but had a set of core tenets and a distinct political ideology.[8] Met with a barrage of criticism, De Felice's work generated the first postwar reevaluation of the state and life under fascism.[9]

The reassessment of the Fascist state that began with De Felice drew on the insights of George Mosse, who argued that the political import of fascism was inextricably linked to cultural expressions.[10] Some scholars set out to look at the production and symbolic meaning of Fascist political culture. Analyzing Fascist rituals, the integration of the myths of war, the idealization of the "soldier-citizen," Emilio Gentile argued that fascism aimed to create a new society where all men and women served the needs of the state. The parades, marches, and speeches did not merely express an ideology, but transformed fascism into a political religion.[11] Although not everyone accepted Gentile's thesis, the focus on culture generated a wealth of literature on the role of ritual, culture, and art in constructing the Fascist state.[12] While some scholars argue that the cultural turn erased politics, the work has encouraged historians to see the regime's social, economic, and foreign policies as expressions of an ideological vision.[13]

The cultural turn accompanied a reconsideration of the contentious debates surrounding questions of support for the regime. In the aftermath of the war, scholars argued that few Italians enthusiastically supported the regime, most submitted to the demands of the dictatorship with quiet resignation mixed with disgust. Over the course of the 1930s, the suppressed hostility grew deeper and wider with the invasion of Ethiopia and intervention in the Spanish Civil War.[14] This line of argument, combined with the comparative "gentleness" of Fascist Italy relative to the horrors of Nazi Germany, contributed to the idea Italians were basically *brava gente* (good people). In 1974, Renzo De Felice offered an alternate argument, suggesting that there was widespread support for the regime between 1929 and 1936. De Felice's work sparked heated debate, and historians set to work to test his assertion.[15]

The work spurred by De Felice's argument found that the regime generated limited consensus. Studies focusing on Fascist efforts to create consensus revealed structural constraints posed by geography, culture, and social divisions. The regime's ability to draw people into the movie theaters or sporting events did not transform them into Fascist subjects or translate into support of the regime's politics.[16] A number of excellent studies on the consumption of Fascist ideology, focusing on women and children, have explored the gap between Fascist social theory and lived experience. Research on work, leisure, and family life attest to the ways family, church, and community continued to shape individual and collective life. Efforts by the regime to remodel Italians into the image of the perfect Fascist man and women—heterosexual, virile, and fertile—also fell short.[17] Historians have also shown the ways mobility undermined the regime's ambition to create a Fascist society.[18] Recognizing the limits on the creation of consensus, however, does not translate into opposition to the regime. Drawing on oral testimonies, memoirs, and diaries, social historians have drawn attention to the complexities of consent that often bled into coercion, and complicity that turned into resistance. These analyses accompanied a growing recognition of the violence employed by the regime in its efforts to forge a Fascist nation.[19]

Underlying the notion of Italians as "*brava gente*" stands the conviction that fascism was less violent and less brutal than German Nazism. This idea is rooted in the belief that anti-Semitism sat lightly on Italy. Erasing Italy's colonial history, scholars insisted that Italy's racial laws were imported from Germany and found little sympathy within the community. The first works on the Italian Holocaust recovered the stories of Italians who risked their own lives to hide Jewish neighbors, of bureaucrats who erased Jews from the official rosters, and of members of the clergy who transformed convents and monasteries into places of refuge.[20] Only a few published Jewish memoirs questioned the heroic narrative. In the last few decades a number of works have challenged the notion of a "gentler" Italian Shoah. Dismissing the notion that Mussolini imported racial theories from Germany, scholars have traced anti-Semitism back into nineteenth-century Italy, linking liberal racial hierarchies to Fascist imperial policies. Works underscoring the racial assumptions behind the brutality of the African wars make it difficult to hold on to any notion that Italians stood outside the wider Western racial systems. New scholarship explores the ties between the colonization of Africa to the implementation of racial laws at home, and the exclusion of Jews from the national body.[21] There is nothing gentle in the genocidal policies in Africa, nor in the histories of Jewish deportations. While there are heroic stories deserving of recognition, the question of Italian complicity in the Holocaust is complicated.[22] Works challenging the myth of the "*brave gente*" have generated interesting reflections on historical memory.[23]

The collapse of Mussolini's dictatorship in the summer of 1943 enabled Italians to reconfigure their country's Fascist past into a story of antifascist resistance. Although the subsequent Cold War precluded any celebrations of the resistance that involved recognizing the role Communists played in liberation, it still allowed for a story of heroic resistance to German oppression to emerge as a foundational myth of the Republic. In the years following the war, the historical narrative that emerged told a story of a people who refused to ally with the Germans. The antifascist resistance encompassed diverse political ideologies, including Catholics, Liberals, Socialists, and Communists, a testimony to the endurance of Italy's humanist traditions. By the 1970s, in the midst of a slight Cold War thaw, a number of historians sought to reclaim the role of the Communists in the partisan movements, but the notion of an antifascist popular front continued to hold sway. Attempts to create a kind of historical middle ground angered those on the left who contended that the resistance was a proletarian revolution, and on the right who sought to discredit the role of the Communists in Italy's liberation.

In the 1970s and 1980s the idea of the resistance as a civil war took hold among the right, promoting an "anti-anti-fascist" story. In this telling, Communists appeared as thugs and terrorists, qualitatively no different from the Fascists. In the early 1990s, the historian Claudio Pavone, a former partisan, published a work reclaiming the idea of civil war, and transforming the historiographical landscape. Pavone maintained that the years of occupation were marked by three interconnected wars: a war of national liberation fought against the Germans; a civil war between Italian antifascists and Fascists; a class war. Pavone's reconceptualization shifted attention off of the resistance, reframing his study around the central question: Why did Italians on all sides join the fight?[24] Pavone's work not only sparked heated debate but also encouraged more nuanced studies of the period of occupation and resistance.

The reassessment of occupation and resistance revealed the weight gender, class, and ideology played in determining individual decisions to fight, and have led to a reconsideration of the violence of the period. The works show the critical role played by women, kin, and neighbors in shaping experiences and politics of occupation. Once scholars shifted attention off of the partisan groups and on to wider networks linking members of the resistance along the lines of work, family, and village, a variety of forms of collaboration and resistance emerged. Oral histories and local studies have enabled historians to better understand the complicated calculations of political idealism, personal circumstances, and moral choices that informed individual actions.[25] Nowhere have the debates between partisans and non-partisans been more fraught than in studies of Nazi massacres. For decades, Communist partisans were blamed for the thousands of civilians killed in Nazi reprisals in both popular memory and official commemorations. Recent works drawing on careful analysis of archival sources and oral testimonies have complicated the picture, uncovering factual evidence countering the accepted accounts. These works highlight the ways that personal experience, familial memory, and ideology shaped the historical narratives underpinning the Republic.[26]

This new scholarship encouraged historians to rethink the politics of reconstruction. Focusing on the underlying fissures, historians have traced how the Republic's antifascist origin myths incorporated the regional, social, and political divides of past Italies, reinforcing tropes of southern dependency, reinscribing gender hierarchies, and concentrating political power within a liberal elite. New histories of the Anglo-Allied occupation show how the antifascist myth erased the southern experience of war and occupation, burying the history of bombings, hunger, and homelessness in the longer history of poverty and failure. Like liberal Italy, Republican Italy would be born in the North.[27] Historians of women and gender highlighted the disjuncture between the constitutional rhetoric of equality for men and women and legislation privileging family and maternity over women's autonomy. The strength of the antifascist foundational myths rehabilitated all Italians, ensuring that few Fascists had to grapple with their past.[28]

The new historical trends depict a postwar Italy at once more fractured and more united. The experiences of war and the collapse of the liberal state did not erase the deeper social and political tensions. Local elites continued to challenge the authority of the state. Class, gender, region, and mobility still defined social relations. Lingering anger and resentment directed at former Fascists, collaborators, and members of the resistance further divided communities. Yet, the experiences of two world wars and fascism also strengthened notions of national identity.

CHAPTER 9
THE GREAT WAR

(Section of Military Censorship—Lecco)
From the Zone of War
To Molteno (Como)
5/6/1917

Do not be surprised at misfortune because we here are all constantly subject to brutal death like so many beasts to slaughter, daily, there is an enormous number of wounded and dead . . . yesterday one grenade alone wounded 17 of my company. . . . We are now bivouacked in the woods (in reserve) there is not even a hole for shelter—extremely demoralized, even the officers are going crazy . . . it is not death that demoralizes us because by now we know that we must die, but the extraordinary circumstances that we face—the carnage—the slaughter—the suffering and then the abuse—the cruelty of Colonel Brigadier F. Cav. Temistocle— which he unfortunately paid for dearly, killed as he was the 2nd of this month by an enemy grenade—who ordered the execution in front of us all of 4 soldiers, two of whom, suffering from thirst, left in order to fill a jug of water, I should say that I, we, had gone for three days without a drop of water. Therefore, let's hope for a good wound or a damned death.[1]

Written shortly before the tenth battle of the Isonzo, the bitter words of this unknown Milanese soldier speak to the disgust, anger, and disillusionment felt by many soldiers. After two years of fighting, few managed to still take "comfort in being one of those who gave their blood to their country and defended it from the eternal hated enemy."[2] By 1917, the idea that war was the culmination of the Risorgimento dream of liberating the *terra irredenta* or a regenerative force for the Italian people had long vanished.

Wartime experiences of suffering, scarcity, cruelty, political ineptitude, and military stupidity experienced by civilians and soldiers united a nation around shared feelings of disgust toward the state. The war fractured the rickety foundation of the liberal state, ushering in a period of fear and insecurity enabling rival political visions—Catholics, Socialists, Nationalists—to fill the growing vacuum. Italy came out of the war in crisis: economic chaos, a morally bankrupt Parliament, social instability, and a deep burning rage pushed the country to the brink of civil war and led to the rise of fascism and the collapse of the liberal state.

Libya and the origins of the First World War

Historians have debated the causes of the First World War since the war began. While German belligerence, Serbian nationalism, Austrian paranoia, and imperialism all played a role, ultimately European statesmen chose to go to war in the summer of 1914. The decision was based on a complex evaluation of the benefits and risks of facing, what many perceived to be, an inevitable European war sooner, rather than later. In the first decade of the twentieth century, a series of colonial struggles in the Balkans and North Africa suggested that a full-scale war was only a matter of time. For many Italians, the Libyan war proved particularly divisive, fueling Nationalist imperialist dreams and disgust with a liberal state seemingly incapable of fulfilling the Risorgimento's promises of physical unification or spiritual regeneration.

By 1910, Nationalists had resurrected Italy's African imperial dreams. The growth of an emigrant community in Libya fueled calls for a formal colony. After securing the support of the European powers to carve out a sphere of influence in Libya, Italy prepared to invade. On September 27, 1911, the government issued an ultimatum demanding Turkey recognize Italian economic claims in Libya and permit its troops to occupy Tripoli and Cyrene. Officials claimed that Italians were insulted and assaulted by Turks on a daily basis: Turkish officials exacted bribes and cargo from Italian merchant vessels, pillaged Italian businesses, and harassed Italian workers, and authorities proved incapable of protecting emigrants from physical assaults.[3] Turkey, given twenty-four hours to respond to the ultimatum, immediately indicated its willingness to recognize Italian economic control, but refused to acquiesce to occupation. On September 29, Italy declared war.[4]

Within the first few weeks Italian forces occupied much of Libya's coastline, including the major cities of Tripoli, Homs, Tobruk, and Benghazi, encountering little resistance. Italy announced the annexation of Libyan territories in November. After these initial easy victories, the offensive came to a halt. Conscripts who expected to be greeted as conquering heroes found themselves attacked by a growing Turkish and Arab resistance, fighting for their lives in an inhospitable desert. Italy responded by sending in more troops, implementing new military strategies, including aerial bombings to quell the resistance, but made little headway.

In November, Italy declared sovereignty over Libya. In the spring of 1912 Italy launched an attack on the Turkish straits. By the summer, Italy occupied the Dodecanese islands and opened peace negotiations with Turkey. In October of 1912, under increasing pressure from Austria and Russia, concerned with the disruption of trade and the increased threat of political disorder in the Balkans, Turkey signed the Peace of Lausanne, granting Italy control over Libya. The withdrawal of Turkish authorities from Libya did not end the war. A year after issuing the ultimatum, Italy had secured roughly 10 percent of the country. The local Arab population continued a guerilla war against the colonialists, and the Italian army retaliated with mass executions and public hangings. Only in 1932 did Italy gain full control of the colony.

Although the Italo-Turkish war is usually a footnote in discussions of the Balkan crisis, Italy's invasion destabilized international relations. The war made clear that the nineteenth-century balance of powers had shifted. Great Britain's refusal to come to the aid of Turkey in 1911 marked their willingness to let Germany police the Turkish straits and contain the Russian navy, and to see Italy as a potential ally. Italy's refusal to heed warnings from Vienna and Berlin that the war could create difficulties for its allies in the Balkans revealed the tenuous nature of Italy's membership in the Triple Alliance.

The Libyan war proved equally disruptive at home. What initially appeared as a victory for Giolitti's government damaged Italy's fragile political balance. Instead of mollifying Nationalists, as Giolitti had hoped, the war fueled their outrage. Nationalist critics blamed the government for the military, moral, and financial costs of a badly fought war. By 1913, Nationalists had carved out a small but forceful opposition party. The war discredited the reformist wing of the Socialist Party aligned with Giolitti's government who had supported the war and strengthened the party's revolutionary wing. In 1912, the militant anti-war wing of the party came to power, appointing Benito Mussolini, a young Socialist leader from Romagna, as editor of the party newspaper, *Avanti!* In editorials and rallies, the Socialist Party berated the corrupt politicians and cowardly generals who sent working-class men to die at home and abroad. The growing extremism and competing political voices challenged the liberal political order.

In the elections of 1913, the first after passage of universal manhood suffrage, increasing the electorate from 3 million to 8.5 million men, Catholics, Nationalists, Socialists, and Radicals gained seats, creating a complicated but powerful opposition. During the elections, rumors circulated that Giolitti had struck a secret deal with the Catholic electoral union, stipulating that liberal candidates would agree to oppose divorce, Socialism and support religious education in exchange for votes. Rumors of the agreement infuriated the left. Although Giolitti vehemently denied the existence of such a pact, the 1913 election left liberals dependent on Catholic support, and unable to bring the left into government. The elections made it difficult for Giolitti to use his consummate political skills to forge a coalition centrist government. In March of 1914, Giolitti resigned, replaced by the conservative Antonio Salandra.

Prime Minister Salandra, far more sympathetic to Nationalist dreams and Catholic visions than Giolitti, came to office amid rising social unrest. In early June, three protesters at an anti-militarist rally were shot dead by the police in Ancona. The killing of the young men sparked nationwide protests, and the Socialist Party called for a general strike. Anarchists, radicals, and Republicans joined in a series of violent demonstrations that spread throughout the northern and central regions. Protesters attacked public buildings, burned tax rolls, cut telephone and telegraph lines, and planted liberty trees. In Milan, the Socialist Mussolini called for revolution, urging his followers to take to the streets. Armed peasants roamed the countryside in Romagna and the Marches. As buildings burned, the trade union called off the strike, but it took days and the mobilization over a thousand troops to restore order. Giolitti's dream of "absorbing" the left was left trampled on the streets of Ancona, and Salandra moved to the right. Two years after the Libyan victory, "Red week" attested to political and social polarization.

War and Italian neutrality

Two weeks after the Ancona riots ended, Austrian Archduke Franz Ferdinand left Vienna for a Balkan tour. As the royals paraded through the streets of the Sarejevo, Gavrilo Princip, a member of a Slavic Nationalist movement, stepped out and shot the Archduke and his consort. A month later, on July 28, Austria-Hungary declared war on Serbia. By August 4, all major European powers, with the exception of Italy, had declared war. According to the terms of the Triple Alliance, Italy had no obligation to go to war if its allies declared war. As Britain, France, Germany, and Austria began to mobilize for war, Italy remained neutral.

There were a host of reasons for Italy to opt to remain on the sidelines. Supporting the cause of Austria would reignite social unrest at home, angering both the *irredentisti* and the Socialists. Despite the alliance, Austria remained Italy's historic enemy. Beyond the question of historic enmity, lurked the question of money. After nearly a decade of budget surpluses, state revenues were shrinking, and could not begin to cover the costs of the Libyan campaigns. The recent war had depleted the military. In the summer of 1914, Italy sorely lacked officers, trained infantry, and artillery. Moreover, few statesmen thought it prudent to declare war against Great Britain. Not only did Britain supply most of the country's coal, but their navy could easily threaten the Italian coastline and cut the nation off from its colonies.

Prime Minister Salandra and Foreign Minister San Giuliano knew that neutrality only postponed war. Both recognized that Italy had to enter the war if it hoped to retain its status as a great power and lay claim to the Austrian territories of Trento and Trieste. Furthermore, Salandra, a committed *irrendentista*, believed that Italy had a duty to take advantage of the conflict to complete the Risorgimento. The "sacred egoism" of Italy, as he explained in a speech to the foreign ministry in the fall of 1914, was the sacrosanct duty of all politicians to put Italy's interests first in all negotiations. But, was it more advantageous to side with Britain or Germany? In October of 1914, Sidney Sonnino replaced the ailing San Giuliano as the foreign minister. Sonnino embraced Salandra's foreign policy and met with representatives of the Alliance and the Entente during the winter of 1914–15, without the knowledge of Parliament, the generals, or even, until the very last minute, the king.[5] Early in 1915, it became clear that the Entente offered Italy the better deal. In April, Sonnino accepted their offer and signed the Treaty of London. In exchange for entering the war, the Entente promised Italy Trentino, Isonzo, Trieste, South Tyrol, Istria, and a portion of Dalmatia.

At home, the question of intervention created odd coalitions. Staunch supporters of neutrality included the Socialist Party, the Vatican, and Giolitti. The leaders of the PSI maintained their position of proletarian internationalism and held to the anti-war principles of the Second International. The pope had no interest in supporting a war that could strengthen the liberal state and weaken the Austrian Empire. Giolitti supported the idea of a "conditional neutrality," arguing that Italy could come to an agreement with Germany and Austria to stay out of the war in exchange for land. Supporters of neutrality echoed the opinion of most Italians, who expressed little desire to go to war again. Prefects reported that most residents viewed the war with a combination of fear and dread.[6]

If Italians were generally reluctant to go to war, a minority of ardent Nationalists denounced neutrality and eagerly embraced intervention. Just weeks after the outbreak of war, Prezzolini reiterated his conviction of the regenerative power of war in an article published in *la Voce* entitled *Facciamo la Guerra* ("Let's Go to War"). From Paris, D'Annunzio added his voice to the chorus seeing in an alliance of France and Italy a "Latin resurrection."[7] In speeches and newspaper articles D'Annunzio emphasized the historic, cultural, and racial ties that bound Italy to France. Inspired by Nationalist rhetoric, young men left their university classrooms to march in the streets of Genoa, Milan, and Turin shouting: "Down with Austria." Some radicals and revolutionary Socialists, including Mussolini, rejected party neutrality, seeing the war as a potential catalyst for revolution. After resigning as editor of *Avanti!* Mussolini promoted war and revolution in the pages of *Popolo d'Italia*. Men and women who held fast to Risorgimento Republican dreams urged Italy to declare war against Austria, seeing the conflict as the final war of unification. Only a small minority of interventionists argued that Italy should join forces with Austria. Some Catholics, in defiance of the Vatican, saw a war against the French as a means for spiritual and moral renewal.

The interventionists pointed to the thousands of young men who volunteered to fight in the Entente armies as evidence of the war's regenerative powers. Over 8,000 Italians living in France and Great Britain appeared in recruitment offices in August, and by December, volunteers from the Americas arrived ready to join the Entente armies. Although Italians abroad volunteered for a variety of reasons—patriotism, Republican ideals, irredentist desires, and the pragmatic considerations of migrants living in a country at war—interventionists cloaked the volunteers in the myths of the Risorgimento and celebrated the efforts of Garibaldi's sons and grandsons to form a volunteer brigade of 50,000 men to fight with the Entente against Austria. Over a thousand volunteers set sail from New York City in August 1914 bound for the battlefields of France. At the end of 1914, roughly 5,000 Italians were fighting in the Argonne forest.

By the spring of 1914, two of Garibaldi's grandsons, Bruno and Costante, had died and, along with the hundreds of others dead and wounded, became martyrs for the interventionist cause. Journalists sympathetic to the Nationalists demanded that Italy honor the blood of the fallen heroes, who had died fearlessly attacking German trenches while shouting "Viva Italia" and "Viva Trieste." Despite their French uniforms, journalists reminded readers; they fought and died for Italy.[8] Speaking to crowds of over 25,000 supporters, pro-war speakers invoked the blood of Italian soldiers who had died in the woods of Argonne to free Trieste to heap scorn on the cowardice and corruption on the country's political leaders.[9]

In late April, Salandra secretly signed the Treaty of London committing Italy to join the Entente, and a few weeks later the rumors of the treaty reached the public. Giolitti rallied his supporters and demanded Salandra's resignation in a last-ditch effort to avoid war, and to leverage neutrality to broker a deal with the central powers. Salandra resigned, and the king asked Giolitti to return as prime minister. Giolitti, however, could not form a government. The king recalled Salandra and Giolitti left town. As the parliamentary struggles drew to climax, interventionists ramped up their calls to war and urged the crowds to back Salandra. Italy declared war against Germany and Austria on May 23, 1915.

Italians at war

The war first affected Italians abroad. In the fall of 1914 thousands of emigrants returned home, many forced to flee leaving their businesses and homes behind. Between August and September nearly half a million Italians repatriated from France, Germany, and the Austrian-Hungarian Empire. After Italy formally declared war in 1915, a new wave of refugees arrived from the Austrian borderlands. The returnees strained social services in Milan and Turin. Officials called on religious and secular charities to come to the aid of refugees. Churches and volunteer groups quickly responded, organizing food kitchens and temporary shelters.[10]

As Italians living in Europe and the northern provinces moved south, millions of men made ready to travel north to the frontlines. Infantryman between twenty and twenty-eight years of age, specialized forces, engineers, the *alpinisti* (mountain troops), cavalry, and artillery were the first to be called into service. Over the course of the war, Italy called up five million men, between eighteen and forty-four years of age. Conscripts comprised over 90 percent of the army, roughly 5 percent were commissioned officers, and the rest were volunteers and noncommissioned officers. Although the army had nearly ten months to plan for the inevitable war, they were ill prepared for actual battle.

The army, like the nation, was divided. The vast majority of senior officers came from Lombardy or Piedmont and graduated from elite academies. They had been born into military families, enjoying close relations with the king that stretched back generations. On the eve of war, the loyalty of the officer corps lay with the king, not the nation. By contrast, the majority of junior officers came from the ranks of large landowners and industrialists. The elites bitterly resented the admittance of these junior officers and resisted any attempt to introduce promotion based on merit. Junior officers had little chance of ever moving up through the military ranks. Despite rancor among the officers, the corps stood united in its contempt of the common soldier.[11]

Early on, Luigi Cadorna, the chief of staff of the army, expressed grave reservations on the quality and loyalty of the troops and insisted the officer corps be given broad disciplinary powers. Officers viewed all conscripts with suspicion, but particularly disdained those from the South, who constituted the highest proportion of frontline soldiers. Recruits from the north were more likely categorized as skilled workers and served in the artillery or engineering corps, or evaded the battlefield altogether working in munitions factories. Decades of scientific and legal arguments insisting on the inherent intellectual, physical, and the moral inferiority of southerners left officers convinced of the apathy and cowardice of the recruits. Cadorna was notorious for his insistence that soldiers be subject to harsh disciplinary measures. Cadorna insisted that commanding officers publicly flog or execute any soldier believed to have been lagging during a military offensive as a warning to others. Officers perceived to be too soft on their men were stripped of command. The army reported among the highest rates of court martial for insubordination, usually desertion.

Although Cadorna was wrong in assuming that soldiers were a feckless lot, he was right in his assessment that conscripts had little enthusiasm for war. Most men called to serve responded with resignation, a few resisted. In the southern regions draft evasion ran close to 12 percent. In the Sicilian village of Milocca, residents recounted how two men blinded themselves to avoid service, while others ate cigars to make themselves ill before their military exam. Few viewed evaders as cowards, most applauded their cleverness in avoiding service. Evasion rates declined over the course of the war, as local draft boards enlisted the assistance of the carabinieri to ensure obedience.[12]

As hard as it was to secure bodies, training and supplying the men was even more difficult. Parliament was well aware of the shortages faced by the military. Italy went to war with barely enough munitions, and no ready supply of additional material. The majority of new recruits were untrained, and the army lacked the weapons necessary to train them. In September 1914, War Minister Dino Grandi reluctantly admitted that the army was short at least 250,000 uniforms, and over 30 field artillery regiments lacked artillery. From the beginning of the war, soldiers complained of inadequate food rations, lack of tobacco and wine. Although industry did eventually shift to war production, shortages plagued the military throughout the war.

On the battlefields

Italian troops crossed into the Austrian border in June of 1915, but their advance soon came to a halt. Unlike the gentle rolling plains of Flanders, Italian and Austrian forces met in steep mountainous terrain. The front ran 400 miles from the Swiss border to the Adriatic. The war on the southern front quickly turned into a war of attrition, where battle lines changed little over the next twenty-nine months. Despite the harsh landscape, and the lessons from the western front, Cadorna clung to his faith that continuous direct frontal attacks would secure victory. Cadorna ordered his troops to advance up the treacherous rock of the Carso without any sort of cover toward a reinforced Austrian army. The slow mobilization of troops enabled the Austrians to bring fresh recruits to the frontlines: between May and June the Austrian army stationed along the border had grown from 70,000 to over 200,000 soldiers. Initially, Italian troops outnumbered Austrians by about 4:1; however, Cadorna's disastrous strategy soon took its toll. In the first month of battle Italians lost close to 20,000 men, whereas Austria reported 5,000 killed.[13] Cadorna blamed the failed offensives on the weakness of the officers and cowardice of the troops. Throughout the spring of 1916 the southern front remained quiet. Dismissing rumors that Austria was preparing for a major offensive, Cadorna refused to order defensive fortifications, and was unprepared when the Austrians attacked in May. By the end of the month Austrian troops had crossed into Italy, capturing the town of Asiago. The Austrian drive was only halted when the Russian army opened a new assault on the eastern front. Four days after the defeat, Parliament ousted Salandra. The new Prime Minister Paolo Boselli assumed control of a fragile coalition government, with little support from crown or nation.

By December of 1916, the Italian front had settled into a sort of routine; generals ordered impossible attacks and soldiers died. As waves of soldiers were mowed down by Austrian guns a growing sense of futility spread among the troops. Poor food rations, low pay, snow, ice, and mud in the trenches compounded the horrors of the battlefield. Cadorna believed that morally weak soldiers and officers were to blame for the failed offensives, and intensified disciplinary measures. Regimental commanders were told to form extraordinary tribunes to mete out punishments for treason or desertion. In one notorious case, soldiers in a regiment ordered into successive attacks on Monte Interotto tried to surrender to the Austrians after being trapped in no-man's-land for days without food or water. The Italian commander ordered their fellow soldiers to open fire. The next day eight men in the company, four of whom had been arbitrarily chosen, were summarily shot.[14]

In the fall of 1917, the war took a dramatic turn for the worse. On October 24, 1917, Austrian forces attacked the small market town of Caporetto. Despite advance warning, General Capello had done nothing to bolster Italian defenses near the town. The artillery and gas attacks began at 2:00 a.m., followed by heavy mortar fire. At dawn German and Austrian soldiers advanced through the fog and smoke, and by mid-afternoon they had reached the outskirts of Caporetto. By the end of the first day, the Austrians had taken over 15,000 prisoners. Cadorna believed the Italian army could regroup along the banks of the Tagliamento River, but the speed with which the Austrians advanced, combined with a collapse in communications and command, made it impossible.

In November 1917, Italian forces were in disarray. Caporetto left 12,000 men dead, 30,000 wounded, 300,000 taken prisoner, and nearly 400,000 had disappeared. In addition to the dead and wounded, the army lost half its artillery, over 3,000 machine guns, 300,000 rifles, and thousands of boots and uniforms. With the assistance of British and French soldiers, the German and Austrian advance stopped along the Piave River, 150 kilometers west of the Isonzo.[15] The defeat of Caporetto meant a loss of 14,000 square kilometers and more than 1 million people. Over 250,000 residents of Friuli and Veneto who suddenly found themselves living behind enemy lines joined the retreating army. The road eastward was soon littered with broken vehicles, dead horses, jettisoned furniture, and wounded soldiers. No one wanted to shelter the new refugees. Rationing, instituted in 1917, made local governments reluctant to take on extra mouths to feed. In diaries and letters, these "exiles at home" complained of the difficulty in finding work and housing[16] (Map 7 and Figure 12).

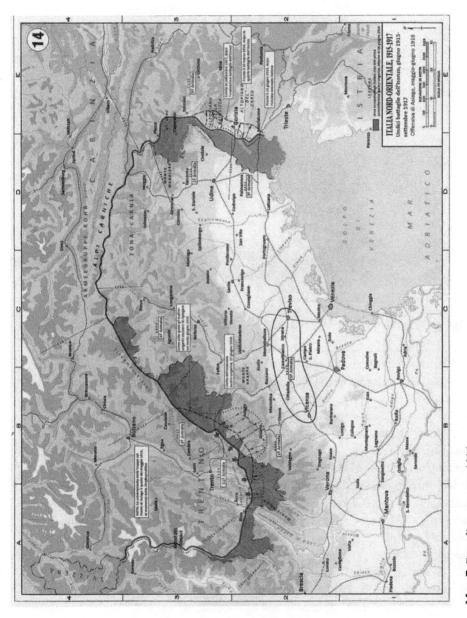

Map 7 Front line, summer 1916.

Figure 12 Italian soldiers in the first line of trenches. Everett Collection Inc/Alamy Stock Photo.

The transformation of a war of liberation into a war of national defense required a wholesale reordering of the civilian and military command. Prime Minister Boselli resigned, replaced by Vittorio Emanuele Orlando. Armando Diaz replaced Cadorna as the chief of staff. Cadorna did not go quietly, insisting that traitors and cowards caused the defeat, not his poor strategy and arrogance; a myth that remained in circulation long after the guns fell silent. Diaz addressed the immediate problem of morale in the military: increasing soldier's pay; improving the quality and quantity of food; upgrading living quarters; increasing annual leave from fifteen to twenty-five days per year. The military streamlined the process for claiming death and disability benefits, linking the amounts to lost wages rather than rank and time in service. The army gave soldiers free life insurance policies and promised land when the war ended. On the frontlines, Diaz opened an office of propaganda, responsible for organizing leisure activities among the troops and publishing trench newspapers. Diaz's implementation of morale building measures did not accompany a relaxation of Cadorna's harsh disciplinary measures, although he urged greater discretion among the officers.[17]

General Diaz also proved more cautious than Cadorna on the battlefield. Diaz spent the summer of 1918 rebuilding the army and improving defensive fortifications. Casualty rates fell dramatically. By autumn, it became increasingly clear that the collapse of the Austrian-Hungarian Empire was only a matter of time. The Germans, facing their own difficulties on the western front, could not spare men or material to reinforce the Austrian army. By August, Prime Minister Orlando, along with British and French commanders, was urging Diaz to attack. Finally, in late October, Diaz ordered an attack on Monte Grappa. Within a week Italian forces reclaimed the town of Vittorio Veneto. By early November troops had taken Trento. On November 4, 1918, Italy and Austria signed an armistice ending the war.

On the home front

Total war transformed the lives of civilians and soldiers alike. Women took on new roles in public and private. In the first months, middle-class women eagerly volunteered for a wide range of charities and aid organizations. Women's associations organized clothing drives for soldier's families, visited wounded soldiers, arranged letter writing campaigns to the soldiers on the frontlines (*madrine dei soldati*). In Milan and Naples, women opened rehabilitation centers for disabled veterans, teaching them braille and new work skills. Middle-class women turned their attention to civilians as well as soldiers, organizing soup kitchens, daycare centers, and aiding refugees. Close to 8,000 women volunteered as Red Cross nurses. Women eagerly participated in war bond drives. In contrast to the war experience of their husbands, elite women often remembered the war as a kind of liberation, an opportunity to prove themselves as worthy citizens in their own right.[18]

The war experiences of working-class and rural women meant more work. As their men marched off to war, women took on the full burden of providing for their families. Wives of shopkeepers ran the shops and dealt creditors and suppliers. Rural women worked the fields, ran their households, and cared for their children. In the factories, women worked long hours for low pay. Working women remembered the war differently than their middle-class counterparts. Women's war work was not a patriotic mission, or an opportunity to take on new public roles, instead, it was a struggle for survival. As one woman from Cuneo recalled, "Yes, we also fought the war, from home. The men were at war, and the women at home fought an even bigger war, a small measured piece of black bread, no sugar, no oil."[19]

The scarcity of food loomed large in the wartime memories of working women, fueling anti-war sentiment and protests. Anger mounted as food shortages forced women to stand in line for hours for a few potatoes or scraps of bread. By the end of 1916, the price of basic foodstuffs had risen by 50 percent. Over the course of the winter of 1916, stories of local elite dining every night on meat and cakes with their husbands and sons at the table, while the poor starved at home and their loved ones died in the trenches, circulated through the working-class neighborhoods. In the summer of 1917 resentment turned to rage. When city authorities announced the closure of a number of bakeries in working-class neighborhoods in response to grain shortages, women took to the streets in protest. In August the demonstrations turned into riots when metalworkers and FIAT workers joined the protesting women, claiming that if they had no food they could not work. Protesters built barricades. Mindful of recent events in Russia, the government sent in troops. By the end of the week, over forty workers lay dead. In the aftermath, the government paid closer attention to civilian food supplies. Rationing did little to quiet rumors of speculation or hoarding. A thriving black-market fueled rumors of state rationing, allocated seven ounces of bread and one ounce of meat per day for war profiteering by the wealthy, increasing distrust and anger at the government.[20]

The Turin bread riot was not an isolated event. Throughout 1917, women took to the streets calling for increased government subsidies. In May, over 4,000 women marched through the streets of Milan, protesting food shortages. By the summer, their demands expanded to include an immediate end to the war and return of their husbands and sons. The "benefits war" coincided with an effort by the Socialists to open negotiations for a peace settlement. In the Po valley, the women refused to harvest the wheat destined for the army. In March 1917, over 9,000 Florentine women working in munitions, cotton, tobacco, and shoe factories went on strike calling for the end of the war. Despite propaganda vilifying deserters, women urged their husbands and sons on leave to stay home and help the family rather than return to the front lines. Prefects complained to their superiors how women protected deserters, provided them with food or work, and kept them hidden from the authorities.[21]

The war shifted the relationship between women and the state, reviving calls for women's suffrage. Women's rights advocates cited their citing wartime contributions as proof; they should be granted equal political and civil rights. Although suffrage failed to pass in 1919, women did come out of the war with more rights. The Sacchi Law of 1919 opened new professions to women and revoking the "marital authorization" stipulation requiring a husband's approval of a woman's financial transactions. The war sparked new forms of political consciousness among working-class women and rural women (Figure 13).

Total war deepened class divisions. From the beginning of the war it was clear that the economy was ill prepared for total war. Adopting the slogan "production at any cost," the state, in concert with industrialists, mobilized industry for war, issuing contracts, setting quotas, and fixing wages. Industry leaders had enormous power in accessing government monies and contracts.[22] The demand for weapons, trucks, cars, boots, and clothing benefited specific sectors of the economy: steel, cement, automotive, chemicals, rubber, textiles. Those companies able to take advantage of wartime opportunities made enormous profits during the war, accelerating the concentration of industrial wealth and power in Turin, Milan, and Genoa. FIAT's capital grew from 25 million to over 125 million during the war. The Ansaldo steel company, profiting from military contracts for the production of artillery and aircraft, also acquired iron mines, hydroelectric plants, and shipping lines. Industrialists took advantage of the war to rationalize work in ways that undermined the status of skilled worker.[23]

Workers gained little during the war. Italy did not suffer from the same labor shortages as other belligerent countries. Wartime bans on emigration increased the available reserve of underemployed male workers, ensuring neither the government nor industry

Figure 13 Some women on fatigue duty, carrying gravel for the construction of the roads, 1916. Gelatin process. Rome, Central Museum of the Risorgimento. Museo Centrale del Risorgimento/ Mondadori Portfolio/Getty Images.

had to make concessions to workers. Although the state did not need to formally draft women into the workforce, the number of women working in agriculture and industry rose during the war, strengthening the size of the workforce. Wartime regulations curtailed labor activism. Emergency legislation forbade workers from quitting a job or taking a new one without permission of regional labor committees. All men employed in war production, and even some women working in munitions, were subject to the military penal code. Absenteeism at work was subject to the same punishments as desertion from the battlefield. Male workers who complained of working conditions could be found guilty of insubordination and sent to the front. Armed soldiers patrolled the factories. Although wages rose during the war, inflation and the rising cost of living left few workers better off. Increased control over labor caused the number of strikes to fall during the war, but did not stop worker resistance. In 1917 over 160,000 workers went on strike.[24]

The war deepened divisions among agricultural workers. While day laborers watched their meager wages shrink, the lives of sharecroppers and renters generally improved. The state fixed rents for the duration of the war, and inflation actually lowered rents and the cost of seed. Sharecroppers, many of whom lived with chronic debt, found themselves making enough to pay off loans and save money. Meanwhile, absentee landowners found their revenues shrinking as rents dried up. Many chose to sell their lands. The possibility of eventually buying land did not seem such an elusive dream.

The exigencies of war accentuated the North/South divide. Conscription pulled nearly half of the active male labor force into the military. The state alleviated the burden on the workforce by excusing some workers from frontline service; industrial workers from the north comprised over 70 percent of those exempted. Factory work was not only marginally safer but also more lucrative. In 1917, an ordinary unskilled worker in industry earned nine lire a day, whereas a soldier made only half a lira. Men from the southern provinces were far more likely to be sent to the front than to work in a factory. Although southerners were numerically underrepresented in the army, the proportional death rate among southerners was higher than the national average. Basilicata reported the highest death rate of over 20 percent. The uneven distribution of military exemptions did not go unnoticed. Southerners bitterly complained that the exemptions ensured that northern workers benefited from higher wartime wages, while southern workers died on the battlefields. The North came out of the war wealthier and with a modern industrial infrastructure; the South emerged more impoverished and grief stricken.[25]

On November 11, 1918, as church bells across Europe rang out peace, Europeans surveyed the dead and damage. Over 450,000 Italian soldiers died in action, from wounds or disease, 947,000 returned from the war wounded, and over half a million were taken prisoner. Over 400,000 civilians died. Peasants had borne the brunt of the war. Over half of the war orphans were children of agricultural workers. The victory had been costly. Mobilization of men, material, and labor cost upward of 140 billion lire: in four years, the government had spent twice what it had between 1861 and 1913. Liberal Italy had won the war, but broke, divided, embittered, and grieving, it would not survive the peace.

The mutilated victory

When Prime Minister Vittorio Orlando and Foreign Minister Sidney Sonnino arrived at the Paris Peace Conference in January 1919, their expectations that the terms of the Treaty of London would be honored were quickly dashed. US President Woodrow Wilson, British prime minister Lloyd George, and French prime minister Clemenceau adopted a condescending attitude toward the Italian delegation, dismissing Italian sacrifices and refusing to honor the terms of earlier treaties. Sonnino and Orlando insisted that Italy receive all territory promised by treaty, plus the Fiume, demanded by Nationalists. France, Britain, and the United States readily granted Italy its border lands, including the culturally German South Tyrol, but refused to cede Dalmatia or Fiume. Wilson was adamant that Dalmatia should remain independent.

The situation came to a head in April, when Wilson circumvented the usual diplomatic channels by publishing his arguments opposing Italian territorial demands in a Paris newspaper. Furious, Orlando, and Sonnino packed their bags and went home. Orlando was greeted as a hero for his refusal to capitulate to the allies. The Italian delegation returned to the table two weeks later, but found little support for their cause. The delegation's humiliation at Versailles strengthened Nationalist calls to annex the lands denied them. In June, Orlando's government fell. Prime Minister Franceso Nitti, an economist by training and a pragmatist by nature, recognized that Italy desperately needed the money and fuel the allies could provide and agreed abandon claims to Dalmatia and Fiume.

In the days leading up to the signing of the treaty, Nationalists organized mass demonstrations, demanding the occupation of the Fiume. Gabriele D'Annunzio brought together a coalition of disaffected veterans, senior generals, Futurists, and members of Mussolini's newly formed *Fasci di combattimento* to plan an invasion of Fiume. As editor of *Il Popolo Italia*, Mussolini used the party's paper to echo D'Annunzio's assessment of the government as cowardly, impotent, and treasonous.[26] Two days after Italy signed the Treaty of Saint Germaine on September 10, 1919, granting Italy Trentino, South Tyrol, and Trieste, D'Annunzio announced he would occupy Fiume. Starting out from Ronchi with 200 men and small fleet of trucks, he made his way south. Along the way, soldiers, veterans, and students joined in. By the time they reached the outskirts of the city, they were some 2,000 strong. The Italian commander ordered to stop D'Annunzio, let the brigade in.

The fifteen-month occupation of the Fiume proved of little political import, but of great symbolic significance. Nitti strategically chose to do nothing. Sending in the army to oust D'Annunzio was out of the question. The seizure of the Fiume was enormously popular among civilians and soldiers alike. His decision to ignore the problem proved effective. The question of Fiume was eventually resolved in 1920 when Giolitti returned to office and negotiated a settlement directly with Yugoslavia, stipulating that Italy would keep Trieste, Istria, and Zara in Dalmatia, along with few scattered islands, and establishing Fiume as a free state. By the end of 1920, Italians had grown weary of D'Annunzio's antics in and most readily accepted the terms of the 1920 Treaty of Rapallo, making Fiume a free state. Only D'Annunzio refused to yield. On Christmas Eve, the army forcibly expelled D'Annunzio and his most ardent supporters from the city. Symbolically, Fiume loomed large. D'Annunzio's defiance of the government and the great powers for nearly two years offered an alternate vision to the decrepit, weak, liberal state. The soldiers of the Fiume stood ready to destroy the old world and sanctify a new one through violence and war. As a mayor and police chief, D'Annunzio performed a new kind of mass politics. In impromptu rallies and speeches, he drew on religious imagery and classical references to draw in the audience, erasing lines between the individual and the collective, equating the sacrifice of one to the martyrdom of a nation. The theatrical displays were taken up by Mussolini and the Fascists.[27]

The peace process eroded what little faith Italians retained in Parliament or democratic institutions. Rather than defending Italian glory, politicians had given the nation a "mutilated victory." The extent of the damage was visible in the results of the first postwar elections held in November 1919. When the votes were counted, the electorate, now including all men over the age of twenty-one, and all veterans regardless of age, had chosen to replace the establishment. Although the Nationalists did not do well, the Fascists won less than 5,000 votes, the Socialists tripled their numbers in Parliament with over 32 percent of the vote and 156 deputies. The Italian People's Party led by the

Sicilian Catholic Priest Don Sturzo won 20 percent of the vote. The government's party, a coalition of democrats, radicals, and liberals, led by Orlando, claimed just 16 percent of the vote.

Biennio Rosso

The return to peace proved difficult for Italy. The dismantlement of wartime economic regulations hit the economy hard. The loss of wartime contracts and a return to a semi-regulated economy meant bankruptcy for some of the largest steel and energy companies. The loss of jobs came as the millions of soldiers returned to the labor force. At the time of the 1919 elections, over two million people were out of work. Meanwhile government debt continued to grow and inflation to rise. By 1920 much of the savings of the middle class had disappeared; the paychecks of civil servants were worth half of what they had been in 1914. The postwar economic crisis combined with political instability proved fertile ground for organizing workers and ushered in the *Biennio Rosso* (The Red Two Years), marked by growing labor militancy and political polarization.

After enduring three years of harsh factory discipline workers came out of the war energized, envisioning a postwar world where workers enjoyed greater freedom and power on the factory floor. Socialist and anarchist leaders returned to the factory floors and began to organize. Millions of workers joined the unions. Worker protests took multiple forms, including factory occupations, riots, demonstrations, and strikes. Worker demands focused on pay, working conditions, and benefits. The government and industrialists responded by passing legislation guaranteeing an eight-hour day, providing old-age pensions, and setting up health and unemployment insurance exchanges.

While reformist Socialists and syndicalists celebrated the victories, revolutionaries campaigned for greater worker control. Many believed that Italy, like Russia, was ready for revolution. In Turin, Antonio Gramsci, a member of the Socialist revolutionary faction of the PSI, organized workers' councils in the factories as models of worker-controlled industry. Gramsci's vision was based on Soviet factory councils. In the spring of 1920 a group of striking metalworkers in the FIAT plant demanded recognition of factory councils in addition to better wages. Hearing rumors that the owners were calling for a lock-out, armed workers took over the factories, organizing collective kitchens and study groups. The occupations spread throughout factories in Milan and Turin.

Giolitti responded to the protests by trying to ignore them, assuming the workers would grow tired and go home. His strategy pleased no one. Attempts to pressure owners into making wage concessions, or to recognize unions left industrialists furious. As the economy drifted into recession the factory occupations ended, but the movement left everyone feeling bad. Factory owners felt betrayed by a government that seemed more sympathetic to workers than owners; workers realized factory occupations would not bring revolution. The occupations divided the Socialist Party. At the Livorno Congress of January 1921 a faction of the Socialist Party, including Antonio Gramsci, ceded from the party to form Italy's first Communist Party, embracing the ideas of Lenin.

In the countryside, agricultural workers occupied the land. Returning soldiers came home expecting to receive the land they had been promised during the war. When the government showed little inclination to fulfill its promise, rural residents claimed uncultivated lands by force. Over the course of 1919 and 1920, nearly 1 million hectares passed into hands of rural workers. In the South, occupations were led by war veterans and Catholic peasant leagues. In the central and northern regions, where demands for lower rents, high wages, and better work contracts overshadowed calls for land, Socialist leagues played a central role in militant actions. In the summer of 1920 over 70 percent of sharecroppers in Emilia participated in strikes and protests. The solidarity between sharecroppers and tenant farmers shocked landowner and organizers alike. Landowners looked on with growing alarm at the spread of rural protests, and the government's apparent acquiescence to their demands. In September of 1919 the government instructed prefects to recognize the right of peasant cooperatives to work occupied lands for at least four years. A year later the minister of agriculture granted permanent rights to the occupiers. Landowners, like factory owners, felt abandoned by the government.

Just days after the 1920 local elections returned significant gains for Socialist candidates, Fascist *squadristi* (action squads) appeared in the cities and towns. In Bologna, they marched through the streets as the Socialist administration took office. By the end of the day at least ten Socialists lay dead. Throughout the fall, the *squadristi* attacked Socialists throughout the Po valley. The *fasci* were local organizations, comprised largely of war veterans and students, led by a commander, or *Ras*. With the assistance of local landowners, the *squadristi* swept through villages disrupting meetings, attacking elected officials, assaulting local labor leaders, and setting fire to Socialist Party headquarters. The police stood by, silently watching. By the spring of 1921, *squadristi* had killed over 200 people and wounded hundreds more. In some areas agricultural cooperatives and unions completely disappeared, and towns in Tuscany and the Po valley became Fascist strongholds. The success of the *squadristi* transformed Benito Mussolini's small Nationalist Party into a political force.

Mussolini was born in 1883 in the small village of Predappio in the province of Romagna. His father, an anarchist blacksmith, and mother, a devout Catholic schoolteacher, instilled in their son a passion for politics and an antipathy toward church. In 1900 he joined the Socialist Party and rose rapidly through the ranks, becoming editor of the party's newspaper, *Avanti!*, at the age of twenty-nine. In 1914, he broke with the party over the war. He founded his own newspaper *Il Popolo d'Italia*, to promote interventionism and the Nationalist cause. Called to the military in 1915, Mussolini served for two years, wounded, he returned home to take up his pen against defeatists and traitors.

On March 23, 1919, Mussolini held the first meeting of the *Fasci di Combattimento* in Milan. One hundred people attended. Early supporters included members of the *arditi* (military shock troops), Nationalists, disgruntled war veterans, and futurists. The party platform included a number of radical demands: the formation of a constituent assembly, the abolition of the Senate, land for peasants, expropriation of church property, and a tax on capital. *Il Popolo d'Italia* publicized the new party's mission, but initially the party attracted few followers. Following the elections in the fall of 1920, membership rose from 1,000 to over 11,000, and by the end of 1921 the party reported over 200,000 members. The first Fascists came from across the political spectrum, including, disillusioned liberals, conservative landowners, factory owners, and even disgruntled peasants, angry at the rigid controls imposed by the leagues. The precipitous growth created difficulties for Mussolini. The *squadristi*, in particular, empowered Mussolini; however, their autonomy and violence threatened his leadership.

Throughout the following year, Mussolini consolidated his power as he expanded the movement. In August of 1921 Mussolini attempted to broker a peace between the Socialists and Fascists in an effort to broaden his appeal. The *Ras* rejected the "pact of pacification," and Mussolini barely managed to hold on to power. In the fall of 1921, Mussolini reorganized the *Partito Nazionale Fascista* (PNF) opening new branches and recruiting new members. By formalizing the structure, Mussolini sought to contain the squads. By May of 1922, party membership had grown to over 300,000, providing a solid base. The new members, like the old, generally came from northern or central regions.

The spring elections of 1922 forced the resignation of Giolitti. Worker occupations and the rise of the *squadristi* had proven too much for Giolitti's fractured coalition government. Over the course of the summer Socialists, Republicans, and anarchists tried to counter Fascist violence, calling for a general strike to protest wage cuts and rising unemployment. The PSI and PCI supported the strike, hoping it would bring an antifascist coalition into power. The strike was a disaster. The workers refused to walk, and Fascist volunteers kept the buses and trains running. The Fascists emerged as the heroes in a war against the Communists. By the fall of 1922, the ascension of the Fascists to government was just a matter of time.

In August 1922, Luigi Facta, a lawyer from Piedmont, became the prime minister. His efforts to build a coalition based on national reconciliation threatened Mussolini. The PNF organized a series of large demonstrations throughout Italy, planning to converge on Rome on October 28, 1922. The prime minister declared martial law, but the king refused to sign the decree. On October 30 Mussolini arrived in Rome, called by the king to form a new government. Mussolini did not seize power. Paramilitary violence supported his political successes, but the terms of his ascension to power were governed by the constitution. Jubilant Fascists celebrated, pouring into the streets singing the Fascist anthem, *Giovinezza*, looting, and rioting.

Although October 30 marked the end of the liberal state, it was not immediately evident. Mussolini initially governed like his predecessors, forming a coalition government, even inviting the CGL to join him. It appeared as if he had adopted a path of reconciliation, tamping down Nationalist extremists and seeking to bring conservatives into the fold. The elections of April 1924 suggested that Mussolini had succeeded in securing his power within the parliamentary system. A month later, however, the murder of Giacomo Matteotti called Mussolini's leadership into question, and proved the death knell of the liberal state.

CHAPTER 10
FASCIST ITALY: CONSENSUS, COERCION, AND OPPOSITION

The year 1924 marked the birth of the Fascist dictatorship under Mussolini, and the end of any attempt to fuse conservatives, Nationalists, and Fascists within a democratic parliamentary system. During celebrations for the third anniversary of the March on Rome, Mussolini defined his vision of the Fascist state: "All in the state, nothing outside the state, nothing against the state."[1] A year later he began the process of transforming his vision into reality, dismantling democratic institutions, merging industry and government, and introducing social reforms designed to undermining religious, class, familial, or regional attachments. Mussolini's attempts to fascistize Italy and Italians were met with limited success. Coercion, violence, propaganda, and material incentives generated enthusiastic support among some, overt resistance among a few, and passive acquiescence among the majority. Fascism ran up against the power of community, kin, and class in its efforts to erase the borders between state and society. The creation of a Fascist state was further undermined by Italians abroad. The vast web of transnational ties that connected communities in Paris, London, Buenos Aires, and New York created new spaces where Fascist totalitarian ambitions vied with antifascist Italian Nationalist visions.

The dictatorship

On the afternoon of June 10, 1924, Deputy Giacomo Matteotti walked along the banks of the Tiber River, heading toward Parliament, when a group of thugs belonging to the Fascist Ceka (secret party policy) wrestled him into the backseat of a waiting car. Matteotti, a member of the Socialist Party, was a vocal leader of the opposition movement, challenging Mussolini's claim that the Fascist state was either normal or respectable. Just a month earlier he had stood outside Parliament denouncing the recent elections as fraudulent and demanding they be annulled. The car sped out of town, and when it stopped some twenty miles outside of Rome, Matteotti was dead. They buried his body in a shallow grave. Within days Dumini and his four accomplices were arrested on charges of kidnapping and murder. Two months later, authorities recovered Matteotti's body.[2]

The killing of Matteotti sparked a governmental crisis. Liberals, Communists, and Socialists blamed Mussolini for the murder and walked out of Parliament in protest. The Aventine secession, a reference to the ancient Roman protest of 493 BCE, aimed to convince the king to restore the rule of law, and force Mussolini to resign. The liberal press joined the secessionists in denouncing the regime. Four cabinet members quit, and opposition leaders called for a popular uprising. Few people heeded the call, and the king remained silent. The failure of the Aventine secession, combined with the lackluster response of the people, enabled Mussolini to consolidate his power among the remaining parliamentarians. While Mussolini refused to confess to any part in the murder, he happily sacrificed Dumini, and brought monarchists and Nationalists into key government positions, in an effort to "normalize" the regime.

Mussolini's conciliatory measures in the wake of the murder infuriated Fascist extremists. When a Fascist deputy was killed on the streets of Rome in September, the discontent among hard-line Fascists turned into open rebellion. On December 31, 10,000 armed *squadristi* rioted in the streets of Florence, their leaders demanding that Mussolini create a true Fascist state. Caught between the conservatives and Fascist extremists, Mussolini chose fascism. On January 3, 1925, in a speech to the Chamber of Deputies, he rejected all accusations that he had ordered Matteotti's murder, denied the existence of the secret police, and insisted that he had always acted in accordance with the law. He declared that as prime minister, he alone accepted "full political and moral and historical responsibility for what happened." In pronouncing these ambiguous words, Mussolini quieted the extremists, and set in motion the dismantlement of democratic processes.

The establishment of the dictatorship came through laws, approved by a rump parliament and the high courts. New censorship laws enabled the government to seize any newspaper deemed seditious. Editors of opposition newspapers were forced out of office, some savagely beaten by the squads, and replaced by loyal Fascists. The Press Law passed in December of 1925 created a registry of approved journalists. Heavily censored versions of the Socialist *Avanti!* and the Communist *l'Unita* continued to appear, but circulation was limited to a few cities, and eventually they were driven underground. Parliament banned secret societies and brought all civil associations directly under state control. Laws expanded the powers of the police and judiciary. The state set up special tribunals to try those accused of political crimes, presided over by military judges, and reinstated the death penalty. Civil court systems remained relatively unchanged. Parliament extended the powers of prime minister, enabling Mussolini to legislate by decree. As head of the government, Mussolini assumed direct control of the ministry of war, the ministry of the navy and the air force. Similar centralizing measures affected local administrations: the *Podestà*, appointed by the state, replaced locally elected mayors. While the laws undermined democratic institutions, the ability of career civil servants to weather the transition and remain in office for the duration limited the state's ability to erase institutional loyalties.

In the first years of the dictatorship, the PNF consolidated its power over the government by expanding the party and silencing the opposition. Party membership rose sharply. In January of 1926, the party agreed to open its membership rolls, and in the first year, the number of card-carrying Fascists rose from 600,000 to nearly a million. Most of the new recruits came from middle classes, clerks, and bureaucrats, who pragmatically recognized the uses of membership for their professional and personal well-being. Between 1927 and 1933, the party only allowed members of youth organizations to enroll. When it reopened in 1933, membership rose from 1.5 million to over 2.5 million by 1939. As Mussolini gained greater control, the party purged the most extreme members from the lists. As the power of the PNF grew, the opposition shrunk. Members of the Aventine secessionist movement returned to Parliament or withdrew from political life. Trade unions sought to reach some sort of accommodation with the regime. Only a few Republican and Radical political associations continued to resist, although with little effect. By the end of 1926 the state banned all opposition parties, closed their journals and withdrew parliamentary immunity from the deputies. By 1928, there were no legal avenues of dissent.

Opposition to fascism went underground or overseas. The Communist Party created an underground resistance network, and continued to print and distribute antifascist literature. The reach of the network was limited by a lack of funds, weapons, and a membership of fewer than 7,000 people. The Comintern provided small subsidies to the PCI, but apart from welcoming exiles, the USSR offered no real support. Despite the constraints, the party laid the groundwork for a more extensive resistance organization. Informally, students, intellectuals, writers, and artists, drawn together by their overlapping political visions, published newspapers, organized reading groups, and undertook antifascist graffiti campaigns in provincial cities and towns. Informal resistance rarely lasted more than a few months. Empowered by their expanded surveillance authority, the police quickly arrested the leaders and suppressed their journals and newspapers.

Diasporic networks facilitated the creation of transnational antifascist networks. For political and geographical reasons France proved the most fertile ground for the resistance. As early as 1923, politicians reached out to the French and Italian emigrants warning them about the dangers Mussolini posed to Italian democracy. The creation of the dictatorship boosted the circulation of antifascist journals and newspapers and made space for exiled Italians to organize. Émigré Republicans joined with radicals, Socialists, and anarchists to form the *Concentrazione Antifascista* (CA). In the summer of 1929, Carlo Rosselli, imprisoned on the Sicilian island of Lipari for helping Mussolini's enemies to escape, broke out of prison, and made his way to Paris. With his brother Nello and colleagues Ernesto Rossi, Emilio Lussu, and Alberto Tarchiani, Carlo founded the noncommunist collective *Giustizia and Liberta* (GL), uniting a coalition of liberal, Socialist, and democratic Italians living abroad. The overseas GL focused on bringing down Mussolini's regime and restoring the liberal state, generating antifascist propaganda and plotting various unsuccessful attempts to assassinate Mussolini. At home, under the leadership of Carlo Levi and Leone Ginzburg, the organization created small resistance cells committed to spreading antifascist propaganda and helping members of the opposition escape.

The formation of a French Popular Front brought more Italian labor migrants into the resistance movement. Although the CA and the PCI continued to focus on resisting fascism at home, they joined the growing broad-based multiethnic movement emerging in France. In 1936, exiled Italians, including Carlo Rossi, organized the volunteer Garibaldi Brigade to fight alongside Spanish Republicans in what they saw as a war against fascism. Broadcasting from Spain in the spring of 1937, Rossi reported the defeat of the Italian Fascist forces at Guadalajara and called for a "Guadalajara on Italian soil."[3] Acutely aware of the growing influence of GL, the police and OVRA (the Fascist secret police force) infiltrated the GL seeking to destroy the movement. In the summer of 1936, OVRA, in collaboration with an extreme right-wing French group, stabbed Carlo and Nello to death in the resort town of Bagnoles-de-l'Orne. The murder of the Rosselli brothers became an international sensation, mobilizing labor migrants to join the movement in ever larger numbers.

Antifascist exiles had a more difficult time in the United States. Fascism had rooted itself within the US emigrant community shortly after the war. The first *fascio* appeared in New York in 1921 attracting Italian war veterans, leading businessmen and local leaders. Radical labor migrants, including Carlo Tresca, warned of the dangers of fascism, and organized the Antifascist Alliance of North America in 1923. The movement grew large enough to attract the attention of the Italian police who maintained dossiers on over 6,000 migrants living in the United States.[4] Yet, despite the growing visibility of antifascism, the vast majority of Italians in the United States proved sympathetic to Mussolini and his anti-communist stance. Italians in the Americas took pride in Mussolini's Italy, where the trains now ran on time, and law and order had been restored. The Catholic Church in the United States trumpeted the glories of Mussolini, urging Italian congregations to recognize the common values linking Fascist Italy and America. Editorial and articles in major Italian American papers praised Mussolini. Influential businessmen used their political connections to persuade the US government to remain neutral when Italy invaded Ethiopia in violation of the League of Nations accord. Both transnational Fascist and antifascist movements strengthened notions of national belonging among migrants in different ways. Fascists drew on arguments of blood and patriotism to bind migrants as colonists within the emigrant empire. The global network of antifascists, tapped into a humanist, Republican, and Risorgimento vision of a democratic Italy to foster a sense of *Italianità*.

The new Fascist state altered the political landscape of Italians at home and abroad. Through violence, fear, and the repression of free speech the regime shattered democratic processes and reconfiguring national and transnational political alliances. Yet, amid the upheaval, much remained the same: Italy under Mussolini was still a monarchy; Parliament survived, although its powers diminished; Key institutions—the courts, the military, and the police—remained. In some ways, the political polarization that accompanied the dictatorship appears as the final death throes of much older struggles that pitted those who imagined a free and democratic Italy and those who envisioned a united Italy as an authoritarian state.

Labor and the corporate state

Mussolini's vision of a totalitarian state depended on a stable economy. The movement had come to power based on its ability to discipline labor. By 1925, the state had destroyed the trade unions, but now faced the more difficult task of winning support of workers and industrialists. Fascist economists sketched out a vision of a "corporatist state," a "third way," between capitalism and communism, where labor and capital worked together to exploit resources for the national good. In practice, the corporatist state proved most beneficial to the wealthy. The implicit violence in the face of any dissent, combined with the expansion of state welfare policies, curbed the power of labor.

Initially the government focused on winning over the support of industrialists, boosting agricultural production and suppressing unions, rather than implementing systemic reforms. In his first years in office Mussolini reduced government spending, eliminated public sector jobs, and lowered taxes. The measures proved a boon to the manufacturing sector. In the countryside, he dismantled postwar land programs dividing the large estates and, in 1925, announced the "battle for grain." Embarking on an ambitious land reclamation program, investing in irrigation systems, roads, and drainage works, the state sought to bring more land into production in an effort to end its dependency on food imports.

The movement toward corporatism began in the fall of 1925. In October Confindustria, the business league signed the Palazzo Vidoni Pact, recognizing the General Confederation of Fascist Syndical Corporations as the sole representative of labor. The pact outlawed all other unions. Business interests were reluctant to sign the agreement fearing a united labor front. Their fears did not materialize. In the spring of April 1926, the minister of justice, Alfredo Rocco passed a more expansive law limiting the power of the unions. The Rocco law on labor contracts confirmed the syndicate's monopoly over labor and ensured compulsory arbitration of disputes by special labor courts, however, that was the extent of worker protections. The law banned strikes, lockouts, and slow-downs. Only the syndicates could represent workers, destroying any possibility of creating a system where employers and workers met as equals to negotiate economic policy.

The new law reassured industrialists that the shift to corporatism posed little threat to their autonomy. The Ministry of Corporations, formed in 1926, initially focused on mediating labor disputes. In 1930, The National Council of Corporations opened, designed to bring owners, workers, and the state together to set wages, settle disputes, allocate labor, and boost the economy. The council mostly existed as propaganda. When Mussolini began to nationalize sectors of the economy, he generally bypassed the council, instead entering into a partnership with owners to set production and wages. Yet, as a marketing tool the concept of corporations was inordinately useful. On paper, Mussolini had solved the vexing issue of class conflict, creating a capitalist system that promised workers equal standing with employers. In reality, the state gifted labor to business.

Limits on labor mobility and a swelling workforce further weakened worker activism. Throughout the 1920s there was a glut of workers, a consequence of heightened immigration restrictions in Europe and the Americas. In 1924 the US Congress passed the Johnson-Reed Act limiting the number of immigrants from any given country to just 2 percent of the number of people from that particular country counted in the 1890 census. This meant 3,600 Italians were allowed into the United States each year. Germany and England also took steps to limit labor migration. France, Argentina, and Brazil continued to welcome Italian laborers, in their efforts to bolster a declining workforce. Emigration dropped from 560,717 men and women in 1920 to 260,878 in 1930.[5] Although Mussolini did not ban emigration, he censored the use of the word "emigrant," requiring that it be substituted with "Italian worker abroad."[6] In the 1920s, roughly one million men and women entered the workforce, even as jobs grew scarce. After 1926, Italians watched wages decline, and jobs growth slow as employers tried to increase production and efficiency through mechanization and rationalization.[7]

Prohibited from taking direct action, syndicates sought other ways of representing workers, and to cushion workers from the worst effects of the depression. Unions ran local labor exchanges and lobbied for a shorter work week. In 1934, they managed to force employers to accept a forty-hour week to combat rising unemployment. A limited work week meant that while many workers saw their weekly wages decline, more remained employed. Unions provided unemployment benefits from monies exacted from workers' wages and employer contributions. Beginning in 1934, the syndicates distributed family allowances in compensation for the forty-hour week limits, as well as bonus and holiday pay.

Beyond limiting labor activism, Fascist economic policies sought to weaken working-class culture. When the syndicates took over the Socialist and Catholic unions, they also took over the recreational and mutual-aid societies. In 1925, all workingmen associations were combined into one network, the *Opera Nazionale Dopolavoro*. The clubs were organized by neighborhood, grouping people by sex and age, rather than political affiliation or occupation. A few of the largest industrial firms set up their own recreational associations, and separate clubs did cater to public employees. The neighborhood clubs had bars, game rooms, libraries, radios; they put on plays and, in the summer, screened outdoor movies. Some of the clubs organized weekend excursions to the mountains or sea.

Corporatism was particularly harmful to women. Even before the passage of the Vidoni Pact, the situation of women in the workforce had deteriorated. The state's response to the glut of workers was to try to reduce the labor pool by sending the urban unemployed back to their birth villages, and to increase restrictions on women's employment. In the Fascist vision of the world, women's work consisted of reproductive labor. Beginning in the late 1920s, the state passed measures to "protect" working mothers, limiting occupations open to women and the hours they could work, justifying the legislation on the grounds that women were physically and psychologically unfit for positions that "involve(d) the exercise of public judicial authority, political rights or power, or the military defense of the state." By the mid-1930s, the state had imposed quotas on the percentage of women in the workforce and prohibited women from working in any business that employed fewer than ten employees.[8] In their efforts to improve working conditions, syndicates lobbied for hiring quotas that favored men. Women had no representation within corporatist organizations or the syndicates. Corporatism incorporated women through auxiliary institutions, such as the *massaie rurali*, unionizing peasant women from all classes. Unlike the male sections, women's associations focused on domestic and familial obligations rather than workplace conditions.

State efforts to exclude women from the workforce accompanied steps to protect working mothers. The 1934 law included stipulations expanding paid maternity leave: every working woman was entitled to a paid four-week maternity leave. Factory workers were eligible for a six-week unpaid leave, and office workers upto three months. The law required factories to provide on-site crèches and space for women to breastfeed their newborns. Working mothers received a bonus for every child, reinforcing the notion that reproduction was work. Despite their efforts to erase women from the official labor force, women continued to work. During the course of the Fascist *ventennio* the percentage of women officially in the labor force declined from 37 percent in 1911 to 31 percent in 1936.[9]

Fascist efforts to control labor shifted internal labor migration circuits. The regime promoted a vision of an idealized rural world, where strong men and fertile women lived deeply attached to family, land, and tradition, as quintessentially Fascist. By contrast, officials depicted cities as decadent, unhealthy, and immoral spaces dangers to the national body. The Fascist idealization of rural life contrasted to a reality where for generations sons and daughters had left their families to find work. In the course of the 1920s, internal migration accelerated as global restrictions made transnational migration more difficult. The state attempted to reconcile its vision of a rural Eden with reality by regulating traditional seasonal migration and urban migration through work and residency permits, and setting up various internal colonization schemes. Massive recruitment campaigns tried to convince peasants to resettle near large land reclamation projects, selling the work as politically, economically, and morally revitalizing. Moving peasants and their families was part of a Fascist vision of creating a world of healthy, loyal, and fertile Italians working the land. One of the largest projects, the Agro Pontine Marsh reclamation works brought over 80,000 workers and their families, mostly from the Veneto region, into the marsh lands south of Rome, although relatively few stayed.[10]

Despite the campaigns to limit mobility, people continued to move. Falling agricultural prices and rural wages encouraged people to seek work in the cities, often following the same circuits that had long linked country and city. Throughout the 1930s, the population of major cities continued to grow: the population of Turin increased by 20 percent, and Milan's grew by 36 percent between 1920 and 1936. The most significant population shift that occurred under fascism was the migration of South Italians to northern cities. Migration under fascism, like past and future circuits, shifted people and wealth northward.

Society and culture in Fascist Italy

Totalitarian efforts to bring all institutions within the purview of the state were grounded in its capacity to remake the Italian people. The ultimate success of the Fascist state lay in its ability to regenerate men and women. Mussolini insisted that fascism would restore natural gender relations, transforming servile, indecisive, undisciplined, and lazy men into hypermasculine, virile, hardworking, men of action.[11] The regime would replace the cosmopolitan, urban, emancipated women (*la donna crisi*) with strong and healthy wives and mothers. Employing multiple strategies, including propaganda, social reforms, urban planning, and cultural programs, the regime sought to reconfigure gender norms by dissolving the boundaries between public and private life.[12]

The totalitarian state had always relied heavily on propaganda, but nowhere was it more crucial to win hearts and minds than in remaking the social body. Political propaganda linking the regime to the Roman Empire, through symbolic and linguistic appropriation—the *fasci, Dux* (Duce)—was instrumental in legitimizing Fascist political rule. The militarization of economic policy—the "battle for grain," the "battle for the lire," the "battle for land," and the "battle for births"—mobilized support for corporatism. Mass media played its most active role in promoting Fascist gender ideals.

The public campaign to forge the new man centered on Mussolini. Beginning in the mid-1920s, an extensive media campaign transformed the politician into a kind of messiah, a charismatic hero with superpowers, the personification of the nation.[13] Newspapers, radio broadcasts, magazines worked assiduously to create an image of Mussolini as someone who never slept, eternally vigilant, selflessly stoic, and capable of making the deaf hear again. Photos of Mussolini on horseback or skiing proved his physical strength, his wife and children testified to his virility, and the rumors of his many and varied sexual adventures attested to his erotic power, and refusal to be tamed by domesticity. The cult of the duce promoted a vision of masculinity anchored in reproduction, where men were defined, but not limited, by marriage and children. The regime insisted on defining masculinity within the bounds of heterosexual conjugal relations, eventually even imposing a tax on bachelors, but not on monogamy. The sexuality of healthy Fascist men could not be contained within marriage. To accommodate men, the regime oversaw a number of state-run brothels. The sexual prowess of the Fascist contrasted with the impotence of the liberal man. The cult of the duce modeled an ideal Fascist man accessible to rich, poor, urban, and rural alike. Mussolini's humble beginnings in Predappio made him an "everyman," while fascism turned him into a real man.[14] (Figure 14).

Fascism did not hold the same mystical powers for women as it did for men. In the Fascist imagination liberalism accounted for the enervated men; whereas, women had only themselves to blame. Women had succumbed to the temptations of modern life and trespassed into the world of men. By facilitating a "return" to domesticity, fascism could revitalize women. Over the next few years the press office sent out reminders to journalists to condemn the modern woman and champion the beauty of the ideal rural peasant woman in articles, stories, and cartoons. In 1931, the press office announced to editors that "the fascist woman must be physically healthy to be able to become the mother of healthy children. . . . Therefore, to be absolutely eliminated are sketches of artificially thin and masculine female figures who represent the type of sterile woman of decadent western civilization."[15] By the 1930s, widespread circulation of images of virile men and fecund women in newspapers, magazines, and movies appeared to testify to the success of fascism in remaking the nation, masking the limitations of the regimen's reforms.

Figure 14 *La Tribuna Illustrata*, 1937. Chronicle/Alamy Stock Photo.

Cinema challenged Fascist gender ideals. The regime came to appreciate the power of film late. Only in 1931 did the state take direct control over the industry, insisting that all films be written by an Italian, produced mainly be Italians and shot on Italian soil. In 1933, the government restricted the importation of foreign films. In 1934, a film division under the *Ministero per la Stampa e la Propaganda*, directed by Mussolini's son-in-law, Galeazzo Ciano, was opened. Three years later construction of the Roman film studio, *Cinecittà*, was completed. The government considered film industry as a critical piece of its propaganda campaigns, yet ultimately failed to control the media. Despite the interference of church and state, films tended to focus on beauty, glamour, wealth, and luxury. The popular "white-telephone" comedies were modeled on Hollywood films, set in middle-class, bourgeoisie homes, with plots revolving around the status symbol of the white telephone. The melodramas in particular subverted the ideal Fascist woman, showcasing independent, rebellious, and sexual women.[16]

The state enlisted the aid of the church in its efforts to win over hearts and minds. Pope Pius XI ascended office in February of 1922. Initially the pope remained wary of the new regime. True, the party and church shared common enemies, the liberal state, and bolshevism, but Mussolini's record of anticlerical vitriol was not easily forgotten. The official Catholic press denounced the party as a danger to the church, and the pope maintained his position as "prisoner of the Vatican." In private, however, Pius XI was willing to consider Mussolini a potential ally in his struggle to balance the demands of intransigent anti-modern factions with those of moderates within the Vatican, and as a means to bring the church back into secular life.[17]

Between 1922 and 1926 relations between church and state grew closer. In December of 1922, the new pope issued his first encyclical, lamenting the removal of religion from the schools and state houses, railing against the immorality of modern women, and mocking the League of Nations. The pontifical themes resonated with those in the speeches of Mussolini. In turn, the prime minister signaled his willingness to reconcile with the Vatican, ordering crucifixes to hang alongside his portrait in government offices and classrooms, and providing government monies to restore church property at home and abroad. After 1924, Mussolini saw the church as a means to normalize the regime. In 1926, the state proposed a reevaluation of the legal relationship between church and state. The pope instructed Francesco Pacelli to establish the first lines of communication between the state and the Vatican since unification. Negotiations lasted two years. In 1929, Mussolini and the pope signed the Lateran Accords, establishing Vatican City as a sovereign territory, reaffirming Rome's position as the spiritual center of the Catholic world, and stipulating compensate the church for the lands and property lost during unification.

The Vatican Concordat was profoundly significant. The pope urged the faithful to support Mussolini's authoritarian state, strengthened the regime's legitimacy by allowing the state to graft its celebrations on to Catholic holidays, and disciplined priests who dared challenge the violence of local Fascist officials. The accord enhanced the Vatican's social and political power within Italy and the world. The relationship between the two leaders was not an easy one. The pope and the duce both considered themselves the unquestioned head of their worlds.

Population concerns stood central to the regime's social projects. In the Ascension Day Speech of May 26, 1927, Mussolini announced the "battle for births," declaring that "the most fundamental, essential element in the political, and therefore economic, and moral influence of the nation lies in its demographic strength."[18] Although presented as means of bolstering the labor force, providing settlers for the colonies, and soldiers for the army, the "battle for births" was also about social regulation. The Ascension Day Speech, announcing the expansion of *Opera nazionale per la maternita' e l'infanzia* (the National Agency for Maternity and Infancy—ONMI), funded by a tax on unmarried men, introduced a series of new laws regulating sex and gender. Among the first measures passed after the announcement was a tax on unmarried men and the outlawing of homosexual acts among men. Fathers who could boast of their many sons and daughter were eligible for expanded government subsidies and jobs. ONMI, founded in 1925, privileged women's roles as mother, offering prenatal and postnatal care for all women, including unmarried mothers. In 1933, in an effort to sanctify state population policies the regime made December 24, *Giornata della Madre e dell'infanzia* (Day of the Mother and Child). There is little evidence that demographic initiatives increased the birth rate or had an impact on a couple's private decision to have more children.[19]

The regime's demographic policies undermined the autonomy of the family. By recruiting women into a variety of party organizations as mothers and housewives, including the *Fasci Femminili, the Giovane Fasciste* and *Sezione Operaie e Lavoranti a Domicilio,* in an effort to exert control over reproduction and maternity, the state politicized domestic roles. By 1939, nearly a quarter of women over the age of fifteen were officially enrolled in the party in some form. The regime also challenged parental authority. In 1926, the party founded the Opera Nazionale Balilla (ONB), to replace Catholic and Socialist youth groups. Children joined the ONB at the age of six and moved up through the ranks as they grew older. Boys engaged in paramilitary training: drills, marching, sports, and camping. Girls learned homemaking skills, first aid, typing, and child care. The ONB operated in close collaboration with the schools, even running kindergartens in some rural districts. Membership was not compulsory until 1939, but parents had to formally request that their sons and daughters be excused, an act that brought the family's loyalty into question (Figure 15).

Schools played a critical role in the regime's efforts to manufacture support. In 1923, the Minister of Public Education Giovanni Gentile introduced a series of reforms

Figure 15 Camp Mussolini, 1935. A crowd of boys seen here climbing up to the entrance of Camp Mussolini at Monte Sacro. Note the tanks attached to the pylon which guards the entrance to the camp. Hulton Archive/Getty Images.

strengthening state controls over schools. The new educational laws required all children to attend school through the age of fourteen and introduced a series of curriculum reforms designed to strengthen individual identification to the nation, and present fascism as the culmination of the Italian spirit. Beginning in kindergarten, lessons emphasized the greatness of Mussolini, militarism, nationalism, and the importance of empire. After the Vatican Concordat of 1929, religious education entered the curricula providing mutually reinforcing lessons on obedience, loyalty, modesty, and morality. The regime tightened controls over school personnel. Any teacher suspect of antifascist sentiment was terminated. In 1929, the state mandated that every primary and secondary teacher swear an oath of loyalty, and four years later limited positions in the schools to party members. A few years later, the restrictions extended to the universities. The molding of minds proved minimally successful; schools could not fully supplant the influence of parents, grandparents, and neighbors. Remembering his childhood in Mussolini's Italy, Gian Franco Romagnoli mused, "As a good and true Italian youth, I had to be loyal to the official line, but my conflicting loyalty to my father and his opinions, no matter how outlandish, was natural and incorruptible."[20]

Efforts to forge a Fascist citizen accompanied the remaking of urban spaces. The demolition of the older, nineteenth-century buildings was tangible evidence of the end of the liberal state. Across the country, architects demolished post offices, town halls, stadiums, and train station, replacing them with rationalist, modern buildings with Fascist symbols embedded in floors and walls. Post offices and train stations were particularly important symbols of state power in private life. In isolated villages, post offices served as institutional proof of the existence of the state. Train stations played an important literal and symbolic role in the making of the nation. On the platforms and in the stations, people from all parts of the nation crossed paths, and the new Fascist facades decorated with winged horses, lions, fasces, and eagles reminded travelers of the strength and power of the regime.

Mussolini concentrated his efforts to legitimize fascism by rebuilding the capital. Urban renewal in Rome focused on linking the modernity of fascism to the glory of the ancient Roman Empire. Mussolini ordered extensive evacuations in the Forum, isolating imperial monuments and surrounding them by broad modern boulevards. In 1931, Mussolini's vision, consolidated in the Master Plan, was to use Rome to prove that fascism had returned Rome to its rightful place as a center of world power. The *Foro Mussolini* is perhaps the best example of Mussolini's architectural hubris. Walking through the main gate, the ground is covered in a mosaic of *Duce, Duce, A Noi*. The EUR remains a testimony to the Master Plan's vision of reclaiming the marshes and linking Rome to the sea. Although the war halted construction, the neighborhood offers some of the best examples of the imagined Fascist city.[21]

The demolitions displaced hundreds of thousands of Romans from the center to the periphery. Some residents secured housing in the new *case popolari*, large apartment buildings divided into hundreds of cramped dark apartments. Others were assigned temporary houses in new residential developments on the edge of the city. These *borgate* generated hostility toward the regime among residents who had lost their family homes and businesses. The regime justified the relocation by arguing that the old neighborhoods were unsanitary and unhealthy, and the new *borgate* were cleaner and lighter. They rarely emphasized that these new neighborhoods also made surveillance easier. The *borgate* and *case popolari* were constructed with only one or two entrances, enabling the police to close off access if necessary.

Despite its best efforts, the ability of fascism to realize its totalitarian vision remained circumscribed. The regime successfully created the appearance of consensus, and convinced millions of men and women of the merits of fascism. Rarely, however, was admiration of the regime unmixed with skepticism and pragmatism. Rival beliefs and ethics did not just wither and disappear. Fascism could not erase individual and collective histories.[22]

The power of place

Regional ties posed a particularly intractable obstacle for the regime. Fascism seemed to sit lightly across the southern provinces and northeastern territories. Residents in the newly acquired lands on the Austrian border, many ethnic Germans, were determined to preserve their culture. Residents continued to speak German at home, and organized clandestine school in attics, barns, and basements. Efforts to isolate and humiliate those who refused to comply with the regime's efforts to erase German heritage in the region deepened antifascist sentiment. In parts of Venezia Giulia, local residents attacked Italian teachers, representatives of the regime, and planted bombs in government buildings. The state responded by redrawing provincial boundaries and implementing relocation schemes to move people in from other regions in an attempt to defuse cultural resistance.

Fascism had difficulty in winning over the hearts and minds of southern Italians. Sicilians initially evinced little enthusiasm for fascism, but as long as the regime effectively left the island to govern itself few protested. In 1925, antifascist sentiment swelled, fueled by anger at new tax policies and the Matteotti crisis. Local politicians and the elite renewed calls for a Sicilian separatist movement. Mussolini responded to the growing resistance by launching a campaign to bring Sicily under state control focusing on the eradication of the mafia. Cesare Mori, the prefect of Palermo, was placed in charge of police operations, and immediately began rounding up residents. Between 1926 and 1928, the police arrested over 11,000 people. In January of 1926, in the midst of a brutally cold winter, Mori surrounded the small town of Gangi, pulling men out of their beds, slaughtering the livestock, and looting homes. Over 150 men were arrested. Fascism's efforts to eradicate the mafia gained international praise, but Mori's tactics failed to break local political and social allegiances. Local power brokers to join the Fascist Party gaining access to state resources they used to maintain control. While some Sicilians donned black shirts out of conviction, most did so out of self-interest. Visible support for Mussolini's law and order campaigns faded quickly in the course of the 1930s.

Fascism, wars, and racism

In October of 1935, Italy invaded Ethiopia. For the most part Italians supported the invasion. The defeat at Adua still stung, lingering as a visible reminder of the failures of the liberal state. Officials saw the war as a chance to prove the military strength of the Fascist state, to carve out an African colony, and resolve the endemic problems of underemployment and land. To achieve his goals, Mussolini needed a quick and decisive victory, mobilizing over 650,000 men against an Ethiopian army half the size. The war was brutal. Mussolini ordered his generals to employ gas attacks on a massive scale and urged commanders to use bacterial warfare if necessary. Within months Italian troops entered the capital of Addis Ababa, forcing the Emperor Haile Selassie to flee.

The Ethiopian war and occupation proved costly. The "gold for the nation" campaign, asking women to donate their wedding rings in exchange for steel bands, did little to offset war debts. Postwar pacification efforts and public works projects added to overall colonial costs. The failure to recruit migrants destroyed dreams of creating a prosperous colony. Ethiopia revealed the violence and brutality at the heart of fascism. In Somalia, the regime opened concentration camps imprisoning over 7,000 Ethiopians who resisted Italian imperial rule. The conditions in the camps were horrific, and almost half of the prisoners died from disease and starvation. Historians have argued that the Ethiopian war was the high point of popular consensus for the regime, and certainly few spoke out against the invasion, but the war eroded support. In the privacy of kitchens and living rooms, some wondered if the war was just an act of aggression and cruelty.[23]

The war left Italy diplomatically isolated and encouraged its friendship with Hitler's Germany. When word of the atrocities leaked out public opinion in the Americas and Europe turned against Mussolini. Publications criticizing the regime by Italian antifascist exiles gained new readers. The League of Nations took sanctions against Italy in 1935, imposing an embargo on imports. European and global alliances drew Mussolini and Hitler closer together. In the fall of 1936, the two dictators announced the Rome-Berlin Axis treaty of friendship. Although Mussolini remained convinced that he stood as the leader of global fascism, the country soon found itself trailing behind Hitler's Germany. When General Franco declared war against the democratically elected government of Spain, Hitler provided support in the form of personnel, aircraft, and armored units. Although unprepared to fight two wars, Mussolini found himself forced to send men and arms. Talk of Italy's military ineptitude resurfaced in the wake of the army's decisive defeat at Guadalajara. To salvage his honor, Mussolini sent more men, material, and money. At home, the deficit continued to grow. The embargo and wars created shortages of most raw materials; as the quality of life grew worse, the grumblings grew louder. After 1936, Italian Fascism increasingly mimicked German National Socialism. Mussolini replaced the handshake with the Roman salute, introduced the *passo romano* (the Italian version of the goose-step), and began to target the Jews.

Italian intellectuals had long embraced European wide assumptions about the inferiority of people of color, but the Ethiopian wars deepened racial assumptions and facilitated the implementation of anti-Semitic laws. Until the wars, Mussolini denied that Jews were a problem for the regime. Jews were deeply assimilated into secular Italy, and many appeared on the list of the first Fascists. Colonial propaganda normalized racial hierarchies, and laws transformed Fascist Italy into a racial state, where race, not *Italianità*, determined national inclusion and citizenship. Racial legislation excised Africans and Jews from the national body. The laws banned marriages between black and white, prohibited Jews from settling in theorists argued that the laws marked the culmination of national regeneration, the final purge of the weak and corrupt. Italy or the colonies, revoked Italian citizenship of Jews if acquired after 1919, banned Jews from employment including government jobs, banking, education, and the practice of law. Jews were forbidden to attend schools, to work as domestics in the houses of non-Jews, or to serve in the military. The law ordered a special census of Jews. In the journal *La Difesa della Razza* (The defense of the Race), Fascist racial theorists argued that the laws marked the culmination of national regeneration, the final purge of the weak and corrupt[24] (Figure 16).

Italian Jews resigned their positions, left schools and universities, and moved into the ghettos. Those who could, left. Over 6,000 Jews emigrated to Palestine, the United States, and Great Britain. The party expelled Jews from social clubs and civic associations. Although most Jews and non-Jews remained silent, a few spoke out, writing letters to the duce protesting the laws. The racial purges eroded support among the regime among students, as they watched their classmates disappear. Mary Teresa Regard recalled

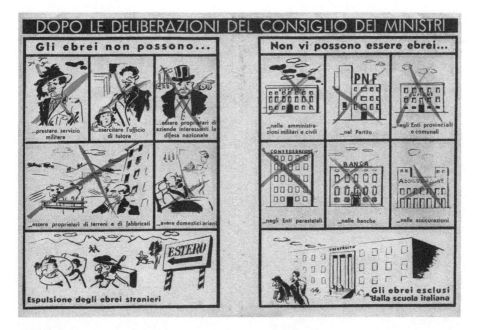

Figure 16 Racial Laws. Explanations of what Jews could not do after the passage of the Racial laws. Published in "La Difesa della Razza," Italy, Rome, November 5, 1938. Fototeca Gilardi/Getty Images.

how "it was then that I became an ardent antifascist. I had so many close friends who were Jewish."[25]

The limits of Mussolini's ability to impose his Fascist vision of regeneration and purification is not an indication that Italians were somehow more resistant to fascism. Over the course of two decades the vast majority of people accommodated themselves to the new regime, and many happily participated in the regime's violence. Rather, the history of fascism reveals the institutional and structural limitations to Mussolini's policies. Family, class, region, and transnational ties created alternate affective, political, and social bonds.

CHAPTER 11
WAR, OCCUPATION, AND RESISTANCE

At 11:00 a.m. on July 19, 1943, Rosario Bentivegna, a second-year medical student, wheeled his bike toward the gates of the *Policlinico Umberto*, near the university. As he climbed on his bike, the air raid sirens began to scream, just like they had every day over the past week. He began to pedal, expecting the pamphlets urging the Italians to surrender to fall from the sky. As he passed through the hospital gates the first bomb fell on the medical clinic, the second destroyed the Department of Chemistry. Rosario returned to the hospital as bombs rained down across the neighborhood:

> Quickly, all those who could be transported were taken to the shelters. . . . Soon the entrance to the hospital, the hallways, paths, every available room, was filled with the wounded, dying and dead. It was the first time I had seen the war. We worked all afternoon and through the night . . . only on the evening of the 20th were we able to return home, tired, heartbroken, desperate. In all my life, I had never seen so much blood and suffering. I pedaled slowly in the summer twilight. A distraught crowd dragged away furniture, clothes, pots and pans, from the ruined houses towards who knows where. I pedaled slowly and cried all the way home.[1]

Six waves of American bombers passed over Rome that morning. In just two hours the allies dropped a thousand pounds of bombs on the neighborhood of San Lorenzo, the cemetery of Campo Verano, the Basilica di San Lorenzo, and the university, leaving 1,500 dead and 6,000 wounded. Despite Mussolini's insistence that not even a swallow could pass through Roman skies, antiaircraft guns remained silent.[2] The next evening, Pope Pio XI held mass amid the ruins. The German and Italian press responded with righteous indignation, pointing to the bombings as evidence of American barbarity and cruelty, but their attempts to rally support fell on deaf ears. Romans who lived in the working-class neighborhood of San Lorenzo reserved their anger for Mussolini. The day after the bomb someone scrawled on the wall along via Casilini *Mejo l'americani su la capoccia che Mussolini tra il cojoni* ("Better the Americans on your head than Mussolini between your balls").[3] A week after the bombings of San Lorenzo, the king accepted Mussolini's resignation.

War proved the undoing of Fascist Italy. As Italy's offensives into Greece and Africa turned into military disasters and the economic costs of war took their toll on daily life, anti-Mussolini sentiment grew. In July of 1943, as allied troops moved across Sicily, Mussolini's war ended, and Italians entered a second, civil war. From September 8, 1943, until May 2, 1945 Italians fought a war to defeat fascism and to reclaim the moral heart of Italy. Members of the resistance saw the struggle as a "second Risorgimento." The second war enabled Italians to see themselves as *brava gente* ("good people"), who stood bravely against fascism, to deny the fact that for nearly twenty years the vast majority had lived complacently with fascism. The civil war generated the founding myths of the Republic shaping postwar political, regional, social, and cultural relations.

Italy at war, 1939–43

Mussolini's descent into war began in 1936, when Hitler compelled him to support Franco's rebellion in Spain. Over the next few years, Mussolini was caught up in Hitler's visions of German territorial expansion. In March of 1938, Hitler's armies crossed into Austria, while Mussolini stood by and watched. Just four years earlier, Mussolini, honoring Italy's agreement to protect Austria's postwar borders, had stopped Hitler's troops from advancing. In a radically reconfigured international political landscape, Italy now stood on the margins. Mussolini tried to navigate through the murky diplomatic waters in an effort to assert Italy's primacy, but to little effect.

In September of 1938, as Hitler moved on Czechoslovakia, the British Prime Minister Neville Chamberlin called on Mussolini to mediate the crisis. Mussolini was widely credited with brokering the Munich Agreement, and seemed to gain some prestige on the international stage. The goodwill Mussolini earned at Munich quickly dissipated as relations between Italy, France, and Great Britain deteriorated the following months. Mussolini tried to assert Italy's independence by announcing the annexation of Albania, shortly after Germany annexed Czechoslovakia in March of 1939, but it was clear that Italy was the weaker power. In May 1939, Italy signed on to the "Pact of Steel," transforming the "Pact of Friendship" into a military commitment to aid Germany in wars of aggression and defense. Although well aware that Italy was not prepared for war, Mussolini agreed to the treaty after German assurances that they would not start a war until 1942. Mussolini grossly underestimated Hitler's ambitions.

In the summer of 1939 Hitler made clear that Italy had no say in Germany's war plans. As German preparations for the invasion of Poland advanced, Mussolini sent his Foreign Minister Galeazzo Ciano to Salzburg to remind Berlin that Italy would not be ready for war for at least another year. Hitler told Ciano that Italy's assistance was not needed. Ciano left the meeting convinced that Italy should abandon the alliance, but Mussolini refused. The Nazi-Soviet pact of nonaggression made war somewhat more palatable for Mussolini. Absent the threat of the USSR, Mussolini saw an opportunity for Italy to advance into the Balkans. On September 1, 1939, German panzer divisions rolled across the Polish border. On September 3 France and Great Britain declared war. Italy remained "non-belligerent."

Throughout the winter months of the "phony war" Italy remained quiet, declaring war only in June of 1940, as Mussolini grew increasingly nervous watching German divisions sweep through Denmark, Norway, Belgium, and Holland. On May 10, German troops crossed into France. It seemed as though Germany would soon win the war, leaving the martial, bellicose regenerated Italy left on the sidelines. If Italy entered the war, perhaps they could sit at the victors table without much sacrifice. On June 10, Mussolini announced that Italy was joining Germany in war in order to secure its empire and its control of the Mediterranean. On June 21 the army crossed over the French border, but their advance soon ground to a halt. The next day, France signed an armistice with Germany and on June 24, signed a truce with Italy. The army had gained little territory, and suffered over 4,000 casualties (the French reported 104). Despite Italy's poor showing, Mussolini tried to claim Nice, Corsica, and French African territories. Hitler advised they wait to divide the spoils until after they had won the war. Mussolini's hope for a quick, lucrative war vanished.[4] Unlike the First World War, this war was not fought on Italy's borders, but in Africa, the Soviet Union, and the Balkans. Multiple front lines in faraway places complicated logistics and put unbearable pressure on the Italian military. The Italian campaigns ended in disaster.

In the fall of 1940, Mussolini ordered the invasion of Greece in an effort to assert his independence and bolster Italy's reputation as a military power; Mussolini rejected Hitler's suggestion that Italy concentrate its war efforts in North Africa, and instead looked for a swift victory in the Balkans. According to military intelligence, the Greek forces, demoralized and divided, could be easily defeated and Mussolini ordered the invasion of Greece. It soon became apparent that victory would not come easy. A wet autumn made roads nearly impassable, slowing the military advance and allowing Greece time to mobilize its forces. Within weeks the Greeks had driven Italian forces back over the Albanian border, and the two armies stretched along a 150-mile frontline were at an impasse. In spring Mussolini brought in reinforcements but could not break through the Greek defenses. In April, Hitler sent in troops from Bulgaria to open a second front and break the stalemate. Two weeks later, Athens fell to the Germans. Over 100,000 soldiers died in the Balkan campaign.

In the midst of the Greek imbroglio, the British overran the Italian African Empire. Early in the war, Italian troops had captured a few British outposts in Sudan, but lacked the fuel to go any further. With the Italians occupied in Greece, the British prepared to advance on Italian African outposts. In November of 1940, the British bombed the port of Taranto, destroying half of the fleet of battleships, and crippling the supply line to Libya. A month later British troops attacked Italian forces in eastern Libya. Over 130,000 Italians were taken prisoner, and nearly 400 tanks. Again, the German army came to Italy's defense. In early February of 1941, British and French forces attacked the East African colonies, and by April the Italians lost control of Eritrea, Somalia, and Ethiopia. Despite the military losses, Mussolini persisted in sending troops to war. In the summer of 1941 he directed an expeditionary force to the Russian front. The three initial divisions arrived at the front in an assortment of requisitioned conveyances, including trucks, horses, and bikes. Only one division had a few light tanks, but nothing that could challenge the strength of the Soviet army. The Italian army in Russia was routed in February of 1943. Nearly half the force was killed in action, thousands more died of frostbite and illness. The remnants of the army were conscripted into the German forces.

Images of long columns of prisoners of war marching in their tattered uniforms made clear to the world just how ill-prepared Italy was to wage war.

Divisions among military commanders and lack of equipment played critical roles in the military defeats. The lack of coordination among senior military command meant that the navy went unprotected by the air force, and civilians had little protection from allied bombers. Shortages of weapons and supplies proved detrimental. When Nazi Germany invaded Poland, Italy had only 1,500 tanks, fewer than 200 fighter jets, 650 bombers, and no long-range bombers. The tanks were light, and the aircraft were slow. The navy was in relatively better shape with 115 submarines. However, they had virtually no aircraft-carriers, planes, or radar. All branches of the military suffered from a lack of fuel, even when they had the equipment. There was little Italy could do to remedy the supply problems; it simply did not have the resources. War had little impact on an economy used to state intervention. Factories had already retooled production in response to increased defense spending in the 1930s. The difficulties lay in the lack of raw materials. The country depended on imports for oil, coal, and ammunitions, and the domestic hydroelectric system could not meet the increased energy demands. Even the most dedicated war manufacturer could do little without oil, iron, or steel. War production remained low in comparison to other countries. The situation worsened by the end of 1942, when the allies began to systemically bomb the northern industrial cities.

Low morale among civilians and soldiers further undermined the war effort. The first defeats were soon followed by a series of bombing raids on the northern industrial cities interrupting wartime production. The first bombs fell in Turin in the summer of 1940. By the end of 1942, allied bombs had destroyed over 25,000 houses in Turin, and over half a million refugees had fled Milan. Food, fuel, clothing, and soap were in short supply. Rationing, instituted in 1941, allotted 1,000 calories a day to each person; however, the legal allotments were difficult to find. The shelves of the government stores sat empty for weeks. Agricultural production fell as laborers were marched off to war, and increasingly farmers chose to sell what they could harvest on the local black markets. Italians could find most staples on the streets if they were able to pay the exorbitant prices. By the spring of 1942, the shortages had sparked bread riots among the women of Venice and Matera. The police in Agrigento wrote to Rome cautioning that the people were on the verge of rebellion. The bread riots turned into labor protests as workers in Turin began walking off the job protesting working conditions and the war.

By the end of 1942, Mussolini was losing his grip on power. Seeking to cast blame on someone for the military defeats and war shortages, he called for the resignation of senior staff and railed at the defeatist attitudes of the people. Few listened. Prefects reported that throughout the provinces and cities people publicly denounced the Germans, Ciano, and Mussolini. Graffiti equating fascism with hunger, and calling for "Death to the Duce" appeared with greater regularity. Mussolini's vaunted rhetorical and journalistic talents failed him. Even the most adapt spin doctor could not find a way to justify this war. It was impossible to cast the war as a struggle for the liberation of an Italian people tyrannized by a foreign power or for the national survival. It was hard to rally the people to fight for the interests of Nazi Germany. Radio broadcasts recounting the brutality and barbarism of the British and Americans made little headway among those listeners who had lived for years in London or New York, or had relatives and friends overseas.[5]

Mussolini was not wrong when he raged at popular defeatism. By the spring of 1943 most people just wanted the war to end. One woman from Turin recalled asking her grandmother what she prayed for every night as she knelt before the picture of Jesus Christ hanging in her bedroom. Her grandmother responded, "I pray for the Russians to win the war . . . because your papa loved the Soviet Union. And then if the Russians win the war, the war will end."[6] The leading Fascist Roberto Farinacci on a trip to Milan at the end of March wrote to Mussolini:

The party is absent and impotent. Now the unimaginable is happening. Everywhere in trams, in the cafes, in the theaters and the movie houses, in the shelters, in trains, people criticize, rail against the regime and denigrate not only the party hierarchy but even the Duce. And the worst thing is that nothing happens. Even the police stay away, as if it was by now a useless job.[7]

Reports filtered back to the British Foreign Office of Sicilians walking around with Union Jack pins hidden under their lapels.

As Fascist power faded, antifascist movements emerged from hiding. In January of 1943 the *Partito d'Azione* ("Party of Action"), a reconstituted version of *Giustizia e Liberta* forced underground after the German occupation of France, began distributing a clandestine newspaper in Italy. The Communist Party newspaper, *L'Unità*, also reappeared in cities and towns. The leadership of the Christian Democratic (DC) Party, including leaders of the former Popular Party, Alcide De Gasperi, and Giovanni Gronchi, created a noncommunist antifascist movement, recruiting from the latent Catholic Action networks. Although the combined effectiveness of these groups was limited, they marked the emergence of a new political alliance between Catholics, Communists, and Socialists.

By the late spring of 1943, the fall of Mussolini was just a matter of time. In May, the Axis surrendered in Africa, and the war on the Russian front was going badly. The allied bombers began to target southern cities. In early June bombing raids on Palermo, Messina, and Catania destroyed the ports and forced residents to evacuate. Meanwhile Mussolini seemed to be losing touch with reality. In February, he fired half of his cabinet, alienating senior party members, and spent most of the spring in the arms of his mistress, Clara Petacci. In Rome, government officials met in quiet corners to discuss the deteriorating situation. Who, or what, could replace Mussolini? Would the war end with the demise of the duce? How would Hitler react? What would the allies do? Nothing was clear. The decision lay in the hands of the king. Vittorio Emanuele III, now in his forty-third year on the throne, was a cautious man who feared a Communist takeover almost as much as he feared Nazi occupation. Reassured by advisers that the army remained loyal to the crown, the king began to contemplate replacing Mussolini with a military government.

On the night of July 9, 1943, Anglo-American forces landed in Sicily, and by the end of the month the government ousted Mussolini. The allied troops crossed the island, meeting virtually no military or civilian resistance. Sicilians were deeply war weary and generally greeted the allies with relief, and at times overt enthusiasm. The allied invasion accompanied the expansion of bombing raids on the major cities. On July 24, less than a week after the bombing of San Lorenzo, the Fascist Grand Council met for the first time since 1939. Dino Grandi, the ex-minister of justice under Mussolini, presented a motion calling on the king to take command of the armed forces, as stipulated in the *Statuto,* and that all other state institution should resume their functions. The wording of the resolution envisioned a Fascist state without Mussolini. After much discussion and debate, lasting until the early hours of the morning, Grandi's motion passed by a vote of 19–8. Even Galeazzo Ciano voted against his father-in-law. The next morning the king fired Mussolini and ordered his arrest. The carabinieri took over the radio stations and occupied the post offices, telephone exchanges, party headquarters, and the Ministry of the Interior. There was no resistance. On the evening of July 25, the king appointed Marshal Badoglio, the disgraced former commander of the armed forces, as prime minister and announced to the people that Mussolini had resigned. Celebrations were muted as Badoglio vowed to continue the war (Map 8).

The king and the prime minister immediately opened talks with the allies to negotiate a surrender. The Allies, preparing for the D-Day invasion, did not have the resources to launch a full-scale invasion of mainland Italy, although they continued to move up the peninsula over the course of the summer. Recognizing the imminent collapse of the Italian army, Hitler sent reinforcements over the Brenner Pass. On September 3, Badoglio and the Allies agreed to the terms of the armistice. Italy would secure all airfields and ports against the Germans and hand over its ships and planes to the Anglo-American forces. The public announcement of the armistice was delayed in order to give the Allies time to reach Rome, but the plan failed. The Germans suspecting that Italy had surrendered immediately took control of the airfields. The armistice was officially announced at 6:00 p.m. on September 8, 1943. The next day, Italians awoke to the news that the war against the Allies was over, and the prime minister and the king had fled to Pescara and Bari, abandoning Rome to the Germans. Neither government nor crown had given instructions to the troops or civilians now living in the German occupied territories.[8]

German troops poured down from the north to occupy as much of the peninsula as they could. On September 12 the Germans staged a daring raid rescuing Mussolini from his mountaintop prison and restored him as the head of a new Fascist state, its capital in the small resort town of Salò, on the banks of Lake Garda. The Fascist faithful made their way to the *Repubblica Sociale Italiana* (Italian Social Republic, RSI), commonly referred to as the Republic of Salò. Some of the soldiers stationed in the north heeded Mussolini's call to continue to fight for Fascist Italy, but many more refused to serve. Italian soldiers abandoned their weapons and uniforms in an effort to avoid being conscripted into the German army and sent to the Russian front, or drafted into the German workforce. Closer to the allied lines, residents and soldiers resisted the German armies. In Rome, residents tried to close off their city, but the Germans quickly overran civilian defenses. Residents in the South were more successful. On September 27 the

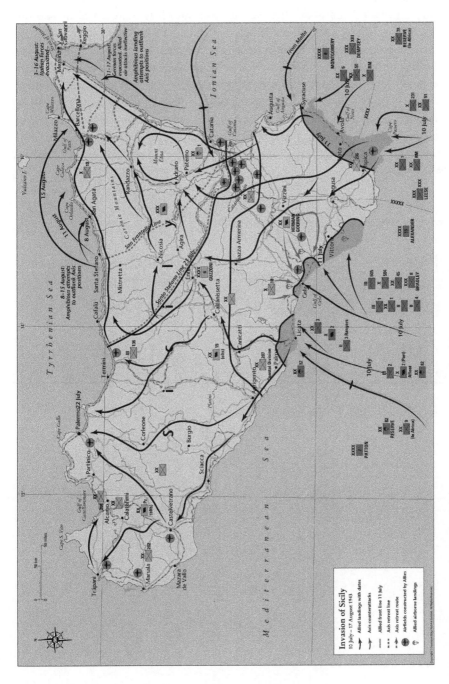

Map 8 Operation Husky invasion, July to August 1943. The Map Archive.

people of Naples drove the German troops out, holding the city until the Allied troops arrived on October 3.

By the fall of 1943, Italy was divided into two: the Allies occupied Sicily and the southern regions under the Allied Military Government (AMGOT); Nazi Germany controlled central and northern Italy. Badoglio's government had official command over Sardinia and four small provinces at the heel of the boot. In reality, the Kingdom of Italy had no power at all. Badoglio tried to renegotiate Italy's position in the war, pleading with the Allies to be allowed to join the war effort. When Churchill refused to allow Italy to switch sides, Badoglio declared war on Hitler as a "co-belligerent." At the end of September, Badoglio signed the full armistice granting the Allies complete control over Italy's economic, military resources, and the right to govern its people, formally ending the Fascist war (Map 9).

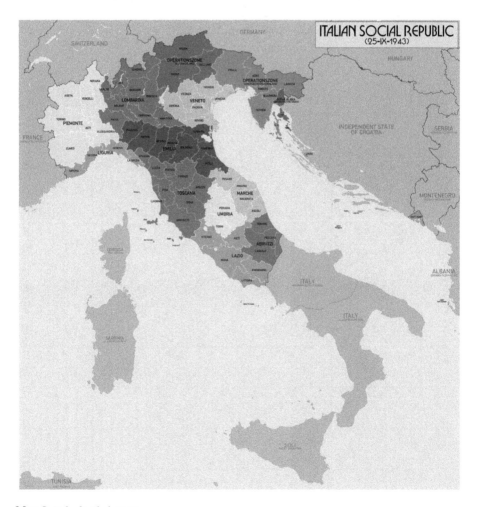

Map 9 Italy divided, 1943.

Allied occupation in the South

From the occupation of the South emerged two of the key issues that would trouble postwar Italy. First, where did political legitimacy lie? The crown? Liberal Republicans? Communists and Socialists? Second, how to reunite a North and South more divided than ever. During the occupation, southern Italians returned to their peacetime lives relatively untouched by the ongoing civil war in the North. Under the Allied occupation local elites returned to power, and the mafia and camorra resurfaced eager to take advantage of available economic and political opportunities. In the eyes of the antifascist coalition it seemed as though occupation had created two distinct Italies: one that embodied the heroism, sacrifice, and moral strength of post-Fascist Italy and a second one mired in corruption and crime with no claim on the nation or loyalty to the state. The very different experiences ensured that postwar Italy would be built on a foundation as fractured as the one that underpinned the liberal state.[9]

Within months after the Allied occupation, it was clear that Italian civic authority was in crisis. The royal government was too deeply implicated in the Fascist dictatorship and too discredited by its flight from Rome in September to wield much authority, while the Italian government faced a crippling struggle between Republicans and monarchists. The liberal, Republican, and Socialists who could legitimize Badoglio's government refused to join the administration, without the abdication of the king. Not surprisingly, the king and his ministers had no interest in wooing the Republicans or abdication. In January of 1944, when the antifascist coalitions met in Bari to hammer out the contours of the postwar state, they agreed to postpone the question of the monarchy until after the war, when an elected constituent assembly could take up the issue, but insisted that regardless of what form the government took, Vittorio Emanuele III had to abdicate. Although the king refused to step down, he agreed to appoint his son Umberto as the lieutenant general of the realm once Rome was liberated.

The political paralysis between monarchists and Republicans was complicated by divisions between Churchill and Roosevelt. Churchill resisted any attempt to topple the monarchy, whereas Roosevelt was much more concerned with securing the votes of Italian Americans in the upcoming election than the fate of the crown. Ultimately Stalin stepped in to break the stalemate, by officially recognizing the legitimacy of Badoglio's government. Stalin's acknowledgment of the Italian government enabled Palmiro Togliatti, the leader of the Italian Communist Party, to return from exile in Moscow to join Badoglio and the king. The *svolta di Salerno* ("the Salerno turn") left many of the party faithful feeling betrayed, but the move brought a minimal degree of political stability. The possibility of the Communist Party gaining institutional influence was too much to bear for liberals and Republicans who quickly agreed to take the ministerial positions with the government. Badolgio's government managed to limp along until June of 1944, when the liberation of Rome shifted the political balance of power. The leaders of the Roman resistance insisted on the resignation of Badoglio, refusing to join in government led by an ex-fascist. The appointment of Ivanoe Bonomi, a leading member of the resistance, ushered in a new government found on the experience of antifascist resistance.

As the antifascists struggled for power on the national level, Allied occupation ensured that local elites and power brokers returned to power across the South. Although the Allies shifted some of the burden of civil administration, the Allied Military Government for Occupied Territories (AMGOT) continued to appoint local prefects, police chiefs, and mayors. Choosing from among those who could claim noncommunist antifascist credentials, the Allies returned mafia bosses to power. Charles Poletti, the head of the Allied government in Sicily, looked on local elites who had championed the separatist cause, even serving time in jail for their political activities, as natural allies, discounting rumors of mafia affiliations. There is no evidence that the United States deliberately reintroduced the mafia, but they certainly facilitated its revival. Poletti, like the Italian government, dismissed the notion of the mafia as an organized society as nothing more than an unfortunate anti-Sicilian stereotype. Like previous governments, the refusal to admit to the existence of the mafia enabled it to flourish. To the extent that authorities recognized mafia power in the ports and markets, the Allies thought they could use it to suppress black-market activities. The combination of AMGOT's naiveté and arrogance enabled the mafia to secure political and economic power in the postwar world.

By 1944, the mafia and camorra had formed a close alliance with the Allied government. AMGOT officials hired Vito Genovese, who had been deported from America in the 1930s for mafia activities, as an official interpreter. Commanders praised him for his willingness to report on black-market activities. Genovese's access to the Allied government ensured that he was able to shut down rival operations, and access valuable information and goods that could be sold or traded. Norman Lewis, a British Intelligence officer posted to the Field Security Service in Naples in 1944 and attached to the American 5th Army, bore witness to the new relationship between mafia and the Allies. Writing in his diary in the spring of 1944, he estimated that roughly a third of allied supplies and equipment disappeared from the bases into the black market. Walking through the market of Via Forcella, he described how the Allied goods were on "blatant display, tastefully arranged with colored ribbon. . . . Tailors all over Naples are taking uniforms to pieces, dying the material and turning them into smart new outfits for civilian wear."[10] The reemergence of organized crime, clientelism, and banditry in the South horrified northern Italians, reinforcing their prejudices and stereotypes.

During the course of 1944, as the Allies worked to establish civilian rule in the occupied territories, the front lines running through central Italy did not move. Allied armies struggled to break through the defensive Gustav line the Germans erected to halt the allied advance. In January of 1944, the Anglo-Australian forces fought a bitter battle in Monte Casino, lasting months. The Americans tried to break through on the beaches of Anzio, South of Rome. Only in late May did the allies finally begin to advance, reaching Rome on June 4, 1944. The complete liberation of Italy would take another year. The slow movement up the peninsula had profound consequences for Italian Jews and the partisan movement.

Italian Shoah

German occupation brought Hitler's genocidal program to Italy. Attacks on Jewish Italians began much earlier but took on horrific dimensions in 1943. In 1922, Italian Jews were well integrated in the liberal state, serving in Parliament, the military, and the civil service. Sidney Sonnino, the son of a Tuscan Jewish landholder, served as minister of finance, foreign minister, and prime minister. Italian Jews had served in the military at all ranks, and in 1907, Ernesto Nathan was elected the mayor of Rome. Although Catholic anti-Semitism ran deep throughout Italian culture, the anticlericalism of the Risorgimento had carved out space for Jews in the liberal state. When Mussolini came to power, generations of Italian Jews and Catholics had grown up together, sitting side by side in public schools, and joining the same youth groups. Mixed marriages between Jews and Catholics were not uncommon. Assimilation, however, did not erase anti-Semitism.

Until the mid-1930s, the Jewish communities expressed little outward concern with the regime. Many embraced Mussolini's promises of moral and military regeneration. Jews from Turin, Bologna, and Milan were among the first to join the party in 1919, attracted by Mussolini's anti-union, anticlerical rhetoric. Jewish Fascists were generally solidly middle-class conservatives, who felt threatened by the specter of communism. Those who opposed the regime went into exile or joined the antifascist movements.

Over the course of the dictatorship, as racial ideologies gained traction, the state made a concerted effort to identify, isolate, and marginalize Jews. The party began to whittle down the number of Jews in public office, limiting the responsibilities of those who remained. Jewish military officials were barred from high-level meetings in Germany. The governor of Libya, Italo Balbo, issued a decree requiring all Jewish shops to remain open on Saturdays. Political efforts to isolate Jews accompanied a widespread propaganda campaign. Anti-Semitic works, including Paolo Orano's *Gli ebrei in Italia*, argued that all who identified with Judaism were enemies of the state. In 1938, the promulgation of the racial laws institutionalized Italian anti-Semitism. The laws forbade Jews from attending public schools, engaging in certain occupations or professions, or joining leisure clubs. The laws segregated Jews from their neighbors.[11] Over the next two years the state refined its racial hierarchy, barring foreign Jews from acquiring citizenship or entering the country, and excluding all Jews from the military. By 1939, Italian Jews had been cut out of the nation.[12]

Mussolini envisioned a general expulsion of Jews. After 1939, Mussolini encouraged Jews to emigrate making passports readily available to those who had the means to leave: over 6,000 Jews emigrated, about 13 percent of the Jewish population.[13] The war intensified government controls on Jews. In the spring of 1940, Mussolini ordered the arrest and interment of all non-Italian Jews, refugees from Nazi occupied Europe. Approximately 9,000 Jews were held in camps in the southern provinces. As a consequence of war and emigration, the size of the Italian Jewish population fell from 45,000 to 33,000 between 1938 and 1943.[14] By 1942, news of the Nazi death camps filtered into Italy, and Germany increased pressure on Mussolini to begin to deport Jews. Italian authorities often resisted

German demands, perhaps, more out of irritation with German arrogance than of concern for the Jews.

When Mussolini fell in September of 1943 the situation of Jews drastically changed In the South, Allied occupation meant liberation for the roughly 300 Italian Jews, and 22,000 foreign Jews in the cities and the internment camps.[15] In the German occupied zone, persecution intensified. On September 9, German troops arrested Jews in Bolzano and Merano. Across the North, community leaders and Rabbis warned Jews to leave or go into hiding. Those who lived close to the southern border of German occupied Italy sought safety in Allied territory. Along the northern border, people crossed over into to Switzerland. The elderly, children, and infirm hiked across the Alpine passes, paying guides close to 5,000 lire a person. The avenues of escape were soon closed off. Many of those who stayed did so because they did not have the means to leave, others decided that they would be safer at home then in exile.

The deportation of Italian Jews began in earnest in the fall of 1943. On October 16 residents of the Roman ghetto were awoken at 5:30 a.m. to the sound of gunfire and SS troops pounding at their doors. The guards ordered everyone into the streets. A few escaped over the roof troops, others barricaded themselves in the apartments and hid until the Nazi's left. Those arrested were given a few minutes to pack food and clothing. The Germans herded the Italians into the piazza behind the synagogue and loaded them on to trucks. After clearing the ghetto, the SS moved out into nearby neighborhoods. By the end of the day they had arrested over 1,200 Romans. During their nine-month occupation of Rome, the Germans deported over 1,700 Jews. Throughout the fall, the SS troops also moved through the cities and towns, rounding up those who appeared on synagogue membership lists or on the lists provided by the local police. The Jews were sent to transit camps then on to the Auschwitz, Buchenwald, and Dachau. According to camp records, on October 23, 1943, 800 Jews arriving from Rome were sent to the gas chambers; 47 women and 149 men were sent to the work camps. Only fifteen of the Roman Jews survived (Map 10).

After the October deportations, the Jews who avoided capture went into hiding and arrest rates fell. Within a few months, the number of Jews handed over to the Nazi's began to rise as more people joined the hunt. On November 30, 1943, the RSI Minister of the Interior Guido Buffarini ordered the police to arrest all Jews and send them to the internment camps. A few days later, the police raided Jewish old-age homes, schools, and hospitals. Over the course of the winter the number of Jews deported rose. In Rome, 49 Jews were arrested in November and December of 1943, while 150 were sent to camps in February of 1944, and over 160 in March. Responding to increased pressure from the Nazi authorities, Italian police made the arrests of Jews a priority, offering rewards and recruiting informers. Employers, housewives, shopkeepers, ex-servants, friends, and even relatives collaborated. Militant Fascists organized bands to find Jews and members of the resistance, raiding private homes, convents, and monasteries. The most infamous was the brutal *banda Koch*. With the backing of the German authorities and the Italian police, Pietro Koch was given free rein to capture and torture prisoners.

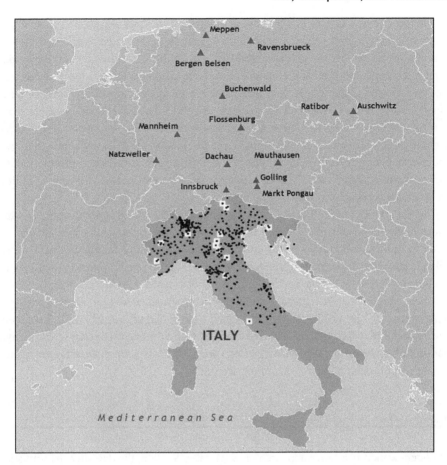

Map 10 Places of arrest and internment camps. Black dots show places of arrest. White squares symbolize internment camps, and the destination camps are marked by triangles. Alberto Giordano/Anna Holian.

Historians estimate that over 85 percent of Italian Jews survived the Holocaust. Their survival was a consequence of a combination of their personal decisions, luck and circumstance. Most of those who survived chose to go into hiding. Jews from the cities sought safety in rural inns or country homes of non-Jewish friends. Small rural towns, with their close-knit communities, posed particular dangers to easily identifiable strangers. The swelling numbers of refugees provided some cover for the Jews. Carlo Milan, a Roman Jew, managed to get papers identifying him as Neapolitan war refugee, enabling him to move his family into an apartment in a neighborhood far from where the family previously lived. Large cities provided an anonymity that rural towns could not.

Critical to the survival of Italian Jews were non-Jewish Italians. Although the papal response to the Holocaust was equivocal at best, priests, nuns, and monks opened the doors of their convents and monasteries. Local village priests warned families hiding in villages of approaching Fascist patrols. The Capuchin Monastery in Rome became the clandestine headquarters of the Jewish emigrant assistance league, *Delegazione per l'assistenza agli emigranti ebrei*, or DELASEM, providing money and shelter to fugitives. Catholic orphanages took in Jewish children, providing false documentation. Stories of civil servants, and even some members of the local police force, offer protection to the Jews abound. Doctors hid Jews and partisans on special wards, marked as highly contagious. Survivors also remembered the teachers, shoemakers, storekeepers, who took in fugitives. Luck and circumstance were as important as social networks in surviving the occupation. Those who stayed in Rome or made their way to the city lived under occupation for only nine months. Those who sought shelter in the mountains around Turin endured German occupation for twenty months, forced to stay in hiding for nearly twice as long.[16]

The experiences of Jews under occupation bear witness to the peculiarities of Italy under German occupation. Despite the presence of informers and other dangers of living in hiding, Italian Jews were better able to evade capture than Jews in France or Poland. Hostility to German occupation drove people to plead ignorance, bankers to forget to list Jewish accounts, and innkeepers to fail to register guests. Local and regional loyalties often outweighed official or military directives, encouraging many to refuse to collaborate. The timing of the Italian Holocaust also limited the number of Jews arrested. The persecution of Italian Jews occurred as the Nazi regime began to collapse and as civil war broke out across the German occupied zone in Italy. The presence of the resistance made the protection of Jews an act of patriotism.

Resistance and civil war

The open, armed resistance appeared on September 9, 1943, the day after the armistice was announced. Over the next few months thousands of men joined the resistance groups, seeking to escape military conscription or the labor draft. Although only slightly more than 200,000 Italians are officially recognized as resistance fights, the number is most likely much higher. The men and women of the resistance represented a wide cross section of society: factory workers and artisans comprised approximately 40 percent of the members of the resistance; peasants and rural workers accounted for 20 percent; professionals, students, and intellectuals made up roughly 25 percent. The number of recognized partisan soldiers fails to include the many men and women who provided food, cover, and support for the resistance.[17]

Women played a critical role in the resistance. By the end of the war over 35,000 women were recognized as partisans. Most were young and, unlike their brothers, were not compelled to join by the threat of military conscription or forced labor. Housewives, students, factory workers, clerks, and civil service workers volunteered to fight. GL member Ada Goberti elegantly described the variety of ways, both domestic and militant, women resisted Nazi occupation, acting as nurses, couriers, recruiters, soldiers, and cooks. With greater freedom of movement, they carried underground newspapers, military orders, weapons, and ammunition in the baskets of their bicycles.

In Milan, the Communist affiliated *Gruppi di difesa della donna e per l'assistenza ai combattenti per la liberta'* (GDD, or Women's Groups for Defense and for the Assistance of Freedom Fighters) organized in 1943, provided food, shelter and raised money for the partisans. Initially the partisans resisted incorporating women into combat roles, but the determination of women, and the exigencies of guerilla war, eroded their prejudices. Women took up arms. Carla Capponi and Marisa Muso, leading members of the Rome *Gruppi Azione Patriottica* (GAP), were involved in bombings and assassinations. While women's auxiliary roles have been celebrated, their combat roles have been erased, deemed incompatible with the postwar gendered visions of women as mothers and wives.

Women's experiences as soldiers and leaders were personally and politically transformative. Equating the political struggle for liberation with women's liberation meant that partisan women claimed a political voice in the postwar world, stepping into local and national government positions[18] (Figure 17).

By the end of 1944 hundreds of small partisan bands moved through the occupied territory. Some bands were affiliated with political parties. The Communist Garibaldi brigades and GAP, accounted for close to 60 percent of the partisans, with over 50,000 members. Many rank-and-file members saw the resistance as the beginning of a social revolution, a dream deferred by the cautious Togliatti, the head of the party. The Party of Action constituted the second largest resistance group, with nearly 28,000 members in the "GL." The leaders of the party envisioned their mission as a new Risorgimento, a movement that would purge Italy of fascism and give birth to an authentic democracy. The DC Party also organized resistance groups, drawing on the remnants of the Catholic

Figure 17 Members of the Italian Resistance, November 1944. Keystone/Getty Images.

Action. The "Green Flame" bands attracted Catholic youth and priests, and provincial clerics. Convents, monasteries, hospitals, and orphanages provided shelter and food, and hid weapons and ammunition.

Geography determined membership in partisan groups more often than ideology. Men and women generally joined the nearest brigades, regardless of their political orientation. The regional multiparty *Comitato di Liberazione Nazionale* (Committee of National Liberation, CLN) coordinated military and political action. In the liberated zones, the CLN stepped in as the civil authority, establishing judicial proceedings and providing social services. The leaders of the CLN, including Ivanoe Bonomi, Giorgio Amendola, Alcide De Gasperi, Ugo La Malfa, and Pietro Nenni, represented a range of political visions. In January of 1944, resistance leaders formed the *Comitato di Liberazione Nazionale Alta Italia* (Committee of National Liberation for Upper Italy [CLNAI]) to coordinate the CLNs and the independent partisan groups. The CLNAI challenged the power of Badoglio's government and forced the Allies to recognize the committee as the representative body of the resistance, and by extension, of Italy. The Allies granted the CLNAI provisionary governmental powers. Within the CLNAI the antifascist powers learned to collaborate in fighting the war against the Germans, and in envisioning a postwar future.

Partisan activities varied depending on gender and location. In the countryside and cities partisan men sabotaged German communications and transportation systems, raided military stores, and carried out assassinations of Fascist and German officials alike. In smaller provincial towns, partisans targeted local Fascist supporters and informers, and escorted fugitives to safety. In the cities, partisans urged factory workers to go on strike or sabotage production. The Germans responded with a vengeance, deporting workers to the German camps. Despite the risks, men and women continued to join the resistance. In April of 1945, the CLNAI called for a general insurrection, and partisans took control of northern cities well before the Allied armies arrived. On April 27, the 52nd Garibaldi Brigade stopped a convoy of trucks and cars. They allowed the Germans to retreat but arrested the Italians. Among those who huddled by the side of the road stood Mussolini and his mistress Clara Petacci. The next day Mussolini and Clara were taken out and shot, the other Fascist leaders appeared before a hastily called military tribunal and then executed. On April 29, the bodies of Mussolini and Pettaci were strung upside down outside of a gas station in Milan; the rest of the bodies were dumped on the ground. Crowds gathered round, kicking, spitting, and beating the dead. The following morning, American military authorities ordered Mussolini's body be buried in an unmarked grave.

German's responded to partisan successes with violence. In the spring of 1944, Carla Capponi, Rosario Bentivegana, Giulio Cortini, and Laura Garroni led an attack on an SS police regiment on via Rasella in Rome. On the morning of March 23, they planted twelve kilograms of dynamite in a trash barrel midway up the street. The bomb killed thirty-two Germans. Nazi reprisal was swift and furious. Two days later the Germans published an announcement in the Roman newspapers denouncing the attack on via Rasella and proclaimed that "for every German killed 10 communists . . . would be killed. The order has already been executed." The day before, the head of the SS in Rome Herbert Kappler and the Chief of Police Caruso plucked 335 men from jails, detention centers, and the streets, and trucked them out to caves along the via Ardeatine. Each group of men were summarily executed, their bodies piled on top of each other, the wounded buried under the dead. That evening Kappler ordered the opening of the cave be dynamited, burying the dead behind a wall of stone. When the Allies marched in two months later, the cave was opened, and the dead identified. The bodies buried in the caves of Ardeatine were a small fraction of all those killed by Germans and Fascists. Historians estimate that over 45,000 partisans were killed between 1943 and 1945.

The Ardeatine massacre makes visible the tensions that swirled around the resistance. In the wake of the massacre, the Vatican published an editorial blasting the partisans, the "guilty who fled," and claiming the Communists let 335 innocents take their place.[19] The Vatican editorial gave life to a rumor running through the streets of Rome that had the partisans turned themselves in; the German's would not have carried out the mass execution. The editorial was just one of the many attempts by noncommunist factions to undermine the moral authority of the Communists in the civil war against the Fascists. The persistent rumors around the Fosse Ardeatine massacre bolstered the notion that the war of the resistance was a patriotic war of liberation, and not a war pitting Italians against Italians, and workers against capitalists. Yet, for many partisans, the war was all those things.

CHAPTER 12
RECONSTRUCTION (1943–48)

Midway through Roberto Rosellini's film *Roma Città Aperta* (Rome Open City) Pina, a widowed mother living in a working-class neighborhood of Rome, sits on the staircase outside her apartment with her fiancé, Francesco, on the eve of their wedding. She recounts how they first met just two years ago, when the war had just begun. Francesco, quietly smiles, "We thought it would end soon, and we would only see it in newsreels." Pina quietly asks, "When will it end? There are moments I cannot go on. This winter seems like it will never end." Seeking to encourage her, Francesco responds:

> It will end, it will end, and spring will come, and it will be more beautiful than ever, because we will be free. . . . We are fighting for something that will come, that cannot fail to come. Maybe the road will be long and difficult, but we will arrive, and we will see a better world, and above all our children . . . will see a better world. This is why you must not be afraid Pina, no matter what happens.

The scene is pivotal, telling a story of how hunger, fear, and exhaustion transform the exigencies of daily life under German occupation into quiet acts of resistance. Pina, Don Pietro, and the neighborhood children testify to the organic antifascism of the average Italian.

When *Roma Città Aperta* opened in Rome in September of 1945, an American critic commented that "if I had known nothing else about it, I could have understood from the audience's reaction 'Open City' was truth." Some walked out, unable to bear to see "their own memories laid open before their eyes." Less than a year had passed since those in the audience had lived under occupation. Only one girl asked: "Why should they show it here? We want to forget?"[1] Forgetting, however, was not an option for Italians faced with the political and social uncertainties of the postwar world. Rossellini's celluloid depiction of life under occupation offered the possibility of a redemptive remembering. The story of Pina and Francesco provided a new ethical and moral foundation for Italy's postwar future that included the partisans, women, and priests who had sacrificed their lives for a new and better Italy. Italian Fascists faded away under the weight of German cruelty and perversion. As in the film, those who collaborated with the Germans were not inherently evil, but weak and cowardly, to be pitied not scorned. Postwar Italy honored the courage, dignity, and compassion of the dead, and nurtured the notion of Italians as *brava gente* ("good people"), innocent victims who did their best to protect each other in the face of Nazi atrocities.[2]

The mythology visible in "*Città Aperta*" shaped the immediate postwar political and social reconstruction. Many hoped the ideals of the resistance could heal the political and regional divisions fostered by fascism and war, and reconstitute a secure economic and social foundation based on equality and liberty. The government designated April 25, the day people drove the Germans out of the northern cities, as the official holiday celebrating the end of the war. Yet, quickly the limits of building a new Italy on the ideals of the resistance became clear. The vision of a pluralistic body politic forged under German occupation fractured under the weight of a global Cold War, a reinvigorated church, and the unresolved tensions inherited from the liberal state. In certain respects, the Italy formed in 1946 looked similar to earlier versions, riddled with a deep-seated fear of democracy and social conflict, split by the same geographic and social divisions. Fears of the revolution and social unrest ensured the inclusion of safeguards into the new constitution. The antifascist mythology, like the foundational myths of the Risorgimento, marginalized the experience of southern Italians. Gender distinctions continued to define citizenship rights and notions of national belonging. Yet, two world wars and fascism had substantially altered the political and social landscape, and forged a more unified and democratic Italy.

Making the republic

On May 2, 1945, the war ended. Nearly five years of war and occupation had taken a toll. From the beginning the war spilled out from the battlefields, sweeping through villages and cities. In nearly every city, government offices, public services, libraries, archives, and public monuments lay in ruin. Every household had been touched by loss. Journalists estimated that there were over 50,000 homeless in Genova in January of 1946. In Rome, the city government estimated that on average there were 1.75 people living in each available room. In Naples, war and allied occupation worsened prewar housing shortages, leaving half the population living in overcrowded conditions. The Allies requisitioned a sizable portion of the housing left habitable for their own use, or to shelter refugees and evacuees. Outside of the cities refugee camps for Italians and foreigners alike lacked running water, electricity, windows, or toilets.[3] The hardships of daily life were made worse by the difficulty in finding work. If one was lucky enough to have a job, transportation posed its own set of problems. The lack of electricity and fuel limited trams, buses, and private vehicles, leaving people to get around on scooters, bicycle, or foot. Despite the troubles, peace brought some semblance of normalcy. People flocked to the theaters, concerts, dance halls, and sporting events, seeking to put the war behind them. Seeing people in restaurants, or strolling through the streets, gave a sense that "something had started, even if its wheels were still squeaky . . . the old automobile of a city began to move."[4]

The renewed spirit of optimism visible in the cities and towns did not erase feelings of acrimony and bitterness. In the immediate aftermath of liberation, the CLNAI set up special tribunals and purge committees, ordering the execution or imprisonment of thousands of politicians, doctors, businessmen, lawyers, and civil servants implicated in the Fascist regime. Even after the resistance ceded authority to the Allies, local attacks on Fascists continued.[5] Over 10,000 people, former Fascists or accused collaborators, were killed in the two months following the end of the war. Even as the first waves of vengeance receded, the bitterness remained. Moral distinctions were difficult to make in a world where nearly everyone had been a Fascist at some point. Neighbors tried to distinguish between the "good" Fascists, those who acquiesced to the regime, and the "bad," those who actively supported Mussolini's vision. Communal memory was long lived. One court sentenced a local official to eight years for a murder committed in 1921 as part of the local Fascist squads.

Attempts to provide a moral foundation for the new nation through the persecution of war criminals, or the purging of Fascists, proved difficult. In July of 1944, Bonomi's government passed decree 159 authorizing the High Commission for Sanctions against fascism to investigate all party leaders who "annulled constitutional guarantees, destroyed popular liberty and created the Fascist regime," sentencing them to life imprisonment or death if found guilty. The decree targeted all those who were members of the *squadristi*, those who collaborated with the Germans, or those who profited from the regime in a way that violated the boundaries of "political decency."[6] As harsh as the sanctions appeared, the decree did little to clarify who should be targeted and what acts could be prosecuted. Furthermore, the decree stipulated that penalties for crimes committed prior to 1943 could be reduced if the accused had participated in the resistance. Few government officials faced sanctions and the majority of bureaucrats managed to avoid prosecution. Many regions never formed commissions, or if the local governments did create them, they were riddled with corruption, and the few who were accused were usually able to have the charges dismissed. Decree 159 only pertained to government officials; the purging of industrialists was left to the resistance.

The CLNAI set up purge commissions in the factories of Turin and Milan and brought many leading industrialists to trial. Few faced sanctions for their profitable wartime contracts with the Germans or the RSI. Factory owners often claimed that they collaborated in order to keep the factories open and provide jobs, and had also funneled monies to local partisan groups. Relying on their antifascist credentials, and support from the anti-communist Allies, few industrialists permanently lost their positions. Formal trials that followed the purges indicted only a fraction of the leading Fascists and collaborators, and sentenced even fewer.

By the fall of 1945 defascization efforts fueled the widening political polarization. No one on the left or right considered the purges or trials a success. Businessmen, conservatives, and the Allies voiced their opposition to the sanctions, arguing the entire process was rendered illegitimate by poorly defined crimes, uneven sentencing, and the illegality of retroactive legislation. The unpurged judiciary also proved an obstacle to the process, dismissing accusations of torture or brutality brought by partisans, letting the accused walk free, or administering absurdly light punishments. Instead, the generally conservative magistrate defined the actions of individual partisans as criminal acts, excluded from the amnesty that covered acts of resistance. Tired of the violence and, perhaps, weighed down by a sense of collective guilt, most people were happy to see the purges end. The trials deepened resistance to the antifascist ideals among the conservative southern landowners. In the years after the war, many voiced their support for the *Fronte Uomo Qualunque* (Common man) party, founded by the Neapolitan Guglielmo Giannini, in 1944. The party rejected the antifascist alliance and called for a purely administrative government focused on the needs of the people. Two years after the war it was clear that Bonomi's idea of using the trials as a means to cleanse the national body and build a new ethical foundation on antifascism had failed. On June 22, the government passed a law introduced by the Communist, and minister of justice, Togliatti granting a general amnesty for all crimes committed by Fascists.

The failure of sanctions accompanied the dissolution of the postwar antifascist coalition governments. Ferruccio Parri, the first postwar prime minister and the leader of the Action Party, a man who in many ways embodied "the values of the resistance," quickly proved the inability of the antifascist coalition to restore public order, unify Italians, or introduce substantive economic or social reforms. In December of 1945, Parri's coalition collapsed, and Alcide De Gaspari, the leader of the Christian Democratic Party, became prime minister. Under his tenure he abandoned the purges, abolished the factory councils, and dismissed partisan appointed prefects and police chiefs. A quarter of a century after the war ended, scholars estimated that of the country's sixty-four prefects, sixty-two had held bureaucratic positions under Mussolini. The vast majority of police chiefs, and military officers in office in 1946, had begun their careers during the Fascist era.

On June 2, 1946, Italians went to the polls for the first time in nearly a quarter of a century. Men, and for the first time, women, decided the fate of the monarchy and elected representatives to the Constitutional Assembly. The vote highlighted the geographic and political divisions. While 54 percent of all Italians supported the republic, the most enthusiastic supporters lived in the north and central regions. Roughly two-thirds of southern Italians voted to keep the monarchy. King Umberto went into exile in Portugal. Similar regional patterns marked the elections. The Christian Democrats won by 35 percent of the vote, the largest single party. The Socialists won 21 percent of the vote, and the Communists claimed 19 percent. Combined, the three parties accounted for 75 percent of the vote. The remaining 25 percent was distributed among the various antifascist parties. In certain respects, the election reflected the creation of a more democratic Italy. Over 52 percent of the voters were women, nearly 90 percent of eligible women. If the victory of the DC marked the end of the antifascist coalitions and the emergence of a new conservative party, the participation women attests to a shifting political landscape. The PCI assiduously courted women's votes, and presented women as candidates in nearly every district. Voters elected 21 women to the constituent assembly and over 2,000 women to local offices. The results also bore witness to the new geopolitical landscape, where the far northern and southern voters stood united in their support for the DC.[7]

Over the next year half delegates worked on writing a new constitution. The "Committee of 75," a smaller subcommittee, consisting of seventy-one men and four women, was tasked with drafting the document to be debated by the entire assembly. The committee readily agreed on many issues: the Republic was antifascist; institutional power had to be decentralized among the judiciary, Parliament, and regional governments; the Senate should be an elected body (with the exception of a few senators appointed for life); the Presidency should be a largely symbolic office. Facing the threat of regional revolt, the constitution granted autonomy to five regions, including Valle d'Aosta, South Tyrol, and Trentino-Alto Adige, the eastern portion of Venezia Giulia, Sardinia, and Sicily. Each of the regions would be allowed to form their own parliaments and granted certain legislative and administrative powers. In the absence of a strong centralized state, the devolution of authority seemed a pragmatic solution to growing calls for secession, a small price to pay for the appearance of unity (Map 11).

The constitution included a host of provisions protecting basic liberties, including freedom of speech, freedom of assembly, freedom of mobility, freedom of religion, freedom of expression, and the right to strike. Yet, in every case, the state also had the right to restrict individual rights. For instance, magistrates could issue warrants for wiretapping phones, nullifying constitutional protections from state surveillance. For the most part, the emancipatory, democratic promise of the constitution was undermined by the insistence that all rights were to be exercised "within the framework of the laws that regulate it," which, in 1947, meant the Fascist legal codes. The equality

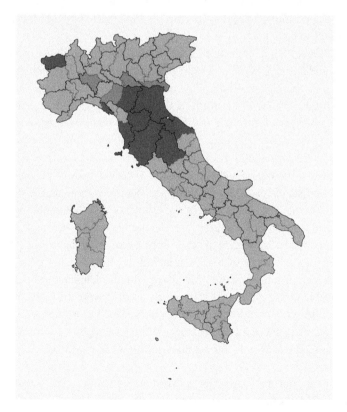

Map 11 Italian general election results, 1946. Light Gray: Christian Democratic majority. Dark Gray: Communist majority. Medium Gray: Socialist majority.

of all religions before the law promised in Article 8 was undermined by stipulations in Article 7 insisting that the Lateran Pacts would remain in effect. The Catholic Church continued to enjoy a privileged position within the Republic. The legal limits placed on constitutional liberties reflected the contradictory impulses of the assembly: to enact mass democracy, while limiting the power of democratic participation.

The constitution explicitly protected social rights, recognizing the right to work, the right to health care, and the right to education. Among the most radical acts was the inclusion of women as full-rights bearing citizens. Article 3 expressly noted that "all citizens have equal social dignity, and are equal before the law, without distinction of sex, race, language, religion, political opinions or personal or social conditions." The constitution ostensibly guaranteed women equal rights in marriage, and in the workplace: Article 29 stated that husbands and wives were legally and morally equal, while Article 37 explicitly guaranteed women equal rights and pay in the workplace. Yet, once again the emancipatory tendencies were curtailed by later clauses distinguishing female citizenship as based on both natural rights and women's roles as mothers and wives. Article 37 included a clause specifying that employers had to respect the "essential familial function of women," while the constitutional guarantee of equality between husband and wives was curtailed by the addendum "within the limits established by law." Despite the limitations, the female delegates ensured that the constitution recognized women as full legal citizens and made discrimination based on sex unconstitutional. The recognition of the natural rights of women, combined with the inclusion of social rights as fundamental to all citizens, made the constitution passed in December of 1945 a more progressive, democratic document.

Global events undermined the fragile consensus of the antifascist coalition. In February of 1947, in the midst of constitutional debates, the Allies signed the Paris Peace Treaty. Italy lost significant swaths of land along the French and Yugoslavian borders. The Allies agreed to let Italy keep South Tyrol, but handed over Dalmatia, Istria, and Fiume to Yugoslavia. The region between Trieste and Capodistria remained occupied by Anglo-American troops and Yugoslavs until 1954, when Trieste was finally returned to Italy. With the exception of Somalia, Italy lost all its colonies. In addition to the territorial punishment, the treaty required Italy to pay reparations to Greece, Yugoslavia, and the Soviet Union. The treaty placed limits on the size and composition of Italy's military. The terms of the treaty made it clear that the Allies refused to recognize the role Italians played in their own liberation. The humiliation cut deep. Some members advocated that the assembly refuse to sign the treaty. The assembly ratified the treaty under protest.

Cold War politics reinforced fears that Italy would remain forever powerless in relation to Europe, the United States, and the USSR. Togliatti denounced the government, accusing the ruling Christian Democratic Party of colluding with the Americans and the church. Members of the PCI threatened revolution, although Stalin made clear that the USSR would not support such a move. Meanwhile the Vatican and the United States urged Prime Minister De Gasperi to oust the Communists from his cabinet. In May 1947, De Gasperi complied. The expulsion of the PCI, the largest Communist Party in western Europe, presented a formidable opposition on the eve of the election.

National and international concerns shaped the 1948 electoral campaigns, ensuring that a centrist, conservative coalition would dominate the government for decades, and tempering the more democratic possibilities embedded in the constitution. The 1948 elections were more than a vote on forming a new government, but a referendum on the goals and aspirations of the Republic. The election marked the final struggle between a popular-front antifascist Republic or an anti-communist state. Both the DC and the PCI had been part of the antifascist alliance and pointed to their wartime experience as evidence of their antifascist credentials. Alcide De Gasperi, branded a traitor by Mussolini, spent the war hidden in the Vatican, while Togliatti found safety in exile in Moscow. In the electoral campaigns of 1948, De Gasperi was acutely aware of the need to present the DC as a broad-based anti-communist coalition capable of governing a democratic Italy: a party that could usher in social stability by providing support to families, and economic prosperity through land reforms and profit-sharing plans. The DC was not conservative, in the sense of safeguarding an older tradition, but envisioned a democracy based on Catholic values, a party that supported social conservative ideas around marriage, divorce, and abortion, while embracing welfare reforms benefiting workers and rural residents. On the left, Togliatti tried to establish the PCI as the party of postwar Italy, by emphasizing the party's commitment to unity, and democratic principles. Togliatti stressed the party's rejection of violence, reminding electors of the party's conciliatory participation in De Gasperi's coalition government, and the compromises it made during the Constitutional Assembly. The divisions between the parties deepened in the months leading up to the elections, as De Gasperi and Togliatti were drawn into a polarized political world.

Despite being exiled from the government, the Communist Party was still strong, with over two million members. Moreover, they had done well in the 1947 regional elections held in Sicily, garnering over 30 percent of the vote. The DC came in a distant second. In the February municipal elections in Pescara, the PCI claimed 10 percent more of the vote than in 1946. In anticipation of the elections, the Socialists agreed to join the Communist Party and run as the Democratic Popular Front Party, adopting Garibaldi as the party's symbol for the ballot. The party drew on their extensive networks among workers and women to mobilize voters, organizing through the trade unions and *Unione donne italiane* (UDI), an antifascist women's movement founded in 1945. The party recruited women to stand for office, sending them out to campaign in provincial towns. The Popular Front billed itself as the party of peace, liberty, and work. Explicitly referencing the wars of independence, the front positioned itself as the enemy of tyranny, oppression, and foreign intervention. Supporters plastered city walls with posters of Garibaldi in his red shirt standing above the people promising liberty and work. In campaign speeches, Togliatti denounced De Gasperi's willingness to sell Italy to the United States, depicting the leaders of the DC as Truman's puppets (Figure 18).

The DC embraced a politics of fear drawing on the rhetoric of the Cold War to bolster its position. In 1947, the party had far fewer members than the PCI, but had the backing of the United States and the Vatican. Throughout the months leading up the April elections, the DC countered the posters of Garibaldi, with ones depicting the brutality

Figure 18 Propaganda election poster issued by the Christian Democracy against the Popular Democratic Front. Getty Images.

of communism, and the imminent threat of a new dictatorship. The party supported the publication of comic books, exploiting the growing popularity of the *fumetti* (photo comics), emphasizing the dangers posed by communism, and the stupidity of those who cast their ballots for the Popular Front. One comic retold the adventures of Pinocchio in a postwar world, where *Italia*, in the form of a fairy, appears to tell the wooden-headed puppet that the only way to become a real man was to vote. Lured first by the Socialists and Communists he is imprisoned and hung, saved by the fairy clutching a ballot, only to be enticed again into the promised land of plenty by Stalin disguised as Garibaldi. At the end, the reader is warned to not be "gullible like Pinocchio," or "put your faith in the appearance of things. In fact, only those with wooden heads ignore the fact the behind the face of Garibaldi—the symbol of the Popular Democratic Front—hides the face of Stalin."[8]

The United States saw the elections as part of the wider Cold War struggle. The United States intervened, sending money, food, and goods to Italy, while making clear that American aid depended on the defeat of the Popular Front. American funded propaganda campaigns emphasized the dangers posed by the "enemy within," and presented the vote as one between dictatorship and democracy. The US State Department mobilized the emigrant community, urging Italian Americans to write home and beg their family to vote against communism. Sample letters appeared in the newspapers, and local organizations provided pre-written postcards that only required a signature. The US Post Office offered "Freedom Flights" from the United State to Italy to publicize the letter writing campaign. The Voice of America issued daily broadcasts praising American aid, and enlisting the help of prominent Italian Americans, including Frank Sinatra. Military assistance accompanied the propaganda efforts. President Truman authorized the covert shipment of arms to Italian security forces in case of revolution.

The Catholic Church entered the political arena with a vengeance, reinforcing the messages coming from the United States. The church used the pulpit and its extensive network of lay organizations, including Catholic Action and the *Centro Italiano Femminile* (Italian Women's Center) to mobilize support for the DC. The Vatican made it clear that the elections of 1948 constituted a vote for good or evil. In the Easter message Pius XII urged Catholics to go vote, warning the faithful of the dangers posed by the Communist menace, and reminding them that at the ballot box they could only stand with Christ, or against Christ. Bishops and parish priests added their voices to the chorus. The archbishop of Milan instructed priests to deny the sacraments to all members of the PCI. In a village near Arezzo the parish priest took advantage of the traditional Holy Week blessings to visit his parishioners in their homes to talk about the dangers of communisms. In the weekly sermons priests publicly prayed for the "good" outcome of the elections. Propaganda posters reinforced the church's message, declaring that that when voters cast their ballot, "Stalin will not see what you do in the ballot box, but God will."[9]

On April 18, 1948, over 90 percent of the eligible population went to the polls. The Christian Democratic Party won by a wide margin, gaining 48.7 percent of the vote and 305 seats. Despite the weight of the church and America, the Popular Front won 30 percent of the vote and 183 seats. Residents in the North and South cast their vote for the church, in the central regions the Popular Front won. The elections marked the end of the postwar dreams of liberal pluralism and multiparty coalitions; instead, they ushered in a polarized political landscape. According to some on the left, Francesco's vision of a better world lay in ruins, stolen by Fascists disguised as Christians, and a cowardly Communist Party (Map 12).

The 1948 election set the pattern for future elections. Until the 1970s, the DC generally returned around 40 percent of the vote, and the left roughly 35 percent. Between 1948 and 1962 the DC governed by forming centrist coalitions with the Republicans and Social Democrats. After 1962, the DC reached an accord with the PSI and formed a series of center-left governments. Despite Italy's reputation for short-lived governments, the DC maintained firm control over the government until the 1960s. Underlying the factional infighting that transformed the government into a strange kind of musical chairs, where one minister replaced another every year or so, postwar political landscape remained stable.

The return to a "one-party regime" did not constitute a return to the past. The elections of 1948 made two things crystal clear. First, while the Republic remained divided between North and South, postwar Italy had brought the South firmly into national politics. Second, although the victory of the DC helped erase the military role women played in the resistance by fusing notions of femininity with family and domesticity, the participation of women in the making of the Republic made visions of greater gender equity central to those of a democracy.[10]

Early in the postwar period the Christian Democratic Party secured their power in the South by forging an alliance with local elites and the mafia. On May 1, 1947, residents of the rural towns of Piana degli Albanesi, San Giuseppe Jato, and San Cipirello, in the

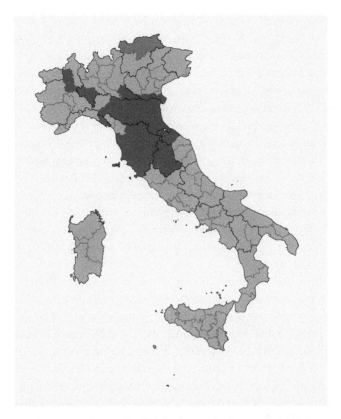

Map 12 1948 Elections for Chamber of Deputies. Light Gray: DC majority; Dark Gray: Popular Front.

province of Palermo, gathered together at Portella della Ginestra, a wide open plain near Monte Pizzuta, to celebrate Labor Day. The holiday first organized by the nineteenth-century *fasci* movements had been banned by Mussolini, and had resumed in 1943. Over 2,000 people had gathered to listen to political speeches by local Communist leaders and activists, and to enjoy the music and food. On this warm spring day of 1947, residents had also come to celebrate the unexpected victory of the People's block coalition (PCI and PSI) in the regional elections held two weeks earlier. In the midst of the festivities, a group of men rushed down from the mountain and opened fire on the crowd, leaving eleven dead and twenty-seven wounded. Within hours, rumors circulated blaming the mafia for the massacre. The next day, Girolamo Li Causi, the secretary of the Sicilian Communist Party, stood up in the Regional Assembly and accused the carabinieri, the mafia, monarchists, and members of the Common Man's Party for the massacre. Outraged, members of the assembly interrupted Li Causi, pointing to endemic lawlessness and banditry in general, and the bandit Salvatore Giuliano in particular, as the guilty parties. The subsequent investigation refused to consider evidence pointing to the involvement of police or politicians. Twelve members of Giuliano's band were eventually found guilty.[11]

The May Day celebrations of 1947 marked the culmination of years of protest and struggle on the island. Since 1943, labor organizers had worked closely with rural residents on land redistribution initiatives and improving labor contracts. In 1944, the government announced land reforms, but did not provide any details. Over the next few years, labor organizers urged residents to go to the polls and demand that the reforms be implemented. The mafia bosses who profited off of the existing land-tenure system responded with violence, murdering hundreds of organizers between 1943 and 1947. Despite the violence and intimidation, victories in the regional elections attested to the success of the labor movement. The inroads made by the activists angered the conservative elite. In the fall of 1944, the separatist party, the *Movimento per l'independenza della Sicilia* (MIS), organized a military wing, *Esercito Volontario Indipendenza Siciliana* (EVIS), to recruit local bandits and members of the mafia to contain postwar democratization. Although MIS lost political momentum with the passage of regional autonomy, the movement continued to serve as a means to discipline left-wing activists and protect the interests of the landed elite.

In the spring of 1947 Salvatore Giuliano was already a legend. Born in Montelepre, a small village in the hills outside of Palermo in 1922, he left school and soon found work trading in olive oil. The arrival of the Anglo-American forces and the expansion of the black market proved lucrative, if dangerous, for the enterprising Giuliano. In the fall of 1943, Giuliano shot and killed a police officer who caught him transporting black-market grain. The carabinieri organized a manhunt, but Giuliano managed to evade arrest. The audacity of his exploits, combined with his good looks and his talent for self-promotion, transformed the bandit into a Sicilian version of Robin Hood. In April of 1945, MIS recruited Giuliano into EVIS. Although the separatist revolt faded, Giuliano's reputation as a man of the people and defender of Sicily did not. Giuliano continued to campaign for the MIS in rural villages, offering interviews to national and international journals, including *Life* magazine. In August of 1946, Giuliano sent an open letter to the Palermo newspaper *L'Ora* insisting: "We are not delinquents, but independents who take thousands of lire from the rich to give to the poor."[12]

Despite Giuliano's populist claims he and his followers were crucial to the expansion of Christian Democratic power in the South. The truth behind the origins of Portella Massacre remains murky; however, it is clear that Giuliano was used by local bosses and politicians to consolidate power on the island. Giuliano helped transform fears of revolution and violence into a political tool to protect the interests of the island's political elite against those calling for land reform, improved working conditions, and the end to the mafia. The Robin Hood mythology surrounding Giuliano casts its shadow across the mafia, enabling politicians to claim that to the extent that the mafia existed, it was a heroic, noble force, providing protection and jobs, not an industry of violence and extortion. In the wake of the massacre, the mafia, writ large, emerged as a bulwark to stop the spread of communism and secure votes for the DC in future elections. The integration of Sicilian separatists into the DC meant that government monies, appointments within public administration, jobs, labor contracts often moved through the offices of local DC politicians and into the hands of the mafia who dispersed it in exchange for kickbacks and favors. Postwar political reliance on clientelism, deployed so effectively by the DC, took on a particular power in Sicily. The postwar political landscape based on institutional decentralization and increased reliance on political parties as a conduit for government resources and electoral support brought the Sicily and the South securely into the nation-state.

The new role of the South in national politics is made evident by the number of southern Italians appointed to civil service and judicial appointments. De Gasperi's government enlarged the still unpurged bureaucrats, nearly doubling the number of workers between 1948 and 1971. By 1954 over half of the senior civil servants were from the south. Ideology motivated few of the newly appointed government workers. Although civil service salaries remained low, the pensions and security that accompanied government jobs made them appealing in a region still suffering from high unemployment. For the parties in power, government jobs proved a lucrative bartering tool to secure votes. The Southern elite expanded its influence through the judiciary. Until the mid-1950s magistrates successfully protected Fascists laws, ensuring that many of the limitations on internal mobility and privacy remained on the books. Magistrates proved particularly useful in protecting the interests of the party, and the southern judges showed themselves eager allies of the Christian Democrats.

Gender and the postwar state

Underlying the story of postwar reconstruction as a struggle to limit the consequences of democratization lies another, more emancipatory, tale. The inclusion of women into the process of reconstruction as citizens and representatives created a new political voice that crossed religious and ideological divides, and proved more difficult to contain. The construction of a new woman, incorporating qualities of the Resistance heroine, worker, and mother as the basis for the Republican female citizen informed laws regarding women's rights, reconfigured gender norms in the postwar world in ways that eroded divisions between public and private sphere.

The increased visibility of women in politics was not unusual in the postwar world. In France and Germany, women entered politics in larger numbers than ever before. However, unlike their northern neighbors, Italian female politicians linked their concerns about women's rights and equity to general debates on the strength of the democratic republic. The women in Parliament argued that older laws limiting women's power had to be revised if Italy wanted to claim its democratic status. In short, they insisted that the law code be reconciled to the constitution, the same law code traditionalists sought to use to curtail the social and political rights written into the constitution. The return of gender normalcy meant the rejection of the virile militaristic Fascist man, replaced instead with fathers and providers, and the continuation of femininity as linked to domesticity, women as managers of children and households. The political inclusion of women, however, separated domesticity from the private sphere. Women made political and labor rights central to the nation's recovery.

Evidence of the changing meanings of female citizenship is visible in the passage of a series of law addressing women's work issues. Shortly after Parliament opened in 1948, the Communist representative Teresa Noce proposed law 860 guaranteeing paid maternity leave and other benefits for working mothers. The image of the working mother, while not the most progressive choice, was effective in countering the demand that women leave the workforce to make room for demobilized men. Italians could understand, or at least empathize, with the struggle of working mothers to navigate between home and work. The Noce Law presented women's wage work as unthreatening to the family. Unlike nineteenth-century politicians and activists who argued that protectionist legislation helped women to better fulfill their duties as wives and mothers, Noce's law rested on the assertion that paid maternity leave was a woman's right as a citizen; a woman's place in the postwar state incorporated both productive and reproductive work.[13] The final law passed in the summer of 1950 was a compromise that wedded the maternalist ideals of the Christian Democrats to the egalitarian values of the Communists. The law guaranteed 100 percent pay during maternity leave for workers, sharecroppers, unemployed women, and wives of workers. It required employers to guarantee a woman could return to her job for a year after childbirth, and mandated that they open day cares in all workplaces with more than fifty married women (although the centers would be available to married or unmarried mothers).

Conservative voices tried to limit the impact of the inclusion of women as full citizens. Despite the efforts of women in Parliament, Italian law continued to prohibit women from certain professions, including the judiciary, the diplomatic corps, or the military. Women could be lawyers, but not judges or sit on a jury. In 1948, women parliamentarians argued that occupational restrictions posed a clear violation of the Article 3 in the constitution that women were equal to men, but the existing laws remained on the books until 1963. The continued predominance of patriarchal family values also ensured that divorce remained illegal, and there was no discussion of the right of women to their own bodies: domestic violence, rape, and sexual harassment.

As tempting as it is to see the ascension of the Christian Democrats as proof of Lampedusa's observation that "for things to remain the same, everything must change," the Republic did create something new. The compromises and alliances underpinning the postwar political system, in many ways as corrupt and fragmented as they were under Depretis, proved remarkably stable. The divisions between North and South, in many ways as deep as ever, accompanied greater integration of the South into political life. Like prewar Italy, the family continued to loom large as a source of identity and stability in Italy, even as the institution itself changed.

PART FOUR
THE REPUBLIC

Historians and postwar Italy

The history of postwar Italy drives home the point that the past is made in the present. The fracturing of postwar political alliances into center-left and center-right coalitions in the post-1992 "second" Republic reinvigorated debates about the meanings and origins of the "first." Politicians and critics wielded the antifascist foundation of the Republic as a weapon to delegitimize political opponents, and justify xenophobia, racism, and neofascism. Historians and scholars waded into the increasingly turbulent waters seeking to wrest Italy's past from the vitriolic rhetoric. Scholars generated new histories, examining how personal and collective memories of the first half of the twentieth century informed the social and political divisions of the second half.[1] The end of the Cold War encouraged historians to reconsider the international dimensions of the postwar political landscape, the economic miracle, the "southern question," and the deeper structural impact of 1968, feminism and mobility.[2]

When the political elite tumbled to the ground in 1992, academics joined with journalists in seeking to assign blame, often pointing to the Resistance and the PCI as the source of the Republic's troubles.[3] Histories of partisan violence seeped into wider debates about the failure of the Republic. The PCI was blamed for appropriating the Resistance in service of its own ideological interests rather than the good of the nation. Other historians sought to rehabilitate fascism, insisting that the weakness of the Republic lay in its refusal to embrace nationalism. The notion that the nation died on September 8, 1943, gained traction, generating its own body of literature.[4] This work proved controversial, generating a wealth of critiques, but took on new significance in the last decade as Nationalist movements laid claim to the past.

If 1992 ushered in a wave of historical studies on the origins of the Republic and the failure of patriotism to thrive, it also occasioned a reappraisal of the role of the Cold War in domestic politics and foreign affairs. Until the 1970s, scholars and the public accepted the notion that through overt and covert channels the United States shaped postwar politics, empowering the Christian Democratic and obstructing the Communist Party.[5] In this telling, Italy itself played only a passive role. Access to new archival sources, combined with the shifting political climate, encouraged scholars to reassess the relationship between Italy, the United States, the Soviet Union, and Europe rescuing Italy from its status as victim. The works draw attention to the limits of superpower influence on domestic politics, and to Italy's active role in positioning itself within the Cold War geopolitical landscape. Increasingly historians uncovered the ways Italy informed US political decisions and strategies, navigating through Cold War rivalries. These works have expanded the historical actors beyond elected representatives to include women, the church, and migrants.[6]

The transnational dimension of this work has been particularly fruitful. Drawing on a wide-ranging cast, including members of religious organizations, business groups, fraternal organizations, and families, historians have traced the various networks that reinforced postwar transatlantic alliance between the DC and the United States. Leading up to the 1948 elections, letter writing campaigns mobilized the Italian American emigrant communities to persuade their family members back home to vote for the DC.[7] Few scholars question that American aid had a profound effect on postwar European reconstruction, but increasingly they argue that the impact was less financial than cultural. Marshall plan monies, combined with Cold War politics, tied modernization to an American vision, manufacturing market demand through advertising, film, and television.[8]

The reevaluation of Italy's place in the Cold War world accompanied a reassessment of historical narratives of democracy. Historians of women have challenged the political narrative arguing that the exclusion of the Communist Party and Cold War policies are evidence of a limited democracy, suggesting, instead, that the inclusion of women into political life attests to the creation of a genuine democratic movement. This "lost wave," of feminism, scholars argue, was instrumental in building a new basis for citizenship that embodied the ideals of the Resistance. Centering histories on the experience of women, and privileging of gender as a category of analysis, makes visible an alternate, slower, process of democratization and civic inclusion. Just as new studies of the Cold War counter narratives of Italian passivity and geopolitical marginalization, the focus on the history of women in the postwar years complicates the story of a republic born from alienation and division.[9]

Economic histories seeking to understand postwar prosperity run counter to political arguments of failure. Within a decade after the end of the war the economy was booming, and although it slowed in the 1960s, it did not stop. A combination of factors including public policy, changing markets, the introduction of new technologies, and an underemployed mobile labor force transformed patterns of production and consumption. There is little disagreement among historians surrounding the causal factors of postwar prosperity, debates center on the relative importance of the individual factors. Historians often credited economic growth to global market forces, insisting that it occurred despite state intervention and trade-union demands. Recent historical studies have reassessed the impact of both foreign markets and domestic policy. The adoption of a wider international framework suggests that the European Market bolstered specific regional industries at the expense of others. Meanwhile, new analyses of the impact of public monies and economic policies suggest that state intervention often had a positive impact, and highlight the regional diversity that characterized the economic miracle.[10]

For decades historians of the "economic miracle" pondered the failure of the South to prosper. Despite the fact that conditions in the South improved between 1945 and 1965 the South still reported much higher rates of unemployment, crime, and poverty. After years of state investment, the gap between the North and South had only grown wider. The South, scholars decreed, had "modernized without development." Economists and historians generally settled on a handful of causes for the persistent uneven development: public investment that focused on the creation of consumer market rather than industrial growth and jobs and an export market dominated by labor. Postwar economic development tied northern and central economic growth to industrial production geared toward foreign and domestic markets, and southern development to exportation of cheap labor. Compounding the difficulties posed by patterns of state investment and market growth was an absence of social capital.[11]

In 1958, the American political scientist Edward Banfield conducted a village-based study in South Italy concluding that southern culture was antithetical to democracy. He argued, the strength of close-knit nuclear families, whose members were motivated solely by short-term gain and familial interests, generated a deep distrust toward those outside the family, especially the state. Banfield maintained that this culture of "amoral familism" left southern Italians incapable of engaging in wider communal or civic initiatives, fostered the growth of the mafia, and resulted in economic stagnation. After an initial warm reception, particularly in the United States, scholars launched a sustained critique of Banfield's argument. Just as acceptance of his thesis began to fade, the political scientist, Robert Putnam, revived Banfield's thesis. In a 1992 study of democracy in Italy, Putnam argued that the problems of the South could be traced back to a distrustful, apathetic citizenry, measured by the scarcity of volunteer associations. Putnam's version gained traction in a new political landscape where northern regional-based political parties decried the South as a parasitical weight on the nation.[12] Common to these economic and sociological analyses stood the notion that the South owed its limited economic and material improvement to the willingness of the North to provide money and support in exchange for cheap labor and access to a growing consumer market.

Putnam's argument generated an immediate backlash.[13] The wealth of studies challenging the trope of southern "backwardness" produced a growing body of work revealing the diversity of southern economies and the development of autonomous ties to local and global markets, and countering the notion that the South profited from northern prosperity.[14] Social historians pointed to the variety of family forms across the region that formed the basis for strong collective identities. Furthermore, while kinship ties proved strong in the South, they were no stronger than those found throughout the country, disproving Putnam's causal link between cooperative social ties and democracy.[15]

Studies of the mafia further undermined assumptions of southern dependency. Recent histories of organized crime and antimafia movements have stressed the complicity of national party systems based on the exchange of public monies for votes that empowered regional government officials to wield state resources in ways that profited private interests. Information revealed by *Tangentopoli* (Bribesville), *manipuliti* (clean hands), and the antimafia judicial investigations in the 1980s opened up new avenues of research on the systemic, rather than geographic origins, of postwar corruption. Scholars have traced the expansion of organized crime through the party system into northern cities and industries. Although born in the South, new historical works argue that the Mafia was shaped by national politics and the Cold War, and global capitalism.[16]

Regionalism has taken on a new importance in the wake of 1992. Historians recognized that any understanding of the rise of Berlusconi and the populist leagues necessitated a reassessment of the regional social, economic, and political developments. New works moved away from seeing regions as fixed entities, each with their own languages, cultures, or foods, and instead looked at the regions as inextricably linked to the formation of the nation-state and transnational communities. Understanding regions as flexible and evolving constructed spaces creates more complicated historical narratives of the Republic and describes a political culture that is in some ways more resilient and in other ways more fragile. These studies underscore how new forms of transportation, communication, globalization, and the rise of the European community created fissures within society and culture often strengthening local allegiances.[17]

Regional studies redirected encouraged scholars to reassess the role of the church and civic associations in postwar life. Historians generally have tended to see the church, as a bulwark against changes associated with modern consumer capitalism, resistant to changing notions of marriage, family, gender norms, or sexuality. Despite its improved position within the Republic, the church remained deeply suspicious of secular civil society. Yet, in the past few years some parishes appeared to champion a limited number of social justice issues (antimafia, immigration, poverty, the environment), and attacking others (LGBT, reproductive rights, etc.). It appears that underlying the broad description of the church as a force of conservatism lurks alternate historic narratives. A few historians have begun to look at the role of faith in civic life and the gap between official church practices and popular Christianity. Looking at how people lived their faith in different times and in different places suggests that the church plays a more complicated role in the making of modern Italy than many have assumed.[18]

Scholars are also attending to the generational and gender changes that transformed Italy in the second half of the twentieth century. Historians tended to dismiss the generation of 1968 as a force of genuine historical change, arguing that the movement was too small and superficial.[19] In the past decade, researchers have moved away from the polarizing debates about the consequences of 1968 (social upheaval, drugs, family dissolution versus liberation, autonomy, community), to consider the longer-term impact of 1968 on society and culture.[20] While it is evident that the movement ushered in a period of renewed authoritarianism, the violence and terror should not erase its emancipatory aspects. The new culture associated with 1968 created space for the voices of marginal social groups, including women and youth. The new histories examine the impact of the movement on personal and collective identities, and the ways that national political mobilization resonated in provincial cities and towns. The year 1968 reverberated in unexpected ways throughout society, culture, and politics.[21]

The history of women and gender relations has taken on greater currency in contemporary historiography.[22] Thematic and chronological works have traced the changing conditions of women's lives and gender norms in the twentieth century.

The work of historians of women and gender explored the impact increased political, educational, and employment opportunities had on society and culture, while recognizing that patriarchal laws, marriage, domesticity, and violence continued to impact women's lives. In Italy, as elsewhere, women's history challenged traditional ideas of periodization and conceptual frameworks. New studies have traced the roots of second wave feminism back to the beginning of the Republic, and reassessed the impact the 1960s and 1970s had on shifting gender and sexual norms. Challenges to familial authority and patriarchy ran throughout the postwar period. Legalization of contraception and divorce may not have undermined the centrality of marriage and family in defining femininity, but did create the possibility of imagining alternate kinds of unions and families.[23]

The arrival of immigrants from Asia, Africa, South America, and Eastern Europe in the past thirty years has encouraged scholars to reconsider assumptions about postwar migration. Adopting new methodologies and interdisciplinary approaches recent scholarship has linked late twentieth-century migration to the longer history of Italy as a crossroads. Recently, a number of chronologically expansive histories of migrations from the eighteenth century to the present have appeared, offering a sweeping overview of the constitutive role internal and transnational migration played in defining urban/ rural relations, national identity, regional identities, and empire. These works challenged distinctions between seasonal, internal, transnational, and permanent migrations. The ways in which regional circuits expanded or contracted in response to changing demands of global capitalism deepen our understanding of the complicated historical ties linking local, regional, national, and transnational communities, and the permeability of state boundaries.[24]

Recognition of historical continuities underpinning the history of migration does not erase the importance of recognizing change. For decades historians identified the postwar period with a shift in emigration away from transatlantic destinations to cities in northern Italy and Europe. Much of the scholarship placed migration within the context of European economic integration, examining the labor politics of the guest worker programs, and casting migrants as hostages of fortune. Contemporary immigration concerns have led historians to reconsider the role of the state in shaping postwar migration policies and processes of migration, paying more attention on the agency of the emigrants. These studies of the back-and-forth movements of people, goods, and ideas make evident the impact of migration on modernization, altering the form and function of families, bolstering consumer markets, and carving out new paths of cultural exchange.[25]

The arrival of labor migrants and refugees has encouraged historians to consider the history of Italian immigration. Recent works have explored how current laws regarding immigration, naturalization, and citizenship were deeply informed by its history of emigration.[26] The focus on immigration has led historians to consider the experiences of emigrants in new ways. Reconsiderations of postwar migration to northern cities uncovered histories of clandestine migrants from Calabria, Sicilia, Veneto, and Piedmont unable to obtain work permits or housing in Turin and Milan. A growing body of interdisciplinary work connects the contemporary resurgence of racial violence and xenophobia to colonialism and the "Southern Question." Combined these works emphasize the centrality of mobility in the making of modern Italy.[27]

The history of the postwar is colored by the political, social, and economic uncertainties of the contemporary world. The palpable discontent of Italians with local and national government, the disillusionment of the youth, the rise of violent neofascist movements could tell a story of social fragmentation and economic fragility. The legacy of a political system mired in corruption, collusion, and criminality could stand as evidence of a failed democracy. Yet, as the new historiographical trends suggest, there is a more progressive narrative woven through Italy's history. Without clinging to the myths of Italians as "*brava gente*," erasing Italy's role in Europe's colonial expansion, downplaying growing social and economic disparities, scholarly attention to the expansion of civil society, changing forms of family, new forms of social and political activism, offer evidence of a more resilient, flexible, and even democratic Italy emerging alongside an increasingly divided, violent, and xenophobic country.

CHAPTER 13
SOCIETY, CULTURE, AND THE "ECONOMIC MIRACLE"

In September 1955, Michelangelo Antonioni's film *Le Amiche* (Girlfriends) premiered at the Venice Film Festival. The Italy that appears in *Le Amiche* is a far cry from Rossellini's rubble strewn streets of *Citta Aperta*. In the opening scene, as the camera pans across a modern, well-ordered cityscape, a young fashionable woman prepares a bath in a nicely appointed hotel. Clelia has returned to Milan, her hometown, to oversee the opening of a new fashion salon. Ambitious, successful, and single, Clelia falls in with a group of wealthy women and men, looking for pleasure and distraction. The war and reconstruction are buried beneath clothes, parties, drugs, villas, and banter. Clelia meets Carlo, an architect's assistant, from a working-class background, similar to the one Clelia left behind when she moved to Rome. When Clelia stands to lose her job, she imagines a future with Carlo, but soon realizes that she belongs "to such a different world." She tells Carlo,

> I'm too used to my independence to be a quiet wife in a modest house. Work is also my way of being a woman, of loving, of participating in life. . . . Maybe, one day, I will be so fortunate as to meet a man I could live with without either one of us having to give up our sense of self. But if you and I stay together, I'm sure one of us would be unhappy.

Clelia's declaration underscores the profound social and cultural changes that accompanied the "economic miracle," that marked the 1950s. The world of Carlo and Clelia stands in stark contrast to the world made whole through love, struggle, and community envisioned by Pina and Francesco just a decade earlier. Work, marriage, family took different forms. The 1950s appear as a period of rapid and sudden transformation. Like Clelia, most Italians seemed to live in a world radically different than that of their childhood. In many respects appearances reflected the reality. The majority of Italians lived in nicer houses, worked more secure jobs, and had access to education and an ever-growing wealth of consumer goods. In the course of the 1950s and 1960s the postwar economic boom and institutionalization of the DC undermined labor, strengthened the power of local elites in the South, encouraged migration, and reconfigured family relations.

The "economic miracle"

Even a cursory survey of economic and social statistics gives a sense of how swiftly the economy grew in the years following the war. Between 1948 and 1958 per capita GDP rose from 4 percent to 7 percent, fueled by Marshall plan aid and rising demand for housing, goods, and food. Although the last years of the war left transportation and communication networks badly damaged, factories and industries were largely intact, requiring relatively little investment to begin production. Reconstruction monies, accompanied by the dismantlement of protectionism, provided investment capital for both private and public sectors. In the late 1940s, the government adopted the *Linea Einaudi* plan, a series of deflationary measures that included restricting the money supply and expanding monetary reserves. To counter the monetary restrictions, the government strategically used ERP funds to boost certain industries. Working through the *Istituto per la Ricostruzione Industriale* (IRI), a government investment body created in 1933 to bail out overextended banks by purchasing industrial debt, the postwar government strategically invested in engineering, chemical, transportation, and communication industries.

By the early 1950s key industries had largely recovered from the war. In the early 1950s, FIAT invested heavily in production for a consumer market. First appearing on the market in 1955, the small, affordable, and innovative FIAT 600 became a best seller. By 1960, FIAT claimed a significant share of the domestic and European car market.[1] Access to raw materials from the United States helped modernize steel and energy industries. The combination of monetary and technical aid aided the growth of Italy's petrochemical industries. By the mid-1950s, steelworks produced enough steel to meet domestic manufacturing demands. Despite fears that the end of protectionist policies would endanger domestic production, the economy thrived. Industrial productivity grew an average of 7.2 percent between 1949 and 1959, a rate only surpassed by West Germany.

The creation of a European common market proved enormously beneficial for industry. After the war Italy eagerly signed on to international trade agreements including the Organization for European Economic Cooperation (OEEC-1948) and the Treaty of Paris (1951), establishing the European Coal and Steel Community. In 1957, Italy became one of the founding members of the European Economic Community (EEC). Greater integration into the global market afforded industries access to foreign consumer markets. The EEC in particular proved a lucrative market for Italian goods; in 1955, 23 percent of exports shipped to western Europe, and in 1965, over 40 percent of Italian goods reached European markets. Italy's success in the export market was based on the entrepreneurial skills of business owners, their willingness to adapt new techniques, and readiness to respond to changing consumer demands. Exports shifted from textiles and food to domestic appliances, typewriters, and cars. Between 1958 and 1964, the number of television licenses rose from 1.2 million to over 5 million. The number of private cars rose from 347,000 in 1950 to 4.3 million in 1964. Italians purchased washing machines and refrigerators in ever-growing numbers as electricity reached into rural regions. Family consumption increased by over 7 percent in the 1950s.[2]

While the postwar government was eager to invest in industry, it was reluctant to intervene in the labor market. At the end of the war over two million people were unemployed, and another four million were classified as underemployed. The largest union, CGIL, attempted to introduce a plan to address the issue of chronic unemployment. In 1949, the leaders rallied support for their *Piano del Lavoro* (National Employment Plan). The union proposed a three-pronged public spending program concentrating on energy, agriculture, and building. The plan called for the nationalization of the electricity industry and the construction of new hydroelectric plants, an extensive land reclamation program, and the building of houses, schools, and hospitals. The union estimated that the plan would employ nearly 700,000 people. De Gasperi summarily dismissed the proposal. The government responded by creating a few programs in the South but did little to address the systemic problem of unemployment. After 1948, the DC saw little need to work with the left-wing unions, and even less reason to intervene in a labor market that provided a large, cheap, flexible workforce. Throughout the 1950s and 1960s real wages remained low and unemployment remained high.

The electoral victory of the DC ushered in *gli anni duri* ("the hard years") for workers as union power declined. Employers took advantage of the government's labor policies to weaken the influence of unions on the factory floor. Between 1946 and 1952 employers purged the most militant workers from their payrolls. When the economy improved, the larger industries hired younger workers, recent migrants, who had no part in the wartime labor struggles. Smaller firms, free from labor regulations, paid low wages. Between 1948 and 1953 unions lost ground. Strikes and occupations organized in response to mass layoffs in the northern industries, some lasting for months ended in defeat for strikers. Union membership fell from nearly 2 million in 1950 to about 800,000 in 1958.[3] Increasingly workers chose to stay out of unions altogether, or joined the DC affiliated union, CISL, or the newly formed Socialist *Unione Italiano del Lavoro* (UIL), both more palatable to industrialists. By the mid-1950s, despite its militant and antifascist history, the power of CGIL had so diminished that they lost the elections in the FIAT factory. The defeat marked the collapse of the centralized bargaining structure and heralded a return to localized negotiations between labor and management. Plentiful cheap labor and weakened unions meant that profits flourished as labor productivity outstripped the costs of wages and benefits.

This "virtuous cycle" between real income growth, productivity, increased investment, and consumption that culminated in material prosperity did not spread evenly across Italy. The "industrial triangle," Milan, Turin, and Genoa, primed postwar industrial growth. The industries born during nineteenth-century industrialization had long benefited from state and private investments and continued to receive the lion's share of public and private investment. This economic region, commonly referred to as the "first Italy," drove the expansion of a wage labor force, and a postwar construction boom. Residents in Piedmont and Lombardy were among the first to purchase houses, cars, refrigerators, and radios. The "third Italy," comprising Veneto, Emilia-Romagna, Tuscany, Marche, and Umbria, witnessed a later economic boom, centered on the expansion of small family firms, light manufacturing, and growth in the service industry. The economic miracle in the north-east looked very different than the one to the west, marked by an increase in self-employed households, and the decline of wage-earning opportunities. In the "second Italy," the South, the "miracle" created labor migrants.

Postwar growth fundamentally changed the structure of the economy. The 1951, census reported that agriculture employed 42 percent of the workforce, as compared to industry that claimed 32 percent. Ten years later 29 percent of people made a living from the land, while 70 percent worked in service, industry, and as professionals. In 1950, agriculture accounted for over 27 percent of GDP, by 1960, only 13 percent. Government policy in part drove the move away from agriculture; the state only invested 29 percent of Marshall plan monies in agriculture.[4] The shift to an economy based on large-scale heavy industry and factory labor systems accompanied an increase in small landholders. The difficulties faced by small-scale agriculture encouraged landowners in the central and southern regions to sell of their lands. Government programs subsidizing rural mortgages encouraged residents to buy land, and the number of small-landowning property holders grew by over 10 percent. In many ways, the increase in land ownership was the fulfillment of dreams and demands stretching back to the nineteenth century; however, few could make a living off their land. Instead, families that had once worked the land now depended on wages from nearby factories, remittances from the north, or government benefits. Those who were able to profit by land sales consolidated their holdings and shifted production to specialized crops for export markets.

Economic growth accompanied a decline in the size of the active workforce. In 1951, 44 percent of all residents worked. In 1961, at the height of the boom, the figure dropped slightly to 40 percent. By 1971 the active workforce accounted for just 37 percent of the population.[5] Even allowing for the impact of mechanization and technological advancements that diminished labor demand, the percentage of Italians working remained lower in comparison to the British, French, or Germans. Women, young adults, and southerners faced the most difficulty in finding work. Between 1951 and 1921 the percentage of women as a proportion of the population fell from 22 percent to 20 percent. The regional distribution of industry, combined with the fall in demand for low-skilled workers, accounted for part of the decline: in the South, far from the "industrial triangle," the active workforce fell from 36 percent to 33 percent by 1971.[6] The disappearance of agricultural jobs and unskilled factory work contributed to the shrinking labor force. In both private and public sectors, the demand for university-educated managers, technical workers, and engineers rose rapidly.

The Milan Clelia walked through in 1955 reflected the postwar reality of some Italians. But, the modern prosperous cities, abundant work, and material prosperity hid more than the bourgeoisie ennui, so elegantly described by Antonioni; it also concealed a world of geographic and wealth disparities, the disappearance of unskilled work, and the transformation of the rural economy.

The South in the age of prosperity

In the South, the "economic boom," largely fueled by public monies, served to tighten the alliance between the Christian Democratic Party and the local elite. In the immediate postwar period a coalition of public and private interests focused attention on the question of southern economic development. In 1946, a group of economists and businessmen formed the *Associazione per lo Sviluppo dell'industria nel Mezzogiorno* (SVIMEZ), a private nonprofit organization concerned with the economic reclamation of the southern regions. The coalition lobbied the government to increase state investments in the South.[7] SVIMEZ's first successful project was the creation of the *Cassa del mezzogiorno* (Fund for the South), designed to funnel money into land reclamation, transportation infrastructure, communication, and hopefully create a dynamic class of entrepreneurs, lawyers, doctors, and accountants. The regional funds allocated for roads, aqueducts, and large drainage projects all passed through the hands of local political networks.

By the late 1950s, infrastructure projects could no longer meet local demands for capital investment. Southern Christian Democratic politicians lobbied the government to increase public monies and provide new incentives for private investment. In 1957, the government announced that 40 percent of the IRI's total investments, and 60 percent of its investment in factories, had to go to the South. The IRI identified specific regions as centers of industrial development (Bari, Brindisi, Cagliari, Salerno, and Taranto), while other communities were designated as smaller development hubs. The state provided generous financial rewards to those industries willing to move to the selected districts, offering government grants to cover up to 20 percent of the initial investment, and low-interest loans to meet the remaining costs. Government investment fueled new industrial growth. Large steelworks grew up on the outskirts of Taranto, and petrochemical works sprung up along the southern Sicilian coast near Gela. Alfa-Romeo opened a factory near Naples, and FIAT built a new plant in Sicily. The new plants provided some jobs, but not enough low-skilled labor-intensive work to meet demand. These "cathedrals in the desert" did little to spark wider economic development.

State investment transfigured the southern urban landscape. Regional and national politicians poured money into urban renewal projects ostensibly to address the housing crisis caused by wartime bombings and postwar urbanization. In Sicily, political autonomy had increased the importance of Palermo, putting additional pressure on the housing market as lawyers, bureaucrats, and politicians poured into the city. The funds financed the construction of new ports, modern apartment buildings, and wide new roads; however, instead of following a planned urban renewal proposal that considered the architectural history of the city and the needs of the residents, the money was used to raze whole neighborhoods, and to cover gardens and parks with concrete.

Il *sacco di Palermo* ("sack of Palermo") was brought about through the close-knit relationship of the mafia and the Christian Democrats. In 1956, the Christian Democrat Salvo Lima became the mayor of Palermo, and Vito Cianciminio took his position as the director of public works. Between 1958 and 1963, these local DC politicians transformed the fund for the South into their private investment account, fueling aggressive real estate speculation across the city. Handing out government funds and contracts in exchange for money and future profits, they oversaw the destruction of seventeenth- and eighteenth-century villas, replaced with shoddily built concrete behemoths. The lack of regulation and oversite encouraged developers to cut corners. The buildings, roads, and walls began to crumble nearly as soon as they were finished. In 1960, over 30 percent of Palermo workers were employed, as compared to roughly 10 percent in the northern cities. Dependent on the contractors for their jobs, Lima and Cianciminio could be counted on to provide a sizable voting bloc for the DC. The close relationship between money and politics brought the southern political elite into the center of national politics.

Migration

Immediately after the war it seemed as though everyone was on the move. Between 1947 and the early 1950s an average of 250,000 rural migrants made their way to nearby cities, or to work in northern Europe or overseas. Despite increased regulations on both internal and transnational labor mobility, Italians left in ever-growing numbers. A 1939 law requiring residents to prove they had work in a new city before they could gain residency remained on the books, even though migrants now had to prove residency to obtain a work permit, thus making it nearly impossible to legally move to the cities. Quota laws and visa requirements made transnational migration equally complicated. Yet, regardless of the difficulties at least nine million people left their homes between 1955 and 1971.

Postwar mass migration broke long-established migratory patterns. By the mid-1950s new labor circuits appeared marked by an overall decline in transoceanic migration, and a predominance of South Italians in transoceanic, transalpine, and internal migrations. These emerging migration patterns that drew people from rural villages to northern cities transformed urban spaces, undermined long-standing regional divides, and strengthened ties between Italy and western Europe.

Between 1958 and 1963 nearly one million southern Italians moved to northern cities. The vast majority of migrants came from Puglia, Sicily, and Campania, and by 1955 southerners outnumbered northern migrants in Milan and Turin. By the end of the 1950s, Turin had become the third largest "southern town" after Palermo and Naples.[8] Between 1950 and 1960, every major city and most provincial towns recorded sharp increases in population. The population of Milan rose by 24 percent between 1951 and 1961, and Turin's grew nearly 43 percent. The influx of workers spilled over into neighboring towns, blurring the boundaries between the cities and countryside. Expanded tram and subway lines linked the growing *periferia* (suburbs) to the urban centers. Cranes crowded the skylines, and the streets were filled with cement dust, as contractors rushed to build new apartments, schools, and factories. Building their new homes were often the first jobs new migrants found.

Although work was plentiful, conditions for the new migrants were precarious. Bosses exploited the new arrivals, refusing to offer legal contracts and paying low wages.[9] The new migrants rarely found positions in the factories; instead, they worked in shops and restaurants for ten or twelve hours a day without benefits or worker protections. Despite fevered construction, recent migrants were hard pressed to find affordable housing. Anti-southern prejudice ran deep in Milan and Turin, and many local residents refused to rent to the *meridionali*. Shantytowns sprang up on the edge of the cities where migrants built their own houses from material scavenged from the nearby dumps. In Milan, contemporary social critics called the neighborhoods *Coree* (Koreas), drawing parallels between rural labor migrants and the Korean War refugees who appeared on the newsreels. By the mid-1960s, conditions had significantly improved. New high-rise apartments built on the outskirts of the cities, replete with electricity and water, satisfied the demand.[10]

As southern Italians settled in the cities, they became part of the fabric of daily life. Over time migrants legalized their status, found better paying jobs, and called for their families. Southern migrants and their northern neighbors mingled at work and in the cafes; they fell in love and married. Working and living next to each other, sharing foods and customs fostered new ties between Lombardi and Calabresi. The social integration accompanying postwar migration mitigated, but did not erase, regional prejudices.

To their northern neighbors, the recent emigrants seemed to prove the stereotypes of southerners as backward, superstitious, and lawless. In the schools, the children of migrants were bullied by classmates and teachers alike. Northerners dismissed the immigrants as *cafoni* ("country boors") or *terroni* ("hayseeds"). Signs appeared on shop doors announcing, "Southerners and dogs prohibited."[11] The more sympathetic northerners condescendingly argued that their more "civilized" culture would temper the "intemperance" of the southerner. In 1964, the journalist Giovanni Russo wrote:

> The talents and habits of Italians in the north can contribute to improving the southerner, whom in exchange bring a vital energy and spiritual vivacity that represents a revitalizing sap. I have the impression, in fact, that we are witnessing the great historical fact of our unified life: the birth, that is, of a new type of Italian."[12]

Postwar South Italian migration to the urban north was part of a reconfiguration of wider transnational migration patterns. Many southern emigrants who settled in Turin or Milan were veteran travelers, part of a network linking emigrant workers in France, Germany, the United Kingdom, and the United States. Some migrants would work for a year or so in Milan, grow disillusioned, return home, and then leave again to try their luck in London or Toronto. From the vantage point of Calabria, Turin, Dusseldorf, and London appeared equally cold and grey. In the aftermath of the war, however, where emigrants chose to go was informed by the state, as well as kin, community.

The government insisted that mobility was indispensable to postwar recovery. By the 1960s, the state had replaced the prewar padrones in rural villages: negotiating contracts, circulating information about migration, and promoting certain destinations. In 1957, Italy signed the Treaty of Rome, establishing the European Economic Community, after having successfully negotiated the inclusion of a commitment to the free circulation of labor within the EEC, and guarantees of equal treatment of all workers regardless of citizenship. State intervention skewed the sex-composition of transnational migration toward men, as the contracts discouraged family emigration. By the mid-1960s, as the economy began to slow, the government actively lobbied on behalf of the emigrants to ease residency requirements and to promote family unification.

Despite the legal obstacles, and increased opportunities in northern cities, emigrants still traveled overseas. In August of 1955, the journalist Giovanni Russo visited the town of Pontelandolfo, eighty miles east of Naples, arriving early one Sunday morning. Outside the church, he described how men, sported brightly colored "American ties," and the children dressed in their Sunday best, appeared to be "American children." Resident in Pontelandolfo received clothes and gifts from kin who had emigrated to Westbury, Connecticut, at the end of the nineteenth century. World wars, fascism, and heightened migration restrictions slowed emigration from the village but did not diminish the desire to go to America. After the United States passed legislation permitting its residents to sponsor the passage of close family members, over 1,000 villagers left for Connecticut. In July of 1955, a rumor circulated through the district that the entire town of Pontelandolfo would be permitted to emigrate to Westbury. Although the rumor turned out to be false, people from across the province wrote to the mayor asking to be registered as official residents of the town.[13]

Existing migratory networks influenced, but did not determine, postwar patterns. Three years later, the migratory trend reversed: by 1965 only 20 percent of emigrants crossed the oceans and the vast majority bought tickets for western Europe or northern cities. The creation of the EEC, trade agreements, state subsidies, all made finding work in European factories a more convenient and easier option. By the mid-1950s, South Italians were traveling in ever-growing numbers to France, Belgium, and Switzerland, despite the lack of a formal treaty. By the early 1960s, West Germany stood out as a popular destination. Most men who decided to emigrate did not usually intend to settle abroad and rarely called their families to join them. The men found work in the building trades and in factories. By the 1960s guest-worker programs ensured a minimum amount of protection for migrants: contracts specifying wages, conditions of work, the transfer of family allowances and pensions. Guaranteed paid-vacations and the improvement of trains ensured that many workers could return home for holidays. In 1964, 2,308,800 Italians worked in Europe, over 900,000 in France, 600,000 in Switzerland, and over 400,000 in Germany.

Despite treaty agreements and government intervention on their behalf, migrants remember the 1950s and 1960s as a difficult time, marked by feelings of sadness, loneliness, and nostalgia for home. The first years were the worst. Crowded together in company barracks, few able to speak the local languages, emigrants formed their own tight-knit communities. Over the years, some migrants managed to navigate through the legal requirements and bring their families to join them. Settling in to their new homes, enrolling their children in school, and learning the language turned them into permanent residents, although still Italian citizens. The permanent migrants strengthened economic, cultural, and social ties between the European community and Italy.

Postwar mass migration had a powerful impact on migrant homeland. Within a few years, journalists noted that the quality of life in the South had markedly improved, measured by increased consumption of sugar and meat, and the decline in childhood illnesses. As in older migrations, remittances brought cash into the economy, fueling the construction of new houses, financing local businesses, even as the rural population continued to decline. The postwar migrations changed the culture and society of southern towns, linking them to the European community. Local feast days or summer holidays transformed small Sicilian hill towns into multicultural parades; children speaking German, French, and English walk the streets alongside their parents and grandparents.

Family

Mobility, industrialization, urbanization, the expansion of state welfare programs, and changing gender norms altered family life. New understandings of femininity, both liberating and limiting, played a critical role in reconfiguring family relations. The expansion of suffrage, and cinematic depictions of modern woman, positioned women in the wider society as full citizens, yet, the "economic miracle" of the 1950s and early 1960s also idealized women as housewives and mothers, diminishing their political and economic standing. Although far from emancipatory, the postwar world gender changes did not signal a return to traditional roles. Expansion of state welfare policies, material prosperity, education, and urbanization altered familial relations in ways that profoundly changed gender norms.[14]

State welfare policies eroded the borders separating the private world of family from public spaces of politics and civil life. Social welfare systems relied heavily on the family. Until the late 1960s, health insurance schemes, pensions, and unemployment benefits were extended in a haphazard fashion, determined by employment, trade unions, and geography. The one thing that the programs all held in common was the expectation that women would provide for their husbands and children. Child allowances, disability subsidies, and pensions assumed that feeding, nursing, and clothing the family was a woman's primary responsibility, and so reinforced the position of men as head of household. Combined, the patchwork of social welfare laws subordinated women to the family. Even the celebrated law 860 requiring paid maternity leave for women, in theory protecting women in the workforce, in practice, proved a disincentive to the hiring of women. Employers tended to fire women once they were married rather than pay for the extended leave. The Catholic Church encouraged women to stay home, reminding them of their duties as mothers and wives.

As a consequence of the new laws and the disappearance of low-skilled, labor-intensive jobs in industry and agriculture, women left the workforce. By 1960, Italy reported one of the lowest rates of female labor participation in western Europe. In spite of the increase of jobs for women in certain sectors, including fashion and civil service, most women found it difficult to find work in the new economy. In 1950 women comprised a quarter of the agricultural labor force, and 20 percent of the industrial labor force. By 1960 only 23 percent of women appeared actively employed. Women continued to take in piece work, sewing dresses for neighbors, or cleaning houses, but their work was rarely counted in employment reports.[15]

The mobility of the postwar world altered family forms. After the war, the average size of the family declined from 4 members in 1951 to 3.6 in 1961, and for the first time over half of all households were comprised of 1 to 3 members. Smaller families and access to modern conveniences (running water and electricity) improved the lives of many of the women who moved to the cities, easing the burden of household chores and provided greater privacy. However, urbanization often accompanied the loss of wider communal networks and increased women's isolation. For women who stayed behind in the southern hill towns daily life remained difficult. Promised modern housing often failed to materialize. Women continued to haul water, chop wood, and tend the land. As remittances filtered in, women's household management chores expanded. Rural women oversaw the family's growing savings and the construction of new homes. While women's increased economic power and their position as social citizens did little to visibly alter the power dynamic between married couples, the 1950s and 1960s did brought significant change in family relations, marked by new forms of authority and challenges to tradition. By 1960 there was a sense that the traditional family was threatened.

Urban life and popular culture created new social networks and provided alternate visions of modern life. Between 1954, when television was first introduced to the market, and 1958, over one million households acquired a television set. By 1965 close to half of all families claimed a television in their house. The DC controlled RAI (Radiotelevisione Italiana S.p.A) the state television monopoly, ensured that the church retained influence over programming. The director of RAI, active in Catholic Action, censored all programs that might be seen to "bring discredit or undermine the institution of the family."[16] Initially religious programming dominated the airwaves, interspersed with quiz shows, and sporting events. RAI imposed controls on advertising, fearing the influence of American products and images. Advertisements were grouped together in a half-hour program, with the product featured at the beginning and end of each two-minute spot. Between the product images aired a sweet fable aimed at children. Initially, watching television was a collective activity. Neighbors and family would bring their own chairs and gather round to watch Mike Buongiorno host one more round of the game show *Lascia o Raddoppia?* (Leave or double). As more families bought their own television sets, the act of watching became a more intimate, private activity.

Despite the popularity of television, the cinema remained an important cultural force. The expansion of movie houses into rural regions meant larger audiences and booming ticket sales. The theaters brought the glamour of Hollywood and images of American modernity into the lives of ordinary people. Although the movies and television shows largely reinforced gender norms, by the 1960s a new generation of filmmakers offered powerful critiques of society. Lucchini Visconti's *Rocco e il suo fratello* and Frederico

Fellini's *La dolce vita* were both released in 1960. In Visconti's story of familial and sexual love, migration, violence, sibling rivalry, and North/South divides is a tale of the disintegration of the traditional family in the modern world. In Fellini's vision, there is no family, only a powerful critique of the beauty and emptiness of a life lived for pleasure alone.

Accompanying the glimpses of alternate worlds visible on screens, the flood of magazines aimed at the postwar woman offered another space to imagine new kinds of intimate and civic roles. In addition to *Grazia*, with its emphasis on housekeeping, celebrity culture and beauty, two of the most widely read publications included the left-leaning *Noi donne* and the more conservative *Famiglia Cristiana*. By the late 1950s new publications, *Epoca* and *Settimana Incom*, modeled on appeared. Women reading across ideological lines turned increasingly to their communities of fellow readers for advice as well as for housekeeping hints, recipes, and news. Letters in the popular advice columns reveal how women were trying to find a foothold in a world of changing sexual mores and gender norms. They wrote asking for help on finding love, navigating marital problems, and addressing sexual concerns (in particular, sex before marriage). An underlying sense of frustration with the limits of women's lives is visible through the letters. The magazines provided a space for women to seek solace, and to debate the meaning of marriage and family. By the 1960s, even the conservative attitudes toward sex, maintained by church and state, began to shift a little as women's magazines challenged the censors and published articles on sex education.[17]

A growing generational divide also marked the postwar family. Schools played an important role in altering intimate relations. The postwar generation was more educated. Throughout the 1950s and 1960s, literacy rates fell sharply, even in the South. Children tended to stay in school beyond the minimum required by law. The number of students earning middle school diplomas more than doubled between 1951 and 1971, as did those who graduated from high school. Although the overall rates still remained low, only 3 percent of Italians finished secondary school, and 2 percent held university degrees, the absolute number of Italians enrolled in university jumped between 1966 (456,000) and 1971 (800,000). Southern Italians in particular attended secondary schools and university in ever-growing numbers. By 1971, the educational gap in higher education between North and South had closed. While factory work pulled northern youth into the workforce at a younger age, southern young men and women went to college.[18] Adolescents in the 1950s grew up with more freedoms than their parents. On weekends teenagers would take scooters, cars, or trains to the local beaches or mountains. In the evenings, they would gather at the cinema, music clubs, bars, and pool halls. Young adults, even daughters, claimed more control over their earnings and their time. The global consumer society targeted young adults, who happily spent their money on American jazz albums, early rock 'n' roll, and blue jeans.[19]

The erosion of patriarchal authority at home accompanied a decline in church attendance. By 1968 less than half of all Italians attended church every Sunday. In the new neighborhoods outside Milan and Turin, attendance was even lower, where 11 percent of men reported going to church. Migration to the north ruptured ties with local saints, and the new parishes often proved unwelcoming to the migrants.[20] Although religion remained compulsory in grade school, and the Vatican had more cultural influence than ever before, the church's hold over social life was on the decline.

Between 1950s and 1960s, Italy experienced an unprecedented economic boom that transformed the world of work, society, and culture. In less than twenty years, Italy emerged as a modern industrial nation-state. Although not everyone lived well, overall, material conditions significantly improved. Urbanization transformed society and culture in ways that challenged traditional values.

CHAPTER 14
1968

The rains began in October of 1966. Violent storms swept across Veneto, Lombardy, Piemonte, Lazio, and the Abruzzi, flooding streets and piazzas, destroying bridges, and downing power lines. In the mountains, the snow piled up in the villages as temperatures plummeted. The water continued to fall and the rivers to rise. On Friday, November 4, the Arno spilled over its banks, rushing through the streets, houses, and museums of Florence, upending rail lines and blocking the autostrada. Over fifteen feet of water scoured the narrow streets of the city center, sweeping through the baptistery, the Uffizi, and the National Library. In some places the mud was over twenty feet deep. By the end of the day over 18,000 houses flooded, 4,000 people were left homeless, 17 people died, 30,000 cars washed away, 1,500 art objects were damaged, and over 1 million manuscripts lay covered in mud. The floods destroyed telephone and telegraph lines and left the city without electricity. The mayor sent out a call on the local radio station for volunteers with boats to join the rescue operations. As word of the flood filtered out, people watched the footage on television with disbelief and horror.[1]

Across Italy and Europe, university and high school students made their way to Florence to help salvage what could be saved. A week after the flood, thousands of young men and women set to work cleaning books, paintings, and statues. Others brought food and water to the elderly and housebound, and cleared the streets of the bloated corpses of cattle and horses. There was no organized appeal for help, volunteers just showed up, sleeping where they could, sharing meals, playing music, making friends, and finding lovers. Those who volunteered remember with fondness the feelings of intimacy that bonded German, British, American, and Italian youth. Two weeks after the flood, the journalist Giovanni Grazzini paid homage to these *Angeli del Fango* ("Mud Angels"), who proved wrong the elders who lamented that the youth of today were "without moral brakes, rebellious to discipline, irreverent toward God, Country, Family, 'savage angels' who came to destroy by the light of the moon, charity and grace. And now? Now they look around astonished, even moved watching these '*bravi ragazzi*'"[2] (Figure 19).

Out of the mud of Florence emerged a new generation of engaged and energized Italians. The government's response to the disaster reaffirmed the conviction of many young adults that the Italy forged by their parents had failed. In the 1960s, students had begun to challenge the cultural conservatism that permeated their schools and families, questioned authorities who privileged conformity and materialism over freedom and community. Their experiences in Florence strengthened their sense of being part of a transnational youth culture, linked by a love of James Dean, Janis Joplin, and Jack Kerouac and new political visions. In 1967, a year after the floods, students in Turin

Figure 19 "Angeli del Fango" (mud angels) at the National Library, 1966. Manuel Litran/Paris Match/Getty Images.

occupied the university, and soon the protests had spread, part of a global youth movement demanding change. Student unrest accompanied growing worker discontent and created new alliances. By the early 1970s, protests led to the emergence of a New Left and the Italian second wave feminist movement. The new politics turned violent. The 1960s and 1970s proved pivotal decades in the history of twentieth century; challenges to authority transformed social relations and fractured postwar political coalitions.

Forces of change

The immediate causes of the cultural and social revolution visible by the late 1960s lay in changes that began earlier in the decade. In 1962 a renewed labor militancy spread through the northern factories. New machinery increased speeds of production, making work more repetitive and stressful. Workers demanded more breaks and greater control of work processes to counter the accelerated rhythms. The influx of southern migrants into the factories had increased membership and energized the trade unions. In 1962, when the contract for metalworkers came up for negotiations, the unions demanded a forty-hour, five-day work week, new pay scales, and a greater union presence on the factory floors. The revitalization of organized labor met with resistance on the part of the owners.

Early in 1962, labor organizers renewed calls for national strikes. Workers at the Lancia and Michelin factories in Turin walked out, demanding long-term contracts and a third week of paid vacation. After a month, Lancia conceded to worker demands. At Michelin, the strikes grew violent as workers clashed with police; the workers gained limited concessions. After the strikes at Lancia and Michelin ended activists shifted their attention to the FIAT factory and its largely quiescent work force. The company paid the highest wages, hired the fewest number of South Italians, and had always swiftly quashed the first signs of worker militancy. Over the spring of 1962, union leaders organized the shop floor, strengthening the voice of the union.

On July 7, 1962, the metal worker sections of CGIL and CISL called for a three-day general strike in Turin. Tens of thousands of workers, including those from the FIAT factory, joined the picket lines and demonstrations. News that FIAT management had negotiated a separate agreement with the *Unione Italiana del Lavoro* (Italian Labor Union—UIL) infuriated workers who gathered in front of the UIL headquarters in Piazza Statuto. Demonstrators built barricades and charged at the police with stones and sticks. The police responded with tear gas and batons. Union officials tried to calm the crowd, but to no avail. The protests lasted for three days. In the aftermath of the demonstrations the trade unions denounced the violence, arguing that paid protesters, students, and anarchists had come to discredit the workers. At the trial, however, it was evident that most of the protesters were young men who worked in the factories, and most had come from the South. The Piazza Statuto protest made evident the existence of a worker's movement based on a new solidarity between northern and southern workers.[3]

The new labor movement transcended the divisions between Communist workers in CGIL and the Catholic workers who comprised the majority of CISL membership. This younger generation of workers rejected the authority of the PCI and PSI in favor of a politics that embraced a different theoretical framework. Just a year earlier a group of militant trade unionists and dissident Socialists and Communists published a new journal, *Quaderni Rossi* (Red Notebooks), arguing that the left had to move away from focusing on contract negotiations and instead attend to the changing working conditions on the factory floor. Over the next year the militant workers' movement grew in size and strength. The number of workers who went on strike rose, from 2,910,000 in 1961 to over 3,694,000 participants in 1962.[4]

Renewed labor militancy accompanied a general trend toward a more open society, fueled, in part, by changes within the Catholic Church. The conservative Pope Pius XII, a staunch supporter of electoral intervention and cultural censorship, died in 1958. The election of Pope John XXIII led to a reorientation of the church's role in society and politics. The new pope urged the church to abandon its interventionist political roles, disbanded the political committees, and remade Catholic Action into a social club. In 1962, Pope John XXIII convened the second ecumenical council of the Vatican, the first in nearly ninety years. Speaking to the assembled priests and bishops, the pope called on the church to address the needs of the world, and to instill a new joy and enthusiasm among Catholics. Vatican II urged the church to return to its spiritual and pastoral role and abandon its anti-communist crusade. In 1963, the pope issued the encyclical *Pacem in Terris* a plea for international reconciliation, and the dismantlement of the ideological barriers that divided the East and West. With demands for greater social justice, John XXIII's papacy paved the way for new alliances between Catholics and the left and laid the foundation for the creation of a center-left political coalition.

The strong electoral victory of the DC in the 1958 elections hid growing factional divides within the party. Amintore Fanfani, appointed prime minister in 1958, insisted that relying on an alliance with neofascists and monarchists left the party vulnerable, and to secure power the DC should invite the Socialists to join the governing coalition. Fanfani argued that by bringing the Socialists into the government, they could isolate the PCI. The right-wing of the party protested his plan and forced his resignation. In the wake of his ouster, a new faction formed within the party, the *Dorotei*, who supported the creation of a center-left coalition. Aldo Moro, a member of the *Dorotei*, took over as party secretary and began to cautiously steer the party in new directions.

In the meantime, the president of the Republic asked Tambroni, a conservative, authoritarian politician, to form a new government with the neofascist party MSI (*Movimento Sociale Italiana*) and the monarchists. Just months after taking office, the MSI announced that they would hold their annual conference in Genoa, a city proud of its antifascist history. To add insult to injury, the invited speakers included Emanuele Basile, the prefect of Genoa during the Salò Republic, famous for ordering the deportations of hundreds of workers and members of the resistance. On June 30, 1960, tens of thousands of Genoese, including former partisans, workers, and students, marched through the streets. By evening, battles raged between the demonstrators and the police. While the police, forced into retreat, called for reinforcements, veterans of the resistance movement organized a liberation committee to take control of the local government. Seeking to restore authority, Tambroni gave permission to the police to open fire on demonstrators. As the struggle in Genoa grew more violent, protests spread into Reggio Emilia and down to Sicily. The violence forced the resignation of the Tambroni, and the return of Fanfani, who formed a government with the support of the PSI and the Republicans.

Changes within the Communist Party contributed to the opening of the political landscape. In 1956 the Soviet Union Communist Party formally denounced Stalin. The revelations of Stalin's crimes roiled the PCI. Togliatti, the leader of the party, tried to minimize the accusations but ultimately was forced to take a stand. Togliatti blamed the Soviet leaders for not denouncing Stalin sooner, but refused to acknowledge his own complicity in supporting Stalin. Although Togliatti's words calmed some of the members of the party, rank-and-file supporters remained demoralized and disillusioned. Their anger at the party was fueled by the Soviet Union's brutal suppression of the Hungarian Revolution a few months later. International events sent the PCI into a crisis. A small dissident minority, led by Antonio Giolitti, demanded that the party recognize the importance of democratic liberties, encourage open debate, and declare its autonomy from all other communist parties. The dissenters lost the vote and were either expelled or resigned. After the Congress closed, hundreds of thousands of members left the party, forming new political coalitions. Between 1955 and 1966 the party lost over a quarter of its membership, and sunk into an existential crisis after the death of Togliatti in 1964: Would the party embrace open revolution or seek to integrate itself within the state?

The crisis in the PCI encouraged Pietro Nenni, the head of the Socialist Party, to break from the Communists. In 1956, the PSI refused to sign the pact of unity for the first time since the war. By 1961, the Socialists announced its allegiance to NATO, and indicated its willingness to enter the government. In January of 1962, Aldo Moro made the case for a center-left coalition at the DC's annual conference, and in February the Social Democrats and Republicans joined the government. In 1963, when Aldo Moro became prime minister, the PSI joined the government, with Nenni as deputy prime minister.

The divided center-left government proved unable to realize its promises of reform. One faction of government, including the Republican Ugo La Malfa, argued for a series of corrective legislative acts addressing the perennial problems of poverty of the South, agricultural backwardness, a disaffected citizenry, and political corruption. The left rejected what they considered cosmetic reforms and insisted on structural changes that shifted power to workers. Finally, there were those, including the *Doroetei* and Moro himself, who argued for the most minimal reforms possible, worried that wider reforms would undermine DC power. Over time positions hardened, and almost by default, the minimalist position emerged victorious. The possibility of political change mobilized workers and students, and the failure to enact real reform deepened their disillusionment with the state and political parties on the left and the right.

1968 in the North and South

The mud angels who came home from Florence in the spring of 1967 returned to schools and universities on the brink of revolt against a repressive, authoritarian system. Even before the Arno flooded students were growing frustrated with the oppressive climate of the schools. On Valentine's Day, 1966, students at *Liceo Parini*, an elite Milanese high school, surveyed their cohort asking questions about women's position in society in relation to family, work, and sex, and published the results in the school newspaper. The story drew the ire of the Catholic Student Association and within days police arrested the three teenage editors on charges of publishing obscene material and corruption of minors. Although the courts absolved the editors and sent them back to school, school administrators responded with draconian measures, heightening censorship and confiscating any pamphlets or books they deemed immoral. Despite their best efforts to control what students read, students continued to read banned books, passing on feminist manifestos and sharing documents from the US civil rights and student movements.

In April 1966, shortly after the student editors were exonerated, a group of neofascist students attacked members of a student Socialist group at the University "La Sapienza" in Rome, in an effort to disrupt student elections. The police arrived and refused to quiet the right-wing students who lined the halls singing Fascist songs and chanting slogans honoring Mussolini. First year architecture student Paolo Rossi, a member of Socialist Party and a Boy-Scout, was pushed down the stairs. He died the next day. Paolo's death sparked demands for a full investigation, but the university administration and the police did nothing. As student protests grew louder their demands moved beyond justice for Paolo to include calls for greater democratic representation within the university and radical curriculum reform.

When the universities opened in the fall of 1967, news of proposed educational reforms sparked widespread protests. Students at the University of Trento, a public

Catholic University founded in 1962, committed to realizing the political vision of the more liberal wing of the Christian Democratic Party, were among the first to stage a sit-in to debate the purpose of higher education. The majority of students rejected the elitist premises of the university and unfair selection processes, and instead, drawing on Marxist theories, they argued for the recognition of students as workers. Authorities squashed the protest in Trento, but the movement continued to grow.

On November 27, 1967, the students of Turin occupied the Faculty of Letters. Like their colleagues in Trento, the students took over the university in protest of the antiquated university structure, where professorial capriciousness had derailed the careers of many students. The Ministry of Education's proposed reforms calling for three distinct degree paths, reinforcing the hierarchical educational system, only infuriated students. In the occupied classrooms students critiqued course content and existing pedagogy, proposing new courses that they believed would better prepare them for the contemporary world. The students demanded a more democratic university that expanded power beyond the small circle of tenured professors, to include the untenured and students. Students interrupted lectures, demanding that professors address their concerns.

Most, but not all students, supported the movement. In Turin, 600 students voted in favor of taking over the university, and 60 opposed the occupation. Those who participated remember the time as personally transformative, providing space to carve out new social relations, to break free from parental expectations and rules. As in Florence in 1966, the university occupations created an open, creative space for young adults to live by their own rules. Rejecting bourgeois suits and dresses, they donned jeans, surplus army gear, parkas, and scarves, moving into student communes or squatting in empty buildings. The students embraced new political, sexual, and cultural freedoms in their political and personal lives.[5]

The student protest movements were marked by a deep commitment to democratization, egalitarianism, and consensus. Through sit-ins, university occupations, and theatrical street actions, students sought to challenge authority and disrupt the complacency of society. Yet, the movement was far from unified. The more radical student contingent insisted that real university reform required systemic social change, while other students limited their demands to the inclusion of students and all faculty into the university structure.

As student protests grew more violent the movement began to fracture. On March 1, 1968, nearly 4,000 student protesters, evicted from the University of Rome, gathered in the Piazza di Spagna and plotted to retake the Faculty of Architecture, located near Villa Borghese. The police attacked, and the students fought back. Over forty policemen were hospitalized. Until the "battle of Valla Giulia," as it was described by journalists, the protests had remained peaceful; the majority of students committed to a politics of nonviolence. In the face of increased police brutality, the student movement responded with increasing violence.[6] The violence divided the movement. By May, a growing number of students complained that they could no longer identify with the movement and were unsure about what or why they were protesting. Many returned to their studies, others moved their political work beyond the confines of the university.

The end of 1968 witnessed a transition in the student movement. As activists worked to create broad-based social coalitions, many of the distinctive characteristics of the movement disappeared. A new focus on organization and theoretical frames replaced the spontaneity and freedom of the 1967–68 protests. The New Left encompassed a multiplicity of political visions and goals, but in general remained committed to social transformation. In the North, activists focused on creating new worker-intellectual alliances; in the South, students challenged clientelism and the mafia, and women across Italy formed feminist movements. The diverse forms of activism reflected some of the important legacies of the Italian 1968 movement: multiple political visions and the creation of new political and social subjects.

In the fall of 1968, the student-worker collectives, *Potere Operaio* (Workers' Power) in Veneto, *Lotta Continua* (Continuous Struggle) in Turin, and *Avanguardia Operaia* in Milan, moved into the factories, organizing worker's committees and liaison groups in support of the worker protests. The failure of unions to resolve worker grievances, combined with the growing militancy of the student movements, culminated in the "Hot Autumn" of 1969, when millions of workers walked off their jobs, decrying factory discipline, brutal work schedules, and pay inequity. Workers argued that wages had to be unhitched from productivity quotas, profits, or the broader economic situation. Wages should be linked to the cost of living and value of labor. The new politics insisted on recognizing the similarities between the student struggle against institutional hierarchies and worker struggles against factory managers. In newspapers and pamphlets, the leaders of the New Left laid out the theoretical ties linking students and labor within the capitalist system. Over the course of the next two years the promise of an authentic revolutionary worker-student alliance faded. Employers responded to the protests by offering wage increases, and traditional unions recruited the most militant labor activists into their organizations. Ultimately the New Left succeeded in strengthening the traditional unions, increasing collaboration among the CGIL, UIL, and CISL.

As labor militancy faded, the New Left expanded their sites of struggle. Building on Mario Tronti's theory of the social factory, arguing that conditions of late capitalism expanded the spaces of repression and oppression into civil society and governmental institutions, members of *Lotta Continua* moved out of the factory and into prisons, government offices, and the community. Recruiting government bureaucrats, activists sought to democratize the bureaucracy and reform the legal system. In prisons, they formed study groups, insisting that the prisoners, mostly young and unemployed, should be brought in as an auxiliary revolutionary force. The expansive understanding of Leninist principles brought *Lotta Continua* into local neighborhoods, spearheading squatting initiatives to resolve housing difficulties, opening day cares, setting up collective restaurants, and running local health clinics. By the early 1970s activists in the North had created an alternate political movement.

Students in the South also voiced their anger at the antiquated universities, but unlike in the North, targeted government corruption and mafia violence in their wider protests. In early February of 1968 students at the University of Palermo occupied the Faculty of Letters. Like in Turin and Bologna, the student initially protested against the university administration, demanding new curriculum and envisioning a new more democratic and equitable politics. The earthquake of 1968 shifted the direction of the movement as it spilled out from university.[7]

On the afternoon of January 14, just a few weeks before the students rose in revolt in Palermo, a series of earthquakes struck western Sicily. The worst of the tremors, registering 6.1 on the Richter scale, destroyed the town of Belice, and left over 200 dead and nearly 100,000 homeless. In the aftermath of the earthquake, students volunteered to help clear the rubble. The experience solidified a sense of solidarity among Sicilian youth and a new political awareness of the failure of the state to meet the needs of the people. The rebuilding necessitated by the earthquake led many students to imagine new social and economic possibilities. Their visions, however, were quickly crushed as they watched government monies allocated for reconstruction siphoned off into the pockets of local politicians and the mafia. Sicilian youth refocused their anger onto political corruption deploying the same strategies as those movements critiquing capitalism and social inequity, including satire, irony, and disruption.

By the 1970s student activists moved into media, recognizing that radio and newspapers provided powerful means to challenge political authority. In Palermo, the newspaper L'Ora became the voice of the New Left, publishing stories linking politicians, industrialists, and the mafia. Southern activists, many who had joined the struggles in the north, turned to journalism and the arts to enact change. In the 1970s, Letizia Battaglia began publishing photos of the dead, and making visible the social and cultural costs of living with mafia violence. In 1977 Giuseppe Impastato founded the pirate radio station Radio Aut to broadcast the crimes of the local mafia. Impastato, born into a mafia family of Cinisi, first joined the student protesters in the late 1960s, and after university worked to enact land reforms through student-peasant alliances. His efforts led to direct confrontations with the local mafia, and soon he began staging satirical performances denouncing political and criminal corruption, before opening Radio Aut and broadcasting a satirical daily show mocking politicians and mafia. Two years later he ran for city council. In the midst of the election campaign the Mafia murdered him.[8] Although the southern student coalitions looked very different from the northern worker/student alliances, both movements shared a common critique of the political status quo and carved out space for new political voices.

Consequences of 1968: New Left and feminism

Student protests and the New Left drew the ire of the political establishment on both the left and right. The PCI deputy Giorgio Amendola dismissed the student protests as infantile. The poet and writer Pier Paolo Pasolini condemned the students as cowardly bourgeoisie, attacking the police, the "sons of the poor." Luigi Lonzo, a PCI leader, offered a more conciliatory approach, acknowledging that the party was partially at fault for having been unable to respond to the concerns of the young. The student movement divided the PCI. In 1969 when the PCI expelled those who shared the New

Left critiques many former party members joined the autonomous groups. The DC was also overwhelmingly hostile to the students, although they were more than happy to use the movement to isolate the PCI. Efforts to dismiss the new politics failed, and the autonomous left undermined the postwar political alliances that had provided stability.

The New Left threatened Moro's coalition. By the early 1970s the Socialists refused to join the DC, unless the PCI also agreed to be a member of the governing coalition. The autonomous parties had made the moderate Socialist position untenable, and their members left to join the PCI, *Lotta Continua* or *Autonomia Operaia*. In an effort to secure power, Aldo Moro opened negotiations with Enrico Berlinguer, the leader of the PCI, to bring the Communists into government. In 1973, Berlinguer outlined a "historic compromise" with the Christian Democrats in a series of articles published in the Communist journal *Rinascita*. The PCI proposed that in exchange for supporting public safety, economic growth, and church privileges, the DC would support comprehensive social reforms. In the following elections, the proportion of Communists elected to Parliament rose rapidly. In 1976, Giulio Andreotti formed the first government that relied on Communist support, and in 1978, the PCI formally entered the government, its members serving as cabinet ministers. Although the compromise opened the possibility of creating a new social democratic alliance, the bargain hardened opposition on both the left and right.

The emergence of women as autonomous political actors in the wake of 1968 transformed the postwar political landscape. The university protests politicized a younger generation of women committed to the creation of a feminist movement who flocked to the local collective or formed new ones. In 1968, women comprised nearly a third of university students, and eagerly joined the occupations, participating in the debates on the nature of power, democracy, freedom, and oppression. As in the global student protest movement, women often found themselves exiled to the margins of power, silenced by their male comrades. Their personal experiences within the movement contradicted the theoretical revolutionary imperatives. Debates focused on class oppression dismissed the subjugation of women. The gap between the experiences of men and women appeared particularly acute around the calls for greater sexual freedom. The emancipatory potential of the politics of sexual liberation in a country that prohibited the sale of contraception and banned abortion were far more complicated for women then for the men. When the students left the university, many women chose to focus their political work on the question of women's oppression.

In the 1970s, women began to form small, locally based collectives, carving out separate spaces. Informed by their own experiences, and the circulation of translations of Betty Friedan's *The Feminine Mystique*, Simone de Beauvoir's *Second Sex*, and the writings of Shulamith Firestone and Juliet Mitchel, women questioned existing gender and sexual hierarchies. Some groups, including *Movemento di Liberazione della Donna* (Movement for the Liberation of Women—MLD) one of the largest of the groups and one of the few linked to a political party (the Radical party), welcomed men, others advocated a separatist stance, insisting that women's autonomy could only be realized in the absence of men. Local groups focused first on the needs and issues of their immediate members, while also building wider networks to share publications, ideas, and information. Although the groups operated independently, reflecting class and regional conditions, they generally shared a conviction that goal of the movement should not be limited to equality, but a recognition of the distinctive subjective condition of women. The *Manifesto Rivolta Femminile*, plastered throughout Rome in July of 1970, opened with the statement that "women must not be defined in relation to man. This awareness is the foundation of both our struggle and our liberty." Common to feminists across the peninsula was the belief that the "personal was political," and that their experiences as lovers, daughters, and wives were of political import.[9]

By the 1970s, women formed hundreds of new collectives reflecting the diversity of the movement. Often meeting in private houses or women's centers, some groups focused on consciousness raising practices and uncovering female subjectivity, while others experimented with new forms of direct political engagement. By the 1970s, the collectives founded new theatrical companies, published newspapers and journals, opened women's clinics, and bookshops. These feminist spaces became centers of intellectual activities, assistance, and politics. Feminists instituted a "wages for housework campaign" in an effort to win compensation for housework and childcare and to draw attention to unacknowledged gendered forms of capitalist labor exploitation.

Deep generational and ideological divides marked the feminist movements. The older generation of "emancipationists," committed to equality, generally aligned with established political parties, viewed the "liberationists" as politically naïve. While the younger generation of feminists dismissed the feminism of the UDI as reformist rather than revolutionary, insisting the movement must be committed to the eradication of patriarchy, not the inclusion of women into the oppressive institutions of family, state, and workplace. Women's liberation, they argued, required the wholesale demolition of the sources of women's subordination.

Divorce and abortion constituted the central legislative victories of the movement and united the disparate camps. The political tactics of the feminist movement, including demonstrations, protests, and performances, mobilized support for legislative agendas, pushed through by the UDI and trade unions. In 1970, the Parliament legalized divorce, with the DC, the monarchists, and neofascists opposing the bill. The first divorce law was admittedly limited in that it allowed divorce only in the instances of criminal insanity, lengthy prison sentences, incest, or bigamy. However, the bill did stipulate that after five-year separation any couple could divorce for any reason. The DC attempted to revoke the law by calling a referendum in 1974, but the effort failed when 59 percent of Italians voted yes. In 1971, Parliament reformed the Noce Law, extending labor protections to home workers, lengthening maternity leave, and creating a national state-funded childcare system. The women's movement also forced through long needed changes to the civil code that stipulated husbands and wives were equal in marriage.

In a world where the church wielded enormous cultural power, abortion proved the most difficult struggle. Women took to the streets demanding the decriminalization of abortion. Alongside the massive demonstrations, women's groups opened local clinics, and helped pregnant women obtain legal abortions abroad. In 1978, the final bill approved by Parliament fell short of feminist demands, but still constituted a major victory. The law decriminalized abortions, made legal abortions through the first trimester if a doctor deemed the pregnancy or birth dangerous to the woman. Conservatives sought to overturn the law by referendum, but suffered a resounding defeat: 67 percent of Italians voted for legal abortion (Figure 20).

Throughout the 1970s, the feminist movement focused on remaking the family, campaigning for wages for housework and against sexual violence. The reform of family law in 1975 (law 151) was a critical step in challenging patriarchal authority within the household. The law abolished marital authority and the legal standing of men as heads of the household. Men and women had the same rights and duties in relation to their children and to each other. Wives were no longer legally required to reside where their husbands told them and were legally entitled to family resources. Unfortunately, feminists were unable to make headway against much of the pervasive sexism embedded in law. Sexual violence against women remained an "offence against morality," not an offense against a person, until 1996. By the late 1970s, the feminist collectives began to

Figure 20 A Feminist Demonstration along Viale Gorizia in Milan, 1977. Getty Images.

decline in number and visibility. Feminists, however, did not disappear. As women in the movement found work in academia, business, civil service, and politics, they altered the culture of the workplace, and challenged institutional hierarchies

By the mid-1970s, the "mud angels" were a decade older, and had helped launch new political movements and transform society and culture. The majority of those involved in the protests moved on with their lives. Many graduated and entered the workforce, bringing their politics with them. The autonomous left began to fade. *Lotta Continua* and *Potere Operaia* dissolved, its members joining either the more moderate wing of the *Avanguardia operaia* pursing a path of political integration or the new *Democrazia Proletaria*. A core group of the most militant protesters continued to fight, choosing a path of revolutionary militancy and violence.

Politics of violence

On the afternoon of December 12, 1969, a bomb exploded outside the *Banca Nazionale dell'Agricoltura* in Piazza Fontana in Milan, leaving sixteen people dead and eighty-eight wounded. On the same day two more bombs exploded in Rome, and a fourth bomb was discovered hidden near another bank in Milan. The police blamed the bombs on anarchists and rounded up the usual suspects. Among others, they brought in Giuseppe Pinelli, a railroad worker, for interrogation. Two days later, on the night of December 15, he fell to his death from the fourth-floor window of police headquarters. The *Carabiniere* declared the death a suicide, despite the presence of multiple officers in the office at the time of his death. Eventually the police charged Pietro Valpreda, a dancer, and anarchist, for the Milan bombings. In Rome, the police arrested fourteen members of the *Circolo Anarchico XII Marzo*. There was no evidence linking Pinelli, Valpreda, or any anarchist to the crimes. As the cases against the anarchists dissolved, signs that the police had ignored evidence pointing to the neofascists came to light. Even more disturbing, information emerged suggesting that the bombing had been coordinated by the neofascist party, the MSI, and the secret service in order to sow fear and panic among the public. The bombing at Piazza Fontana was the first salvo in a right-wing "strategy of tension," designed to use violence to rally support for the state, to justify the implementation of authoritarian measures. Calls to open an investigation flooded into Parliament, but the president refused on the grounds of national security concerns, and instead chose to cover up the evidence, and obstruct the judicial process.[10]

A year later, on December 7, 1970, Prince Junio Valerio Borghese, a former commander during the Republic of Salò, attempted a coup d'état. The coup failed, but Borghese and his small cadre of men succeeded in occupying the Ministry of the Interior before he was quietly escorted away. The political establishment covered up the plot, and news of the attempted coup filtered out months later. Even more disquieting was evidence that Borghese was connected to much broader network of politicians, secret service agents, and generals. The extent of the wider conspiracy to destabilize the state and to create the conditions for a military takeover did not come to the surface for another ten years. Throughout the 1970s the extreme right continued their campaigns of violence, targeting trains and public spaces. Although their efforts faded in the late 1970s, they returned with a vengeance in 1980, planting a bomb in the waiting room of the Bologna train station, killing more than eighty people.

Escalating right-wing violence, increased state repression, and the decline in labor militancy encouraged some on the extreme left to form an armed clandestine army. Violence, they argued, could only be met with violence. The *Brigate Rosse* (Red Brigades—BR), established in October of 1970, became the most effective and infamous of the groups advocating for armed resistance. Renato Curcio was raised by a single mother, who worked as a house cleaner on the outskirts of Rome. In 1962, he won a scholarship to study at the University of Trento where he became a leader in the student movement. He later joined *Lavoro Politico*. At the university, he met and married Margherita Cagol, born into a middle-class Sardinian family, and equally involved in the autonomous movements. Cagol and Curcio were disillusioned with the failure of the New Left to effect change through demonstrations and reforms, and began to insist on the need for revolution. Their message resonated among the disaffected members of the left.

Modeling themselves on Latin American guerilla groups and the Second World War partisans, the BR organized small independent cells in northern and central cities. Early in 1972, the BR carried out a series of highly publicized kidnappings of industrialists and union managers. Initially their actions tended toward the theatrical, setting fire to the cars of their hostages, holding mock trials and then releasing their victims physically unharmed a few hours later. The BR's activities were largely confined to North, and intended to win support among militant workers. In the South, a separate militant movement emerged, the *Nuclei Armati Proletari*, who moved through prisons and poor neighborhoods calling for armed insurrection. The police arrested the leaders of the NAP, and the movement soon faded. The authorities found the BR more difficult to suppress.

In 1974 the violence escalated. The BR targeted higher profile victims, and the state responded with greater force. In April of 1974 the BR kidnapped Judge Mario Sossi, keeping him captive for over a month. The abduction of Sossi brought the BR into the national spotlight, inciting both anger and approval. The visibility of the Sossi kidnapping, and the BR's growth, brought the full weight of the state down on the organization. The police infiltrated local cells, uncovered hiding places, and identified leaders. The BR responded by opening fire on the police and attacking the headquarters of the MSI. In September, the police arrested Renato Curcio, and a few months later Mara Cagol led a raid on the jail and freed him. In need of money, the BR returned to kidnapping. In June of 1975 the carabinieri discovered where the BR was holding a prominent businessman, and the ensuing firefight left two policemen and Cagol dead. The growing number of dead made the possibility of peace ever more elusive.

The elections of 1976, the first held after the historic compromise, polarized the electorate and strengthened the BR. Between 1976 and 1977 the BR recruited more members from disillusioned members of the PCI, underwent a structural reorganization, and prepared to open a new offensive. In 1977, they implemented a "strategy of annihilation," targeting civil servants, industrialists, and politicians from both the DC and the PCI. Between 1976 and 1977 the BR killed fifteen people and wounded fifty-six.

On the morning of March 16, 1978, Aldo Moro set out for Parliament. As he rode through the streets of Rome surrounded by his security detail, a car suddenly braked, forcing Moro's driver to stop. Moro's bodyguard pushed him to the floor as gunfire opened around them, all members of the police escort died. The kidnappers took Moro and drove away. The news of Moro's kidnapping shocked the public, who poured into the streets in a show of support for the minister. According to communiques from the BR, they had targeted Moro for his central role in orchestrating the PCI and DC alliance. Soon after, however, they proposed a prisoner exchange, suggesting an ulterior motive for the kidnapping. Andreotti refused to negotiate his colleague's release. During his fifty-five days in captivity, Moro wrote a series of letters to his wife, children, and colleagues pleading for his freedom, and condemning his own party. On May 9, 1978, Aldo Moro's body was discovered in the trunk of a car left half way between the DC and PCI headquarters.

Although the kidnappings and bombings on the right and left continued until the end of the decade, the kidnapping of Aldo Moro marked the beginning of the end of the "years of lead." The murder galvanized public opinion in support of the state. Few people protested the implementation of a series of emergency measures undermining civil liberties if they would bring an end to the violence. Authorities passed new laws requiring all tenants and residents to register with the local police in an effort to uncover the BR's clandestine apartments. The newly formed anti-terrorist squad under

Figure 21 Demonstration Against Terrorism in Piazza Duomo, Milan, March 16, 1978. Adriano Alecchi/Mondadori Portfolio/Getty Images.

the command of General Carlo Alberto Dalla Chiesa expanded wiretapping efforts, executed countless warrantless arrests, and widened the searches of private homes and vehicles. The number of *brigatisti* behind bars rose. In February 1980, Parliament passed the *Legge Cossiga* enabling magistrates to offer reduced sentences to members of subversive organizations in exchange for full cooperation. In March, the carabinieri arrested Patrizio Peci, who agreed to talk. Over the course of the spring he outlined in detail the organizational structure of the RB, destroying the entire organization. The *pentiti* program proved invaluable in breaking up the remaining cells, and within a few years, the state had virtually dismantled the Red Brigade (Figure 21).

By the beginning of 1980, the political, social, and cultural turmoil of the 1960s and 1970s began to fade. In some respects, it is difficult to see what the student protests and New Left had accomplished. More than a decade later, the unions were in decline. In October of 1979, FIAT fired sixty militant labor leaders. When the unions called a strike, the workers refused to join. The students were quiescent; membership in the autonomous groups was on the decline. The anti-terrorist campaigns strengthened the authoritarian and repressive state, silencing voices for reform. Yet, despite the apparent return to "normalcy," 1968 proved transformative, radically reconfiguring social relations, cultural mores, and the political landscape.

CHAPTER 15
A CHANGING WORLD (1980–2000)

As the generation born between the 1950s and 1960s reached adulthood in the 1980s, it seemed as though the youth movements had altered their worldviews but had done little to change the worlds they lived in. Costanza, born in 1963 in the province of Grossetto, recognized the importance of second wave feminism for a girl coming of age in a provincial city. Costanza remembers her youth as a time of freedom, where "sex was not taboo," and she lived in a world apart from her parents. She went to university, joined the student movement, and believed her degree would enable her to realize the ideals of liberty entwined in feminism and the new politics. Yet, within a few years of enrolling in the university, Costanza fell in love, married, dropped out of university, and became a mother at the age of twenty-two. Her early political activities fell by the wayside, and when Berlinguer, the leader of the PCI, died in 1984, she withdrew from politics altogether. She remembered how "we tried so hard . . . and then many [of us], growing up, reproduced the same models that we tried to destroy."[1]

Costanza's story was not unique. Many of those who took to the streets in the 1970s, embracing the revolutionary promises embedded in sexual liberation and new political visions, found themselves living lives that appeared very similar to those of their parents. By the mid-1980s, it seemed as though the passions, dreams, and struggles of their youth only survived in the songs of Fabrizio de Andre and Francesco de Gregori. Yet, in 1992, the political coalitions held in place by memories of fascism and the Cold War unraveled. The political and social movements of the 1960s and 1970s, combined with shifts in global capitalism and new migrations, undermined postwar stability. By the end of the century, it was clear that Italians lived in a world marked by new social relations and notions of individual and collective identities.

Politics on the margins

One of the significant consequences of the political struggles of the 1970s was the emergence of new voices challenging the authority of the governing parties and the power of Rome. Regional reforms undertaken in the 1970s fostered the creation of local political movements across the peninsula. Although the constitution of 1948 made provision for greater regional autonomy, the actual devolution of power to regional governments took hold after 1970. These ordinary regions, as compared to the autonomous regions designated in 1948, held their first elections for regional assemblies in June of 1970. Although ostensibly responsible for overseeing local health services, education, and urban planning, the central government still funded regional initiatives and retained the power to overrule their deliberations.

Despite their limitations, the reforms strengthened the autonomy of provincial politicians. Toward the end of the decade, under pressure from the left, Parliament passed a series of reforms transferring more control over public agencies, civil servants, and monies to the regional assemblies. Each region could use state funds to implement their own development projects, youth employment programs, childcare centers, charity initiatives, and arts programs. Access to government monies and contracts transformed local political offices into lucrative and powerful positions, benefiting smaller regional parties. The Christian Democrats, Socialists, and Communists continued to dominate the larger regional assemblies, but in the provinces, the additional resources enabled grassroots organizations to carve out wider spheres of influence. By the mid-1980s, the devolution of power to the regions had led to the emergence of new political movements. These geographically and ideologically disparate movements undermined the fragile postwar political coalitions.

In the 1983 regional elections of Veneto the *Liga Veneta* won 4 percent of the vote, and a seat in Parliament. *La Liga* was one of the several regional movements, demanding greater fiscal, economic, and social autonomy for the communes. The northern leagues embraced a patchwork of political and social philosophies, ranging from libertarian fiscal policies to social conservative views, although they shared a vaguely federalist vision of Italy where government services and jobs should go first to northern residents. Underlying league politics stood the conviction that the languages, customs, and histories of the regions provided ample evidence that the people of Lombardy and Veneto comprised a separate, and superior, nation, forcibly annexed by Italy. The cultural rhetoric celebrating the northern peoples turned racist, devolving into attacks on immigrants and South Italians. The *Liga Veneta*, founded by Franco Rocchetta, drew on long simmering anger toward the central government stretching back when Mussolini sought to nationalize the provinces, and fueled by postwar migrations, industrialization, and a state bureaucracy that seemed to target small family firms and entrepreneurs. Rocchetta's arguments for regional self-determination echoed calls for a federalist state emanating from populist autonomous movements in Val d'Aosta and South Tyrol.[2]

Although ideologically opposed to the Marxist-Leninist groups of the 1970s, the leagues shared the New Left's rejection of postwar political coalitions, corruption, and clientelism. Many of the founding members of the leagues had honed their political skills within the student movements. In his twenties, Umberto Bossi, a leader of the *Lega Lombarda*, was active in the autonomous movement, a member of *Il Manifesto* and the *Partito di Unita' Proletaria*. In the early 1980s he turned away from Marxism, but continued to frame his politics as a struggle against hegemonic power. Roberto Maroni, an early member of the *Lega Lombarda,* joined a Marxist-Leninist group in Varese at the age of sixteen and remained active in the movement until 1979, when he met Bossi. The northern leagues appropriated many of the strategies of the earlier movements, publishing newspapers, opening radio stations, organizing mass rallies and demonstrations, and holding colorful historical reenactments of Medieval and Renaissance battles celebrating their distinct cultures.

Within a few years, these provincial political parties emerged as an influential bloc. In 1982, Umberto Rossi founded the *Lega Lombarda*, and under his charismatic leadership, the movement grew, spreading into Piedmont, Emilia-Romagna, and Tuscany. The earliest parties, including the South Tyrolean's People's Party, List for Trieste, and the Valdostan movement, presented candidates for elections in 1979, claiming a handful of seats. In 1983, the *Liga Veneta* won its first seat in the Senate. In 1987, voters returned Bossi to Parliament, and the *Lega Lombarda* carried administrative elections in Bergamo and Varese. In 1989, six northern leagues joined together to form the *Lega Nord per l'Independenza della Padania*, a political party committed to advancing the interests of the northern states. The *Lega Nord* became a player on the national political scene. In the 1990 elections the *Lega Nord* won 5 percent of the national vote, and nearly 20 percent in Lombardy. In 1993, Milanese elected a member of the *Lega Nord* Mayor. By the 1990s, the *Lega Nord* stood poised to challenge the political elites.[3]

In the South, local political movements challenged the collusion between state and organized crime in the face of growing mafia violence. In 1981, nearly two decades after the first mafia wars in the early 1960s, Toto Riina, the leader of the Corleone clan, started the second mafia war, known simply as *la mattanza* (the killings). For years, Riina had recruited dissatisfied members of the other clans, forged regional alliances, isolated and discredited the Palermo families, in an effort to eliminate all rivals. In the late 1970s, Riina began the war by targeting politicians, and then moved on to massacre the Palermitano bosses. In just two months Riina's clan killed over 200 people, establishing control over Palermo and the surrounding regions. By 1983, the killings waned, but never stopped.[4]

Unlike previous wars, Riina targeted politicians as well as mafia bosses and antimafia activists. The murders of high profile politicians and magistrates, the *cadaveri eccellenti* (eminent cadavers), were intended to prove to corrupt politicians that the old alliances no longer offered rewards or protection, and to intimidate those who challenged the mafia. In the spring of 1979 Riina's men shot Michele Reina, the secretary of the provincial Christian Democrat Party who had the temerity to support Moro's historic compromise. In July, they assassinated Giorgio Ambrosoli, a Milanese lawyer working on the case against Michele Sindona, a banker linked to the Vatican, the mafia, and politicians. A few months later, they killed Cesare Terranova, a leader in the antimafia movement and member of the independent left, who had recently returned from Rome to serve as chief examining magistrate in Palermo. In January 1980 they killed Piersanti Mattarella, the leader of the Sicilian regional government and a Christian Democratic committed to party reform. In May, they murdered Emanuele Basile a young Carabiniere captain stationed in Monreale investigating the links between heroin traffic and the mafia. As the number of "eminent cadavers" grew, so did calls for the government to respond. Beyond obfuscation and attempts to shift blame on to the extreme left, the state did little to stop the violence.

In 1980, the Communist Deputy, Pio La Torre, requested a transfer back home to Palermo. Born into a poor family in rural Sicily in the 1920s, war and reconstruction drew him into politics as a young man. In the 1940s he joined the Communist Party, becoming a leader in the postwar peasant movements. In 1962, he was elected regional secretary of the party, and a decade later he was elected to the national Parliament. While in government La Torre continued to work for land reforms and against state corruption, in Rome, he joined the antimafia parliamentary commission and lobbied hard for the passage of an Italian version of the US RICO laws (Racketeer Influenced and Corrupt Organizations Act). Members of the DC fiercely resisted La Torre's bill. A year later, La Torre returned to Sicily as regional secretary of the PCI.

In Palermo, La Torre entered into the escalating mafia wars. He advocated for the appointment of General Carlo Aberto dalla Chiesa as Prefect of Palermo. Although the conservative Dalla Chiesa, the son of an ardent Fascist, stood for all he hated, La Torre realized that the tactics Dalla Chiesa had used against the *Brigate Rosse* could be directed against organized crime. Recognizing the formidable threat posed by these two men, the mafia ordered La Torre's execution. On April 30, 1982, just two days after Dalla Chiesa arrived in Palermo, the mafia opened fire on La Torre and his driver, Rosario Di Salvo, killing both. Over 100,000 mourners attended La Torre's funeral. Despite the enormous outpouring of grief and rage, Rome remained silent. Hampered by a vague mandate and little support from Rome, Dalla Chiesa soon realized he was isolated and powerless. In Rome, politicians opposed to Dalla Chiesa's work that spread rumors questioning the prefect's integrity and ethics. In September of 1982 the mafia executed Dalla Chiesa.

The deaths of Matarella, Basile, La Torre, and Dalla Chiesa, combined with the failure of the political establishment to act, sparked grassroots movements. Residents funneled their rage into local organizations determined to break the mafia hold over their city. Students staged rallies in support of the police, often on the frontlines of the struggle against the mafia. *L'Ora* publishes investigative reports detailing the nexus between mafia, industry, and politics that held the city hostage. The stark and stunning photos of Letizia Battaglia that appeared on the front page forced residents to see the violence that surrounded them. Faced with mounting public rage, the government finally took action and passed the Rognoni-La-Torre law. The Rognoni-La Torre bill provided magistrates with two important tools to fight the mafia: mandatory prison sentences for anyone guilty of membership in the mafia; the power to confiscate mafia assets.

The popular protests and legislative initiatives energized the Palermo antimafia pool. Rocco Chinnici, appointed after the death of Terranova, implemented a series of reforms making the squad more efficient and efficacious. Insisting on full collaboration, Chinnici ensured that all information was shared, so if one member of the squad was killed, the investigations no longer came to a halt. In 1983, Chinnici was killed when a car bomb exploded outside his house. His successor, Antonio Caponnetto continued to strengthen the pool. Working alongside magistrates Giovanni Falcone and Paolo Borsellino, Caponnetto made full use of the new Rognoni-La Torre law: the expanded surveillance laws still in place from the 1970s, and the Cossiga Law, enabling prosecutors to offer prisoners immunity for testifying.

In 1984 the antimafia pool achieved a major breakthrough when Falcone convinced Tommaso Buscetta to turn state's witness. Born into a poor Palermo family, Buscetta rose through the ranks of the local mafia, working the black market during the war years, before becoming a hit-man for the Palermo mafia. Forced into exile in the 1950s, he was instrumental in expanding the clan's transnational drug trade. In 1972, he was arrested for heroin possession in Brasil and extradited to Italy. From his prison cell, he watched the rise of the Corleonese with growing concern. In 1982, released on probation, he fled back to Brasil where he was rearrested. Locked in a Brazilian prison, aware that Riina had ordered the execution of his family, Buscetta realized he had no protection and agreed to talk. Over a year, Buscetta described the structure of the mafia, its initiation rites, and the history of the clans to Falcone. Buscetta served as a kind of interpreter for the magistrates, making sense of the complicated relationships born of money, power, and blood that defined mafia relations. Buscetta's collaboration remained secret until September 1984 when the magistrates issued 366 arrest warrants and arrested hundreds of *mafiosi* in predawn raids.

The arrests empowered popular and institutional antimafia movements. Centers opened to honor the work of Danilo Dolci and Giuseppe Impastato. The Archdiocese of Palermo broke its silence, speaking out forcefully against the mafia. A new generation of politicians won elections on platforms that challenged the long-standing relationship between the state and the mafia. In the 1985 regional elections, Sicilians elected LeoLuca Mayor, ushering in the *primavera di Palermo* (Palermo Spring). Orlando, a long-time member of the DC, was part of a new generation of Catholic loyalists who embraced principles of social justice. Orlando entered Palermo politics under the mentorship of Mattarella and enthusiastically participated in the administration's efforts to end municipal corruption. Rebelling against his party, Orlando refused to deny the existence of the mafia. As the mayor, he mobilized city resources to build a bunker-like courtroom for the impending maxi-trials and made the city a civil complainant in the trial. Under his administration, city government hosted outdoor concerts and cultural exhibits in an effort to reclaim public spaces and civil society.[5]

When the maxi-trial opened in February of 1986, approximately 475 men faced charges. Falcone and Borsellino buried the defense with mountains of carefully prepared evidence, and the testimony of Buscetta. The trial lasted nearly two years. In December of 1987, the judge and jury returned over 300 guilty verdicts: a stunning victory for the prosecution. Although many of the verdicts were overturned on appeal, ultimately the Supreme Court upheld the original rulings. The maxi-trials severely damaged the Palermo mafia, making it impossible to ignore the link between mafia and politicians.

Mafia investigations in Palermo lent credence to rumors that leading politicians had subverted democratic processes for much of postwar period. In the spring of 1981, magistrates in Milan, investigating the collapse of the Banca Ambrosiano and the ties between the Vatican banker Michele Sindona and the mafia, uncovered evidence of the existence of a secret Masonic lodge, *Propaganda Due* (P2). The P2 first emerged as a patriotic secret society in the Risorgimento, but had long since disappeared. In the early 1970s, the Masonic leadership tasked Licio Gelli with resurrecting the P2 lodge to counter the New Left. Gelli, a provincial business man, had long been a supporter of the Far Right. He had volunteered for the Italian expeditionary forces in Spain and worked as a liaison officer with the German SS during the Salò Republic. Only in 1944, when it became clear he had chosen the losing side, did he join the resistance and volunteer to work with American military intelligence. Gelli's political sympathies never changed; he remained a staunch Nationalist and anti-communist. Gelli recruited bankers, regional and national politicians, secret service agents, generals, admirals, former prime ministers, industrialists, prefects, and journalists into the resurrected P2, many of whom were linked to Borghese's failed coup d'état in 1970, or the mafia. The discovery of the documents made evident that P2 was far more than a lodge committed to working "solely for the good of humanity." In 1982 the lodge was closed.[6]

The mission of Gelli's P2 was to eradicate communism and create a more "stable" Italy. The lodge placed its people in key economic and political positions through bribery and corruption, unleashing extensive propaganda campaigns against the left. Members of the P2, including the chief of the secret service, Pietro Musumeci, and Gelli were eventually implicated in the campaigns to blame the anarchists for the Bologna bombing in 1980. The full extent of P2's activities remains murky, although as the 1984 commission concluded, the lodge clearly sought to pollute "public life," and "undermine democracy." A minority report, issued at the end of the investigation, went farther, claiming that P2 was an intrinsic part of the political system. Contrary to the parliamentary findings, the judicial inquiry, moved from Milan to the more agreeable magisterial climate of Rome, determined that the men involved were merely business associates.

The revelations of P2, the judicial ruling, and evidence of mafia collusion in Palermo, deeply discredited the Christian Democratic Party and the entire political system. In 1990, 76 percent of Italians reported that they were dissatisfied with the way democracy worked in their country.[7] Popular disgust grew when a Venetian magistrate came across documents in 1990 outlining the existence of *Gladio*, a clandestine "stay-behind," quasi military organization created in partnership with the CIA and Italian secret services as a last-ditch defense against communism. The documents identified Gelli as the central figure, and linked munitions held by *Gladio*, to the bombings undertaken by members of the extreme right. In October of 1990, Prime Minister Giulio Andreotti admitted the existence of Gladio. Over 600 people, including Francesco Cossiga, the president of the Republic, were implicated in the scandal. The left-wing accusations that politicians were actively seeking to bring down the democracy, that so many had dismissed as paranoia, had been confirmed.

The DC-PSI alliance could not withstand the growing evidence of systemic corruption. When the Palermo maxi-trials opened, the national political landscape was in chaos. The party coalitions crumbled; and individual politicians traded contracts, monies, and political appointments for votes, or plundered public resources for private gain. Craxi, the leader of the Socialist Party, who served as prime minister from 1983 to 1987, distributed patronage with unrestrained abandon, accruing a large personal fortune in the process. The cumulative effect of the political movements of the 1980s strengthened *partitocrazia*, a term coined by the journalist Roberto Lucifero in 1949, referring to systems where parties wielded greater power than the constitution or Parliament. The only thing that politicians seemed able to agree on was the danger posed by magistrates. In response to the judicial investigations uncovering widespread collusion and bribery, the government limited the powers of the judiciary and extended legal protections to defendants.

The expansion of the European community further undermined political alliances. Although Italy signed the Treaty of Rome in 1957, it was at best a reluctant participant, little interested in working to European integration. Recognizing that their power rested in local networks, politicians saw little benefit in representing Italy's interests as the European community moved toward economic and political unification. By the 1980s, Italy found itself reacting to European directives, rather than shaping them. Through a combination of indifference, disorganization, and hostility, local and regional governments often refused to take on European funded projects. The European community controls on monies challenged the clientelistic networks that shored up parties and politicians. The attitude of politicians stood in stark contrast to that of the people, who expressed unwavering support for the European project since the 1970s. The gap between popular opinion and political practice grew untenable as domestic political discontent rose and the European community grew stronger.[8]

By 1980 leading politicians within the DC-PSI alliance sought to counter the declining reputation of their political parties at home by trumpeting their commitment to integration. Andreotti, Craxi, and others championed the European Monetary System (1979), linking all European currencies through a restricted foreign exchange rate, supported the move toward a single market, signed on to the Schengen agreement (1985) guaranteeing freedom of movement within the boundaries of the EEC. Italy played a central role in shaping the Maastricht treaty creating the European Union in 1992. Securing its place in the wider world redounded well on individual politicians, but failed to resolve domestic conflicts. Italy's ties with the European community and the European Union exacerbated the sense that the state did not function, and neither political parties nor Parliament could fix it.

Society

The mounting dissatisfaction with public life accompanied an increased satisfaction with personal life. Net average income more than doubled between 1965 and 1991. Over 65 percent of Italians owned at least one home, and over 75 percent owned a car, refrigerator, and a washing machine. People were, in general, healthier and better educated. Infant mortality rates declined and life expectancy rose. The passage of the National Health Service law in 1979, expanding the number of doctors and clinics, improved access to health care across the nation. Although the passage of legislation in 1962 making education compulsory through the age of fourteen did not eradicate class and regional educational differences, it did raise literacy rates. Material security and greater disposable wealth encouraged Italians to spend more on travel and entertainment. Increased longevity, personal mobility, and a growing consumer culture, combined with the changing nature of family, widened social networks and further eroded traditional forms of political power.[9]

Family continued to anchor society, but its form and function changed. While the number of households rose over the course of the 1980s, the size of families shrunk: the average household fell from 3.0 people in 1981 to 2.8 people in 1991. By 1991, nearly half of all households were comprised of one or two people. Falling birth rates and rising divorce rates contributed to changing the shape of families. On average women were having fewer children and having them later. Italy's fertility rate of just 1.3 children stood among the lowest fertility rates in Europe, and many couples were choosing not to have children at all.[10] Although divorce rates remain low, the legalization of divorce accompanied a rise in the number of single parent households. Throughout the 1980s and 1990s, the number of people who chose to live together outside of marriage also rose. By the 1990s, the traditional heterosexual legal family had lost its primacy in regulating sexuality and reproduction, although they continued to anchor social networks. The new households remained embedded in tightly woven kin networks, and relied on family for childcare, financial assistance, and psychological support.

Feminism, sexual liberation, and changes in the workplace all played a role in the transformation of the family. Feminist critiques of patriarchal power, domestic violence, and the burdens of unpaid labor redefined ideals of intimate partner relations. The Family Reform Law of 1975 stipulated that husband and wife shared authority within the family, acquiring the same civil rights and obligations. Wives were no longer required by law to acknowledge their husband as head of household with the sole right to determine where and how the family lived. Husbands and wives now held equal legal standing in relation to family life, children, and property, and responsibility for the family's economic and emotional well-being. Changing cultural norms shaped the impact of the legal reforms on family life.[11]

Liberalization of sexual mores, access to contraception, and the ability to divorce strengthened expectations that conjugal unions constituted an equitable and emotional partnership. Greater access to education and the increased number of women in the workforce played a critical role in shifting familial gender roles. More women delayed marriage and children until they established their careers. When women did marry or entered domestic unions they did so with greater financial security and wider social networks. The move toward more equitable relations between wives and husbands accompanied a shift to more liberal relations between parents and children. Children enjoyed greater freedom and independence as adolescents, and parents continued to provide housing and financial support well into adulthood.

The changing affective and physical contours of the family did not eradicate gender inequities in public or private. The fusion of femininity with maternity diminished women's standing in the workforce. Discriminatory, and often illegal, practices continued to women's work in private and public sectors precarious. Women recounted stories of employers asking them to sign an undated letter of resignation when they started work, so that if they become pregnant or ill, the employer could present the letter of resignation and avoid paying benefits. The tendency to regard women's work as auxiliary and the changing decline in the number of permanent jobs left women vulnerable to the whims of their employers.[12] Despite substantial increases in the number of women wageworkers by the 1990s, the proportion of women active in the workforce remained among the lowest in Europe. At home, patriarchal authority did not disappear. Although husbands assumed a greater portion of chores and care-work within middle-class families, women continued to shoulder the bulk of domestic labor. New kinds of domestic arrangements did not make the family safer for women. Despite efforts to define rape and domestic violence as crimes, the government did not pass a comprehensive sexual assault bill until 1996. According to a government report published in February of 2007, over 30 percent of women experienced physical or sexual violence in their lives, often at the hands of partners or kin.[13]

Changing forms of family and work fueled volunteerism widening social networks and undercutting the traditional sources of political power. By the end of the century men and women offered their time and energy to a variety of volunteer efforts, including drug-counseling clinics, criminal rehabilitation, needy families, animal rescue, immigrants, and people with disabilities. The associations provided advice, material assistance and helped people access services.[14] The 1980s saw an increase in participation in church-based activities, after decades of falling attendance at mass and parish events. For many, the church provided a welcome respite from the sordid world of politics, and the materialism of daily life. The expansions of new civil associations, often funded by regional monies, strengthened grassroots politics and encouraged issue oriented voting patterns. Legislative struggles around divorce, abortion, and family reform split the center-left ruling coalition, creating new alliances between liberals and the left, and between the DC, Monarchists, and Fascists.

Economy

Globalization also disrupted postwar politics. Between 1976 and 1992, real GDP grew by nearly 50 percent, well above the average for the European community. Economic growth, however, was no longer fueled by the industries that had driven the first "economic miracle." Manufacturers of automobiles, domestic appliances, and chemical industries had difficulty competing in the global market and watched their profits fall. In the course of the 1980s over one million factory jobs disappeared. The shrinking factory workforce eroded union power. By the end of the decade, union membership declined; in 1986 unions represented 1.5 million fewer workers than in 1976, and over a quarter of the members were retired. Agricultural jobs also disappeared. Agro-industries, including Parmalat and Barilla, prospered throughout the 1960s and 1970s, but as global demand for Italian wines, cheeses, and fruits grew, multinational corporations moved in to the markets. By the 1980s agro-industries faced competition from Nestle and Kraft for control over production and distribution networks.

Many of the unemployed found work in smaller manufacturing firms, the service sector, and civil service. Small-scale manufacturing, quick to adopt more flexible, innovative strategies, proved enormously profitable, offsetting declines in traditional industries and corporate agriculture. The changing economy shifted the industrial center eastward. The people of Lombardy, Veneto, Trentino, Marche, and Emilia Roma grew wealthier. By the mid-1980s, Lombardy boasted over 350,000 companies, and nearly a quarter were small, family run firms, manufacturing jewelry, textiles, and ceramics. The growth of both domestic and global consumer markets fueled prosperity. The expansion of the common market benefited the smaller cottage industries. More people also found work in service industries. Increased entrepreneurship accompanied growth in tourism, commerce, financial services, advertising, and accounting. Public sector jobs continued to provide jobs for many.

The large corporations adapted to shifting markets by adopting new technologies, developing different products, and eliminating unskilled jobs. The retooling did not come cheap, and much of the cost fell on the state, a major shareholder in many of the firms. Throughout the economic boom, the state had invested in steel, airlines, shipbuilding, banks, and electricity through the IRI. Unfortunately, their investment choices were often driven more by political expediency and private greed rather than sound fiscal policy. As the industries began to fail, the state increased government subsidies, providing generous retirement packages and unemployment benefits to the newly unemployed. The close relationship between state and industry meant that the declining profits of private firms resulted in greater public debt. By the last few years of the decade, interest payments weighed heavily on the national budget, but the possible remedies seemed too politically fraught. Attempts to raise money through new taxes lowered domestic demand and contributed to the economic decline of the early 1990s. The shifting economy deepened geographical and gender divides within the workforce.

The late twentieth-century industrial landscape accentuated divisions between North and South. The emerging economy restructured employment in ways that made it increasingly difficult for unskilled labor and educated youth just entering the market to find work. As the northern manufacturing industries required workers with technical or specialized skills, the demand for construction workers and unskilled labor fell. Unskilled workers in the North usually ended up working in low-paying retail jobs, and the southern economy had less to offer unskilled workers, since most of the government subsidized factories had closed. Recent university graduates also found it difficult to find work in the public or private sector. Despite the system of national exams (*concorsi*) put in place to ensure state jobs went to the best qualified, public sector jobs remained part of the political system. Political connections and kin continued to determine who worked in local government offices. The long-term contracts made for little turnover. The politics of clientelism, the presence of the mafia, and the corruption of the state hindered independent entrepreneurs from opening new businesses. By the mid-1990s, it became apparent that few private investors were willing to invest in the South. Even tourism, one of the few sectors that did grow, suffered inadequate public and private investment.

The economic consequences of global capitalism and European integration deepened regional divisions and distrust of the state. In the South, the changing economy meant underemployment or joblessness. In 1990, 21 percent of southern Italians between fifteen and seventy-four years of age were unemployed, as compared to roughly 3 percent in the northwest. The gap was even higher among the youth. In the northwest 12 percent of residents between the ages of fifteen and twenty-four were unemployed as compared to 52 percent in the South.[15] Although residents in Lombardy and Piedmont may have been able to find work, the jobs were more precarious than those of their parents. The loss of well-paying secure jobs, sharp rise in youth unemployment, and the gridlock and corruption visible in the public sector generated support for the regional parties.

New mobilities

New migrations played a pivotal role in reshaping society and politics at the end of the century. Since the Risorgimento, Italy had defined itself as an emigrant nation, but in 1973, the number of immigrants outnumbered emigrants. Those who first noticed the shift focused on explaining why Italians seemed to be staying home. Experts pointed to the global economic crisis of the 1970s and the condition of the domestic economy in the 1980s as causal factors of diminishing emigration. Demographers noted that many emigrants who had spent their working lives in Germany and the United Kingdom had reached retirement age and moved home. Slowing rates of emigration and a rising number of returnees accounted for only a portion of the population increase. French, British, and German managers, who came to work for the multinational manufacturing and agro-industries, comprised a significant portion of the immigrants, although few experts seemed to notice them. Only when the number of immigrants from outside the European Union began to grow did Italians begin to take note of immigrants.[16]

Between 1984 and 1987 the number of immigrants rose from 400,000 to 572,103, with the majority identified as *extra-communitari*, coming from outside of the European community. Official estimates, based on those who registered for a *permesso di soggiorno* (residency permit), underestimate the number of immigrants. Experts believe that at least another 400,000 undocumented migrants crossed the borders in the 1980s. In the 1990s, Croatian, Slovenian, and Albanian war refugees joined the growing number of labor migrants from Eastern Europe, Africa, and Asia. Over the course of the 1990s nearly one million people arrived from China, Philippines, Morocco Senegal, Tunisia, Poland, Romania, and Albania. Women comprised over half of the new immigrants.[17]

Migrants found work in the expansive underground cash economy. Moroccans, Tunisians, Eritreans, Senegalese, and Filipinos worked the fields, cleaned houses, and watched the children. In the South, men worked as poorly paid seasonal or day laborers in agricultural or fishing industries. Women took jobs as housecleaners, nurses, and nannies. Few immigrants stayed in the South, most gravitated to the northern industrial regions, seeking work in manufacturing, agro-industry, retail, and service industries. Volunteer organizations and social service agencies helped immigrants find housing, jobs, and language classes, easing the difficulties of integration.

The government paid little attention to policing its borders or the legal status of immigrants. Until the 1980s there was one Fascist-era law requiring all foreigners to report to the local police but no other regulations. The first legislation passed in 1986 regulated access to the labor market and required employers to offer all the same benefits to legal workers. Although motivated by a desire to create equity between undocumented and documented labor, the unintended consequence of the law was to expand the informal labor market, as employers sought to avoid paying benefits for immigrant workers. The law did little to facilitate the integration of the growing number of immigrants. In 1990, Parliament passed the Martelli Law, guaranteeing immigrants the same social rights as Italians. The law offered legal amnesty for both immigrants and employers; hundreds of thousands of immigrants took advantage of the law and obtained their *permesso di soggiorno*, and work permits. The law addressed the needs of the immigrants but did not provide a means of legal entry, or a pathway to citizenship. Clandestine migration continued to rise throughout the 1990s.

The European Union pressured Italy to secure its borders and create a coherent immigration policy in advance of the implementation of the Schengen agreement. Italy responded by passing The Turco-Napolitano law in 1998 which in addition to introducing quotas tied to labor needs and deportation proceedings that provided the state to order "temporary" administrative detention if it deemed necessary, also provided permanent residence cards and expanded access to benefits for documented immigrants. The question of citizenship proved contentious as the country's immigration needs collided with those of its emigrant nation. Citizenship laws, anchored in a combination of blood and birth right, had been shaped by the needs of emigrants, not immigrants. In the 1990s politicians passed laws acknowledging dual citizenship making it easier for those of Italian origin to gain citizenship in an effort to bind the Italian diaspora to the nation, but did not create a pathway to citizenship based on work or residency alone.

The new laws helped immigrants acquire legal status, but did little to mitigate structural inequities, cultural misunderstandings, and everyday prejudices. Many people welcomed the immigrants offering them shelter and work, referencing their own history as strangers in strange lands. In the course of the 1980s, however, sympathy often turned to fear. As migrants from Asia and Africa arrived in ever-growing numbers, newspapers began to refer immigration as "an emergency," or as a "mass invasion." The term *extra-communitari* took on a racial cast, code for Africans, Filipinos, and Chinese. Despite the word's geographic designation, few Italians viewed foreigners from the United States or Canada as *extra-communitari*. Newspaper stories linking crime and immigration fueled underlying racial fears, and stories of attacks on immigrants soon began to circulate. In August 1989, a group of local thugs murdered Jerry Essan Masslo, a refugee from apartheid South Africa in an immigrant camp in Villa Literno, in Caserta, where he had gone to work the harvest. Horrified by Masslo's death, local groups organized demonstrations against racism, and campaigned for greater legal and economic protection for migrants. Although their efforts did little to slow the rise of xenophobic violence, the antiracist movements enabled immigrants to make their voices heard.

In the aftermath of Masslo's murder, Alagi Mangu, from Ghana, told a journalist with *La Stampa*, that when he first arrived he thought it was paradise, despite the stories of his friends. Mangu recounted, "The trouble began when I began to look around. Then I became aware that I was black, an inferior being. . . . I am a pariah. I cannot speak to a white person, I can't sit at a table in a bar without being afraid of bothering someone."

Mangu dreamed of traveling on to Germany or Great Britain, but without proper papers he was stuck; only in Italy could he remain hidden in plain sight.[18] Salah Methnani came to Italy in 1987 at the age of twenty-four. Methnani studied linguistics in Tunisia and was eager to experience another country and culture. In Italy, he became one of many North African immigrants, illegal, homeless, marginalized, and isolated. In his memoir he recounted the daily discriminations faced by migrants, baristas who refused to serve them, landlords who would not rent to them, and the constant harassment by the police.[19]

By end of the millennium public debate about immigration overshadowed the rising numbers of emigrants. Young adults traveled to northern Europe, Asia, and the Americas in ever-growing numbers. The new migration pattern reflected the demands of late twentieth-century capitalism and the influence of well-established migration networks. In general, those who emigrated to the United States and South America were more educated, and more likely to be employed as managers, or as corporate employees, while those who made their way to Germany or Great Britain tended to find work in low-skill sectors, aided by diasporic communities. Experts warned that contemporary emigration patterns resembled a brain drain rather than a "global circulation" of "brains." As a generation of doctors, lawyers, scientists, and academics were leaving to work abroad, there was no concurrent influx of highly skilled immigrants into the country. The growing fears that accompanied the new migrations added to the economic uncertainties, the sense of social dislocation all proved too much for the postwar political alliances to bear.

The collapse

In February of 1992, the magistrates in Milan, now controlled by the northern leagues, arrested Mario Chiesa, a Socialist, on bribery charges. The party leader, Bettino Craxi, denounced Chiesa, and a few weeks later, just before the March elections, an infuriated Chiesa turned against the party and agreed to cooperate with the magistrates. His testimony depicted a vast network of kickback schemes, linking national politicians, local officials, large corporations, and small family run firms in a web of bribes and payouts. The subsequent *Mani Pulite* (clean hands) investigations led by the magistrate Antonio di Pietro made the scope of the *Tangentopoli* (Bribesville) clear. By September over 2,600 people were arrested, and over 300 Members of Parliament were under investigation. In many respects, the discoveries of the magistrates uncovered nothing new. Rampant corruption was no secret, nor was the existence of a politics of collusion. But, awareness of corruption was not the same as recognizing that it was an integral part of the political system. Until 1992, few journalists examined the ways in which local corruption was linked to national politics. As the news came out, people grew angrier at both the extent of the dishonesty, and at the utter failure of the corrupt system to function. In April 1992, a disgusted electorate went to the polls and voted the old guard out of power. The Christian Democrats won less than 30 percent of the popular vote, and the Socialist Party came away with just 14 percent. The Northern League emerged as the winner, with 9 percent of the vote. Two weeks after the elections, President Cossiga resigned.

On May 23, 1992, as Parliament debated Cossiga's successor, the leading magistrate of the Antimafia Pool, Giovanni Falcone and his wife Francesco Morvilla landed at Punta Raisi airport. Climbing into their armored car, surrounded by an armed escort, the couple made their way toward their house by the sea in Addaura. Crossing an overpass near the town of Capaci a sudden explosion ripped through the air opening a deep crater in the road, destroying all of the cars in the convoy. Three members of the police escort died in the blast, and Falcone and Movillo died later that evening. At Falcone's funeral, attended by thousands of people, his friend and colleague Paolo Borsellino spoke:

> Falcone began working a new way here. By that I don't just mean his investigative techniques. . . . Falcone believed that the fight against the mafia was the first problem that had to be solved in our beautiful and wretched land. But that fight could not just be a detached, repressive undertaking: it also had to be a cultural, moral and even religious movement. Everyone had to be involved, and everyone had to get used to how beautiful the fresh smell of freedom is when compared to the stench of moral compromise, of indifference of living alongside the mafia, and therefore of being complicit with it.[20]

Two months later, on July 19 Borsellino paid a visit his mother, as was his custom on Sunday afternoons. As he walked up to the door a car bomb exploded, ripping through bodies and buildings, shattering windows five stories above the street, killing Borsellino and his escort. *Palermitani* responded to the bombings with a visceral rage. At the public funeral for the bodyguards, thousands of people gathered outside of the Cathedral in Palermo to pay their respects and voice their anger at the politicians who had let this happen. Even the police began to speak out against the state. Throughout the summer, the people of Palermo took to the streets, holding torch lit parades. The mourning and rage spilled out across the nation. Falcone and Borsellino became symbols of the failure of the state, of the complicity of the politicians in the violence that racked the South, and the corruption of the North. Within a matter of months, the governing parties had collapsed. In the spring of 2018, the courts confirmed the rumors, convicting high ranking state officials and mafiosi of collusion in the 1990s (Figure 22).

The murders of Falcone and Borsellino ended attempts by the old guard to rebuild the old coalitions. In the wake of the Capaci bombing, Parliament approved Oscar Scalfaro as president of the Republic, over the objections of both the PSI and the DC. Efforts to maneuver Andreotti back into power crumbled with Scalfaro's appointment. In June, at the end of the legislative session Prime Minister Andreotti tendered his resignation ending a political career spanning six decades. Scalfaro appointed Giuliano Amato, a Socialist, as prime minister. Amato's efforts to squelch the *mani puliti* investigations forced his resignation after a year. In the wake of Amato's ouster, Scalfaro brought in an independent, Carlo Azeglio Ciampi, to form a government comprised of experts rather than politicians. Ciampi's "technical government" oversaw the dismantlement of the postwar Republic and the creation of a new political order.

Figure 22 Antimafia Demonstration, June 28, 1992. Franco Origlia/Getty Images.

The April elections and the deaths of Falcone and Borsellino proved the death knell for the DC and the PSI. The Christian Democrats had been crumbling for years, as leading members had left to form rival parties. After being ousted by the DC for his antimafia work in 1990, Leoluca Orlando helped found a new democratic party, *La Rete* (the Network), an antimafia and anticorruption party comprised of a coalition of disaffected members of the DC and the left. In 1992, frustrated with the party's unwillingness to enact systemic reform, Mario Segni formed a new coalition to tackle questions of electoral reform. In the 1993 local elections the DC won 19 percent of the vote. Seeing the writing on the wall, leaders of the Christian Democratic Party sought to head off the collapse by changing the party's name to the *Partito Popolare Italiano* (PPI). The new name did not convince the electorate that the party had changed. In the 1994 elections the PPI and Segni's party together garnered just 16 percent of the vote. By 1995, most members of the DC had joined other parties, and those who remained in the PPI found themselves marginalized from the corridors of power. The Socialist Party disbanded months after the DC Party. In February of 1993, magistrates indicted Bettino Craxi, the secretary of the PSI, on bribery charges. At his trial Craxi admitted to the bribes, but insisted that they were just the cost of doing business. Found guilty in 1994, the former prime minster, and party leader, fled into exile in Tunisia to avoid serving his sentence. In the elections of 1994, the first under the new system, the Socialists garnered less than 3 percent of the vote, and within a few months the party dissolved.

As the DC-PSI coalition crumbled, members of Parliament worked on a full-scale reform of the electoral law and the Senate. Mario Segni, the head of the *Popolari per la Riforma* who had been elected to Parliament on his promises of political reform, led the campaign. In April of 1993, Italians enthusiastically endorsed Segni's reforms, abolishing a number of ministries, prohibiting state appointments to private boards, ending state financing of political parties, and decriminalizing drug possession.

The voters supported the reforms, approving a majority system for 75 percent of the seats, and a proportional system for the remaining 25 percent. To sit a candidate in Parliament, parties had to secure at least 4 percent of the votes in the Chamber of Deputies and at least 10 percent in the Senate. Support for the reforms was stronger in the North where the leagues had long been championing systemic reforms. Over 70 percent of the electorate in Lombardy, Veneto and Piemonte voted in favor of reform, as compared to roughly 30 percent in the South. In the first elections held after the introduction of the new electoral system a reconstructed left, a cleansed Fascist Party and a brand new party claimed power.

The Italian Communist Party and the Fascist Party were among the few prewar parties that managed to claim a stake in post-1992 politics. The PCI had been the first of the major parties to fall in 1991. However, unlike the PSI and the DC it was not brought down by corruption and greed. The demise of the Soviet bloc sent an already weak and confused party into an existential crisis. The party had never succeeded in regaining support after the 1960s, and failed to align itself with the interests of the New Left. With the collapse of the USSR and the end of the Cold War, the party lost its larger, international reason for existence. In 1991, Achille Occhetto proposed changing the name of the party to the *Partito Democratico della Sinestra* (PDS). His proposal pleased no one. A large contingent of party members left, and created a rival Communist Party, the *Partito della Rifondazione Comunista* (Communist Refoundation Party—PRC). The party entered the 1990s, divided, its members fleeing to rival parties including *I Verdi* (the Greens) and *la Margherita* (the Daisy party). Yet, the fragmentation of the PCI offered the possibility of creating a larger leftist coalition.

The Fascists emerged relatively unscathed into the post-1992 world. Under the leadership of Gianfranco Fini, the leader of the *Movimento Sociale Italiano* (Italian Social Movement—MSI), formed in 1946 by ex-fascists, had generally supported the DC from the sidelines. During the 1970s and 1980s, Fini sought to marginalize the extremists and minimize the historic links to Mussolini. Many of the most ardent Fascists left the party, leaving the more moderates to shape policy. As the bribery scandals grew, bringing down the governing parties, the MSI emerged unscathed. Party members had little opportunity to profit from the kickback schemes as few occupied significant positions. Cleansed of its Fascist past and free from the taint of corruption, the MSI appealed to many of the politicians fleeing the DC. In 1994, the MSI voted to rename the party the *Alleanza Nazionale* (National Alliance—AN), allied with the new *Forza Italia* party won 14 percent of the vote.

The 1994 elections brought new political voices to power. The corruption scandals and resurgence of mafia violence fueled the growth of the *Lega Nord*. In the regional elections of 1993, the *Lega* won 16 percent of the vote, just 2 percent less than the DC. *Lega* politicians won a number of mayoral victories; the regional movement had become a national presence. In the 1994 elections the *Lega* emerged as a member of the governing coalition. The willingness of the electorate to reject the old was manifest in the victory of a brand new party, *Forza Italia* (Go Italy). Formed in 1993, the party led a coalition ticket that won 43 percent of the vote.

Silvio Berlusconi, the leader of the *Forza Italy*, was born into a middle-class Milanese family in 1936. As soon as he graduated from university, he invested in the burgeoning construction industry of the 1960s. His first venture, *Milan due*, an enormous apartment complex, proved enormously lucrative. He invested his profits from construction into local television stations. Although the state controlled all national licenses, local licenses were available for sale. Frustrated by the government's hold over the media, Berlusconi founded Fininvest in 1978, an umbrella group that bought up a variety of print, television, and publishing outlets. Berlusconi's strategy was to break the national monopoly by purchasing local channels across the country, and then broadcasting the same programs, in essence creating a national network. When the government charged him with violating state monopoly laws, he successfully lobbied for the laws to change. By 1986, Berlusconi's empire controlled 60 percent of the media, and Berlusconi himself had amassed a large private fortune. Alarmed by the fall of the Craxi and the growing corruption investigations, Berlusconi decided to form his own party.

The goal of *Forza Italia* was to attract conservative and moderate voters alienated from the DC and the PSI. They ran on a program of denouncing corruption and cronyism, promising to bring "good government" back to Parliament. Before the elections of 1994, he formed a coalition of conservative and right-wing parties, including the AN and the *Lega Nord*, entitled *Polo delle liberta-Polo del buon governo* ("Pole of Freedom and Pole of Good Government"). In the wake of the 1994 elections, the president appointed Berlusconi as prime minister. As soon as Berlusconi began to use his institutional power for personal gain the coalition began to crumble. When his brother came under judicial investigation Berlusconi issued a special decree that made it illegal for the judiciary to arrest people for political corruption and fraud. Thousands of defendants were freed. Umberto Bossi, an avid supporter of the magistrates, resigned in disgust.

In April of 1996, new parliamentary elections were held and a center-left coalition, l'*ulivo*, came to power. Romano Prodi, the ex-president of the IRI, brought together the reconstructed Communist Party (PDS), the former DC (PPI), *I Verdi* (Greens), *la Rete* (Network), liberals, and Republicans to win the elections. The elections proved that Segni's reforms had failed in their fundamental purpose, to shrink the number of parties and break the dependency on coalitions. Over twenty-two parties gained seats in the Chamber in 1996. Under Romano Prodi, an ardent Europeanist, Italy moved closer to the European Union and committed to the single currency. Prodi implemented a series of austerity measures, raising taxes, cutting pensions, and privatizing a few state firms, in an effort to bring the budget in line with the requirements of the EU. In many respects, Prodi's strategies proved successful in stabilizing the economy, even if his policies often proved unpopular.

The most vocal opposition to Prodi's government came from the growing northern federalist movements led by Bossi. Elated by his party's strong showing in the local and national elections, Bossi launched a call for an independent Padania, envisioning an autonomous region within the European Union that would encompass the Po valley, stretching across Veneto, Lombardy, and into Piedmont. The union refused to support Bossi's proposal, but his demands reinvigorated calls for greater regional autonomy.

In 1996 a bicameral constitutional commission formed to discuss the creation of federal structure based on regions. The commission collapsed under the weight of competing and conflicting ideological positions and Berlusconi's personal interests. The *Lega* sought to complete federalism; the National Alliance defended a centralized state, while Berlusconi focused on limiting the power of the magistrates. The paralysis of the commission accompanied the collapse of the Prodi's government.

The resignation of Prodi did not signal the end of the center-left government. In 1998, the former Communist, Massimo D'Alemo stepped in to lead the coalition, serving as prime minister until the spring of 2000. D'Alemo's first order of business was to prove that a Communist-led coalition could govern wisely, and he immediately set out to strength ties to the European Union, extend regional autonomy, and pass reforms abolishing or streamlining a host of hated bureaucratic practices. Within months after taking office, NATO attacked Serbia in defense of Kosovo. For D'Alema, the war offered the perfect opportunity to prove his loyalty to NATO and his alliance with the United States. The majority of Italians, however, opposed the war. D'Alemo's own coalition was deeply divided over the wisdom of Italy's participation in NATO. A year later, D'Alemo could boast of securing the country's standing within the EU, and proving its military strength, but at the cost of a disaffected electorate. In the fall of 1999, D'Alemo's government fell.

As Italians celebrated the new millennium they looked back at three decades of rapid change. The political system that had begun to fray in the 1970s collapsed, appearing to have left Italy more divided than ever. Postwar visions of peace, of prosperity, of an Italy defined by democratic and egalitarian values seemed a distant dream. Physical and social divisions remained, but they cut across different geographical, racial, class, and gendered axes, troubling long-standing notions of individual and collective belonging. The judicial investigations had made clear that crime and corruption were not just southern problems. New generational and gendered ties transcended older divisions of family, kin, and place. As the fireworks faded on January 1, 2000, Italians entered into a new millennium debating the meaning of Italy and what it meant to be Italian.

CHAPTER 16
TWENTY-FIRST-CENTURY ITALY

In 2003, Igiabo Scego's story *Salsiccie* (*Sausages*) won the Eks&Tra prize for migrant literature. The short story opens on a morning in the middle of August, a young Italian-Somalian woman walked into her neighborhood butcher to buy sausages. Buying sausages on a Roman summer morning is far from unusual, yet Rosetta, who knew the young woman for years, looked up from behind the counter with some surprise, asking if she had perhaps converted. Assuring her friend that the sausage was for a neighbor, the young woman took it home intending to eat it for lunch. Rosetta was right, our narrator had never eaten a sausage. So, why on this very ordinary day did she feel compelled to buy sausages she did not know how to cook, and that would defile her cookware, and break her mother's heart? She bought the sausages as an experiment, wondering, "If I swallow these sausages one by one, will people know that I am Italian like them? Identical to them? Or will this all be a futile gesture?"[1] A gesture brought on by the passage of the 2002 Bossi-Fini Law imposing stricter regulations on all immigration, including a fingerprint requirement to renew papers. A decision brought on by an examiner at a recent *concorso* who asked her if she was more Italian or more Somalian:

> "Maybe," she thinks, beginning to panic, "¾ Somalian and ¼ Italian? Or maybe it is really the reverse? I don't know how to respond! I have never 'fractioned' myself before now . . . naturally I lied. I did not like it, but I was forced . . . and I said 'Italian.' And then despite being the color of the night, I turned red like a pepper. I felt like an idiot even if I had said Somalian. I am not one hundred percent. I have never been and don't believe I can now become that person. I believe I am a woman without an identity. Or better yet, with multiple identities."[2]

She lists all that makes her Somalian: drinking spiced tea, performing her daily prayers, wearing her Dirac, or eating bananas and rice. And then inventories all that make her Italian: when she eats sweets for breakfast, goes to museums, watches the films of Monica Vitti, or listens to the music of Gianni Morandi. She is all of it, and yet at times is erased both by the Italians, who dismiss her as a foreigner, and the Somalis, who see her as a westerner. She gives up, throws out the sausage, and watches television. Scego's story offers an eloquent reflection on what it means to be Italian. If Italy was first imagined through the eyes of cosmopolitan Europeans, two centuries later, it is being reimagined through the eyes of multicultural Italians.

Twenty-first-century Italy is in many respects a "new Italy," but it is also a very old Italy. The mobilities that shape social relations and polarize politics are a continuation of the centrality of mobility in the making of the modern Italy. The tensions entwined in the history of a nation that has always been in motion forged from a multiplicity of cultures, customs, and languages.[3] Yet, there is something different about contemporary mobility: for Italians at home and abroad, the idea of homeland is no longer solely defined by Italy's political borders but has expanded to include those of countries in Africa, Asia, and Latin America. This multiethnic Italy has opened up the possibility of imagining a more inclusive, diverse Italy, but it has also fueled xenophobic and racist visions of a fixed, unchanging mythical Italy.

The new Italians

Recent reports estimate that there are over five million resident immigrants currently living in Italy comprising roughly 10 percent of the resident population.[4] The statistical portrait of settled immigrants describes a geographically diverse, but demographically similar, population, who have gravitated toward the northern regions. Although it is nearly impossible to chart the ebbs and flows of immigrants crossing the nation's borders, *permessi di soggiorni* provide a fairly accurate portrait of people who have chosen to make Italy their home. In 2007 nearly 2.5 million Europeans, Africans, and Asians held legal residency. Eastern Europeans comprised 31 percent of resident foreigners, with nearly 200,000 Albanians making up the largest single group. Since the 1990s, Moroccans, Tunisians and Senegalese, Filipinos, Indians, and Chinese have outnumbered Eastern Europeans among those seeking permanent residence.[5] The immigrant community is comprised of roughly equal numbers of men and women, although in the last decade women have begun to outnumber men. The majority of migrants are young, about two-thirds are between fifteen and forty-four years of age. Although immigrants came from different places, with wildly different resources and experiences, the majority eventually found homes in the cities and manufacturing towns of the northern and central regions. Well over half of people who requested residency permits reside in the North.

Immigrants transformed the cities. At first, those who arrived found housing in the cheap hotels and boarding houses near the train stations. In the late 1980s and throughout the 1990s, large migrant enclaves expanded out from the central train stations. The new arrivals found cheap housing in dilapidated apartments and rundown hotels. Recently arrived migrants turned to their communal networks to find rooms and work. By the early 2000s many emigrants, in particular Filipinos, Peruvians, Somalians, and Moroccans, began to move to other neighborhoods and to the suburbs. Settlement patterns encouraged integration. Immigrants joined neighborhood sports club, soccer teams, and bridge clubs. The number of marriages between foreigners and Italian-born residents has also been on the rise.[6] Although Italians still maintain a deep attachment to regional pastas, meats, and cheeses, recent migrants have altered the nation's food culture, introducing new spices, fruits, and vegetables. Once nearly impossible to find, tortillas, black beans, peanut butter, or curries appear on the shelves of neighborhood grocery stores. Eritrean, Peruvian, and Chinese restaurants cater to immigrants and nonimmigrants alike.

The legal and social integration of immigrants improved the working conditions for many. For those who arrived in the 1990s, a series of government amnesties offered the opportunity to secure temporary resident work paper. Over 200,000 migrants took advantage of the amnesty offered by the Martelli Law in 1990, and nearly 670,000 applied for papers with the amnesty offered by the Bossi-Fini Law in 2002.[7] Amnesties enabled many of those who arrived without papers to move into better paying jobs or open their own businesses. The culture of entrepreneurship aided immigrant prosperity. Moroccans, Chinese, Albanians, Egyptians, Bangladeshi, and the Swiss account for half of the business licenses issued to immigrants. They have applied for licenses to open service businesses (cleaning, childcare), construction companies, catering firms, as well as larger textile or manufacturing factories. Since 2007, the number of immigrant business owners has increased by 53.6 percent. Black-market work has not disappeared, nor has the exploitation of undocumented migrants working in seasonal trades, the textile industries, or service.

As immigrants settled into their Italian lives many called for their families. The average number of requests for residency permits on the basis of family reunification rose from 21 percent between 1995 and 1999 to nearly 56 percent between 2005 and 2009. Others found love in their new home, married, and had children. Over the past decade nearly a million children have been born to immigrant parents.[8] Migrant children, and second-generation immigrants, born and raised in Italy, play a critical role in the creation of a multiethnic society. They have come of age attending Italian schools, speaking Italian, immersed in Italian pop music, art and literature. In 2015, over half of students enrolled in public schools born to foreign parents entered the school system before the age of ten. As they moved through elementary, middle, and high schools, they formed social networks that often crossed ethnic and racial lines.

The children of immigrants belong to multiple worlds. According to recent studies, only 38 percent of Italians born to immigrants feel Italian, and 33 percent continue to see themselves as foreigners. Even among those who have lived their whole lives in Italy, 23 percent still feel as though they are not truly Italian. The sense of being an outsider is strongest among children of Asian and Latin American immigrants. Less than 30 percent of Chinese Italian youth consider themselves to be Italian or speak Italian well, and only about half say they have Italian friends and frequent parties and events organized by Italians. By contrast, over half of those claiming ties to Albania, Romania, Ukraine, and Moldova reported that they felt fully Italian, think in Italian, and socialize with Italians. Outside of Europe, Moroccans and Ecuadorians report the deepest sense of affinity with Italy.

Despite feelings of alienation, children born to immigrant parents have chosen to become citizens. In 2011, 56,000 immigrants became citizens, and in 2014, the number soared to 130,000. Many of those who are claiming citizenship are children born in Italy to foreign parents who when they reach eighteen years of age are eligible to apply for citizenship; nearly 90 percent of those children born in Italy in 1995 became citizens when they reached the age of eighteen. Tens of thousands of residents under the age of thirty legally become citizens each year, making a younger and more diverse Italy.[9] As generations of immigrants have settled into cities and towns, the question of immigration has grown more contentious, polarizing and violent (Figure 23).

Figure 23 Denny Mendez, 1996. Miss Italy. ROBERTO SCHMIDT/AFP/Getty Images.

Refugees

The Arab Spring revolts brought more migrants and refugees to Italy. In the first months of 2011, antigovernment rallies brought down governments in Tunisia and Libya. The struggles between the various factions jockeying for power, following the collapse of authoritarian regimes, turned increasingly violent, and tens of thousands of people sought refuge in Europe. The sea route from North Africa to Italy had long been popular among African migrants. Italy's relatively porous borders, relatively mild deportation laws, and geographic proximity fueled profitable smuggling industries along the Tunisian and Libyan coasts. The sea routes concerned EU officials, who only admitted Italy into the Schengen Area after the government passed the 1998 Turco-Napolitano law strengthening conditions for expulsion and immigrant detention.

The Libyan refugee crisis had been brewing before the Arab Spring. Deteriorating conditions in sub-Saharan Africa brought hundreds of thousands of emigrants to the edge of the Mediterranean to try to find passage to Europe. Libya's leader, Muammar el-Qadaffi, recruited labor migrants from Africa and Asia to work in the oil fields and construction. Work conditions were abysmal and most were eager to leave. In 2008,

Prime Minister Silvio Berlusconi's center-right government tried to negotiate with the Libyan government, pledging $5 billion to Qaddaffi, if he cracked down on clandestine emigration from Libya. Much to the horror of human rights activists, the deal also allowed Italy to deport all immigrants intercepted by the coast guard, without allowing migrants to apply for asylum, in violation of the United Nations Refugee Convention. Despite the condemnation of Berlusconi's tactics, the agreement seemed to work: the number of clandestine migrants arriving by boat fell. By 2010, EU officials met with Qadaffi to negotiate a European version of the Rome-Tripoli agreement. Qadaffi, playing on European racial fears, warned that if Europe did not want to "turn black" it needed to pay another 5 billion dollars to secure its borders.[10]

In the following months, European deals dissolved as Libya sunk into civil war. The collapse of Qadaffi's regime in August of 2011 brought a temporary halt to the flow of migrants, as smugglers worked to reestablish their routes. The lull was not for lack of demand. By 2013, smugglers had reorganized and the number of migrants arriving by sea began to climb again. When civil war broke out in Syria, hundreds of thousands of Syrians joined the Ethiopian, Nigerians, Eritreans, Ghanaians, and Somali coming through Tunisia and Libya. In 2014, more than 170,000 immigrants sought refuge in Italy, many first arriving on the small island of Lampedusa. The receiving centers were soon overburdened, and struggled under the weight of caring for the survivors.

The journey across the Mediterranean Sea is extraordinarily dangerous and every year thousands die. Smugglers crowd the migrants, many of whom paid over $4,000 a piece for passage, on to rickety fishing boats or rubber rafts that quickly take on water. Sometimes the traffickers hire refugees as crewmembers; other times they send them out as "ghost ships," lacking captain or crew. The stories of survivors are harrowing, telling of engines bursting into flame, boats filling with water, and the surrounding seas covered by the dead. In October 2013, a ship carrying over 500 Eritreans and Somalians caught fire and sank off not far off the island of Lampedusa. Hundreds of passengers jumped into the water and drowned, others died still in the boat, only 150 people survived. The tragedy, just one of many, left people horrified, grief-stricken, and angry at the European Union and their government.

In wake of the disaster Enrico Letta's government announced the creation of a new search and rescue program: operation *Mare Nostrum*. A joint mission involving the air force, coast guard, finance police, and the port authorities sent out ships to intercept and rescue the migrants from the sinking boats. If authorities could identify the smugglers, they were arrested and held for questioning. A year later the number of deaths had plummeted; the operation was credited with saving over 100,000 lives.[11] Letta was well aware that Italy could not pay for the costly program alone, and appealed to the wider European Union for support. He warned that if the European Union failed to recognize that the refugees constitute a humanitarian crisis and ended the program more would die. France and Germany, irritated with what they perceived as Italy's unwillingness to secure its borders, refused to listen to Letta, insisting that *Mare Nostrum* had only encouraged more people to set sail. The EU's decision to replace *Mare Nostrum* program with *Operation Triton*, under control of the European Union's border agency, Frontex, proved Letta right.

The new program shifted the focus off of search and rescue and on to border control. The *Triton* patrols limited their patrols to thirty kilometers off the coast of Italy, and had no authorization to assist any boat beyond that line. Foreseeing the dangers, some European leaders insisted that they expected Italy to continue funding the humanitarian portion. Unable to afford the estimated nine million euros per month, Italy ended the rescue operations on October 31, 1914. The shift to *Operation Triton* had an immediate impact. According to the *Missing Migrants Project*, the number of dead through the central Mediterranean route rose from 3,184 in 2014 to 3,712 in 2015, and 4,967 in 2016. Despite European Union's efforts to control the borders, refugees continue to show up on the shores of Lampedusa.

The government responded to the crisis in an ad hoc manner, opening reception centers in various communities. The government created three different centers: Center for first assistance (CDA); CARAs identification centers for immigrants without documents, who requested asylum; Centers for identification and expulsions (CIEs), for all immigrants taken in by the authorities without documentation. The centers were soon overflowing. In 2013 there were over 22,000 people held in the reception centers, by 2015, the number had risen to over 100,000, and in 2016, there were over 176,000 refugees held in the camps. There were no standard procedures governing the reception of migrants. Each community had the power to implement their own systems; although they were encouraged to follow a similar protocol for assessing each person's legal status, they were free to create their own. The chaotic system left many refugees in physical and legal limbo, trapped in the centers for weeks and months at a time.

Horror stories of conditions in the camps circulated through the press, and calls for reforms began to grow, as images of the overcrowded camps, infested with cockroaches, filthy bathrooms, and rancid food appeared in the papers and on the news. Aid-workers decried the lack of social services, language classes, or work programs that isolated an already vulnerable and traumatized population. In 2014 the government restructured the system. The CARAs were replaced with collection points called HUBs where officials were to quickly determine the legal status of the migrants. Within a few weeks the refugees were supposedly sent to one of the new centers or towns that formed the SPRAR system, the System of protection of Asylum Seekers and Refugees. Under SPRAR, private charities, volunteer associations, and city governments applied to host migrants. Each community or organization could determine the type of accommodation and services for migrants, although all would receive European Union subsidies to providing an allowance for clothes, food, and housing. Some towns transformed empty buildings into receiving centers; others recruited local citizens to open their houses to refugees.[12]

The new system provided a wealth of opportunities for those seeking to assist the migrants on humanitarian grounds and those eager to profit from the government programs. Lack of oversight transformed the government contracts with the cooperative social organizations into lucrative sources of income for the mafia. In December of 2014, a year after the new system had been put into place, authorities issued an arrest warrant in Rome, including the president of Rome's city council and the head of the city's public housing division for fraud. The "Mafia Capital" investigation uncovered evidence of politicians giving Mafia cartels the contracts to manage immigrant reception centers. One Mafia boss boasted the clan had made more money off the immigrant than off of drugs. It appeared that the relationship between politicians, neofascists, businessmen, and the mafia formed in the 1970s and 1980s continued to operate.[13] Despite the arrests the Mafia has continued to profit from immigration. In July of 2017, authorities arrested the managers of one center in Calabria who had siphoned off over thirty million euros for personal use. The arrival of the refugees not only made evident that the political system based on reciprocity and party loyalties remains intact but has also stoked fears of immigrants in general, unleashing a dangerous torrent of xenophobic and racist rhetoric.

Xenophobia, race, and politics

Despite the continued cries that Italy is "not a country for racists" by politicians and cultural critics, racist attitudes are growing. A commission comprised of Italian deputies, European Union representatives, the United Nations, and a number of other NGOs undertook a comprehensive study of race, entitled *La piramide dell'odio in Italia* ("the pyramid of hate in Italy"). In the final report delivered to Parliament in the summer of 2017, the authors concluded that among all Europeans, the Italians were the most ill-informed about immigration. Despite their own history of mobility, Italians, more than other Europeans, were quick to see immigration as a dangerous threat, and to believe that their country was being overrun by people from Africa and Asia. According to the survey data, over 50 percent of Italians were convinced that immigrants comprised 30 percent of the population (whereas they actually make up roughly 8 percent) and that Muslims account for 20 percent of the migrants (in reality far less). Over half agreed with the sentiment that immigrants cause crime, and that the arrival of immigrants degrades neighborhoods. Over 65 percent of Italians believed that refugees are a burden on the state, stealing jobs and benefits from residents. The commissioners discovered that negative attitudes toward the Roma and Sinti were particularly strong, despite the fact that Romani had lived in Italy for generations.[14]

Prejudicial sentiments toward perceived foreigners accompanied an increase in physical and verbal racial attacks. Just in the summer of 2017, according to a report in *Corriere della Sera*, an African-Italian woman, seven months pregnant, was attacked at a bus stop in Rimini. In Ravenna, a hotel refused to hire a young man when they found out he was African, writing to the applicant "I'm sorry Paolo but I cannot place young men of color in the lobby, here in Romagna the people have a backward mentality I am sorry I cannot bring you here, ciao." In Turin, a young woman was refused a job because of her Nigerian boyfriend, "I will not trust the cash register to someone who shares her life with an African." In Milan, someone had scrawled "No Entrance for Africans" (*vietato L'ingresso ai negri* in front of playground. Italians of color regularly report being denied housing, jobs, or even the right to participate in competitions. Right-wing racist websites have proliferated since 2010.[15]

The reports from the summer of 2017 were not new. In 2008 a group of thugs violently attacked a gypsy community outside of Naples. In the autumn, a barrista shot and killed Abdoul Guiebre, an Italian originally from Burkina Faso. In 2013, Prime Minister Enrico Letta appointed Cécile Kyenge minister of integration. Born in the Republic of Congo, Cécile came to Italy to study medicine in 1983. In 1994, she married an Italian man and settled in Emilia, working as an ophthalmologist in Modena. She volunteered in a number of migrant organizations and worked to promote cooperation between Italia and Africa. In 2004 she entered local politics, and in 2013, joined Parliament. Her appointment to a ministerial position was met with fierce attacks A representative of the Northern League, Roberto Calderoli, vice president of the Senate, called her an orangutan, others threatened her life.

The rise of racist verbal and physical attacks sparked a fierce backlash. Horrified at what many consider the fundamental betrayal of the values of the resistance and the Risorgimento, people organized antiracist campaigns, opened migrant assistance centers, held demonstrations, concerts and parades in support of open borders and multiculturalism. As part of the reorganization of the migrant reception centers a number of small towns volunteered to join the program. In exchange for government subsidies the towns vowed to create open humane spaces for the migrants, free from corruption or collusion. New foundations committed to promoting a multicultural vision of Italy have countered the racist propaganda with evidence of the economic and social benefits that have accompanied rising immigration rates. On social media and in the press the antiracist and pro-immigrant associations are raising their voices, starting hashtag movements such as *#italianisenzacittadinanza* to mobilize support or opposition to proposed citizenship legislation and to organize community actions. Websites, such as *Cronache di ordinario razzismo*, seek to collect and disseminate information to counter racial prejudice and stereotypes. Students in high schools and universities, retired factory workers, lawyers, and doctors organized local candlelight vigils to honor those who died trying to cross the sea, and reaffirm the country's humanitarian values. Newspapers and websites have tried to counter lies with facts: emphasizing the demographic and economic benefits of immigration, pointing out that the arrival of the immigrants offsetting the difficulties posed by an aging population, and how immigrant workers have already increased state pension plans and welfare benefits through their tax contributions.

Since 2000, the question of immigration polarized the political landscape. Post-1992 populist parties were the first to embrace immigration as a potent political weapon, but after 2001, the center-right parties also included migration as a central plank in their electoral campaigns. When Berlusconi returned as prime minister in 2001, his government made good on its promises to tighten border controls, passing the Bossi-Fini Law a year later. Global terrorism and the economic downturn of 2008 strengthened efforts of politicians to recast anti-immigrant politics as effective governance. Decrying accusations of racism, members of the Lega Nord and the AN argued that restricting immigration and deporting all migrants without papers was nothing more than taking appropriate measures to improve the economy, public security, and eliminate government abuse. If anti-immigration politics defined the right, center-left coalitions embraced a multicultural vision of Italy, and a more humanitarian approach to immigration. Romano Prodi's government (2006–08) passed a series of laws expanding family reunions, amnesty, and emphasizing search and rescue missions over border controls. In 2008, Italians returned Berlusconi to power for a third time, in a coalition government with the Lega Nord. Their victory came in no small part to their willingness to promote harsher sentences on crimes committed by immigrants as opposed to legal residents, and facilitating the arrest of foreigners in an effort to lower crime rates.[16] The fusion of immigration reforms with fears of crime and terrorism expanded the reach of the debates into a wide range of political concerns, including support for the European Union and questions of regional autonomy.

The power of migration to shape politics reasserted itself in the election campaigns of 2017. In the summer regional elections, the center-right gained power in leftist strongholds, largely on the issue of immigration. Berlusconi, attempting a fourth comeback with *Forza Italia*, campaigned throughout Sicily on a promise to halt immigration. Candidates warned that if Italy did not stop accepting migrants it would end up like Libya, riven by sectarian violence. In Pistoia, voters elected a right-wing mayor. The town, proud of its history as a center of antifascist resistance, had initially embraced the immigrants, but over the past four years, sympathies had soured. Community resistance to a refugee center sparked protests. In response to growing anti-immigrant sentiment the center-left is moving toward the right on immigration issues. Within days of the municipal elections Matteo Renzi flipped his position on emigration. While continuing to support rescue missions, he declared that the government must stop people from leaving in the first place. Echoing the arguments on the Far Right, Renzi insisted that immigrants must be helped at home. The ex-mayor of Rome, Gianni Alemanna, noted that Renzi "suddenly discovered the right, adopting our slogans on immigration. He has forgotten the fact that laws approved by his government are the cause of the invasion that afflicts our country."[17]

Immigration debates continued to fuel populist parties on the left and right. In 2009, Beppe Grillo, a comedian, founded *Movimento 5 Stelle* (Five Star Movement). Grillo began the grassroots movement calling to end political corruption and collusion in resistance to Berlusconi's government. The movement had no clear ideological orientation, beyond being vaguely environmentalist, anti-globalist, skeptical of the European Union, and decidedly anti-establishment. In March 2009, Grillo transformed the movement into a party, presenting candidates for regional, national, and European wide elections. The flexibility, openness, and ideological confusion of the Five Star Movement enabled politicians holding radical ideas to enter the political mainstream. Within a few years, the movement's platform seemed to have much in common with the *leghisti* and the neofascists. At Cinque Stelle rallies politicians used migration to fuel populist anger at the European Union and the government.

Racism, xenophobia, fear, Euroscepticism, and populism are not unique to Italy. In Great Britain, supporters of Brexit focused on fears of unrestricted immigration to convince British voters to leave the European Union. In Austria, Sebastian Kurz, a young candidate with the far-right Freedom Party, made a strong showing in the fall elections of 2017, gaining support by running an anti-immigrant campaign, reminding voters that he had closed the overland route from Turkey to Europe in 2016. Yet, the divisive political rhetoric has had a powerful impact on the political landscape. In the elections of 2018, immigration emerged as the touchstone issue that ushered the Five Star Movement and the neofascist right into power.

Fuga dei cervelli (Brain Drain)

Until recently, the divisive politics of immigration overshadowed the fact that Italians are leaving in ever-growing numbers. The decline among emigrants that began in the 1970s reversed in recent years, as more youth seek work in Northern Europe or the Americas. In 2014, over 136,000 people between the ages of fifteen and thirty-nine moved abroad. This is the highest number in a decade. According to one recent survey, over 40 percent of youth dream of moving away. The United States still looms as the preferred destination, followed by Great Britain and Germany.[18] A slowing economy, combined with the precarity of work at home, is driving many to leave.

Italy's entrance into the Eurozone in January 1999, and the adaptation of the Euro in 2002, weighed heavily on the country's economy. The EU's commitment to the free circulation of people and capital made Italy a more attractive destination for immigrants, but also took a toll on domestic industries. Since 2002, the economy has been lethargic at best. The smaller family firms that drove the economy in the 1980s seemed unable to meet the technological demands of the world market. The sluggish economy at home encouraged many graduates to seek work in Europe. The financial crisis of 2008 pushed more young professionals to go abroad. In the wake of the global crisis of 2008, youth unemployment sky-rocketed to 44 percent nationally, and reaching over 70 percent in the southern regions.

The slowing economy and global crisis exacerbated the difficulties in finding entry level professions. A new college graduate was considered fortunate to find work as an unpaid intern or a temporary position. According to a 2013 study, the average salary for Italians in their twenties was less than 1,400 dollars a month.[19] Young adults grew frustrated with the politics of favoritism, the lack of meritocracy, and a labor market that offers only low-paid part-time work. Twenty and thirty-year-olds took their professional skills and headed north. The new emigration brings to mind the early nineteenth-century patterns when the educated elite dominated the migrant streams. And yet, the current generation of migrants, clutching their diplomas, are global-labor migrants like their grandparents and great-grandparents who worked in the mines and factories.

National and regional governments tried to stem the exodus of young professionals by passing a series of employment reforms. The reforms tried to free the labor market by authorizing more flexible work contracts, with fewer job protections, expanding unemployment benefits, offering tax breaks for companies hiring works on permanent contracts. Local governments implemented local programs to slow the "*fuga dei cervelli.*" Piedmont began offering subsidies to students and graduates to gain experience abroad, but requiring they return home to work.[20] Governmental efforts seem to have had effect. In 2016, over 100,000 people left, and nearly 40 percent were between the ages of eighteen and thirty-four. More recently, older Italians are joining their children abroad. The new emigrants are comprised of people from Lombardy, Veneto, Lazio, Sicily, and Piedmont, countering the geography of past migrations.[21] Generational divides have replaced geographical ones in shaping emigration patterns.

Looking toward the future

Sutera, a small hill town in central Sicily, sits wrapped around the base of Monte Paolino, on the edge of the province of Caltanisetta. Walking through the heavy silence that fills the narrow streets on a hot summer day, one might feel as though the town exists in splendid isolation, cut off from the sounds of the modern world.

Occasionally a shout is heard. A woman looks out a window, and eyes the stranger with more than a touch of suspicion, calling out, "who are you," insisting on knowing how you are tied to the village. Yet, this insular world is tightly linked to a much wider world. It is the history of Italy writ large, and one face of the future.

For centuries Suteresi have left their hilltop homes to work in the mines, factories, and fields in the United States and Europe. Nearly every family has kin in the United States, Great Britain, or Germany. In the aftermath of the war, the town nearly disappeared, its population falling from 4,600 to 1,436 in 2010. By the 1990s, it seemed that all who remained were the elderly, and a handful of doctors and civil servants. The number of children enrolled in the schools shrunk fall. Houses stood empty for most of the year, only coming alive in the summer when the emigrants came home. Each August, Sutera appeared as a multicultural, cosmopolitan community, filled with residents speaking German, Italian, Sicilian, and English, catching up on family gossip and sharing news of their lives.

In 2013, Sutera welcomed nearly thirty families, mostly from sub-Saharan Africa as part of the SPRAR program. The local government promoted the plan by emphasizing the humanitarian concerns and the economic possibilities. The migrants were paired with local families, who welcomed them into their homes, shared meals, and taught them Italian. Suteresi converted an old convent into classroom space, offering language, computer, and sewing lessons. In exchange, the European Union provided some funding for food, clothing, and housing. The initial fears about the program soon disappeared. In the mornings, African migrants join the older men in the coffee bars to talk over the news of the day, share jokes, and drink espresso. The schools have expanded to accommodate the children, and once again the classrooms are growing. Each summer the town organizes a multicultural festival in Rabato, a neighborhood built by the Arabs in the ninth century, featuring Nigerian foods, music, and dance.[22]

The decision to welcome migrants is just one of many cultural and economic initiatives the local government has undertaken in the past few years. Those who have chosen to stay in Sutera have entered city government and encouraged the city to take advantage of EU opportunities, investing in tourist infrastructures and environmental programs, and developing local attractions. Over the past decade Suteresi organized a living nativity event, transforming Rabato, one of the oldest neighborhoods, into Jerusalem. The event references the Sicilian *presepio* tradition by integrating local customs and traditions into the story of Christ's birth. Surrounding the manager, locals dressed as nineteenth-century peasants weave, bake bread, build furniture, make olive oil, and thresh wheat just as their great-grandparents had done. Each year tens of thousands of tourists arrive to see the Sutera's living history museum.

Tucked away deep in Sicily, Sutera is one face of the future Italy. Fiercely proud of its local history, culture, and traditions, Suteresi also see themselves and their future prosperity as inextricably tied to the nation and the European Union. Yes, Italy today is politically polarized and anti-immigrant, Nationalist attitudes seem on the ascendency. Yet, looking beneath the rhetoric of hate, and anger, there is a more progressive, cosmopolitan, and tolerant Italy.

NOTES

Part One

1. Adriano Roccucci, ed., *La Costruzione dello stato-nazione in Italia* (Roma: Viella, 2012); Maurizio Isabella, "Rethinking Italy's Nation-Building 150 Years Afterwards: The New Risorgimento Historiography," *Past & Present* 217, no. 1 (November 1, 2012): 247–68; Silvana Patriarca and Lucy Riall, "Introduction: Revisiting the Risorgimento," in *The Risorgimento Revisited Nationalism and Culture in Nineteenth-Century Italy,* eds., Silvana Patriarca and Lucy Riall (Palgrave Macmillan, 2011), 1–17.

2. Examples of these histories include Carlo Botta, *Storia d'Italia continuata da quella del Guicciardini sino al 1814 con annotazioni* (Milano: Tipi Borroni e Scotti, 1842); *Pio IX e l'Italia, ossia storia della sua vita e degli avvenimenti politici del suo pontificato* (Stab. naz. tip. di Carlo Turati, 1848); L. C., *Serie di biografie contemporanee,* Vols. I and II (Torino: De Agostini, 1853); Cesare Balbo, *Sommario della storia d'Italia: dalle origini fino ai nostri tempi* (Firenze: Felice Le Monnier, 1856); Giuseppe La Farina, *Storia d'Italia dal 1815 al 1850* (Società editrice italiana, 1860).

3. Alfredo Oriani, *La lotta politica in Italia: origini della lotta attuale: (476-1887)* (Torino: Roux, 1892); Gioacchino Volpe, *La storia degli italiani e dell'Italia* (Milano: Treves, 1934); Giulia Albanese and Roberta Pergher, eds., *In the Society of Fascists: Acclamation, Acquiescence, and Agency in Mussolini's Italy* (New York: Palgrave Macmillan, 2012).

4. Benedetto Croce, *Storia d'Italia dal 1871 al 1915* (Bari: G. Laterza & Figli, 1928); Benedetto Croce, *Storia d'Europa: nel secolo decimonono* (Bari: Gius. Laterza & Figli, 1932).

5. Examples include Gino Luzzatto, *L' età contemporanea* (Padua: Cedam, 1952); Rosario Romeo, *Il Risorgimento in Sicilia* (Bari: Gius. Laterza, 1950); Rosario Romeo, *Risorgimento e capitalismo* (Bari: Laterza, 1959); Federico Chabod, *L'Italia Contemporanea (1918-1948)* (Torino: Einaudi, 1961). For a critique of the Crocean position see Giovanni Sabbatucci, "Il Fallimento Del Liberalismo e Le Crisi Del Primo Dopoguerra," *Mélanges de l'École Française de Rome. Italie et Méditerranée,* no. 2 (2002): 711–21, and Roberto Vivarelli, *Il fallimento del liberalismo: studi sulle origini del fascismo* (Bologna: Il Mulino, 1981). On the historiographical debates see: Walter Maturi, *Interpretazioni del Risorgimento: lezioni di storia della storiografia* (Torino: Einaudi, 1965); *Rosario Romeo e Il Risorgimento in Sicilia: bilancio storiografico e prospettive di ricerca* (Soveria Mannelli: Rubbettino, 2002).

6. Antonio Gramsci, *Opere di Antonio Gramsci* (Torino: Einaudi, 1947).

7. Examples include Emilio Sereni, *Il capitalismo nelle campagne (1860-1900)* (Turin: G. Einaudi, 1947), and Giorgio Candeloro, *Storia dell'Italia moderna. Vols 1-4* (Milano: Feltrinelli, 1956–64).

8. Denis Mack Smith, *Garibaldi: A Great Life in Brief* (New York: Alfred A. Knopf, 1956); Denis Mack Smith, *Italy: A Modern History* (Toronto: University of Michigan Press, 1959).

9. Franco della Peruta, *Mazzini e i rivoluzionari italiana. Il partito d'azione, 1830-1845* (Milano: Feltrinelli, 1974); Franco Della Peruta, *Democrazia e socialismo nel Risorgimento: saggi e*

ricerche (Roma: Editori Riuniti, 1977); Rosario Romeo, *Cavour e il suo tempo (1810-1842)* (Bari: Laterza, 1969).

10. Alberto Mario Banti and Paul Ginsborg, "Per una nuova storia del Risorgimento," in *Il Risorgimento*, Annali 22, *Storia d'Italia*, eds. Alberto Mario Banti and Paul Ginsborg (Turin: Einaudi, 2007), XXIII–XLI.

11. David Laven and Lucy Riall, eds., *Napoleon's Legacy: Problems of Government in Restoration Europe* (Oxford: Berg, 2000); David Laven, *Restoration and Risorgimento: Italy 1796-1870* (Oxford: Oxford University Press, 2010); Marco Meriggi, *Milano borghese: circoli ed elites nell'Ottocento* (Venezia: Marsilio, 1992); Marco Meriggi, *Gli Stati italiani prima dell'Unità: una storia istituzionale* (Bologna: Il Mulino, 2002); John A. Davis, *Naples and Napoleon: Southern Italy and the European Revolutions, 1780-1860* (Oxford: Oxford University Press, 2006).

12. Marco Meriggi, *Il Regno Lombardo-Veneto* (Turin: UTET libreria, 1987); Alberto Mario Banti, *Terra e denaro: una borghesia madana dell'Ottocento* (Venezia: Marsilio ed., 1989); Paolo Macry, *Ottocento: famiglia, élites e patrimoni a Napoli* (Turin: Giulio Einaudi, 1988); David Laven, *Venice and Venetia under the Habsburgs, 1815-1835* (Oxford; New York: Oxford University Press, 2002).

13. Alberto Mario Banti, *La nazione del risorgimento: parentela, santità e onore alle origini dell'Italia unita* (Turin: G. Einaudi, 2000); Silvana Patriarca, *Numbers and Nationhood: Writing Statistics in Nineteenth-Century Italy* (Cambridge: Cambridge University Press, 2002); Alberto Mario Banti and Roberto Bizzocchi, *Immagini della nazione nell'Italia del risorgimento* (Roma: Carocci, 2002); Patriarca and Riall, eds., *The Risorgimento Revisited.*

14. Mario Isnenghi and Eva Cecchinato, eds., *Fare l'Italia: unità e disunità nel Risorgimento* (Turin: UTET, 2008).

15. Elena Doni, *Donne del Risorgimento* (Bologna: Il Mulino, 2011); Nadia Maria Filippini, *Donne sulla scena pubblica società e politica in Veneto tra Sette e Ottocento* (Milano: FrancoAngeli, 2006). Simonetta Soldani, "Il Risorgimento delle donne," in *Il Risorgimento*, eds., Banti and Ginsborg, 184–224; Gian Luca Fruci, "Cittadine senza cittadinanza: la mobilitazione femminile nei plebisciti del Risorgimento (1848-1870)," in *Una donna un voto*, ed. Vinzia Fiorino, Special Issue, *Genesis* v (2006). Also see Patriarca and Riall, eds., *The Risorgimento Revisited.*

16. Silvana Patriarca, "Indolence and Regeneration: Tropes and Tensions of Risorgimento Patriotism," *The American Historical Review* 110, no. 2 (April 1, 2005): 380–408; Lucy Riall, "Eroi maschili, virilità e forme della guerra," in *Il Risorgimento*, eds., Banti and Ginsborg, 253–88.

17. Among the earlier works by cultural historians emphasizing the transnational dimension of the cultural Risorgimento see Franco Venturi, "L'Italia Fuori d'Italia," in *Storia d'Italia*, eds., Ruggiero Romano and Corrado Vivanti, vol. 3 *Dal primo Settecento all'Unita* (Torino: Einaudi, 1973), 987–1481. On migration see: Donna R. Gabaccia, *Italy's Many Diasporas* (Seattle: University of Washington Press, 2000); Maurizio Isabella, *Risorgimento in Exile: Italian Émigrés and the Liberal International in the Post-Napoleonic Era* (Oxford: Oxford University Press, 2009); Laura Guidi, "Donne e uomini del Sud sulle vie dell'esilio. 1848-60," in *Il Risorgimento*, eds., Banti and Ginsborg; Marcella Pellegrino Sutcliffe, *Victorian Radicals and Italian Democrats* (Woodbridge, UK: Boydell & Brewer Ltd., 2014); Oliver Janz and Lucy Riall, *The Italian Risorgimento: Transnational Perspectives* (Abingdon: Routledge, 2014); Emilio Franzina e Matteo Sanfilippo, eds., *Risorgimento ed emigrazione* (Viterbo: Edizioni Sette Città, 2014).

18. Isnenghi and Cecchinato, *Fare l'Italia: unità e disunità*.

19. Pietro Stella "Religiosità vissuta in Italia nell'800," in *Storia vissuta del popolo Cristiano*, eds., Jean Deumeau and Franco Bolgiani (Torino: Società Editrice Internazionale, 1985); Gian Luca Fruci, "Il sacramento dell'unita nazionale, linguaggi, iconografia e pratiche dei plebisciti risorgimentale 1848-1870," in *Il Risorgimento*, ed. Banti and Ginsborg, 567–605; Laven, *Restoration and Risorgimento: Italy 1796-1870*.

20. John Dickie, "A Word at War: The Italian Army and Brigandage 1860-1870, *History Workshop*, no. 33 (Spring, 1992), 1–24; Lucy Riall, *Sicily and the Unification of Italy: Liberal Policy and Local Power, 1859-1866* (Oxford: Clarendon Press, 2002); Nelson Moe, *The View from Vesuvius: Italian Culture and the Southern Question* (Berkeley: University of California Press, 2006); Salvatore Lupo, *L'unificazione italiana: Mezzogiorno, rivoluzione, guerra civile* (Roma: Donzelli, 2011); Lucy Riall, *Under the Volcano: Revolution in a Sicilian Town* (Oxford: Oxford University Press, 2013).

Chapter 1

1. Madame de Staël, *Corinne, Or Italy*, trans. Sylvia Raphael (Oxford University Press, 1998), 19; Robert Casillo, *The Empire of Stereotypes: Germaine de Staël and the Idea of Italy* (New York: Palgrave Macmillan, 2006).

2. Johann Wolfgang von Goethe, *The Flight to Italy: Diary and Selected Letters*, trans. T. J. Reed (Oxford; New York: Oxford University Press, 1999), 117.

3. Jeremy Black, *Italy and the Grand Tour* (New Haven, CT: Yale University Press, 2003); Cesare De Seta, ed., *Grand Tour viaggi narrati e dipinti* (Napoli: Electa Napoli, 2001); Cesare De Seta, *L'Italia nello specchio del Gran Tour* (Milano: Rizzoli, 2014).

4. Johann Wilhelm von Archenholz, *A Picture of Italy* (London, 1791).

5. Quoted in Moe, *The View from Vesuvius*, 24.

6. Quoted in Jeremy Black, *Italy and the Grand Tour*, 148; Silvana Patriarca, *Italian Vices: Nation and Character from the Risorgimento to the Republic* (New York: Cambridge University Press, 2010), offers a brilliant analysis of the cultural narratives of indolence and decadence in the making of modern Italy.

7. Jean-Charles-Léonard Simon de Sismondi, *Storia delle repubbliche italiane dei secoli di mezzo*, Vol. 16 (Capolago: Tipografia Elvetica, 1832), 197–200; Paula Findlen, Wendy Wassyng Roworth and Catherine M. Sama, eds., *Italy's Eighteenth Century Gender and Culture in the Age of the Grand Tour* (Stanford: Stanford University Press, 2009); Roberto Bizzocchi, *Cicisbei: morale privata e identità nazionale in Italia* (Roma: Laterza, 2008).

8. Reinhard Strohm, *Dramma Per Musica: Italian Opera Seria of the Eighteenth Century* (New Haven, CT: Yale University Press, 1997), 1–29.

9. Carlantonio Pilati, quoted in Patriarca, *Italian Vices*, 21.

10. Venturi, "L'Italia Fuori d'Italia," 987–1481.

11. Stuart Woolf, *A History of Italy 1700-1860: The Social Constraints of Political Change* (London; New York: Routledge, 1992); Franco Venturi, "L'Italia Fuori d'Italia," in *Storia d'Italia*, eds. Ruggiero Romano and Corrado Vivanti, Vol. 3, *Dal primo Settecento all'Unita* (Torino: Einaudi, 1970), 200.

12. Patriarca, *Italian Vices*, 20–50.

Notes

13. Maria Pia Donato, Davi Armando, Massimo Cattaneo and Jean-Françaois Chauvard, *Atlante storico dell'Italia rivoluzionaria e napoleonica* (Rome: École française de Rome, 2013), 33.

14. F. Nicola Badaloni, "La Cultura," in *Storia d'Italia 3 Dal primo Settecento all'unita*, eds., Ruggiero Romano and Corrado Vivanti (Torino: Einaudi, 1973), 699–888.

15. Davis, *Naples and Napoleon: Southern Italy and the European Revolutions, 1780-1860*; and Donato et al., *Atlante storico*.

16. Stuart Woolf, "La storia politica e sociale," in *Storia d'Italia: Dal Primo Settecento all'Unità*, eds., Ruggiero Romano e Corrado Vivant (Torino: Einaudi, 1972).

17. Quoted in Woolf, *A History of Italy*, 159.

18. Ibid., 161.

19. "Proclamation to the Cisalpine Republic, Nov. 17, 1797," in *Napoleon: Life, Addresses and Expeditions*, ed. Ida M. Tardell (Volendam, NL: LM Publishers, 2017), 37.

20. Christopher Duggan, *The Force of Destiny: A History of Italy since 1796* (Boston: Houghton Mifflin, 2008), 12.

21. Melchiorre Gioia, *Dissertazione di Melchiorre Gioja sul problema quale dei governi liberi meglio convenga alla felicità dell'Italia* (1831), 100.

22. D. A. Bingham, *A Selection from the Letters and Dispatches of the First Napoleon* (London: Chapman and Hall, 1884), 85.

23. Donato et al., *Atlante*, 304–305.

24. "Napoleone ad Eugenio, da Saint-Cloud, 21 luglio 1805," Eugéne de viceré d'Italia Beauharnais (viceré d'Italia), *Il principe Eugenio memorie del Regno d'Italia* (Corona e Caimi, 1865), 252–53.

Chapter 2

1. Woolf, *A History of Italy 1700-1860*; Laven and Riall, *Napoleon's Legacy: Problems of Government in Restoration Europe*.

2. Riall, *The Italian Risorgimento*, 11–23.

3. Banti, *La nazione del risorgimento: parentela, santità e onore alle origini dell'Italia unita*, 3–55, for a list of canonical texts, see, 45.

4. Vincenzo Cuoco, *Platone in Italia* (Napoli: Tip. M. Lombardi, 1861), 356; Duggan, *The Force of Destiny*, 24–29.

5. Ginevra Canonici Fachini, *Prospetto biografico delle donne italiane rinomate in letteratura dal secolo decimo quarto fino a giorni nostri: Con una risposta a Lady Morgan risguardante alcune accuse da lei date alle donne italiane nella sua opera L'Italie* (Dalla tipografia di Alvisopoli, 1824).

6. Madame de Staël, "Letteratura ed arti liberali: Sulla maniera e la utilità delle traduzioni," *Biblioteca italiana, ossia Giornale di letteratura, scienze ed arti*, Vol. 1 (Milano, 1816), 10, 17–18.

7. Giovanni Ragone "La letteratura e il consumo: un profilo dei generi e dei modelli nell'editoria italiana (1845-1925)," *Letterature italiana*, Vol. II (Torino: Einaudi, 1983), 690–95.

8. Gianna Proia, *Cristina di Belgiojoso: dal salotto alla politica* (Roma: Aracne, 2010); Doni, *Donne del Risorgimento.*

9. Maurizio Isabella, "Emotions, Rationality and Political Intentionality in Patriotic Discourse," *Nations and Nationalism* 15, no. 3 (July 2009): 427–33.

10. Laven, *Restoration and Risorgimento*; C. A. Bayly and E. F. Biagini, *Giuseppe Mazzini and the Globalization of Democratic Nationalism, 1830-1920* (Oxford: Oxford University Press/ British Academy, 2008).

11. John Davis, *Naples and Napoleon.*

12. Gabaccia, *Italy's Many Diasporas*, 45.

13. Ibid., 35.

14. Luch Riall, *Risorgimento: The History of Italy from Napoleon to Nation-State* (New York: Palgrave Macmillan, 2009), 125. Gabaccia, *Italy's Many Diasporas*, 35–52.

15. Maurizio Isabella, "Italian Exiles and British Politics before and After 1848," in *Exiles from European Revolutions: Refugees in Mid-Victorian England*, ed., Sabine Freitag (New York; Oxford: Berghahn, 2003), 59–87. Also see Maurizio Isabella, *Risorgimento in Exile*; Maurizio Isabella, et al., eds., *Mediterranean Diasporas: Politics and Ideas in the Long 19th Century* (London: Bloomsbury, 2016).

16. Emilio Cecchi, *Il primo scritto di Giuseppe Mazzini "Dell'amor patrio di Dante," seconda metà del 1827* (Marzocco, 1911).

17. Denis Mack Smith. *Mazzini* (New Haven, CT: Yale University Press, 2008), 41.

18. Duggan, *The Force of Destiny*, 142; Luigi Carci, *La spedizione e il processo dei fratelli Bandiera: con una appendice di documenti* (Modena: Società tipografica modenese, 1939), 28–35, 158–66.

19. Emanuele Celesia, *Sul martirio dei fratelli Bandiera discorso* (tip. Ferrando, 1848), 6.

Chapter 3

1. Luigi Settembrini, *Protesta del popolo delle Due Sicilie* (Morano, 1891); Finocchiaro and Maag, *La rivoluzione siciliana del 1848-49 e la spedizione del generale Filangieri*, 59.

2. Vincenzo Finocchiaro and Albert Maag, *La rivoluzione siciliana del 1848-49 e la spedizione del generale Filangieri* (F. Battiato, 1906), 63.

3. Riall, *Sicily and the Unification of Italy*, 30–61.

4. Simonetta Chiappini, "From the People to the Masses: Political Developments in Italian Opera from Rossini to Mascagni," in *The Risorgimento Revisited*, eds. Patriarca and Riall, 56–76; Bruno Sanguanini, *Il pubblico all'italiana: formazione del pubblico e politiche culturali tra Stato e teatro* (Milano: F. Angeli, 1989).

5. Giuseppe La Farina, *Storia d'Italia dal 1815 al 1850*, Vol. II (Società editrice italiana, 1861), 178–79.

6. Bernardino Biondelli, *Le cinque gloriose giornate di Milano esattamente descritte da un lombardo, testimone oculare: con interessanti documenti editi ed inediti* (Torino: Presso G. Pomba e compagnia, 1848), 6.

7. Riall, *Risorgimento*, 72.

8. Giuseppe Monsagrati, *Roma senza il Papa: La Repubblica romana del 1849* (Bari: Gius. Laterza & Figli Spa, 2014).

Notes

9. Lucy Riall, *Garibaldi: Invention of a Hero* (New Haven: Yale University Press, 2007); Fanny Tedeschi, "Sulla Tomba di Anita Garibaldi," *Poesie di Fanny Tedeschi* (Tipografia di F. Bencini, 1867).

10. David Kertzer, *The Kidnapping of Edgardo Mortara* (New York: Alfred Knopf, 1997), 139.

11. Anonymous, "Dell'unione Italiana," *L'Indipendente. Giornale politico italiano* (Cecchini, 1848).

12. Marina D'Amelia, "Between Two Eras: Challenges Facing Women in the Risorgimento," in *Risorgimento Revisited*, eds. Riall and Patriarca, 115–33; Patriarca, *Italian Vices*, 20–49.

13. Paolo Mencacci, *Memorie documentate per la storia della rivoluzione italiana* (Tip. di M. Armanni, 1886).

14. Giacomo Oddo, *I mille di Marsala: scene rivoluzionarie* (G. Scorza di Nicola, 1863).

15. Riall, *Under the Volcano*, 144.

Chapter 4

1. Francesco De Sanctis, *Scritti politici di Francesco de Sanctis* (A. Morano, 1900), 23–24.

2. Giorgio Candeloro, *Il movimento cattolico in Italia* (Roma: Riuniti, 1974); Guido Verucci, *L'Italia laica prima e dopo l'Unità, 1848-1876* (Roma: Laterza, 1996); Arturo Carlo Jemolo, *Chiesa e stato: dalla unificazione ai giorni nostri* (Turin: G. Einaudi, 1977); David Kertzer, *Prisoner of the Vatican the Popes' Secret Plot to Capture Rome from the New Italian State* (Boston: Houghton Mifflin, 2004).

3. Mark Seymour, *Debating Divorce in Italy: Marriage and the Making of Modern Italians, 1860-1974* (New York: Palgrave Macmillan, 2006), 11–26.

4. David Kertzer, "Religion and Society, 1789-1892," in *Italy in the Nineteenth Century: 1796-1900*, ed. John A Davis (Oxford: Oxford University Press, 2007), 190–200.

5. Fulvio Cammarano, *Il nuovo stato e la società civile: 1861-1887* (Roma: Laterza, 1995); Giorgio Candeloro, *La costruzione dello stato unitario 1860-1871* (Milano: Feltrinelli, 1994). Giovanni Sabbatucci and Vittorio Vidotto, *Il nuovo stato e la società civile: 1861-1887*, Vol. 2, *Storia d'Italia* (Bari: Laterza, 1995).

6. Patriarca, *Numbers and Nationhood*, 178.

7. Ibid., 189–97.

8. Rudolph M. Bell, *Fate and Honor, Family and Village: Demographic and Cultural Change in Rural Italy since 1800* (Chicago: University of Chicago Press, 1979), 151–53.

9. On regionalism see *Storia d'Italia: le regioni dall'Unità a oggi* (Turin: Giulio Einaudi, 1977–2002); Carl Levy, *Italian Regionalism: History, Identity and Politics* (Oxford: Berg, 1996).

10. Massimo Montanari, *Italian Identity in the Kitchen, or, Food and the Nation* (New York: Columbia University Press, 2013).

11. Ministro d'Agricoltura, Industria e Commercio (MAIC), *Statistica Del Regno d'Italia. Popolazione. Censimento Generale (31 Dicembre 1861)*, Vol. II (Torino: Tip. Letteraria, 1865), XVIII, IX.

12. Ibid., XVII.

13. Piero Bevilacqua, *Storia della questione meridionale* (Roma: Editrice sindacale italiana, 1974); Marta Petrusewicz, *Come il meridione divenne una questione: rappresentazioni del*

Sud prima e dopo il Quarantotto (Soveria Mannelli (CZ): Rubbettino, 1998); Francesco Barbagallo, *La questione italiana: Il Nord e il Sud dal 1860 a oggi* (Bari; Roma: Laterza, 2017).

14. John Dickie, *Cosa Nostra: A History of the Sicilian Mafia* (New York: Palgrave Macmillan, 2004), 74.

15. Nelson Moe, *The View from Vesuvius*; and Aliza Wong, *Race and the Nation in Liberal Italy, 1861-1911: Meridionalism, Empire, and Diaspora* (New York: Palgrave Macmillan, 2006).

16. Moe, *The View from Vesuvius*, 235.

17. Dickie, *Cosa Nostra*, 59.

18. Riall, *Sicily and the Unification of Italy,* 224.

19. Riall, "Men at War: Masculinity and Military Ideals in the Risorgimento," in *The Risorgimento Revisited: Nationalism and Culture in Nineteenth-Century Italy,* eds. Lucy Riall and Silvana Patriarca (Houndmills, Basingstoke, Hampshire; New York: Palgrave Macmillan, 2011), 158; Patriarca, *Italian Vices*, 51–78; on masculinity in general see Sandro Bellassai and Maria Malatesta, *Genere e mascolinità: uno sguardo storico*, Biblioteca di cultura, 595 (Roma: Bulzoni, 2000).

20. Massimo D'Azeglio, *I miei ricordi*, Vol. 1 (Firenze: G. Barbèra. 1867), 6.

21. Ibid., 16.

22. Ibid., 15–35; Giuseppe Levi, *Autobiografia di un padre di famiglia* (Firenze: Successori Le Monnier, 1868).

23. Giuseppe Mazzini, *Doveri dell'uomo* (London, 1860).

24. Ministero dei Deputati, 1 tornata del 18 luglio, 1862, "Svolgimento delle proposte di legge del deputato Petruccelli sul matrimonio civile, sulle condanne delle curie vescovili," in *Atti del parlamento*, 3368–69.

25. Anna Maria Mozzoni, *La donna e i suoi rapporti sociali* (Milano, 1864), 30; Franca Pieroni Bortolotti, *Alle Origini Del Movimento Femminile in Italia, 1848-1892* (Torino: Einaudi, 1963), 285.

26. Mozzoni, *La donna e i suoi rapporti sociali*, 97.

Part Two

1. Nick Carter, "Rethinking the Italian Liberal State," *Bulletin of Italian Politics* 3, no. 2 (2011), 225; Nick Carter, *Modern Italy in Historical Perspective* (London; New York: Bloomsbury Academic, 2011); John A. Davis, "Remapping Italy's Path to the Twentieth Century," *The Journal of Modern History* 66, no. 2 (1994): 291–320.

2. Croce, *Storia d'Italia dal 1871 al 1915*; Federico Chabod, *Storia della politica estera italiana dal 1870 al 1896: volume primo: Le premesse: [Presentazione]* (Bari: G. Laterza & figli, 1951); Rosario Romeo, *L'Italia unita e la prima guerra mondiale* (Roma; Bari: Laterza, 1978); William Salomone, *Italian Democracy in the Making: The Political Scene in the Giolittian Era, 1900-1914*, 2nd edn. (Philadelphia: University of Pennsylvania Press, 1960); Alexander De Grand, *The Hunchbacks Tailor: Giovanni Giolitti and Liberal Italy from the Challenge of Mass Politics to the Rise of Fascism, 1882-1922* (Westport: Praeger, 2001).

3. Paolo Favilli, *Marxismo e storia: saggio sull'innovazione storiografica in Italia (1945-1970)* (Milano: FrancoAngeli, 2006).

4. Raffaele Romanelli, *Il comando impossibile: stato e società nell'Italia liberale* (Bologna: Il Mulino, 1995); Susan A. Ashley, *Making Liberalism Work: The Italian Experience, 1860-1914*

(Westport, CT: Praeger, 2003); Sabina Donati, *A Political History of National Citizenship and Identity in Italy, 1861–1950* (Palo Alto, CA: Stanford University Press, 2013).

5. John A. Davis, "Introduction," in *Italy in the Nineteenth Century: 1796-1900*, ed. John Davis (Oxford: Oxford University Press, 2007), 18–20; Simonetta Soldani and Gabriele Turi, *Fare gli Italiani: scuola e cultura nell'Italia contemporanea*, vol. 1 (Il Mulino, 1993); Donna R. Gabaccia, *Italy's Many Diasporas*; Linda Reeder, *Widows in White Migration and the Transformation of Rural Italian Women, Sicily, 1880-1920* (Toronto: University of Toronto Press, 2003); Emilio Gentile, *La grande Italia: il mito della nazione nel XX secolo* (Roma; Bari: Laterza, 2006); Alberto Mario Banti, *Sublime madre nostra: la nazione italiana dal Risorgimento al fascismo* (Roma: Laterza, 2011); Arianna Arisi Rota, et al. eds., *Patrioti si diventa: luoghi e linguaggi di pedagogia patriottica nell'Italia unita* (Milano: Angeli, 2009); Axel Korner, *The Politics of Culture in Liberal Italy: From Unification to Fascism* (London: Routledge, 2008).

6. Banti, *Terra e denaro: una borghesia madana dell'Ottocento*; Alberto Mario Banti, *L'età liberale* (Roma: Donzelli, 1996); Marco Meriggi and Pierangelo Schiera, *Dalla città alla nazione: borghesie ottocentesche in Italia e in Germania* (Bologna: Il Mulino, 1993); Axel Korner, *The Politics of Culture in Liberal Italy: From Unification to Fascism* (London: Routledge, 2008); Steven C. Soper, *Building a Civil Society: Associations, Public Life, and the Origins of Modern Italy* (Toronto: University of Toronto Press, 2013); Macry, *Ottocento: famiglia, élites e patrimoni a Napoli*; Maria Malatesta, *Society and the Professions in Italy, 1860-1914* (Cambridge: Cambridge University Press, 2002).

7. Davis, "Remapping Italy's Path to the Twentieth Century," 310–11.

8. Donald H. Bell, *Sesto San Giovanni: Workers, Culture, and Politics in an Italian Town, 1880-1922* (New Brunswick: Rutgers University Press, 1986); Maurizio Gribaudi, *Mondo operaio e mito operaio: spazi e percorsi sociali a Turin nel primo Novecento* (Turin: Einaudi, 1987); Dora M. Dumont, "Strange and Exorbitant Demands': Rural Labour in Nineteenth-Century Bologna," *European History Quarterly* 30, no. 4 (October 1, 2000): 467–91; Donna R. Gabaccia, *Militants and Migrants: Rural Sicilians Become American Workers* (New Brunswick, NJ: Rutgers University Press, 1988); Donna R. Gabaccia and Fraser M. Ottanelli, *Italian Workers of the World: Labor Migration and the Formation of Multiethnic States* (Urbana, IL: University of Illinois Press, 2001).

9. Franca Pieroni Bortolotti, *Alle origini del movimento femminile in Italia: 1848-1892* (Turin: G. Einaudi, 1963); Franca Pieroni Bortolotti, *Socialismo e questione femminile in Italia 1892-1922* (Milano: Gabriele Mazzotta, 1976); Annarita Buttafuoco, *Suffragismo femminile e istituzioni politiche dall'Unità al fascismo* (Roma: Associazione degli ex parlamentari della repubblica, 1988); Annarita Buttafuoco, *Questioni di cittadinanza: donne e diritti sociali nell'Italia liberale* (Siena: Protagon Editori Toscani, 1995).

10. Simonetta Soldani and Gabriele Turi, *Fare gli Italiani*.

11. Silvana Patriarca, "Gender Trouble: Women and the Making of Italy's 'Active Population,' 1861-1936," *Journal of Modern Italian Studies* 3, no. 2 (1998): 144–63; Donna Gabaccia, "In the Shadows of the Periphery: Italian Women in the Nineteenth Century," in *Connecting Spheres: Women in the Western World, 1500 to the Present*, eds. Marilyn J. Boxer and Jean H. Quataert (New York: Oxford University Press, 1987), 166–76; Anna Cento Bull, "Lombard Silk-spinners in the Nineteenth Century: An Industrial Workforce in a Rural Setting," in *Women and Italy: Essays on Gender, Culture and History*, eds. Zygmunt G. Barański and Shirley Vinall (London: Macmillan, 1990); 11–42; Elda Gentili Zappi, *If Eight Hours Seem Too Few: Mobilization of Women Workers in the Italian Rice Fields* (Albany: State University of New York Press, 1991); Patrizia Audenino, *Donne e libere professioni: il Piemonte del Novecento* (Milano: Angeli, 2007). On the relationship between public and private spheres

see: Michela De Giorgio, *Le italiane dall'unità a oggi: modelli culturali e comportamenti sociali* (Bari: Laterza, 1992); Katharine Mitchell and Helena Sanson, *Women and Gender in Post-Unification Italy: Between Private and Public Spheres* (Oxford: Peter Lang, 2013); Margherita Pelaja, *Matrimonio e sessualità a Roma nell'ottocento* (Bari: Laterza, 1994); Perry Willson, ed., *Gender, Family, and Sexuality: The Private Sphere in Italy 1860-1945* (New York: Palgrave Macmillan, 2004); Mark Seymour, "Epistolary Emotions: Exploring Amorous Hinterlands in 1870s Southern Italy," *Social History* 35, no. 2 (May 1, 2010): 148–64.

12. On gender see Silvana Patriarca, *Italian Vices: Nation and Character from the Risorgimento to the Republic* (Cambridge; New York: Cambridge University Press, 2010), 51–107; Suzanne Stewart-Steinberg, *The Pinocchio Effect: On Making Italians 1860-1920* (Chicago: University of Chicago Press, 2007); Donna R. Gabaccia and Franca Iacovetta, *Women, Gender and Transnational Lives Italian Workers of the World* (Toronto; Buffalo: University of Toronto Press, 2002). On sexuality see: Mary Gibson, *Prostitution and the State in Italy: 1860-1915* (New Brunswick, NJ: Rutgers University Press, 1986); Paolo Sorcinelli, *Storia e sessualità: casi di vita, regole e trasgressioni tra Ottocento e Novecento* (Milano: Mondadori, 2001); Bruno P. F. Wanrooij, *Storia del pudore: la questione sessuale in Italia, 1860-1940* (Venezia: Marsilio, 1990); Valeria Paola Babini, Fernanda Minuz and Annamaria Tagliavini, *La donna nelle scienze dell'uomo: immagini del femminile nella cultura scientifica italiana di fine secolo* (Milano: F. Angeli, 1986); Domenico Rizzo, "Marriage on Trial: Adultery in Nineteenth-Century Rome," in *Gender, Family and Sexuality* (Palgrave Macmillan, London, 2004), 20–36; Valeria Paola Babini, *Il caso Murri: una storia italiana* (Bologna: Il Mulino, 2004); Valeria P. Babini, Chiara Beccalossi, and Lucy Riall, *Italian Sexualities Uncovered, 1789–1914* (London: Palgrave Macmillan UK, 2015).

13. Sereni, *Il capitalismo nelle campagne (1860-1900)*, and *Capitalismo e mercato nazionale in Italia* (Roma: Editori riuniti, 1974). Also see Alexander Gerschenkron, *Economic Backwardness in Historical Perspective a Book of Essays* (New York: F. Praeger, 1962).

14. Gianni Toniolo, *Storia economica dell'Italia liberale: (1850-1918)* (Bologna: Il Mulino, 2001); Vera Zamagni, *Dalla periferia al centro: la seconda rinascita economica dell'Italia, 1861-1981* (Bologna: Il Mulino, 1990); Vera Zamagni, *Introduzione alla storia economica d'Italia* (Bologna: Il Mulino, 2007); Stefano Fenoaltea, *The Reinterpretation of Italian Economic History: From Unification to the Great War* (Cambridge UK; New York: Cambridge University Press, 2011).

15. Giuseppe Giarrizzo, ed., *La Modernizzazione difficile: città e campagne nel Mezzogiorno dall'età giolittiana al fascismo* (Bari: De Donato, 1983); Marta Petrusewicz, *Latifondo: economia morale e vita materiale in una periferia dell'Ottocento* (Venezia: Marsilio, 1990).

16. Rosario Villari, *Il Sud nella storia d' Italia. 2: Antologia della questione meridionale* (Roma-Bari: Laterza, 1971); Bevilacqua, *Storia della questione meridionale.* The most influential postwar analyses blaming southern poverty on the people is Edward C. Banfield, *The Moral Basis of a Backward Society* (Glencoe, IL: Free Press, 1958).

17. Robert Lumley and Jonathan Morris, *The New History of the Italian South: The Mezzogiorno Revisited* (Exeter, Devon: University of Exeter Press, 1997); Piero Bevilacqua, *Breve storia dell'Italia meridionale: dall'Ottocento a oggi* (Roma: Donzelli, 2005).

18. Paolo Pezzino, *Una certa reciprocità di favori: mafia e modernizzazione violenta nella Sicilia postunitaria* (Milano: FrancoAngeli, 1990); Salvatore Lupo, *History of the mafia* (New York: Columbia University Press, 2011); and Dickie, *Cosa Nostra: A History of the Sicilian Mafia.*

19. Jane Schneider, ed., *Italy's "Southern Question": Orientalism in One Country* (Oxford: Berg, 1998); John Dickie, *Darkest Italy: The Nation and Stereotypes of the Mezzogiorno, 1860-1900* (New York: Macmillan, 1999); Wong, *Race and the Nation.* For a general history of Italian

positivism and social Darwinism see Mary Gibson, *Born to Crime: Cesare Lombroso and the Origins of Biological Criminology* (Westport, CT: Praeger, 2002).

20. Macry, *Ottocento: famiglia, élites e patrimoni a Napoli;* Umberto Santino, *Storia del movimento antimafia: dalla lotta di classe all'impegno civile* (Editori Riuniti, 2000); Paolo Macry, "Rethinking a Stereotype: Territorial Differences and Family Models in the Modernization of Italy," *Journal of Modern Italian Studies* 2, no. 2 (June 1, 1997): 188–214.

21. Patrizia Audenino, *Un mestiere per partire: tradizione migratoria, lavoro e comunità in una vallata alpina* (Milano: F. Angeli, 1992); Andreina De Clementi, *Di qua e di là dall'oceano: emigrazione e mercati nel Meridione (1860-1930)* (Roma: Carocci, 1999); Donna R. Gabaccia, *Italy's Many Diasporas*; Piero Bevilacqua, Andreina De Clementi and Emilio Franzina, *Storia dell'emigrazione italiana* (Roma: Donzelli Editore, 2001); Reeder, *Widows in White*; Patrizia Audenino and Maddalena Tirabassi, *Migrazioni italiane: storia e storie dall'ancien régime a oggi* (Milano: Mondadori, 2008); Emilio Franzina, *Una patria espatriata. Lealtà nazionale e caratteri regionali nell'immigrazione italiana all'estero (secoli XIX e XX)* (Viterbo: Edizioni Sette Città, 2014); Maurizio Isabella, *Mediterranean Diasporas*.

22. Elizabeth Zanoni, *Migrant Marketplaces: Food and Italians in North and South America* (Urbana: University of Illinois Press, 2018); Mark I. Choate, *Emigrant Nation: The Making of Italy Abroad* (Cambridge, MA: Harvard University Press, 2008).

Chapter 5

1. Nuto Revelli, "Una lira al giorno per sedici ore di lavoro," *Il mondo dei vinti: testimonianze di vita contadina* (Torino: Einaudi, 1997), 348.

2. ISTAT, *Sommario delle statistiche storiche* (Roma, 1968), 13; *Censimento 31 dicembre 1871: Popolazione classificata per professioni, culti e infermità principali* (Stamperia Reale, 1876), XIX.

3. Stefano Jacini, *Relazione finale sui risultati dell'inchiesta agraria, pubblicata nel vol. 15, fasc. 1 degli Atti della Giunta per la inchiesta agraria e sulle condizioni della classe agricola* (Roma: Forzani, 1884), 65–67.

4. Zamagni, *Dalla periferia*, 55–66; Istat statistiche storiche, *Produzione delle principali coltivazioni industriali e foraggere- Anni 1861-2015*.

5. Istat, *Statistiche Storiche*, "Popolazione Tavola 10.4 - Popolazione attiva in condizione professionale per settore di attività economica e regione ai Censimenti 1861-2011."

6. Gabaccia, "In the Shadows," 194–203.

7. Statistica del Regno D'Italia, *Censimento 31 dicembre 1871: Popolazione classificata per professioni, culti e infermità principali* (Stamperia Reale, 1876), XIX.

8. Petrusewicz, *Latifondo*.

9. Gabaccia, "In the Shadows," 194–203.

10. Zamagni, *Dalla periferia*, 129; Valerio Castronovo, "La storia economica," in *Storia d'Italia*, 4, 1 *Dall'Unita ad Oggi*, eds. Ruggiero Romano and Corrado Vivanti (Torino: Einaudi, 1972), 5–129.

11. Stefano Gallo, *Senza attraversare le frontiere: le migrazioni interne dall'unità a oggi* (edizione digitale: Roma: Laterza, 2012), part 1.

12. Gallo, *Senza attraversare*, paragraph 96.

13. Zappi, *If Eight Hours*, 34–37; Amarella Quasi, "Le mondine delle risaie vercellesi," in *1* (Bologna: Il Mulino, 1992), 165–80.

14. Giovanni Montroni, *La società italiana dall'unificazione alla Grande Guerra* (edizione digitale: Roma; Bari: Laterza, 2002), paragraphs, 31–34.

15. Montroni, *La società italiana*, paragraphs, 75–94; Mario Sanfilippo, *San Lorenzo 1870-1945: storia e storie di un quartiere popolare romano* (Roma: Edilizio, 2003), 1–34.

16. Giorgio Mortara, *Le popolazioni delle grandi città italiane studio demografico* (Turin: Unione tipografico-editrice Torinese, 1908), 373.

17. David Kertzer, *Amalia's Tale: An Impoverished Peasant Woman, an Ambitious Attorney, and a Fight for Justice* (Boston: Houghton Mifflin Co., 2008), 3–5.

18. Giovanni Bolis, *La polizia e le classi pericolose della società studi dell'avv. Giovanni Bolis* (Zanichelli, 1871), 461; Translation from Mary Gibson, *Prostitution and the State in Italy, 1860-1915* (Columbus, OH: Ohio State University Press, 1999), 20.

19. David Forgacs, *Italy's Margins* (Cambridge: Cambridge University Press, 2016), 14–44.

20. Quote from G. Tammeo, *La prostituzione: saggio di statistica morale* (L. Roux, 1890), 146.

21. Marzio Barbagli, "Three Household Formation Systems in Eighteenth- and Nineteenth-Century Italy," in *The Family in Italy: From Antiquity to the Present*, eds. David I. Kertzer and Richard P. Saller (New Haven, CT: Yale Univ. Press, 2008), 250–70; Bell, *Fate, Honor*, 67–112. Also see Marzio Barbagli and David Kertzer, eds., *Storia della famiglia Italiana, 1750-1950* (Bologna: Il Mulino, 1992).

22. Ida Fazio, "Trasmissione della proprietà, sussistenza e status femminile in Sicilia (Capizzi, 1790-1900)," in *Società rurale e ruoli femminili in Italia fra '800 e '900, Annali Istituto «Alcide Cervi» vol. 17-18 (1995-1996)*, ed. Paola Corti (Bari: Dedalo, 1998), 181–99.

23. Istituto centrale di statistica, *Annali di statistica* (Istituto centrale de statistica, 1885), 92. On schooling in general see Soldani and Turi, *Fare gli Italiani: scuola e cultura nell'Italia contemporanea*.

24. Gaetano Bonetta, *Istruzione e società nella Sicilia dell'Ottocento* (Sellerio, 1981), 56.

25. Duggan, *The Force of Destiny*, 280.

26. Giudo Fabiani, *Casa Mia! Patria Mia! Libro di lettura per la 3a classe elementare* femminile (Milano: A. Vallardi, 1903), 147. On nationalism and education see Anna Ascenzi, *Tra educazione etico-civile e costruzione dell'identità nazionale: l'insegnamento della storia nelle scuole italiane dell'Ottocento* (Vita e Pensiero, 2004).

Chapter 6

1. Reeder, *Widows in White*, 55–57.

2. Commissariato generale dell'emigrazione, *Annuario statistico della emigrazione italiana dal 1876 al 1925: con notizie sull'emigrazione negli anni 1869-1875* (Roma: Edizione del commissariato dell'emigrazione, 1927), 10–12.

3. Ibid., 167–84.

4. Giovanni Lorenzoni, *Inchiesta parlamentare sulle condizioni dei contadini nelle province meridionali e nelle Sicilia*, vol. 6, *Sicilia*, tomo 1, parte 5 (Roma: Tip. Naz. G. Bertero, 1910), 812.

5. Reeder, *Widows in White*, 89–102, 142–67.

6. Lorenzoni, *Inchiesta*, parte 3, 26.

7. Charlotte Gower Chapman, *Milocca; a Sicilian Village* (London: Allen and Unwin, 1973), 109.

8. Lorenzoni, *Inchiesta*, parte 5, 754.

9. Gower Chapman, *Milocca; a Sicilian Village*, 109.

10. For a history of the *Fasci* movement see Francesco Renda, *I Fasci siciliani: 1892-94* (Turin: G. Einaudi, 1977); Gabaccia, *Militants and Migrants*.

11. Lorenzoni, *Inchiesta*, parte 5, 754.

12. Reeder, *Widows in White*, 95–97.

13. Patrizia Audenino, *Un mestiere per partire*; Patrizia Audenino, Paola Corti and Ada Lonni, *Imprenditori biellesi in Francia tra Ottocento e Novecento* (Milano: Electa, 1997).

14. Matteo Sanfilippo and Paola Corti, *L'Italia e le migrazioni* (Edizione digitale; Roma-Bari: Gius. Laterza & Figli Spa, 2013), chapter 4; Patrizia Audenino, *Un mestiere per partire*.

15. Robert Foerster, *Italian Emigration of Our Times* (Cambridge: Harvard University Press, 1919), 299.

16. Donna R. Gabaccia, *From Sicily to Elizabeth Street: Housing and Social Change among Italian Immigrants, 1880-1930* (Albany: State University of New York Press, 1984); Samuel L. Baily, *Immigrants in the Lands of Promise: Italians in Buenos Aires and New York City, 1870-1914* (Ithaca, NY: Cornell University Press, 1999).

17. Foerster, *Italian Emigration of Our Times*, 475–76.

18. Ibid., 478.

19. Choate, *Emigrant Nation*, 59–62.

20. Ibid., 189–93.

21. Antonio Mangano, "The Effect of Emigration upon Italy: Ci manca la mano d'opera," we lack the working hand, in *Charities and Commons* XX, no. #1 (April 4, 1908), 16.

22. Ibid.

23. Commissariato dell'emigrazione, Bolletino dell'emigrazione, 18 (1910), 51, quoted in Betty Boyd Caroli, *Italian Repatriation from the United States, 1900-1914* (New York: Center for Migration Studies, 1973), 65.

24. Lorenzoni, *Inchiesta*, parte 5, 514.

25. Reeder, *Widows in White*, 202–31.

26. Zanoni, *Migrant Marketplaces*, 73–100, 183–90.

27. Samuel L. Baily and F. Ramella. *One Family, Two Worlds: An Italian Immigrant Family's Correspondence across the Atlantic, 1901-1922* (New Brunswick, NJ: Rutgers University Press, 1988), and Sonia Cancian, *Families, Lovers, and Their Letters* (Winnipeg: University of Manitoba Press, 2010).

Chapter 7

1. Denis Mack Smith, *Modern Italy: A Political History* (New Haven, CT: Yale University Press, 1997), 108–115.

2. Daniela Melfa, *Migrando a Sud: coloni italiani in Tunisia, 1881-1939* (Aracne, 2008); Julia Ann Clancy-Smith, *Mediterraneans: North Africa, Europe, and the Ottoman Empire in an Age of Migration, c. 1800-1900* (Berkeley, CA; London: University of California Press, 2012).

3. Ernesto Ragionieri, "La storia politica e sociale," in Storia d'Italia, 4, 1 Dall'Unita a Oggi (Turin: Einaudi, 1972), 1744–52; Fulvio Cammarano, *Storia dell'Italia liberale* (edizione digitale: Roma-Bari: Gius. Laterza & Figli Spa, 2014), paragraph 244–47.

4. Daniele Natili, *Un programma coloniale: La Società Geografica Italiana e le origini dell'espansione in Etiopia* (Gangemi Editore spa, 2011), 176–80.

5. Raymond Jonas, *Battle of Adwa: African Victory in the Age of Empire* (Cambridge: Belknap Harvard, 2015), 34–57, 69–74.

6. Choate, *Emigrant Nation*, 30–36.

7. Jonas, *Battle of Adwa*, 158–93; Sean McLachlan, Lorenza Lanza, Patrizia Vicentini and Raffaele Ruggeri, *La battaglia di Adua: marzo 1896* (Gorizia: LEG, 2012).

8. Choate, *Emigrant Nation*, 39–56.

9. Luigi Einaudi, *Un Principe Mercante;Studio Sulla Espansione Coloniale Italiana* (Torino, 1900), 18; Choate, *Emigrant Empire*, 49–53; Zanoni, *Migrant Marketplaces*, 14–21.

10. Peter R. D'Agostino, *Rome in America: Transnational Catholic Ideology from the Risorgimento to Fascism* (Chapel Hill: The University of North Carolina Press, 2003), 53–82; Choate, *Emigrant Nation*, 129–46.

11. Quoted in Choate, *Emigrant Nation*, 54.

12. Donati, *A Political History*, 69–151.

13. Spencer Di Scala, ed., *Italian Socialism: Between Politics and History* (Amherst: University of Massachusetts Press, 1996).

14. Gabaccia and Ottanelli, *Italian Workers of the World*; Jennifer Guglielmo, *Living the Revolution: Italian Women's Resistance and Radicalism in New York City, 1880-1945* (Chapel Hill: University of North Carolina Press, 2010).

15. Alexander J. De Grand and Giovanni Giolitti, *The Hunchbacks Tailor: Giovanni Giolitti and Liberal Italy from the Challenge of Mass Politics to the Rise of Fascism, 1882-1922* (Westport: Praeger, 2001).

Chapter 8

1. Giuseppe Prezzolini and Giovannni Papini, *La colture italiana* (F. Lumachi, 1906), 10.

2. Emilio Praga, *Penombre* (Milano: Casa editrice degli autori, 1864).

3. Ilaria Crotti and Ricciarda Ricorda, *Scapigliatura e dintorni* (Padova: Piccin Nuova Libraria, 1992); David Del Principe, *Rebellion, Death, and Aesthetics in Italy: The Demons of Scapigliatura* (Fairleigh Dickinson University Press, 1996); Albert Boime, *The Art of the Macchia and the Risorgimento: Representing Culture and Nationalism in Nineteenth-Century Italy* (University of Chicago Press, 1993); Fernando Mazzocca and Carlo Sisi, eds., *I macchiaioli prima dell'impressionismo* (Venezia: Marsilio, 2003).

4. Alberto Asor Rosa, "La Cultura," in *Storia d'Italia* (4) 2 *Dall'unità a oggi*, eds. Ruggiero Romano and Corrado Vivanti (Turin: Einaudi, 1972), 850–78. For an overview of modern Italian philsophy see: Brian P. Copenhaver and Rebecca Copenhaver, *From Kant to Croce: Modern Philosophy in Italy, 1800-1950* (Toronto: University of Toronto Press, 2012).

5. Asor Rosa, "La Cultura," 878–900.

6. Linda Reeder, "Unattached and Unhinged: The Spinster and the Psychiatrist in Liberal Italy, 1860–1922," *Gender & History* 24, no. 1 (April 1, 2012): 187–204; Linda Reeder, "The Making of the Italian Husband in Nineteenth-Century Italy," in *Italian Sexualities Uncovered, 1789–1914*, eds. Valeria P. Babini, Chiara Beccalossi and Lucy Riall (London: Palgrave Macmillan UK, 2015), 272–90.

7. Mary Gibson, *Born to Crime: Cesare Lombroso and the Origins of Biological Criminology* (Westport, CT: Praeger, 2002); Delia Frigessi *Cesare Lombroso* (Turin: Einaudi, 2003); For an excellent translation of *L'uomo criminale* see Mary Gibson and Nicole Hahn Rafter, *Criminal Man* (Durham, NC: Duke University Press, 2006).

8. John Dickie, *Darkest Italy*; Wong, *Race and the Nation*.

9. Alfredo Niceforo, *L'Italia barbara contemporanea: studi ed appunti* (Milano; Palermo: Remo Sandron, 1898); Alfredo Niceforo, *Italiani del nord e italiani del sud* (Turin: Bocca, fratelli, 1901).

10. Napoleone Colajanni, *Ire e spropositi di Cesare Lombroso* (Tropea, 1890); Napoleone Colajanni, *La delinquenza della Sicilia e le sue cause* (Palermo, 1885).

11. Asor Rosa, "La Cultura," 955–79.

12. Wendy Griswold, *Regionalism and the Reading Class* (Chicago: University of Chicago Press, 2008), 116–20; Lucienne Kroha, "The Novel, 1870-1920," in *A History of Women's Writing in Italy*, eds. Letizia Panizza and Sharon Wood (Cambridge: Cambridge University Press, 2000), 164–76. Katharine Mitchell, *Italian Women Writers: Gender and Everyday Life in Fiction and Journalism, 1870-1910* (Toronto: University of Toronto Press, 2014).

13. Alan Mallach, *The Autumn of Italian Opera: From Verismo to Modernism, 1890-1915* (Boston: Northeastern University Press, 2007).

14. Sarah Patricia Hill and Giuliana Minghelli, *Stillness in Motion: Italy, Photography, and the Meanings of Modernity* (Toronto: University of Toronto Press, 2014); Maria Antonella Pelizzari, *Photography and Italy* (London: Reaktion Books, 2010).

15. Giovanni Ragone, "La letteratura e il consumo; un profilo dei generi e dei modelli nell'editoria italiana (1845-1925)," *letteratura italiana*, 761; David Forgacs, *Italian Culture in the Industrial Era, 1880-1980: Cultural Industries, Politics, and the Public* (Manchester: Manchester University Press, 1990).

16. For an overview of Italian women writers and domesticity see, Mitchell, *Italian Women Writers*.

17. Martin Clark, *Modern Italy, 1871 to the Present* (London: Routledge, 2014), 200–202. Antonio Morosi, *Il teatro di varietà in Italia* (G. Calvetti, 1901).

18. Goffredo Plastino and Joseph Sciorra, eds., *Neapolitan Postcards: The Canzone Napoletana as Transnational Subject* (Lanham: Rowman & Littlefield, 2016).

19. On the early years of Italian cinema see Gian Piero Brunetta, *Il cinema muto italiano: Da "La presa di Roma" a "Sole." 1905-1929* (Bari: Gius. Laterza & Figli Spa, 2014).

20. Filippo Tommaso Marinetti, *Critical Writings: New Edition* (New York: Farrar, Straus and Giroux, 2007), 14.

21. Quoted in Duggan, *Force of Destiny*, 378. On futurism and modernity in general see Emilio Gentile, *The Struggle for Modernity: Nationalism, Futurism, and Fascism* (Westport, CT: Greenwood Publishing Group, 2003).

Part Three

1. Examples of the Gramscian and liberal interpretations include Chabod, *L'Italia Contemporanea (1918-1948)*; Piero Pieri, *L'Italia Nella Prima Guerra Mondiale (1915-1918)* (Torino: G. Einaudi, 1968); Giuseppe Talamo, *Da Cavour alla fine della prima guerra mondiale* (Torino: Unione, 1965); European analyses include Gail Braybon, *Evidence, History and the Great War: Historians and the Impact of 1914-18* (New York: Berghahn Books, 2003); Stéphane Audoin-Rouzeau and Annette Becker, *14-18: Understanding the Great War* (New York: Farrar, Straus and Giroux, 2014).

2. Mario Isneghi and Giorgio Rochat, *La Grande Guerra: 1914-1918* (Bologna: Il Molino, 2008); Mario Isnenghi and Daniele Ceschin, *La Grande guerra: uomini e luoghi del '15-18* (Torino: UTET, 2008); Antonio Gibelli, *La guerra grande: Storie di gente comune* (Bari: Gius. Laterza & Figli Spa, 2016); Angelo Ventrone, *Piccola storia della Grande Guerra* (Roma: Donzelli, 2005); Marco Mondini, *Alpini: parole e immagini di un mito guerriero* (Roma: Laterza, 2008); Vanda Wilcox, *Morale and the Italian Army during the First World War* (Cambridge: Cambridge University Press, 2016); John Gooch, *The Italian Army and the First World War* (Cambridge: Cambridge University Press, 2014).

3. Revelli, *Il mondo dei vinti*; Federico Adamoli, *Lettere Dal Fronte: La Grande Guerra Raccontata Nelle Pagine Del Corriere Abruzzese* (Federico Adamoli, 2013); Fabio Caffarena, *Lettere dalla Grande Guerra: scritture del quotidiano, monumenti della memoria, fonti per la storia: il caso italiano* (Milano: Unicopli, 2005); Alberto Cavaciocchi and Andrea Ungari, *Gli italiani in guerra* (Milano: Mursia, 2014).

4. Barbara Curli, *Italiane al lavoro: 1914-1920* (Venezia: Marsilio, 1998); Augusta Molinari, *Una patria per le donne: la mobilitazione femminile nella Grande Guerra* (Bologna: Il Mulino, 2014); Paola Antolini et al., eds., *Donne in guerra 1915-1918: la grande guerra attraverso l'analisi e le testimonianze di una terra di confine* (Tione di Trento (TN); Museo storico italiano della guerra: Rovereto (TN): Centro studi Judicaria: 2006); Allison Scardino Belzer, *Women and the Great War: Femininity under Fire in Italy* (Basingstoke: Palgrave Macmillan, 2010).

5. Bruna Bianchi, *Crescere in tempo di guerra: il lavoro e la protesta dei ragazzi in Italia, 1915-1918* (Venezia: Cafoscarina, 2016); Antonio Gibelli, *Il popolo bambino: infanzia e nazione dalla Grande Guerra a Salò* (Turin: G. Einaudi, 2005); Fabiana Loparco, *I bambini e la guerra: il Corriere dei piccoli e il primo conflitto mondiale (1915-1918)* (Firenze: Nerbini, 2011).

6. Daniele Ceschin, *Gli esuli di Caporetto: I profughi in Italia durante la Grande Guerra* (Bari: Gius.Laterza & Figli Spa, 2014).

7. On Fascist historiography see: Nick Carter, *Modern Italy*; and Richard J. B. Bosworth, *The Italian Dictatorship: Problems and Perspectives in the Interpretation of Mussolini and Fascism* (London: Arnold, 2007).

8. Renzo De Felice, *Mussolini il duce*, vol. 1, *Gli anni del consenso* (Turin: Einaudi, 1974).

9. On the critical reception of De Felice see Pasquale Chessa, Francesco Villari and Denis Mack Smith, *Interpretazioni su Renzo De Felice* (Milano: Baldini & Castoldi, 2002); Richard J. B. Bosworth, *The Italian Dictatorship*; Nick Carter, *Modern Italy*, 89–96.

10. On the reception of Mosse see, Lorenzo Benadusi and Giorgio Caravale, *George L. Mosse's Italy: Interpretation, Reception, and Intellectual Heritage* (Springer, 2014).

11. Emilio Gentile, *Storia del partito fascista* (Roma: Laterza, 1989); Emilio Gentile, *La via italiana al totalitarismo: il partito e lo Stato nel regime fascista* (Roma: NIS, 1994); Emilio

Gentile, *Il culto del littorio: la sacralizzazione della politica nell'Italia fascista* (Roma: Laterza, 1993); Simonetta Falasca-Zamponi, *Fascist Spectacle: The Aesthetics of Power in Mussolini's Italy* (Berkeley: University of California Press, 1997).

12. Mabel Berezin, *Making the Fascist Self: The Political Culture of Interwar Italy* (Ithaca, NY: Cornell University Press, 1997); Ruth Ben-Ghiat, *Fascist Modernities: Italy, 1922-1945* (Berkeley: University of California Press, 2001); David G. Horn, *Social Bodies: Science, Reproduction, and Italian Modernity* (Princeton: Princeton University Press, 1994).

13. Critiques of Gentile include R. J. B Bosworth, *Mussolini's Italy: Life under the Dictatorship, 1915-1945* (New York: Penguin Books, 2006); R. J. B. Bosworth and Patrizia Dogliani, *Italian Fascism: History, Memory and Representation* (Springer, 2016).

14. Luigi Salvatorelli and Giovanni Mira, *Storia del fascismo: l'Italia dal 1919 al 1945* (Roma: Novissima, 1952), 743.

15. Renzo De Felice, *Gli Anni Del Consenso, 1929-1936* (Turin: G. Einaudi, 1974); Philip V. Cannistraro, *La fabbrica del consenso: fascismo e mass media* (Roma: Laterza, 1975).

16. Philip V. Cannistraro, *La fabbrica del consenso*; Victoria De Grazia, *The Culture of Consent: Mass Organization of Leisure in Fascist Italy* (Cambridge, etc.: Cambridge University Press, 1981; Philip Morgan, "The Years of Consent? Popular Attitudes and Forms of Resistance to Fascism in Italy,1925-1940," in *Opposing Fascism : Community, Authority and Resistance in Europe*, eds. Tim Kirk and Anthony McElligott (Boston: Cambridge University Press, 1999), 163–79; Giulia Albanese and Roberta Pergher, eds., *In the Society of Fascists*; Paul Corner, *The Fascist Party and Popular Opinion in Mussolini's Italy* (OUP Oxford, 2012); Joshua Arthurs, Michael R. Ebner and Kate Ferris, eds., *The Politics of Everyday Life in Fascist Italy: Outside the State?* (New York: Palgrave Macmillan, 2017).

17. Luisa Passerini, *Fascism in Popular Memory: The Cultural Experience of the Turin Working Class* (Cambridge: Cambridge University Press, 1987); Victoria De Grazia, *How Fascism Ruled Women: Italy, 1922-1945* (University of California Press, 1992); Kevin Passmore, *Women, Gender, and Fascism in Europe, 1919-45* (Manchester: Manchester University Press, 2003); Gigliola Gori, *Italian Fascism and the Female Body: Sport, Submissive Women and Strong Mothers* (Routledge, 2012);Perry Willson, *The Clockwork Factory: Women and Work in Fascist Italy* (Oxford; New York: Clarendon Press; Oxford University Press, 1993); Perry Willson, *Peasant Women and Politics in Fascist Italy: The Massaie Rurali* (New York: Routledge, 2002); Lorenzo Benadusi, *The Enemy of the New Man: Homosexuality in Fascist Italy* (Madison: The University of Wisconsin Press, 2012).

18. Arnd Bauerkämper and Grzegorz Rossoliński-Liebe, *Fascism without Borders Transnational Connections and Cooperation between Movements and Regimes in Europe from 1918 to 1945* (New York: Berghahn Books, 2017); Franca Iacovetta and Lorenza Stradiotti, "Betrayal, Vengeance, and the Anarchist Ideal: Virgilia D'Andrea's Radical Antifascism in (American) Exile, 1928–1933," *Journal of Women's History* 25, no. 1 (2013): 85–110; *La vera Italia è all'estero: Esuli antifascisti a Ginevra e nell'Alta Savoia* (Diacrone, 2011); Gabaccia, *Italy's Many Diasporas*, 129–52; Carlo Rosselli, *Scritti dell'esilio: "Giustizia e libertà" e la concentrazione antifascista (1929-1934)* (Torino: Einaudi, 1988); Patrizia Gabrielli, *Col freddo nel cuore: uomini e donne nell'emigrazione antifascista* (Roma: Donzelli Editore, 2004).

19. Nuto Revelli, *Le due guerre: guerra fascista e guerra partigiana* (Einaudi, 2003); Revelli, *Il mondo dei vinti*; Michael R. Ebner, *Ordinary Violence in Mussolini's Italy* (Cambridge University Press, 2010): Emilio Franzina and A. Parisella, eds., *La Merica in Piscinara: emigrazione, bonifiche e colonizzazione veneta nell'agro Romano e pontino tra fascismo e post-fascismo* (Padova: Francisci, 1986).

20. Renzo De Felice, *Storia degli ebrei italiani sotto il fascismo* (Turin: Mondadori Editore, 1977); Susan Zuccotti, *The Italians and the Holocaust: Persecution, Rescue, and Survival* (New York: Basic Books, 1987); Jonathan Steinberg, *All or Nothing: The Axis and the Holocaust, 1941-1943* (London: Routledge, 1990).

21. Angelo Del Boca, *Le guerre coloniali del Fascismo* (Bari: Laterza, 1991); Angelo Del Boca, *Italiani, brava gente?: un mito duro a morire* (Vicenza: N. Pozza, 2005); Ruth Ben-Ghiat and Mia Fuller, eds., *Italian Colonialism* (New York: Palgrave Macmillan, 2008); Roberta Pergher, *Fascist Borderlands: Nation, Empire and Italy's Settlement Program, 1922-1943* (New York: Cambridge University Press, 2017).

22. Primo Levi, *Se questo è un uomo; Le tregua* (Torino: Einaudi, 1958); Michele Sarfatti, *Gli ebrei nell'Italia fascista: vicende, identità, persecuzione* (Torino: G. Einaudi, 2000); Robert Gordon, *The Holocaust in Italian Culture, 1944–2010* (Palo Alto, CA: Stanford University Press, 2012); Angelo Ventura, *Il fascismo e gli ebrei: il razzismo antisemita nell'ideologia e nella politica del regime* (Roma: Donzelli, 2013).

23. Claudio Fogu, "Italiani Brava Gente: The Legacy of Fascist Historical Culture on Italian Politics of Memory," in *The Politics of Memory in Postwar Europe*, ed. Richard Ned Lebow (Durham, NC: Duke University Press, 2007); John Foot, *Italy's Divided Memory* (Basingstoke: Palgrave Macmillan, 2009). For recent interpretations see: Emanuele Sica and C. Carrier, *Italy and the Second World War: Alternative Perspectives* (Leiden: Brill, 2018).

24. Claudio Pavone, *Una guerra civile: saggio storico sulla moralità nella Resistenza* (Torino: Bollati Boringhieri editore, 1991).

25. Anna Bravo and Anna Maria Bruzzone, *In guerra senza armi: storie di donne: 1940-1945* (Roma: Laterza, 1995); Perry R. Willson, "Saints and Heroines: Rewriting the History of Italian Women in the Resistance," in *Opposing Fascism: Community, Authority and Resistance in Europe*, eds. Antony McElligott and Tim Kirk (Cambridge: Cambridge University Press, 1999), 180–98. Revelli, *Le due guerre: guerra fascista e guerra partigiana*; Noemi Crain Merz, *L'illusione della parità. Donne e questione femminile in Giustizia e Libertà e nel Partito d'azione: Donne e questione femminile in Giustizia e Libertà e nel Partito d'azione* (Milano: FrancoAngeli, 2013); Francesca Volpi and Bianca Fiori Verona, *La donna mantovana nella Resistenza* (Mantova: Sometti, 2010); Ferruccio Vendramini, *Occupazione tedesca e guerra partigiana nel Longaronese (1943-1945): memorie e documenti* (Belluno: Istituto storico bellunese della Resistenza e dell'età contemporanea, 2005); Donna M. Budani, *Italian Women's Narratives of Their Experiences during World War II* (Lewiston, NY: Edwin Mellen Press, 2003); Ada Gobetti, *Partisan Diary: A Woman's Life in the Italian Resistance*, trans. Jomarie Alano (New York: Oxford University Press, 2014); Gabriella Gribaudi, *Combattenti, sbandati, prigionieri: esperienze e memorie di reduci della seconda guerra mondiale* (Roma: Donzelli Editore, 2016).

26. Alessandro Portelli, *L'ordine è già stato eseguito: Roma, le Fosse Ardeatine, la memoria* (Roma: Donzelli, 1999); Paolo Pezzino, *Anatomia di un massacro: controversia sopra una strage tedesca* (Bologna: Il Mulino, 1997). On memory in general see: Bosworth and Dogliani, *Italian Fascism: History, Memory and Representation*.

27. Victoria Belco, *War, Massacre, and Recovery in Central Italy, 1943-1948* (Toronto: University of Toronto Press, 2010); Piero Bevilacqua, *Le Campagne del Mezzogiorno tra fascismo e dopoguerra: il caso della Calabria* (Torino: G. Einaudi, 1980); Guido Quazza et al., eds., *L'altro dopoguerra: Roma e il Sud 1943-1945* (Milano: Fr. Angeli, 1985); Gabriella Gribaudi, *Guerra totale: tra bombe alleate e violenze naziste: Napoli e il fronte meridionale, 1940-44* (Torino: Bollati Boringhieri, 2005).

Notes

28. Laura Derossi and Anna Bravo, eds., *1945, il voto alle donne* (Milano: FrancoAngeli, 1998); Molly Tambor, *The Lost Wave: Women and Democracy in Postwar Italy* (Oxford: Oxford University Press, 2014); Patrizia Gabrielli, *Il 1946, le donne, la Repubblica* (Roma: Donzelli Editore, 2009); Patrizia Gabrielli, *La pace e la mimosa: l'Unione donne italiane e la costruzione politica della memoria (1944-1955)* (Roma: Donzelli, 2005); Anna Bravo, Caterina Caravaggi and Teresa Mattei, eds., *La prima volta che ho votato: le donne di Piacenza e le elezioni del 1946* (Scritture, 2006). On the endurance of the Fascists see, Roy Palmer Domenico, *Italian Fascists on Trial, 1943-1948* (Chapel Hill: University of North Carolina Press, 2011).

Chapter 9

1. Giovanna Procacci, *Soldati e prigionieri italiani nella Grande guerra: con una raccolta di lettere inedite* (Roma: Editori Riuniti, 1993), 465; Giovanna Procacci, *La società italiana e la Grande Guerra* (Roma: Gangemi, 2014).

2. Teodoro Capocci, *Diario di guerra del sottotenente Teodoro Capocci: Assalto a monte Sabotino* (1915), 1.

3. "Italy States Her Case to the Times: Reasons for Going to War Cabled by Her Foreign Minister at the Request of The New York Times," *New York Times* October 1, 1911, 1.

4. Luca Micheletta and Andrea Ungari, eds., *The Libyan War, 1911-1912* (Newcastle upon Tyne, UK: Cambridge Scholars Pub., 2013).

5. Antonio Salandra, *I Discorsi Della Guerra Con Alcune Note* (Milano: Fratelli Treves, 1922). 4.

6. Fulvio Cammarano, *Abbasso la guerra: neutralisti in piazza alla vigilia della prima guerra mondiale in Italia* (Milano: Mondadori, 2015).

7. Gabrielle D'Annunzio, "Un'ode di D'Annunzio, "per la resurrezione latina," *Corriere della Sera,* 14 Agosto, 1914, 3.

8. Rossi, "Fra I volontari Italiani al campo di Nimes" *Corriere della Sera,* Sabato 17, Ottobre 1914.

9. "25,000 interventisti a Genova in una dimostrazione a Peppino Garibaldi," *Corriere della sera*, 8 Aprile, 1915, 2.

10. Choate, *Emigrant Nation,* 210; Direzione Generale di Statistica e del Lavoro, *Annuario Statistico Italiano-Anno 1914* (Roma: Tip. Naz. di G. Bertero, 1915), 300; Luciana Palla, *Profughi fra storia e memorie: 1915-1919* (Istitut cultural ladin "Cesa de Jan," 2017).

11. Gooch, *The Italian Army,* 17–24; Giorgio Rochat, *Ufficiali e soldati: l'esercito italiano dalla prima alla seconda guerra mondiale* (Udine: P. Gaspari, 2000); Giorgio Rochat, *L'esercito italiano in pace e in guerra: Studi di storia militare* (Milano: RARA 1991).

12. Gooch, *The Italian Army,* 63–105; Chapman, *Milocca; a Sicilian Village,* 155.

13. Mark Thompson, *The White War: Life and Death on the Italian Front 1915-1919* (Basic Books, 2009).

14. Thompson, *The White War,* 289; Procacci, *Soldati e prigionieri,* 54–55.

15. Gooch, *The Italian Army,* 236–56.

16. Ceschin, *Gli esuli di Caporetto.*

17. Wilcox, *Morale and the Italian Army.*

18. Molinari, *Una patria per le donne: la mobilitazione femminile nella Grande Guerra*; Belzer, *Women and the Great War*; Antolini et al., *Donne in guerra, 1915 - 1918*; Stefania Bartoloni, *Donne di fronte alla guerra: Pace, diritti e democrazia* (Bari: Gius. Laterza & Figli Spa, 2017).

19. Nuto Revelli and Anna Rossi-Doria, *L'anello forte: la donna: storie di vita contadina* (Torino: Einaudi, 2012), 23.

20. Homer Folks, *The Human Costs of the War* (New York: Harper & Brothers, 1920), 181–82; Istituto centrale di statistica "Indice del movimento economico, prezzi di alcuni principali generi di consumo," *Annuario Statistico Italiano 1917-1918*, ser 2, 215.

21. Simonetta Ortaggi, "Italian women during the Great War," in *Evidence, History and the Great War: Historians and the Impact of 1914–18*, ed. Braybon Gail (New York: Berghahn Books, 2003), 223–25.

22. Bruno Bezza and Giovanna Procacci, eds., *Stato e classe operaia in Italia durante la prima guerra mondiale* (Milano: Angeli, 1983).

23. Zamagni, *Dalla periferia*, 288–91.

24. Ufficio Centrale di Statistica, *Annuario Statistico Italiano 1917-1918*, Serie 2, vol. 7 (Roma: Tip. Naz. Bertero, 1917), 331.

25. Piero Bevilacqua, *Breve storia dell'Italia meridionale: dall'Ottocento a oggi* (Roma: Donzelli, 2005), 99; Sean Brady, "From Peacetime to Wartime: The Sicilian Province of Catania and Italian Intervention in the Great War, June 1914-September 1915," in *Other Combatants, Other Fronts: Competing Histories of the First World War*, eds. James E. Kitchen, Alisa Miller and Laura Rowe (Newcastle: Cambridge Scholars Publishing, 2011), 3–28.

26. Christopher Duggan, *Fascist Voices: An Intimate History of Mussolini's Italy* (Oxford: Oxford University Press, 2013), 23.

27. Mimmo Franzinelli, *Fiume: l'ultima impresa di D'Annunzio* (Milano: Mondadori, 2009); Claudia Salaris, *Alla festa della rivoluzione: artisti e letterati con D'Annunzio a Fiume* (Bologna: Il Mulino, 2008).

Chapter 10

1. Benito Mussolini, *Opera omnia di Benito Mussolini: Dal delitto Matteotti all'attentato Zaniboni, (14 giugno 1924-4 novembre 1925)*, 21 (Firenze: La Fenice, 1956), 425.

2. Mauro Canali, *Il delitto Matteotti* (Bologna: Il Mulino, 2015); Bosworth, *Mussolini's Italy: Life under the Dictatorship, 1915-1945*; Bosworth and Dogliani, *Italian Fascism: History, Memory and Representation*.

3. Joel Blatt, "Carlo Rosselli's Socialism," in *Italian Socialism: Between Politics and History*, ed. Spencer di Scala (Amherst: University of Massachusetts Press, 1996), 87.

4. Gabaccia, *Italy's many Diasporas*, 144–52.

5. Istat. *Serie Storiche*, "Popolazione," *Tavola 2.9.- Espatriati per sesso e condizione professionale - Anni 1876-1990*.

6. Quoted in Victoria De Grazia, *How Fascism Ruled Women*, 179.

7. ISTAT, *Serie Storiche*, "Mercato del Lavoro: Censimento generale della popolazione e delle abitazioni," *Table 10.1 -Popolazione attiva, popolazione attiva in condizione professionale e tassi di attività per sesso ai Censimenti 1861-2011 (a) (in migliaia e per 100 persone)*.

Notes

8. De Grazia, *How Fascism Ruled Women*, 179.

9. Ibid., 180; ISTAT, *Serie Storiche*, Table 10.1

10. Emilio Franzina and A. Parisella, eds., *La Merica in Piscinara*.

11. Patriarca, *Italian Vices*, 133.

12. Natasha Chang, *The Crisis-Woman: Body Politics and the Modern Woman in Fascist Italy* (Toronto: University of Toronto Press, 2015); Gigliola Gori, *Italian Fascism and the Female Body: Sport, Submissive Women and Strong Mothers* (London, New York: Routledge Press, 2004); David Horn, *Social Bodies* (Princeton, NJ: Princeton University Press, 2001); Sandro Bellassai, "The Masculine Mystique: Antimodernism and Virility in Fascist Italy," *Journal of Modern Italian Studies* 10, no. 3 (September 1, 2005): 314–35.

13. Bosworth, *Mussolini's Italy: Life under the Dictatorship, 1915-1945*.

14. Stephen Gundle, Christopher Duggan and Giuliana Pieri, *The Cult of the Duce: Mussolini and the Italians* (Manchester; New York: Manchester University Press, 2015).

15. Quoted in Chang, *The Crisis-Woman*, 13.

16. Jacqueline Reich and Piero Garofalo, *Re-Viewing Fascism: Italian Cinema, 1922-1943* (Indiana University Press, 2002).

17. David I. Kertzer, *The Pope and Mussolini: The Secret History of Pius XI and the Rise of Fascism in Europe* (Oxford: Oxford University Press, 2014).

18. *Il popolo d'italia*, 26, May 1927, 1.

19. Passerini, *Fascism in Popular Memory*, 150–82.

20. G. Franco Romagnoli, *The Bicycle Runner: A Memoir of Love, Loyalty, and the Italian Resistance* (New York: Thomas Dunne Books, 2009), 47; On Fascism and education see Tracy H. Koon, *Believe Obey Fight: Political Socialization of Youth in Fascist Italy* (Chapel Hill, NC; London: University of North Carolina Press, 1985).

21. Borden Painter, *Mussolini's Rome: Rebuilding the Eternal City* (Springer, 2016), 3; Paul Baxa, *Roads and Ruins: The Symbolic Landscape of Fascist Rome* (Toronto; Buffalo: University of Toronto Press, 2010).

22. Duggan, *Fascist Voices*, 148–78.

23. Romagnoli, *Bicycle Runner*, 47; Del Boca, *Le guerre coloniali del Fascismo*; Angelo Del Boca, *Italiani, brava gente: un mito duro a morire* (Vicenza: N. Pozza, 2005), chapters 9–10.

24. Alberto Burgio, ed., *Nel nome della razza: il razzismo nella storia d'Italia, 1870-1945* (Bologna: Il Mulino, 2000); Ventura, *Il fascismo e gli ebrei: il razzismo antisemita nell'ideologia e nella politica del regime*; Silvana Patriarca and Valeria Deplano, "Nation, 'Race,' and Racisms in Twentieth-Century Italy," *Modern Italy* 23, no. 4 (November 2018): 349–53.

25. Patrick J. Gallo, *For Love and Country: The Italian Resistance* (Lanham, MD: University Press of America, 2003), 80.

Chapter 11

1. Anthony Majanlahti and Amedeo Osti Guerrazzi, *Roma occupata, 1943-1944: itinerari, storie, immagini* (Milano: Il Saggiatore, 2010), 26.

2. Majanlahti and Guerrazzi, *Roma occupata*, 24.

3. Majanlahti and Guerrazzi, *Roma occupata*, 41.

4. Emanuele Sica, *Mussolini's Army in the French Riviera: Italy's Occupation of France* (Champaign, Il: University of Illinois Press, 2016.)

5. Bosworth, *Mussolini's Rome*, 490–91. Also see Philip Morgan, *The Fall of Mussolini: Italy, the Italians, and the Second World War* (Oxford: Oxford University Press, 2008).

6. Miriam Mafai, *Pane nero. Donne e vita quotidiana nella seconda guerra mondiale* (Roma: Ediesse, 2008), 140.

7. Mafai, *Pane Nero*, 143.

8. Paolo Sorcinelli, *Otto settembre* (Milano: Mondadori, 2013).

9. On the war in the South see: Quazza et al., eds., *L'altro dopoguerra: Roma e il Sud 1943-1945*.

10. Norman Lewis, *Naples '44: A World War II Diary of Occupied Italy* (New York: Open Road Media, 2013), 123; Dickie, *Cosa Nostra*, 206–32.

11. Michele Sarfatti, *The Jews in Mussolini's Italy: From Equality to Persecution* (Madison: University of Wisconsin Press, 2006), 168; Zuccotti, *The Italians and the Holocaust: Persecution, Rescue, and Survival*.

12. Sarfatti, *The Jews in Mussolini's Italy*, 116.

13. Ibid., 161; Patrizia Guarnieri, *Italian Psychology and Jewish Emigration under Fascism: From Florence to Jerusalem and New York* (Springer, 2016); Joshua D. Zimmerman, *Jews in Italy under Fascist and Nazi Rule, 1922-1945* (Cambridge; New York: Cambridge University Press, 2005); Zuccotti, *The Italians*.

14. Sarfatti, *The Jews in Mussolini's Italy*, 164.

15. Ibid., 178.

16. Settimio Sorani and Francesco Del Canuto, *L'assistenza ai profughi ebrei in Italia (1933-1941): contributo alla storia della Delasem* (Carucci, 1983); Susan Zuccotti, *Under His Very Windows: The Vatican and the Holocaust in Italy* (New Haven, CT: Yale University Press, 2000).

17. Pavone, *A Civil War*, 5–53; Jonathan Dunnage, *Twentieth Century Italy: A Social History* (London; New York: Routledge, 2002), 129–30.

18. Gabrielli, *Il 1946, le donne, la Repubblica*: Marina Addis Saba, *Partigiane: le donne della Resistenza* (Milano: Mursia, 2007); Ilenia Carrone, *Le donne della Resistenza: la trasmissione della memoria nel racconto dei figli e delle figlie delle partigiane* (Formigine, MO: Infinito, 2014).

19. Alessandro Portelli, *L'ordine è già stato eseguito: Roma, le Fosse Ardeatine, la memoria* (Milano: Feltrinelli, 2012), 4.

Chapter 12

1. Bill McElwain, A "Ringside Report" on "Open City," *The Pittsburgh Press*, May 8, 1946, 15.

2. Saverio Giovacchini, "Soccer with the Dead: Mediterraneo, the Legacy of Neorealismo and the Myth of Italiani Brava Gente," in *Repicturing the Second World War: Representations in Film and Television*, ed. Michael Paris (New York: Palgrave, 2007), 55–69.

3. Gabrielli, *Il 1946*, 10–11.

4. Quoted in Gabrielli, *Il 1946*, 11.

5. Domenico, *Italian Fascists on Trial*, 152–53; Belco, *War, Massacre, and Recovery*, 185–213.

6. Mirco Dondi, "The Fascist Mentality after Fascism," in *Italian Fascism: History, Memory and Representation*, eds. R. J. B. Bosworth and Patrizia Dogliani (Secaucus: Springer, 2016), 142–45.

7. Patrizia Gabrielli, *Il primo voto: elettrici ed elette* (Roma: Castelvecchi, 2016).

8. http://pinocchio-e-pinocchiate.blogspot.com/2012/07/pinocchio-anticomunista-elezioni-del.html

9. Robert Ventresca, *From Fascism to Democracy: Culture and Politics in the Italian Election of 1948* (Toronto: University of Toronto Press, 2004); Anne O'Hare McCormick "Italy in the Throes of Political Warfare," *New York Times*, March 19, 1948, 26; "War of Words Rages in Italian Campaign: Both Sides Are Stepping up Efforts as Election Day Draw Nears," *New York Times*, March 27, 1948.

10. Tambor, *The Lost Wave*, 24.

11. Francesco Renda, *Salvatore Giuliano: una biografia storica* (Sellerio, 2002); Mario Calivà, *Portella della Ginestra, Primo maggio 1947: nove sopravvissuti raccontano la strage* (Navarra Editore, 2017).

12. "Il bandito Giuliano fa l'uomo politico," *Corriere d'informazione* 14–15 Agosto, 1946, 4.

13. Tambor, *The Lost Wave*, 78–79.

Part Four

1. Foot, *Italy's Divided Memory*; Claudio Fogu, "Italiani Brava Gente: The Legacy of Fascist Historical Culture on Italian Politics of Memory." Richard Ned Lebow, Wulf Kansteiner and Claudio Fogu, *The Politics of Memory in Postwar Europe* (Duke University Press, 2006); Paolo Pezzino, "The Italian Resistance between History and Memory," *Journal of Modern Italian Studies* 10, no. 4 (December 1, 2005): 396–412.

2. Daniele Pipitone, "Settant'anni Dopo. Ripensare La Storia Dell'Italia Repubblicana," *Passato e Presente*, no. 103 (January 2018): 17–46. Recent general histories of the period include S. J. Woolf and Alastair Davidson, *L'Italia repubblicana vista da fuori (1945-2000)* (Bologna: Il Mulino, 2007); *Storia dell'Italia repubblicana Vols 1-3* (Turin: G. Einaudi, 1995–97); Giorgio Vecchio and Paolo Trionfini, *Storia dell'Italia repubblicana (1946-2014)* (Monduzzi, 2014); Andrea Di Michele, *Storia dell'Italia repubblicana: 1948-2008* (Milano: Garzanti, 2008); Stephen Gundle and Simon Parker, *The New Italian Republic: From the Fall of the Berlin Wall to Berlusconi* (Routledge, 2002).

3. On historiographical debates see Giovanni Orsina, "The Republic after Berlusconi: Some Reflections on Historiography, Politics and the Political Use of History in Post-1994 Italy," *Modern Italy* 15, no. 1 (2010): 77–92; Nick Carter, *Modern Italy in Historical Perspective* (London: Bloomsbury Academic, 2011), 178–89; and Jader Jacobelli, *Il fascismo e gli storici oggi* (Roma: Laterza, 1988).

4. Ernesto Galli Della Loggia, *La morte della patria: la crisi dell'idea di nazione tra Resistenza, antifascismo e Repubblica* (Roma: Laterza, 1996). Emilio Gentile, *La Grande Italia: The Myth of the Nation in the Twentieth Century* (Madison, WI: University of Wisconsin Press, 2009), ix–xi.

5. Roberto Faenza and Marco Fini, *Gli Americani in Italia* (Milano: Feltrinelli, 1976); Ennio Di Nolfo and Myron C. Taylor, *Vaticano e stati uniti 1939-1952* (Milano: FrancoAngeli Editore, 1978); Bradley F. Smith and Elena Aga Rossi, *Operation Sunrise: The Secret Surrender* (New York: Basic Books, 1979); David William Ellwood, *L'alleato nemico: la politica*

dell'occupazione anglo-americana in Italia : 1943-1946 (Milano: Feltrinelli, 1977); Severino Galante, *La politica del PCI Partito Comunista Italiano e il Patto Atlantico* (Padua: Marsilio, 1973).

6. Silvio Pons, *L'impossibile egemonia: l'URSS, il PCI e le origini della guerra fredda (1943-1948)* (Roma: Carocci, 1999); Daniele Caviglia and Massimiliano Cricco, *La diplomazia italiana e gli equilibri mediterranei: la politica mediorientale dell'Italia dalla guerra dei sei giorni al conflitto dello Yom Kippur (1967-1973)* (Rubbettino Editore, 2006); Ilaria Poggiolini and Ralf Dahrendorf, *Alle origini dell' Europa allargata: la Gran Bretagna e l'adesione alla CEE (1972-1973)* (Milano: Unicopli, 2004); Kaeten Mistry, *The United States, Italy and the Origins of Cold War: Waging Political Warfare 1945–1950* (Cambridge: Cambridge University Press, 2014); Wendy Pojmann, *Italian Women and International Cold War Politics, 1944-1968* (Fordham University Press, 2013).

7. Mistry, *The United States, Italy and the Origins of Cold War: Waging Political Warfare 1945–1950*. See works by Maddalena Marinari and Joseph Sciorra in eds., Laura E. Ruberto, Joseph Sciorra and Anthony Julian Tamburri, *New Italian Migrations to the United States. Volume 2, Volume 2* (Champagne: University of Illinois Press, 2017), 32–64.

8. Gian Piero Brunetta, Rob Kroes and David W. Ellwood, *Hollywood in Europe: Experience of a Cultural Hegemony* (Amsterdam: VU University Press, 1994); Victoria De Grazia, *Irresistible Empire: America's Advance through Twentieth-Century Europe* (Cambridge, London: The Belknap Press of Harvard University Press, 2006); David Forgacs and Stephen Gundle, *Mass Culture and Italian Society from Fascism to the Cold War* (Bloomington: Indiana University Press, 2007); Carlo Spagnolo, *La stabilizzazione incompiuta: il piano Marshall in Italia (1947-1952)* (Roma: Carocci, 2001). On Italian autonomy see Alessandro Brogi, *A Question of Self-Esteem: The United States and the Cold War Choices in France and Italy, 1944-1958* (Westport, CT: Praeger, 2001); Mario Del Pero, *L'alleato scomodo: gli USA e la DC negli anni del centrismo (1948-1955)* (Roma: Carocci, 2001). On the impact of the Cold War on the economy, society, and culture see: Emanuele Bernardi and Paul Ginsborg, *La riforma agraria in Italia e gli Stati Uniti guerra fredda, Piano Marshall e interventi per il Mezzogiorno negli anni del centrismo degasperiano* (Bologna: Il Mulino, 2006); Silvia Cassamagnaghi, *Immagini dall'America: mass media e modelli femminili nell'Italia del secondo dopoguerra, 1945-1960* (Milano: F. Angeli, 2007); Laura E. Ruberto, "'Hot Blooded Eye-Taliano' Women: The Lascivious and Desperate Post-World War II Italian Immigrant in U.S. Cincema," in *New Italian Migrations to the United States. Volume 2*, eds. Laura E. Ruberto, Joseph Sciorra and Anthony Julian Tamburri (Champagne: University of Illinois Press, 2017).

9. Anna Rossi-Doria, *Diventare cittadine: il voto delle donne in Italia* (Taylor & Francis, 1996); Laura Derossi and Anna Bravo, eds., *1945: il voto alle donne*; Gabrielli, *La pace e la mimosa: l'Unione donne italiane e la costruzione politica della memoria (1944-1955)*; Bravo, Caravaggi and Mattei, *La prima volta che ho votato: le donne di Piacenza e le elezioni del 1946*; Tambor, *The Lost Wave;* Patrizia Gabrielli, *Il primo voto: elettrici ed elette* (Roma: Castelvecchi, 2016).

10. Paul Ginsborg, *Italy and Its Discontents: Family, Civil Society, State, 1980-2001* (Palgrave Macmillan, 2001), 243–44; Marta Petrusewicz, "The Mezzogiorno: A Bias for Hope?" *Modern Italy* 6, no. 1 (2001): 63–67; Vera Zamagni, *Introduzione alla storia economica d'Italia* (Bologna: Il Mulino, 2007).

11. Augusto Graziani, *L'economia italiana: 1945-1970* (Bologna: Il Mulino, 1972); Vittorio Valli, *L'economia e la politica economica italiana dal 1945 ad oggi* (Milano: Etas libri, 1982); Rosaria Rita Canale and Oreste Napolitano, "National Disparities and Cyclical Dynamics

in Italy (1892–2007): Was the Mezzogiorno a Sheltered Economy?" *International Review of Applied Economics* 29, no. 3 (May 2015): 328–30.

12. Banfield, *The Moral Basis of a Backward Society*; Robert D. Putnam, Robert Leonardi and Rafaella Y. Nanetti, eds., *Making Democracy Work* (Princeton, NJ: Princeton University, 1992). Critiques include, J. Davis, "Morals and Backwardness," *Comparative Studies in Society and History* 12, no. 3 (1970): 340–53.

13. Gabriella Gribaudi, *Donne, uomini, famiglie: Napoli nel Novecento* (L'ancora, 1999); Salvatore Lupo, "Usi e abusi del passato: le radici dell'Italia di Putnam," *Meridiana*, no. 18 (1993), 181–16; Schneider, *Italy's "Southern Question."*

14. Canale and Napolitano, "National Disparities and Cyclical Dynamics in Italy (1892–2007): Was the Mezzogiorno a Sheltered Economy?" 328–48; Giuseppe Giarrizzo, *Mezzogiorno senza meridionalismo: la Sicilia, lo sviluppo, il potere* (Marsilio, 1992); Giuseppe Barone, *Mezzogiorno e modernizzazione elettricità, irrigazione e bonifica nell'Italia contemporanea* (Turin: G. Einaudi, 1986); Vittorio Daniele, *Una modernizzazione difficile: l'economia della Calabria oggi* (Soveria Mannelli: Rubbettino Editore, 2002).

15. Anna Cento Bull, *Social Identities and Political Cultures in Italy: Catholic, Communist, and Leghist Communities between Civicness and Localism* (New York: Berghahn Books, 2000).

16. Alexander Stille, *Excellent Cadavers: The Mafia and the Death of the First Italian Republic* (New York: Pantheon, 1995); John Dickie, *Cosa Nostra;* Salvatore Lupo, *Storia della mafia: dalle origini ai giorni nostri* (Donzelli Editore, 2004); Salvatore Lupo, *Potere criminale: intervista sulla storia della mafia* (Roma: GLF editoria Laterza, 2010); Nando dalla Chiesa, *Passaggio a Nord: La colonizzazione mafiosa* (Associazione Gruppo Abele Onlus - Edizioni Gruppo Abele, 2017).

17. Ilvo Diamanti, *La Lega: geografia, storia e sociologia di un nuovo soggetto politico* (Roma: Donzelli, 1993); Levy, *Italian Regionalism: History, Identity and Politics;* Anna Cento Bull and Mark Gilbert, *The Lega Nord and the Northern Question in Italian Politics* (Houndmills, Basingstoke, Hampshire; New York: Palgrave, 2001); John Dickie, "Imagined Italies," in *Italian Cultural Studies: An Introduction*, eds. David Forgacs and Robert Lumley (Oxford: Oxford University Press, 1996). The publication of the *Storia d'Italia* series, *I regioni*, provides the most comprehensive source for understanding the history of Italian regions.

18. Bull, *Social Identities;* Guido Verucci, *Cattolicesimo e laicismo nell'Italia contemporanea* (Milano: Angeli, 2001); Franco Garelli, *La Chiesa in Italia* (Il Mulino, 2007); Antonio Acerbi, *La Chiesa e l'Italia: per una storia dei loro rapporti negli ultimi due secoli* (Vita e Pensiero, 2003); Jeff Pratt, "Catholic Culture," *The New History of the Italian South: The Mezzogiorno Revisited*, eds. Robert Lumley and Jonathan Morris (Exeter, Devon: University of Exeter Press, 1997), 129–43.

19. For an overview of the historiography of 1968 see the introduction to Marcello Flores and Alberto De Bernardi, *Il Sessantotto* (Bologna: Il Mulino, 2003).

20. Francesca Chiarotto, ed., *Aspettando il Sessantotto: continuità e fratture nelle culture politiche italiane dal 1956 al 1968*, 2017; Alessandro Breccia, ed., *Le istituzioni universitarie e il Sessantotto* (Bologna: CLUEB, 2013).

21. Anna Bravo, *A colpi di cuore: storie del sessantotto* (Bari: Laterza, 2008); A. Bull, *Speaking Out and Silencing: Culture, Society and Politics in Italy in the 1970s* (New York: Routledge, 2017); Pina La Villa, "I Sessantotto di Sicilia: linee d'indagine," *Annali Istituto Gramsci*, no. 2–3 (1998): 1000–26; Lina Severino and Gabriele Licciardi, *Il Sessantotto in periferia: Catania fra il movimento studentesco e la svolta a destra degli anni Settanti: caratteri*

locali e tendenze nazionali (Acireale, (Catania): Bonanno, 2009); Sergio Failla and Pina La Villa, *I Sessantotto di Sicilia* (Catania: Zerobook, 2016).

22. For overviews of historiographical trends in Italian women's history see: Louisa Passerini, "Gender Relations," in *The New History of the Italian South: The Mezzogiorno Revisited*, eds. Robert Lumley and Jonathan Morris (Exeter, Devon: University of Exeter Press, 1997), 144–59; Giovanna Fiume, "Women's History and Gender History: The Italian Experience," *Modern Italy* 10, no. 2 (November 2005): 207–31; Perry Willson, "From Margin to Centre: Recent Trends in Modern Italian Women's and Gender History," *Modern Italy* 11, no. 3 (2006): 327–37.

23. Wendy Pojmann, "Emancipation or Liberation?" Women's Associations and the Italian Movement," *Historian* 67, no. 1 (Spring 2005), 75; Perry R. Willson, *Women in Twentieth-Century Italy* (Basingstoke: Palgrave Macmillan, 2010), 112–48; Bravo, *A colpi di cuore: storie del sessantotto*; Maud Anne Bracke, *Women and the Reinvention of the Political: Feminism in Italy, 1968-1983* (Routledge, 2014).

24. Piero Bevilacqua, Andreina De Clementi and Emilio Franzina, *Storia dell'emigrazione italiana* (Donzelli Editore, 2001); Matteo Sanfilippo, *Emigrazione e storia d'Italia* (Cosenza: L. Pellegrini, 2003); Patrizia Audenino and Maddalena Tirabassi, *Migrazioni italiane: storia e storie dall'ancien régime a oggi* (B. Mondadori, 2008); Ercole Sori and Anna Treves, *L'Italia in movimento: due secoli di migrazioni, XIX-XX* (Forum, 2008); Matteo Sanfilippo and Paola Corti, *L'Italia e le migrazioni* (Gius. Laterza & Figli Spa, 2012).

25. Badino and Inaudi, *Migrazioni femminili attraverso le Alpi. Lavoro, famiglia, trasformazioni culturali nel secondo dopoguerra: Lavoro, famiglia, trasformazioni culturali nel secondo dopoguerra* (FrancoAngeli, 2013); Michele Colucci, *Lavoro in movimento: l'emigrazione italiana in Europa, 1945-57* (Donzelli, 2008); Elia Morandi, *Governare l'emigrazione: lavoratori italiani verso la Germania nel secondo dopoguerra* (Torino: Rosenberg & Sellier, 2011); Grazia Prontera and Sandro Rinauro, *Partire, tornare, restare? l'esperienza migratoria dei lavoratori italiani nella Repubblica federale tedesca nel secondo dopoguerra* (Milano: Guerini e associati, 2009); Laura E. Ruberto, and Joseph Sciorra, *New Italian Migrations to the United States: Vol. 1: Politics and History Since 1945* (Champaign: University of Illinois Press, 2017).

26. Patrizia Audenino, *La casa perduta: la memoria dei profughi del Novecento* (Roma: Carocci editore, 2015); Patrizia Audenino, "I Profughi Italiani: «una Pagina Strappata» Della Storia Nazionale," no. 50 (January 2015): 56–70; Luca Einaudi, *Le politiche dell'immigrazione in Italia dall'unità a oggi* (Laterza, 2007); Nando Sigona, "The Governance of Romani People in Italy: Discourse, Policy and Practice," *Journal of Modern Italian Studies* 16, no. 5 (December 1, 2011): 590–606.

27. On the notion of internal immigration: Sandro Rinauro, *Il cammino della speranza: l'emigrazione clandestina degli Italiani nel secondo dopoguerra* (Ebook; Turin: G. Einaudi, 2009); Nazareno Panichella, *Meridionali al Nord: migrazioni interne e società italiana dal dopoguerra ad oggi*, 2014. Recent studies connecting late twentieth-century immigration, racism, and xenophobia to Italy's colonial past include Cristina Lombardi-Diop, *Postcolonial Italy: Challenging National Homogeneity* (Springer, 2012). Miguel Mellino, *Cittadinanze postcoloniali: appartenenze, razza e razzismo in Europa e in Italia* (Roma: Carocci, 2013); Jacqueline Andall and Derek Duncan, *National Belongings: Hybridity in Italian Colonial and Postcolonial Cultures* (Peter Lang, 2010); Patrizia Palumbo, *A Place in the Sun: Africa in Italian Colonial Culture from Post-Unification to the Present* (University of California Press, 2003).

Notes

Chapter 13

1. Valerio Castronovo, *FIAT: una storia del capitalismo italiano* (Rizzoli, 2005), 438–42.

2. Zamagni, *Introduzione*, 416–24.

3. Roberto Franzosi, *The Puzzle of Strikes: Class and State Strategies in Postwar Italy* (Cambridge: Cambridge University Press, 2006), 111.

4. Istat, *Serie Storiche*, Mercato di Lavoro, "Tavola 10.4 Popolazione attiva in condizione professionale per settore di attività economica e regione ai Censimenti 1861-2011"; Vera Zamagni, *The Economic History*, 328.

5. Istat, *Serie Storiche*, Mercato di Lavoro, "Tavola 10.1 - Popolazione attiva, popolazione attiva in condizione professionale e tassi di attività per sesso ai Censimenti 1861-2011," and Struttura ed evoluzione della popolazione ai censimenti: "Tavola 2.1 - Popolazione residente per sesso ai confini dell'epoca e ai confini attuali ai censimenti 1861-2011 e al 2014 e popolazione presente ai censimenti 1861-2011."

6. Vittorio Daniele and Paolo Malanima, *Il divario Nord-Sud in Italia, 1861-2011* (Edizione digitale; Soveria Mannelli: Rubbettino Editore, 2011), paragraphs 75–76.

7. Zamagni, *The Economic History*, 335.

8. Stefano Gallo, *Senza attraversare le frontiere: le migrazioni interne dall'unità a oggi* (Edizione digitale: Roma: Laterza, 2012), paragraphs, 399–404.

9. Rinauro, *Il cammino della speranza: l'emigrazione clandestina degli Italiani nel secondo dopoguerra*, paragraph, 440.

10. John Foot, "Immigration and the City: Milan and Mass Immigration, 1958–98," *Modern Italy* 4, no. 2 (November 1999): 159–72.

11. "Eravamo tutti meridionali. La migrazione sui Treni del Sole," *Corriere della Sera* (10 Luglio, 2016).

12. Russo, "Nord e sud si mescolano," *Corriere della Sera*, 24–25 Marzo, 1964, 3.

13. Giovanni Russo, "A Pontelandolfo i contadini sognano il giorno in cui potranno emigrare in America," *Corriere della Sera*, 24 agosto, 1955, 3.

14. See introduction in Penelope Morris, ed., *Women in Italy, 1945-1960: An Interdisciplinary Study* (New York: Palgrave Macmillan, 2006); Chiara Saraceno, "The Italian Family from the 1960s to the Present, in *Gender and the Private Sphere in Italy since 1945*, eds. P. Filippucci and P. Willson, *Special Issue of Modern Italy* 9 (2004), 47–57.

15. Antonio Chiesi, Alberto Martinelli, and Sonia Stefanizzi, *Recent Social Trends in Italy, 1960-1995* (Montreal: McGill-Queen's Press - MQUP, 1999).

16. Quoted in Ginsborg, *A History of Contemporary Italy*, 240; Antonio Chiesi, et al., *Recent Social Trends*, 372–76. On the impact of new technology on private life see Emanuela Scarpellini, *Material Nation: A Consumer's History of Modern Italy* (Oxford: Oxford University Press, 2011), 157–65.

17. Penelope Morris, "A Window on the Private Sphere: Advice Columns, Marriage and the Evolving Family in 1950s Italy," *Italianist* 27 (2007): 304–32; Penny Morris, "From Private to Public: Alba de Céspedes' Agony Column in 1950s Italy," *Modern Italy* 9, no. 1 (May 2004): 11–20; Simonetta Piccone Stella, *Tra un lavoro e l'altro: vita di coppia nell'Italia postfordista* (Roma: Carocci ed., 2007).

18. Antonio Chiesi, et al., *Recent Social Trends*, 432–33. Simonetta Piccone Stella, *La prima generazione: ragazzi e ragazze nel miracolo economico italiano* (Milano: Angeli, 1993).

19. Stella, *La prima generazione: ragazzi e ragazze nel miracolo economico italiano*.

20. Ginsborg, *A History of Contemporary Italy*, 245.

Chapter 14

1. Erasmo D'Angelis, *Angeli del Fango: La "meglio gioventù" nella Firenze dell'alluvione a 50 anni di distanza* (Firenze: Giunti, 2016).

2. Giovanni Grazzini, "Nel diluvio il fuoco della gioventù," *Corriere della Sera*, 16 novembre 1966, 11.

3. Dario Lanzardo, *La rivolta di Piazza Statuto: Torino, luglio 1962* (Milano: Feltrinelli economica, 1979).

4. Istat, *Serie Storiche*, Retribuzione e conflitti a Lavoro, "Tavola 10.22 - segue Conflitti di lavoro, lavoratori partecipanti e ore non lavorate per settore di attività economica - Anni 1949-2009."

5. Luisa Passerini, *Autobiography of a Generation: Italy, 1968* (Middletown, CT: Wesleyan, 1996); For a gendered analysis of the experience see Rebecca Clifford, "Emotions and Gender in Oral History: Narrating Italy's 1968," *Modern Italy* 17, no. 2 (May 2012): 209–21.

6. Stuart J. Hilwig, *Italy and 1968: Youthful Unrest and Democratic Culture* (Basingstoke: Palgrave Macmillan, 2009); Marcello Flores and Alberto De Bernardi, *Il sessantotto* (Bologna: Il Mulino, 2003).

7. Francesca Colella, *Napoli frontale nel Sessantotto: narrazioni di rivolte e speranze* (Napoli: Libreria Dante & Descartes, 2008); Sergio Failla and Pina La Villa, *I Sessantotto di Sicilia* (Lulu.com, 2016).

8. Jane Schneider and Peter T. Schneider, *Reversible Destiny: Mafia, Antimafia, and the Struggle for Palermo* (University of California Press, 2003), 168–71; Letizia Battaglia and Alexander Stille, *Passion, Justice, Freedom: Photographs of Sicily* (New York: Aperture, 1999); Letiza Battaglia, *Palermo amore amaro* (Palermo: Associazione Siciliana della Stampa, 1986).

9. Paola Bono and Sandra Kemp, *Italian Feminist Thought: A Reader* (B. Blackwell, 1991), 37; Bracke, *Women and the Reinvention of the Political: Feminism in Italy 1968-1983*; Perry Willson, *Women in Twentieth-Century*; Giovanna Miceli Jeffries, *Feminine Feminists: Cultural Practices in Italy* (Minnesota: University of Minnesota Press, 1994).

10. General histories include, Indro Montanelli and Mario Cervi, *L'Italia degli anni di piombo - 1965-1978: La storia d'Italia #19* (Bur, 2013); Robert Lumley, *States of Emergency: Cultures of Revolt in Italy from 1968 to 1978* (New York: Verso, 1989).

Chapter 15

1. Redazione, "Com'era Essere Giovani in Italia Negli Anni Ottanta," *Vice*, 20 Novembre, 2015 (https://www.vice.com/it/article/vd5wg8/comera-avere-30-anni-negli-anni-ottanta-383).

2. Anna Bull and M. Gilbert, *The Lega Nord and the Politics of Secession in Italy* (Houndsmills, Basingstoke, Hampshire; New York: Palgrave, 2001); Francesco Jori, *Dalla Liga alla Lega: storia, movimenti, protagonisti* (Venezia: Marsilio, 2009).

3. Bull and Gilbert, *The Lega*.

4. Stille, *Excellent Cadavers*.

5. Schneider and Schneider, *Reversible Destiny*, 235–89.

6. Ginsborg, *Italy and Its Discontents: Family, Civil Society, State, 1980-2001*, 146.

7. Antonio Chiesi, et al., *Recent Social Trends in Italy, 1960-1995*, 472.

8. Ginsborg, *Italy and Its Discontents*, 39–248. On Italian attitudes toward the European Community see Standard Eurobarometer surveys from 1974–1996.

9. Martinelli et al., *Recent Social Trends*, 362, 368, 374–76, 420–21, 471–72; David Forgacs, *Italian Culture*, 173.

10. ISTAT, Serie Storiche, *Tavola 3.1 - Famiglie residenti per ampiezza e numero medio di componenti per famiglia ai censimenti 1901-* 2011; Martinelli et al., *Recent Social Trends*, 56, 97–98.

11. Valerio Pocar and Paola Ronfani, "Family Law in Italy: Legislative Innovations and Social Change," *Law and Society Review* 12, no. 4 (Summer, 1978): 607–44.

12. Willson, *Women in Twentieth-Century Italy*, 168–85.

13. Istat, "La violenza e i maltrattamenti contro le donne dentro e fuori la famiglia" (21 febbraio, 2007), 1, 4.

14. Clark, *Modern Italy*, 488; Martinelli, et al., *Recent Social Trends*, 120–21.

15. Istat, *Serie Storiche*, Mercato del Lavoro, "Tavola 10.8.1 segue - Tassi di occupazione, di disoccupazione e di attività per classe di età, sesso, regione e ripartizione geografica - Isole - Anni 1977-2015."

16. Judith Adler Hellman, "Immigrant 'Space' in Italy: When an Emigrant Sending Becomes an Immigrant Receiving Society," *Modern Italy* 2 (August 1997): 34–51.

17. Sanfilippo and Corti, *L'Italia e le migrazioni*: Istat *Serie Storiche*, Stranieri, "Tavola 2.15-Stranieri residenti in Italia secondo le principali cittadinanze ai censimenti 1981, 1991, 2001, 2011 e al 31 dicembre 2012, 2013 e 2014."

18. "La storia di nessuno," *La Stampa*, 26 agosto, 1989, 3.

19. Mario Fortunato and Salah Methnani, *Immigrato* (Roma: Napoli, 1990).

20. Quoted in Dickie, *Blood Brotherhoods*, 577.

Chapter 16

1. Igiaba Sceco, "Slasicce," in Gabriella Kuruvilla, Ingy Mubiayi, Igiaba Scego and Lalia Wadua, *Pecore Nere* (Roma: Laterza, 2005), 26.

2. Scego, "Salsicce," 28.

3. Asher Colombo and Giuseppe Sciortino, *Gli immigrati in Italia* (Bologna: Mulino, edizione ebook, 2010), paragraphs, 101 and 102.

4. ISTAT, *Annual Report 2016*.

5. ISTAT, *Serie Storiche*, Stranieri, "Tavola 2.15-Stranieri residenti in Italia secondo le principali cittadinanze ai censimenti 1981, 1991, 2001, 2011 e al 31 dicembre 2012, 2013 e 2014."

6. ISTAT, Matrimoni fra stranieri, statistiche storiche; Asher Colombo, Giuseppe Sciortino, *Gli immigrati in Italia, Assimilati o esclusi: gli immigrati, gli italiani, le politiche* (Bologna: Il Mulino, edizione-ebook, 2010), paragraphs, 86–90.

7. ISTAT, *Gli stranieri in Italia: gli effetti dell'ultima regolarizzazione: Stima al 1 gennaio 2005.*

8. ISTAT, *Annual Report, 2016*, 91.

9. Ibid., 95–96; Eva Garau, *Politics of National Identity in Italy: Immigration and "Italianità"* (New York: Routledge, 2014).

10. Ian Traynor, "EU Keen to Strike Deal with Muammar Gaddafi on Immigration," *The Guardian*, 1 September, 2010.

11. Stefania Panebianco, *Sulle onde del Mediterraneo: Cambiamenti globali e risposte alle crisi migratorie* (EGEA spa, 2017); Pietro Castelli Gattinara, *The Politics of Migration in Italy: Perspectives on Local Debates and Party Competition* (New York: Routledge, 2016).

12. William Spindler, "Italy Reception Centres under Strain as Thousands Rescued at Sea," *UNHCR*, May 6, 2015.

13. Francesca Sironi, "Gli immigrati rendono più della droga" la mafia nera nel business accoglienza," *L'Espresso*, Dicembre 2, 2014; "Ecco la 'mafia Capitale": 37 arresti per appalti del Comune. Indagato anche Alemanno, *Repubblica.it*, 2 Dicembre, 2014.

14. Camera dei deputati, Commissione "Jo Cox," su fenomeni di odio, intolleranza, xenofobia, e razzismo, *La piramide dell'odio in Italia*, July 6, 2017.

15. "l'Italiana Razzista, cronache di un'estate di discriminazioni," *Corriere della Sera*.

16. Human Rights Watch "l'intolleranza quotidiana: la violenza razzista e xenofoba in Italia," Marzo 21, 2011.

17. David Allegranti, "Aiutiamoli a casa loro," L'immigrazione secondo Matteo (non Salvini), *ilfoglio.it*, luglio 7, 2017.

18. Istat, *Annual Report* 2016, 98–99.

19. Lucrezia Sanes and Carlo Ladd, March 16, 2016 "Italian Brain Drain," *Brown Political Review*, March 16, 2016, bloghttp://www.brownpoliticalreview.org/2016/03/italian-brain-drain/.

20. "Un Milione per Far Rientrare i 'Cervelli in Fuga' All'estero." *LaStampa.it*, June 29, 2012.

21. Anna Martinelli, "Italian Brain Drain Speeds up: In 2016 +15%." *LaStampa.it*.

22. "Modello Sutera paese salvato dei migranti," *Repubblica*, Agosto 20, 2017.

SELECTED BIBLIOGRAPHY AND
SUGGESTED READINGS

General Histories

Acerbi, Antonio. *La Chiesa e l'Italia: per una storia dei loro rapporti negli ultimi due secoli.* Milano: Vita e Pensiero, 2003.

Bosworth, R. J. B. *Italy and the Wider World, 1860–1960.* London: Routledge, 1996.

Bellassai, Sandro, and Maria Malatesta. *Genere e mascolinità: uno sguardo storico.* Biblioteca di cultura, 595. Roma: Bulzoni, 2000.

DiScala, Spencer. *Italy: From Revolution to Republic: 1700 to the Present.* Boulder, CO: Westview Press, 2009.

Duggan, Christopher. *The Force of Destiny: A History of Italy since 1796.* Boston: Houghton Mifflin, 2008.

Gabaccia, Donna R. *Italy's Many Diasporas.* London: Routledge, 2005.

Mack Smith, Denis. *Italy; A Modern History.* Ann Arbor: University of Michigan Press, 1997.

Romano, Ruggiero, and Corrado Vivanti. *Storia d'Italia.* Vol. 1–3, *Dall'Unità a Oggi.* Torino: Einaudi, 1972.

Romano, Ruggiero, and Corrado Vivanti. *Storia d'Italia: Dal Primo Settecento all'Unità a Oggi.* Torino: G. Einaudi, 1972.

19th Century Histories

Banti, Alberto Mario, and Paul Ginsborg. *Il Risorgimento.* Torino: Einaudi, 2007.

Beales, Derek, and Eugenio F. Biagini. *T eh Risorgimento and the Unification of Italy.* Abingdon: Routledge, 2013.

Candeloro, Giorgio. *Storia dell'Italia moderna*, Vols. 1–4. Milano: Feltrinelli, 1956–1964.

Cervi, Mario, and Indro Montanelli. *L'Italia del Risorgimento - 1831-1861: La storia d'Italia #8.* Milano: Rizzoli, 2010.

Sabbatucci, Giovanni, and Vittorio Vidotto. *Il nuovo stato e la società civile: 1861–1887.* Storia d'Italia. Vol. 2. Bari: Laterza, 1995.

Sabbatucci, Giovanni, and Vittorio Vidotto. *Storia d'Italia. 1887–1914.* Vol. 3. Roma; Bari: Laterza, 1995.

Volpe, Gioacchino, and Francesco Perfetti. *Italia moderna. 1815–1898.* Vol. 1. Milano: Le Lettere, 2002.

20th Century Histories

Banti, Alberto Mario, Walter Barberis, Carlo Marco Belfanti, Carlo Bertelli, Giulio Bollati, Alberto Capatti, Francesco Cassata, et al. *Storia d'Italia. Annali: Guerra e pace.* Torino: Einaudi, 2001.

Carter, Nick. *Modern Italy in Historical Perspective.* London; New York: Bloomsbury Academic, 2011.

Clark, Martin. *Modern Italy, 1871 to the Present*. London: Routledge, 2014.

Domenico, Roy Palmer. *Remaking Italy in the Twentieth Century*. Lanham, MD; Oxford: Rowman & Littlefield, 2002.

Ginsborg, Paul. *A History of Contemporary Italy: 1943–80*. London: Penguin, 1990.

Sassoon, Donald. *Contemporary Italy: Politics, Economy and Society since 1945*. Routledge, 2014.

Part One: Italy 1800-1876

Amatangelo, Susan. *Italian Women at War: Sisters in Arms from the Unification to the Twentieth Century*. Rowman & Littlefield, 2016.

Banti, Alberto Mario. *Il Risorgimento italiano*. Roma: Laterza, 2013.

Banti, Alberto Mario. *Nel nome dell'Italia: il Risorgimento nelle testimonianze, nei documenti e nelle immagini*. Roma: Laterza, 2010.

Banti, Alberto Mario. *Sublime madre nostra: la nazione italiana dal Risorgimento al fascismo*. Roma: Laterza, 2011.

Banti, Alberto Mario, and Roberto Bizzocchi. *Immagini della nazione nell'Italia del Risorgimento*. Roma: Carocci, 2002.

Banti, Alberto Mario, and Paul Ginsborg. *Storia l'Italia. Annali 22, Il Risorgimento*. Torino: G. Einaudi, 2007.

Battaglia, Antonello. "Italian Risorgimento and the European Volunteers." *Academic Journal of Interdisciplinary Studies* 2, no. 1 (March 1, 2013): 87.

Bizzocchi, Roberto. *Cicisbei: morale privata e identità nazionale in Italia*. Roma: Laterza, 2008.

Black, Jeremy. *Italy and the Grand Tour*. New Haven: Yale University Press, 2003.

Blumberg, Arnold. *A Carefully Planned Accident: The Italian War of 1859*. London; Cranbury, NJ: Associated University Presses, 1990.

Boneschi, Marta, and Mondadori. *Senso: i costumi sessuali degli italiani dal 1880 ad oggi*. Milano: Mondadori, 2000.

Bouchard, Norma. *Risorgimento in Modern Italian Culture: Revisiting the Nineteenth-Century Past in History, Narrative, and Cinema*. Madison: Fairleigh Dickinson University Press, 2005.

Capuzzo, Ester. *Cento anni di storiografia sul Risorgimento: atti del LX Congresso di Storia del Risorgimento Italiano; (Rieti, 18–21 ottobre 2000)*. Roma: Istituto per la Storia del Risorgimento Italiano, 2002.

Casillo, Robert. *The Empire of Stereotypes: Germaine de Stael and the Idea of Italy*. New York: Palgrave Macmillan, 2006.

Cecchinato, Eva. *Camicie rosse: i garibaldini dall'Unità alla Grande Guerra*. Roma; Bari: Laterza, 2011.

Clark, Martin. *The Italian Risorgimento*. London: Routledge, 2015.

Davis, John A. *Naples and Napoleon: Southern Italy and the European Revolutions, 1780–1860*. 1 edition. Oxford; New York: Oxford University Press, 2006.

Davis, John A., and Paul Ginsborg. *Society and Politics in the Age of the Risorgimento: Essays in Honour of Denis Mack Smith*. Cambridge: Cambridge University Press, 2002.

Dickie, John. "A Word at War: The Italian Army and Brigandage 1860–1870." *History Workshop Journal* 33, no. 1 (1992): 1–24.

Doni, Elena. *Donne del Risorgimento*. Bologna: Il Mulino, 2011.

Dovere, Ugo. *Chiesa e Risorgimento nel Mezzogiorno*. Napoli: Verbum Ferens, 2011.

Dumont, Dora M. "Workers in Risorgimento Bologna." *Canadian Journal of History* 40, no. 1 (April 2005): 25.

Embree, Michael. *Radetzky's Marches: The Campaigns of 1848 and 1849 in Upper Italy*. Havertown: Helion, 2014.

Selected Bibliography and Suggested Readings

Falchi, Federica. "Beyond National Borders; 'Italian' Patriots United in the Name of Giuseppe Mazzini: Emilie Ashurst, Margaret Fuller and Jessie White Mario." *Women's History Review* 24, no. 1 (January 2, 2015): 23–36.

Feldman, Martha. *Opera and Sovereignty: Transforming Myths in Eighteenth-Century Italy*. Chicago: University of Chicago Press, 2010.

Filippini, Nadia Maria. *Donne sulla scena pubblica società e politica in Veneto tra Sette e Ottocento*. Milano: FrancoAngeli, 2006.

Findlen, Paula, Wendy Wassyng Roworth, and Catherine M. Sama. *Italy's Eighteenth Century Gender and Culture in the Age of the Grand Tour*. Stanford, CA: Stanford University Press, 2009.

Francesco, Antonino De. *The Antiquity of the Italian Nation: The Cultural Origins of a Political Myth in Modern Italy, 1796–1943*. Oxford: Oxford University Press, 2013.

Franzina, Emilio, and Matteo Sanfilippo. *Risorgimento ed emigrazione*. Viterbo: Ed. Sette Città, 2013.

Freitag, Sabine. *Exiles from European Revolutions: Refugees in Mid-Victorian England*. New York; Oxford: Berghahn, 2003.

Gilbert, M. "History as It Really Wasn't: The Myths of Italian Historiography (A Roundtable with Ruth Ben-Ghiat, Luciano Cafagna, Ernesto Galli Della Loggia, Carl Ipsen and David I. Kertzer." *Journal of Modern Italian Studies* 6, no. 3 (FAL 2001): 402–19.

Gramsci, Antonio. *Opere di Antonio Gramsci*. Torino: Einaudi, 1947.

Isabella, Maurizio. *Mediterranean Diasporas: Politics and Ideas in the Long 19th Century*. London: Bloomsbury, 2016.

Isabella, Maurizio. "Review Article Rethinking Italy's Nation-Building 150 Years Afterwards: The New Risorgimento Historiography." *Past & Present* 217, no. 1 (November 1, 2012): 247–68.

Isabella, Maurizio. *Risorgimento in Exile: Italian Émigrés and the Liberal International in the Post-Napoleonic Era*. Oxford; New York: Oxford University Press, 2009.

Isnenghi, Mario, and Eva Cecchinato. *Fare l'Italia: unità e disunità nel Risorgimento*. Torino: UTET, 2008.

Janz, Oliver, and Lucy Riall. *The Italian Risorgimento: Transnational Perspectives*. Abingdon: Routledge, 2014.

Körner, Axel, and Lucy Riall. "Introduction: The New History of Risorgimento Nationalism." *Nations & Nationalism* 15, no. 3 (July 2009): 396–401.

Lang, A. *Converting a Nation: A Modern Inquisition and the Unification of Italy*. Springer, 2008.

Laven, David. *Restoration and Risorgimento: Italy 1796–1870*. Oxford: Oxford University Press, 2010.

Laven, David. *Venice and Venetia under the Habsburgs, 1815–1835*. Oxford; New York: Oxford University Press, 2002.

Laven, David. "Why Patriots Wrote and What Reactionaries Read: Reflections on Alberto Banti's La Nazione Del Risorgimento." *Nations & Nationalism* 15, no. 3 (July 2009): 419–26.

Laven, David, and Lucy Riall, eds. *Napoleon's Legacy: Problems of Government in Restoration Europe*. Oxford: Berg, 2000.

Lupo, Salvatore. *La questione: come liberare la storia del Mezzogiorno dagli stereotipi*, Roma: Donzelli Editore, 2015.

Lupo, Salvatore. *L'unificazione italiana: Mezzogiorno, rivoluzione, guerra civile*. Roma: Donzelli Editore, 2011.

Luzzi, Joseph. "Italy without Italians: Literary Origins of a Romantic Myth." *MLN* 117, no. 1 (2002): 48–83.

Mack Smith, Denis. *Cavour and Garibaldi 1860: A Study in Political Conflict*. Cambridge: Cambridge University Press, 1954.

Mack Smith, Denis. *Garibaldi: A Great Life in Brief*. New York: Alfred A. Knopf, 1956.

Macry, Paolo. *Ottocento: famiglia, élites e patrimoni a Napoli*. Torino: Giulio Einaudi, 1988.

Manfredini, Matteo. "Families in Motion: The Role and Characteristics of Household Migration in a 19th-Century Rural Italian Parish." *The History of the Family* 8 (January 1, 2003): 317–43.

Marwil, Jonathan. *Visiting Modern War in Risorgimento Italy*. Basingstoke: Palgrave Macmillan, 2011.

Mazzini, Giuseppe. *A Cosmopolitanism of Nations: Giuseppe Mazzini's Writings on Democracy, Nation Building, and International Relations*. Princeton: Princeton University Press, 2009.

Mazzocca, Fernando, and Carlo Sisi. *I macchiaioli prima dell'impressionismo*. Venezia: Marsilio, 2003.

Meriggi, Marco. *Gli Stati italiani prima dell'Unità: una storia istituzionale*. Bologna: Il Mulino, 2002.

Montanari, Massimo. *Italian Identity in the Kitchen, or, Food and the Nation*. New York: Columbia University Press, 2013.

Montroni, Giovanni. *Gli uomini del re: la nobiltà napoletana nell'Ottocento*. Catanzaro: Meridiana Libri, 1996.

Montroni, Giovanni. *La società italiana dall'unificazione alla Grande Guerra*. Roma; Bari: Laterza, 2015.

Morandini, Maria Cristina. *Scuola e nazione: maestri e istituzione popolare nella costruzione dello Stato unitario, 1848–1861*. Milano: Vita e Pensiero, 2003.

Mori, Maria Teresa. *Salotti: La sociabilità delle élite nell'Italia dell'Ottocento*. Roma: Carocci, 2000.

Patriarca, Silvana. "Indolence and Regeneration: Tropes and Tensions of Risorgimento Patriotism." *The American Historical Review* 110, no. 2 (April 1, 2005): 380–408.

Patriarca, Silvana. *Numbers and Nationhood: Writing Statistics in Nineteenth-Century Italy*. Cambridge; New York: Cambridge University Press, 1996.

Patriarca, Silvana. *Italian Vices: Nation and Character from the Risorgimento to the Republic*. Cambridge; New York: Cambridge University Press, 2010.

Patriarca, Silvana, and Lucy Riall. *The Risorgimento Revisited: Nationalism and Culture in Nineteenth-Century Italy*. Basingstoke: Palgrave Macmillan, 2011.

Peruta, Franco Della. *Il giornalismo italiano del Risorgimento. Dal 1847 all'Unità: Dal 1847 all'Unità*. Milano: FrancoAngeli, 2011.

Peruta, Franco Della. *Mazzini e i rivoluzionari italiana. Il partito d'azione, 1830–1845*. Milano: Feltrinelli, 1974.

Pieroni. Bortolotti, Franca. *Alle Origini Del Movimento Femminile in Italia, 1848–1892*. Torino: Einaudi, 1963.

Proia, Gianna. *Cristina di Belgiojoso: dal salotto alla politica*. Roma: Aracne, 2010.

Riall, Lucy. *Sicily and the Unification of Italy: Liberal Policy and Local Power, 1859–1866*. Oxford: Clarendon Press, 1998.

Riall, Lucy. *The Italian Risorgimento: State, Society and National Unification*. London: Routledge, 2006.

Riall, Lucy. *Garibaldi: Invention of a Hero*. New Haven: Yale University Press, 2007.

Riall, Lucy. *Risorgimento*. London: Macmillan Education UK, 2009.

Riall, Lucy. *Under the Volcano: Revolution in a Sicilian Town*. Oxford: Oxford University Press, 2013.

Roberts, John M. "Venice and Venetia Under the Habsburgs, 1815–1835." *The English Historical Review* 118, no. 477 (June 1, 2003): 808–10.

Roccucci, Adriano, ed. *La Costruzione dello stato-nazione in Italia*. Roma: Viella, 2012.

Romani, Roberto. *Sensibilities of the Risorgimento: Reason and Passions in Political Thought*. Leiden; Boston: Brill, 2018.

Sabbatucci, Giovanni, and Vittorio Vidotto. *Storia d'Italia. Le premesse dell'unità. Dalla fine del settecento al 1861 1 1*. Bari: Laterza, 1994.

Selected Bibliography and Suggested Readings

Salvatorelli, Luigi. *Pensiero e Azione Del Risorgimento*. Torino: Einaudi, 1974.

Sanfilippo, Matteo, Emilio Franzina e Matteo. *Risorgimento ed emigrazione*. Viterbo: Edizioni Sette Città, 2014.

Sanguanini, Bruno. *Il pubblico all'italiana: formazione del pubblico e politiche culturali tra Stato e teatro*. Milano: FrancoAngeli, 1989.

Scaramuzza, Emma. *Politica e amicizia: relazioni, conflitti e differenze di genere, 1860–1915*. Milano: FrancoAngeli, 2010.

Scarpellini, Emanuela. *Material Nation: A Consumer's History of Modern Italy*. Oxford: Oxford University Press, 2011.

Schwegman, Marjan. "Amazons for Garibaldi: Women Warriors and the Making of the Hero of Two Worlds." *Modern Italy* 15, no. 4 (2010): 417–32.

Seta, Cesare De. *L'Italia nello specchio del Grand Tour*. Milano: Rizzoli, 2014.

Sutcliffe, Marcella Pellegrino. *Victorian Radicals and Italian Democrats*. London: Royal Historical Society, 2014.

Tafuro, Azzurra. *Madre e patriota: Adelaide Bono Cairoli*. Firenze University Press, 2011.

Woolf, Stuart. *A History of Italy 1700–1860: The Social Constraints of Political Change*. London; New York: Routledge, 1992.

Zucca Micheletto, Beatrice. "Reconsidering the Southern Europe Model: Dowry, Women's Work and Marriage Patterns in Pre-Industrial Urban Italy (Turin, Second Half of the 18th Century)." *The History of the Family* 16 (January 1, 2011): 354–70.

Part Two: Liberal Italy

Acerbi, Antonio. *La chiesa e l'Italia: per una storia dei loro rapporti negli ultimi due secoli*. Milano: Vita e pensiero università, 2003.

Arisi Rota, Arianna, Monica Ferrari, and Matteo Morandi. *Patrioti si diventa: luoghi e linguaggi di pedagogia patriottica nell'Italia unita*. Milano: FrancoAngeli, 2009.

Ascenzi, Anna. *Tra educazione etico-civile e costruzione dell'identità nazionale: l'insegnamento della storia nelle scuole italiane dell'Ottocento*. Milano: Vita e Pensiero, 2004.

Ashley, Susan A. *Making Liberalism Work: The Italian Experience, 1860–1914*. Westport, CT: Praeger, 2003.

Audenino, Patrizia. *Democratici e socialisti nel Piemonte dell'Ottocento*. Milano: FrancoAngeli, 1995.

Audenino, Patrizia. *Donne e libere professioni: il Piemonte del Novecento*. Milano: FrancoAngeli, 2007.

Audenino, Patrizia, ed. *Milano e l'Esposizione internazionale del 1906: la rappresentazione della modernità*. Milano: FrancoAngeli, 2008.

Audenino, Patrizia, and Paola Corti. *L'emigrazione italiana*. Milano: Fenice, 1994.

Audenino, Patrizia, Paola Corti, and Ada Lonni. *Imprenditori biellesi in Francia tra Ottocento e Novecento*. Milano: Electa, 1997.

Audenino, Patrizia, and Maddalena Tirabassi. *Migrazioni italiane: storia e storie dall'ancien régime a oggi*. Milan: B. Mondadori, 2008.

Avagliano, Lucio. *La Modernizzazione difficile: città e campagne nel Mezzogiorno dall'età giolittiana al fascismo*. Bari: De Donato, 1983.

Babini, Valeria Paola. *Tra sapere e potere: la psichiatria italiana nella seconda metà dell'Ottocento*. Bologna: Il Mulino, 1982.

Babini, Valeria Paola. *Il caso Murri: una storia italiana*. Bologna: Il Mulino, 2004.

Babini, Valeria Paola, Fernanda Minuz, and Annamaria Tagliavini. *La donna nelle scienze dell'uomo: immagini del femminile nella cultura scientifica italiana di fine secolo*. Milano: FrancoAngeli, 1986.

Babini, Valeria Paola, and Raffaella Simili. *More than Pupils: Italian Women in Science at the Turn of the 20th Century*. Firenze: L.S. Olschki, 2007.

Babini, Valeria P., Chiara Beccalossi, and Lucy Riall, eds. *Italian Sexualities Uncovered, 1789–1914*. London: Palgrave Macmillan UK, 2015.

Banti, Alberto Mario. *Terra e denaro: una borghesia padana dell'Ottocento*. Venezia: Marsilio ed., 1989.

Barański, Zygmunt G, and Shirley Vinall. *Women and Italy: Essays on Gender, Culture and History*. London: Macmillan, 1990.

Beccalossi, Chiara. *Female Sexual Inversion: Same-Sex Desires in Italian and British Sexology, c. 1870–1920*. Basingstoke: Palgrave Macmillan, 2012.

Beccalossi, Chiara. "The Origin of Italian Sexological Studies: Female Sexual Inversion, ca. 1870–1900." *Journal of the History of Sexuality* 18, no. 1 (January 1, 2009): 103–20.

Beer, Marina, Anna Benvenuti Papi, Gérard Delille, Maria Pia Di Bella, Lorenzo Fabbri, Ida. Fazio, Daniela Lombardi, et al. *Storia Del Matrimonio*. Roma: Laterza, 1996.

Bell, Donald H. *Sesto San Giovanni: Workers, Culture, and Politics in an Italian Town, 1880–1922*. New Brunswick: Rutgers University Press, 1986.

Bell, Rudolph M. *Fate and Honor, Family and Village: Demographic and Cultural Change in Rural Italy since 1800*. Chicago: University of Chicago Press, 1979.

Bevilacqua, Piero. *Breve storia dell'Italia meridionale: dall'Ottocento a oggi*. Roma: Donzelli, 1993.

Bevilacqua, Piero. *Le Campagne del Mezzogiorno tra fascismo e dopoguerra: il caso della Calabria*. Torino: G. Einaudi, 1980.

Bevilacqua, Piero. *Storia della questione meridionale*. Roma: Editrice sindacale italiana, 1974.

Bevilacqua, Piero, Andreina De Clementi, and Emilio Franzina. *Storia dell'emigrazione italiana*. Roma: Donzelli Editore, 2001.

Bonelli, Franco. *Il capitalismo italiano: linee generali di interpretazione*. Torino: Einaudi, 1978.

Bortolotti, Franca Pieroni. *Alle origini del movimento femminile in Italia: 1848–1892*. Torino: Einaudi, 1975.

Bravo, Anna, et al. eds. *Storia sociale delle donne nell'Italia contemporanea*. Roma: Laterza, 2001.

Buttafuoco, Annarita. *Le mariuccine storia di un'istituzione laica, l'Asilo Mariuccia*. Milano: FrancoAngeli, 1985.

Buttafuoco, Annarita. *Questioni di cittadinanza: donne e diritti sociali nell'Italia liberale*. Siena: Protagon Editori toscani, 1995.

Buttafuoco, Annarita. *Suffragismo femminile e istituzioni politiche dall'Unità al fascismo*. Roma: Associazione degli ex parlamentari della repubblica, 1988.

Cafagna, Luciano. *Dualismo e sviluppo nella storia d'Italia*. Venezia: Marsilio, 1990.

Cafagna, Luciano, and Carlo M Cipolla. *The Fontana Economic History of Europe Vol. 4 Sect. 6 Vol. 4 Sect. 6*. London: Collins, 1971.

Cammarano, Fulvio. *Il nuovo stato e la società civile: 1861–1887*. Roma [u.a.]: Ed. Laterza, 1995.

Cammarano, Fulvio. *Storia dell'Italia liberale*. Roma: Laterza, 2014.

Candeloro, Giorgio. *Il movimento cattolico in Italia*. Roma: Riuniti, 1974.

Candeloro, Giorgio. *La costruzione dello stato unitario 1860–1871*. Milano: Feltrinelli, 1994.

Cardoza, Anthony L. *Aristocrats in Bourgeois Italy: The Piedmontese Nobility, 1861–1930*. Cambridge: Cambridge University Press, 2002.

Choate, Mark I. *Emigrant Nation: The Making of Italy Abroad*. Cambridge, MA: Harvard University Press, 2008.

Clementi, Andreina De. *L'assalto al cielo: donne e uomini nell'emigrazione italiana*. Roma: Donzelli Editore, 2014.

D'Agostino, Peter R. *Rome in America: Transnational Catholic Ideology from the Risorgimento to Fascism*. Chapel Hill: The University of North Carolina Press, 2003.

Daniele, Vittorio, and Paolo Malanima. *Il divario Nord-Sud in Italia, 1861–2011*. Soveria Mannelli: Rubbettino Editore, 2011.

Davis, John A. *Conflict and Control: Law and Order in Nineteenth-Century Italy*. Atlantic Highlands, NJ: Humanities Press International, 1988.

Davis, John A. *Italy in the Nineteenth Century: 1796–1900*. Oxford: Oxford University Press, 2007.

De Clementi, Andreina. *La società inafferrabile: protoindustria, città e classi sociali nell'Italia liberale*. Roma: Lavoro, 1986.

De Giorgio, Michela. *Le italiane dall'unità a oggi: modelli culturali e comportamenti sociali*. Bari: Laterza, 1992.

De Grand, Alexander. *The Hunchbacks Tailor: Giovanni Giolitti and Liberal Italy from the Challenge of Mass Politics to the Rise of Fascism, 1882–1922*. Westport, CT: Praeger, 2001.

Dickie, John. *Darkest Italy: The Nation and Stereotypes of the Mezzogiorno, 1860–1900*. Basingstoke: Macmillan, 1999.

Dickie, John. *Cosa Nostra: A History of the Sicilian Mafia*. New York: Palgrave Macmillan, 2004.

Dickie, John. *Blood Brotherhoods: A History of Italy's Three Mafias*. New York: PublicAffairs, 2014.

Dickie, John, John Foot, and Frank M Snowden. *Disastro!: Disasters in Italy since 1860: Culture, Politics, Society*. New York: Palgrave, 2002.

Di Scala, Spencer, ed. *Italian Socialism: Between Politics and History*. Amherst: University of Massachusetts Press, 1996.

Donati, Sabina. *A Political History of National Citizenship and Identity in Italy, 1861–1950*. Stanford: Stanford University Press, 2013.

Dumont, Dora M. "Strange and Exorbitant Demands': Rural Labour in Nineteenth-Century Bologna." *European History Quarterly* 30, no. 4 (October 1, 2000): 467–91.

Dumont, Dora M. "The Nation as Seen from below: Rome in 1870." *European Review of History: Revue Européenne d'histoire* 15, no. 5 (October 1, 2008): 479–96.

Fenoaltea, Stefano. *The Reinterpretation of Italian Economic History: From Unification to the Great War*. Cambridge: Cambridge University Press, 2011.

Ferrante, Lucia, Maura Palazzi, Gianna Pomata, eds. *Ragnatele di rapporti: patronage e reti di relazione nella storia delle donne*. Torino: Rosenberg & Sellier, 1988.

Finaldi, Giuseppe Maria, and Giuseppe Finaldi. *Italian National Identity in the Scramble for Africa: Italy's African Wars in the Era of Nation-Building, 1870–1900*. New York: Peter Lang, 2009.

Fiume, Giovanna, "*Madri: storia di un ruolo sociale*. Venezia: Marsilio, 1995.

Franzina, Emilio. *Gli italiani al Nuovo mondo: l'emigrazione italiana in America: 1492–1942*. Milano: Mondadori, 1995.

Franzina, Emilio. *Una patria espatriata. Lealtà nazionale e caratteri regionali nell'immigrazione italiana all'estero (secoli XIX e XX)*. Viterbo: Edizioni Sette Città, 2014.

Frattini, Claudia. *Il primo congresso delle donne italiane, Roma 1908: opinione pubblica e femminismo*. Roma: Biblink, 2009.

Gabaccia, Donna R. *From Sicily to Elizabeth Street: Housing and Social Change among Italian Immigrants, 1880–1930*. Albany, NY: State University of New York Press, 1984.

Gabaccia, Donna R. *Militants and Migrants: Rural Sicilians Become American Workers*. New Brunswick, NJ: Rutgers University Press, 1988.

Gabaccia, Donna R., and Franca Iacovetta. *Women, Gender and Transnational Lives: Italian Workers of the World*. Toronto; Buffalo: University of Toronto Press, 2002.

Gabaccia, Donna R, and Fraser M Ottanelli. *Italian Workers of the World: Labor Migration and the Formation of Multiethnic States*. Urbana, IL: University of Illinois Press, 2005.

Giarrizzo, Giuseppe. *La Modernizzazione difficile: città e campagne nel Mezzogiorno dall'età giolittiana al fascismo*. Bari: De Donato, 1983.

Giarrizzo, Giuseppe. *Mezzogiorno senza meridionalismo: la Sicilia, lo sviluppo, il potere.* Venezia: Marsilio, 1992.

Gibson, Mary. *Prostitution and the State in Italy, 1860–1915.* Columbus: Ohio State University Press, 2000.

Gibson, Mary. *Born to Crime: Cesare Lombroso and the Origins of Biological Criminology.* Westport, CT: Praeger, 2002.

Gibson, Mary. "Women's Prisons in Italy: A Problem of Citizenship." *Crime, Histoire & Sociétés/ Crime, History & Societies* 13, no. 2 (2009): 27–40.

Gibson, Mary. "Forensic Psychiatry and the Birth of the Criminal Insane Asylum in Modern Italy." *IJLP International Journal of Law and Psychiatry* 37, no. 1 (2014): 117–26.

Goglia, Luigi, and Fabio Grassi. *Il colonialismo italiano da Adua all'impero.* Roma: Laterza, 2008.

Gori, Claudia. *Crisalidi. Emancipazioniste liberali in età giolittiana.* Milano: FrancoAngeli, 2003.

Gribaudi, Maurizio. *Mondo operaio e mito operaio: spazi e percorsi sociali a Torino nel primo Novecento.* Torino: Einaudi, 1987.

Griswold, Wendy. *Regionalism and the Reading Class.* Chicago; London: University of Chicago Press, 2008.

Guarnieri, Patrizia. *La storia della psichiatria: un secolo di studi in Italia.* Firenze: L.S. Olschki, 1991.

Guarnieri, Patrizia. *A Case of Child Murder: Law and Science in Nineteenth-Century Tuscany.* Cambridge: Polity Press, 1993.

Guglielmo, Jennifer. *Living the Revolution: Italian Women's Resistance and Radicalism in New York City, 1880–1945.* Chapel Hill: University of North Carolina Press, 2010.

Iacovetta, Franca, and Lorenza Stradiotti. "Betrayal, Vengeance, and the Anarchist Ideal: Virgilia D'Andrea's Radical Antifascism in (American) Exile, 1928–1933." *jowh Journal of Women's History* 25, no. 1 (2013): 85–110.

Ipsen, Carl. *Italy in the Age of Pinocchio: Children and Danger in the Liberal Era.* New York: Palgrave Macmillan, 2006.

Jemolo, Arturo Carlo. *Chiesa e stato: dalla unificazione ai giorni nostri.* Torino: G. Einaudi, 1977.

Jonas, Raymond. *Battle of Adwa: African Victory in the Age of Empire.* Cambridge: Belknap Harvard, 2015.

Kertzer, David I. *The Kidnapping of Edgardo Mortara.* New York: Alfred Knopf, 1997.

Kertzer, David I. *Prisoner of the Vatican the Popes' Secret Plot to Capture Rome from the New Italian State.* Boston: Houghton Mifflin, 2004.

Kertzer, David I. *Amalia's Tale: An Impoverished Peasant Woman, an Ambitious Attorney, and a Fight for Justice.* Boston: Houghton Mifflin Co., 2008.

Kertzer, David I., and Richard P. Saller. *The Family in Italy from Antiquity to the Present.* New Haven; London: Yale University Press, 1991.

Korner, Axel. *The Politics of Culture in Liberal Italy: From Unification to Fascism.* London: Routledge, 2008.

Lombroso, Cesare, Guglielmo Ferrero, Nicole Hahn Rafter, and Mary Gibson. *Criminal Woman, the Prostitute, and the Normal Woman.* Durham: Duke University Press, 2004.

Lombroso, Cesare, Guglielmo Ferrero, Nicole Hahn Rafter, and Mary Gibson. *Criminal Man.* Durham: Duke University Press, 2006.

Luconi, Stefano. "Emigration and Italians' Transnational Radical Politicization." *Forum Italicum* 47, no. 1 (May 1, 2013): 96–115.

Lumley, Robert, and Jonathan Morris. *The New History of the Italian South: The Mezzogiorno Revisited.* Exeter, Devon: University of Exeter Press, 1997.

Lupo, Salvatore. *Il tenebroso sodalizio: il primo rapporto di polizia sulla mafia siciliana.* XL, 2011.

Lupo, Salvatore. *Storia della mafia: dalle origini ai giorni nostri.* Roma: Donzelli Editore, 2004.

Malatesta, Maria. "Le professioni e la citta. Bologna 1860–1914." *Società e storia* 29, no. 111 (2006): 51.

Selected Bibliography and Suggested Readings

Malatesta, Maria. *Society and the Professions in Italy, 1860–1914*. Cambridge: Cambridge University Press, 2002.

Mallach, Alan. *The Autumn of Italian Opera: From Verismo to Modernism, 1890–1915*. Boston, MA: Northeastern University Press, 2007.

Mazzocca, Fernando, and Carlo Sisi. *I macchiaioli prima dell'impressionismo*. Venezia: Marsilio, 2003.

Meriggi, Marco, and Pierangelo Schiera. *Dalla città alla nazione: borghesie ottocentesche in Italia e in Germania*. Bologna: Il Mulino, 1993.

Mitchell, Katharine. *Italian Women Writers: Gender and Everyday Life in Fiction and Journalism, 1870–1910*. Toronto: University of Toronto Press, 2014.

Mitchell, Katharine, and Helena Sanson, eds. *Women and Gender in Post-Unification Italy: Between Private and Public Spheres*. Oxford: Peter Lang, 2013.

Morris, Jonathan. *The Political Economy of Shopkeeping in Milan, 1886–1922*. Cambridge; New York: Cambridge University Press, 1992.

Pelaja, Margherita. *Matrimonio e sessualità a Roma nell'ottocento*. Bari: Laterza, 1994.

Pelaja, Margherita, and Lucetta Scaraffia. *Due in una carne: Chiesa e sessualità nella storia*. Roma; Bari: Laterza, 2014.

Petrusewicz, Marta. *Come il meridione divenne una questione: rappresentazioni del Sud prima e dopo il Quarantotto*. Soveria Mannelli (CZ): Rubbettino, 1998.

Petrusewicz, Marta. *Latifondo: economia morale e vita materiale in una periferia dell'Ottocento*. Venezia: Marsilio, 1990.

Pezzino, Paolo. *Una Certa Reciprocità Di Favori: Mafia e Modernizzazione Violenta Nella Sicilia Postunitaria*, 1990.

Pieroni Bortolotti, Franca. *Alle origini del movimento femminile in Italia: 1848–1892*. Torino: G. Einaudi, 1963.

Pieroni Bortolotti, Franca. *Socialismo e questione femminile in Italia 1892–1922*. Milano: Gabriele Mazzotta, 1976.

Plastino, Goffredo, and Joseph Sciorra, eds. *Neapolitan Postcards: The Canzone Napoletana as Transnational Subject*. Lanham: Rowman & Littlefield, 2016.

Pretelli, Matteo. *L' emigrazione italiana negli Stati Uniti*. Bologna: Il Mulino, 2011.

Quine, Maria Sophia. *Italy's Social Revolution: Charity and Welfare from Liberalism to Fascism*. Houndmills, Basingstoke, Hampshire; New York: Palgrave, 2002.

Reeder, Linda. *Widows in White: Migration and the Transformation of Rural Italian Women, Sicily, 1880–1920*. Toronto: University of Toronto Press, 2003.

Riall, Lucy. "Progress and Compromise in Liberal Italy." *The Historical Journal* 38, no. 1 (March 1995): 205–13.

Rizzo, Domenico. "Marriage on Trial: Adultery in Nineteenth-Century Rome." In *Gender, Family and Sexuality*, 20–36. London: Palgrave Macmillan, 2004.

Roccucci, Adriano, ed. *La Costruzione dello stato-nazione in Italia*. Roma: Viella, 2012.

Romanelli, Raffaele. *Il comando impossibile: stato e società nell'Italia liberale*. Bologna: Il Mulino, 1995.

Sanfilippo, Matteo. *Emigrazione e storia d'Italia*. Cosenza: L. Pellegrini, 2003.

Sanfilippo, Matteo, and Paola Corti. *L'Italia e le migrazioni*. Roma: Laterza, 2012.

Schneider, Jane, and Peter Schneider. *Culture and Political Economy in Western Sicily*. New York: Academic Press, 1975.

Serra, Ilaria. *Immagini di un immaginario: l'emigrazione italiana negli Stati Uniti fra i due secoli (1890–1924)*. Verona: Cierre, 1997.

Seymour, Mark. *Debating Divorce in Italy: Marriage and the Making of Modern Italians, 1860–1974*. New York: Palgrave Macmillan, 2006.

Seymour, Mark. "Epistolary Emotions: Exploring Amorous Hinterlands in 1870s Southern Italy." *Social History* 35, no. 2 (May 1, 2010): 148–64.

Snowden, Frank M. *Naples in the Time of Cholera, 1884–1911*. Cambridge: Cambridge University Press, 2010.

Soldani, Simonetta. "The Construction of a New Feminine Identity in Italy through the School from the Unification to Fascism." *Education and the Construction of Gender* (1991): 26–40.

Soldani, Simonetta, and Gabriele Turi. *Fare gli Italiani: scuola e cultura nell'Italia contemporanea*. 1–2, Bologna: Il Mulino, 1993.

Soper, Steven C. *Building a Civil Society: Associations, Public Life, and the Origins of Modern Italy*. Toronto: University of Toronto Press, 2013.

Sorcinelli, Paolo. *Storia e sessualità: casi di vita, regole e trasgressioni tra Ottocento e Novecento*. Milano: Mondadori, 2001.

Stewart-Steinberg, Suzanne. *The Pinocchio Effect: On Making Italians 1860–1920*. Chicago: University of Chicago Press, 2007.

Toniolo, Gianni. *Storia economica dell'Italia liberale: (1850–1918)*. Bologna: Il Mulino, 2001.

Toniolo, Gianni. ed. *L' Italia e l'economia mondiale: dall'unità a oggi*. Venezia: Marsilio, 2013.

Toniolo, Gianni. *Economic History of Liberal Italy: 1850–1918*. London: Routledge, 2014.

Verucci, Guido. *Cattolicesimo e laicismo nell'Italia contemporanea*. Milano: FrancoAngeli, 2001.

Willson, Perry R. *Gender, Family, and Sexuality the Private Sphere in Italy 1860–1945*. Houndmills; Basingstoke; Hampshire; New York: Palgrave Macmillan, 2004.

Wong, Aliza S. *Race and the Nation in Liberal Italy, 1861–1911: Meridionalism, Empire, and Diaspora*. New York: Palgrave Macmillan, 2006.

Zanoni, Elizabeth. *Migrant Marketplaces: Food and Italians in North and South America*. Urbana: University of Illinois Press, 2018.

Zamagni, Vera. *Dalla periferia al centro: la seconda rinascita economica dell'Italia, 1861–1981*. Bologna: Il Mulino, 1990.

Zamagni, Vera. *Introduzione alla storia economica d'Italia*. Bologna: Il Mulino, 2007.

Zamagni, Vera. *The Economic History of Italy 1860–1990*. Oxford: Clarendon Press, 1993.

Zappi, Elda Gentili. *If Eight Hours Seem Too Few: Mobilization of Women Workers in the Italian Rice Fields*. Albany: State University of New York Press, 1991.

Part Three: Wars and Fascism

Adamoli, Federico. *Lettere Dal Fronte.: La Grande Guerra Raccontata Nelle Pagine Del Corriere Abruzzese*. Federico Adamoli, 2013.

Agosti, Aldo. *Storia del Partito comunista italiano: 1921–1991*. Roma: Laterza, 1999.

Alano, Jomarie. "Armed with a Yellow Mimosa: Women's Defence and Assistance Groups in Italy, 1943–45." *Journal of Contemporary History* 38, no. 4 (2003): 615–31.

Albanese, G., and R. Pergher. *In the Society of Fascists: Acclamation, Acquiescence, and Agency in Mussolini's Italy*. New York: Palgrave Macmillan, 2012.

Antolini, Paola. *Donne in guerra, 1915 - 1918: la Grande Guerra attraverso l'analisi e le testimonianze di una terra di confine*. Rovereto: Centro Studi Judicaria, 2007.

Arthurs, Joshua, Michael R. Ebner, and Kate Ferris. *The Politics of Everyday Life in Fascist Italy: Outside the State?* New York: Palgrave Macmillan, 2017.

Audenino, Patrizia. *Il prezzo della libertà Gaetano Salvemini in esilio, 1925–1949*. Soveria Mannelli Catanzaro: Rubbettino, 2009.

Audenino, Patrizia. *La casa perduta: la memoria dei profughi del Novecento*. Roma: Carocci editore, 2015.

Barrera, Giulia. "Mussolini's Colonial Race Laws and State-Settler Relations in Africa Orientale Italiana (1935–41)." *Journal of Modern Italian Studies Journal of Modern Italian Studies* 8, no. 3 (2010): 425–43.

Selected Bibliography and Suggested Readings

Bartolini, Stefania Bartoloni. *Donne di fronte alla guerra: Pace, diritti e democrazia*. Roma; Bari: Laterza, 2017.

Bauerkämper, Arnd, and Grzegorz Rossoliński-Liebe. *Fascism without Borders Transnational Connections and Cooperation between Movements and Regimes in Europe from 1918 to 1945*. New York: Berghahn Books, 2017.

Belzer, A. *Women and the Great War: Femininity under Fire in Italy*. Basingstoke: Palgrave Macmillan, 2010.

Ben-Ghiat, Ruth. *Fascist Modernities: Italy, 1922–1945*. Berkeley: University of California Press, 2004.

Bentivegna, Rosario, and Michela Ponzani. *Senza far di necessità virtù: memorie di un antifascista*. Torino: Einaudi, 2011.

Bentivegna, Rosario, and Alessandro Portelli. *Achtung banditen!: prima e dopo via Rasella*. Milano: Mursia, 2004.

Bentivegna, Rosario, and Bruno Vespa. *Via Rasella: la storia mistificata: carteggio con Bruno Vespa*. Roma: Manifestolibri, 2006.

Benadusi, Lorenzo. *Il nemico dell'uomo nuovo: l'omosessualità nell'esperimento totalitario fascista*. Milano: Feltrinelli, 2005.

Benadusi, Lorenzo. *The Enemy of the New Man: Homosexuality in Fascist Italy*. Madison: The University of Wisconsin Press, 2012.

Benadusi, Lorenzo, and Giorgio Caravale. *George L. Mosse's Italy: Interpretation, Reception, and Intellectual Heritage*. Basingstoke: Palgrave Macmillan, 2014.

Berezin, Mabel. *Making the Fascist Self: The Political Culture of Interwar Italy*. Ithaca, NY: Cornell University Press, 1997.

Bevilacqua, Piero. *Le Campagne del Mezzogiorno tra fascismo e dopoguerra: il caso della Calabria*. Torino: Einaudi, 1980.

Bezza, Bruno, and Giovanna Procacci, eds. *Stato e classe operaia in Italia durante la prima guerra mondiale*. Milano: FrancoAngeli, 1983.

Bezza, Bruno, and Giovanna Procacci, eds. *Lezioni sull'Italia repubblicana*. Donzelli Editore, 1994.

Bianchi, Bruna. *Crescere in tempo di guerra. Il lavoro e la prostesta dei ragazzi in Italia 1915–1918*. Libreria Editrice Cafoscarina, 2016.

Bianchi, Bruna. *La follia e la fuga: nevrosi di guerra, diserzione e disobbedienza nell'esercito italiano (1915–1918)*. Roma: Bulzoni Ed., 2001.

Bianchi, Bruna, and Geraldine Ludbrook. *Living War, Thinking Peace (1914–1924): Women's Experiences, Feminist Thought, and International Relations*. Newcastle upon Tyne: Cambridge Scholars Publishing, 2016.

Bono, Salvatore. *Morire per questi deserti: lettere di soldati italiani dal fronte libico: 1911–1912*. Catanzaro: Abramo, 1992.

Bosworth, R. J. B. *Mussolini's Italy: Life under the Dictatorship 1915–1945*. London: Allen Lane, 2005.

Bosworth, R. J. B. *Mussolini*. London: Arnold, 2002.

Bosworth, R. J. B. *The Italian Dictatorship: Problems and Perspectives in the Interpretation of Mussolini and Fascism*. London: Arnold, 2007.

Bosworth, R. J. B., and Patrizia Dogliani. *Italian Fascism: History, Memory and Representation*. London; New York: Palgrave Macmillan, 2016.

Bravo, Anna, and Anna Maria Bruzzone. *In guerra senza armi: storie di donne: 1940–1945*. Roma: Laterza, 1995.

Bravo, Anna, Caterina Caravaggi, and Teresa Mattei. *La prima volta che ho votato: le donne di Piacenza e le elezioni del 1946*. Piacenza: Scritture, 2006.

Bravo, Anna, and Silvia Paggi. *Storia e memoria di un massacro ordinario*. Roma: Manifestolibri, 1996.

Bravo, Anna, and Lucetta Scaraffia. *Donne del '900*. Firenze: Liberal Libri, 1999.

Braybon, Gail. *Evidence, History and the Great War: Historians and the Impact of 1914–18*. Berghahn Books, 2003.

Brunetta, Gian Piero. *Il cinema neorealista italiano: Da "Roma città aperta" a "I soliti ignoti."* Roma: Laterza, 2014.

Budani, Donna M. *Italian Women's Narratives of Their Experiences during World War II*. Lewiston, NY: Edwin Mellen Press, 2003.

Caffarena, Fabio. *Lettere dalla Grande Guerra: scritture del quotidiano, monumenti della memoria, fonti per la storia: il caso italiano*. Milano: Unicopli, 2005.

Caffarena, Fabio, Rosalba Sapuppo, and Carlo Stiaccini. *La Grande Guerra in archivio: testimonianze scritte e fotografiche*. Università di Genova, Centro Stampa, 2006.

Caldwell, Lesley. *Italian Family Matters: Women, Politics and Legal Reform*. Basingstoke Macmillan, 1991.

Camanni, Enrico. *Il fuoco e il gelo: La Grande Guerra sulle montagne*. Roma: Laterza, 2016.

Canali, Mauro. *Il delitto Matteotti*. Bologna: Il Mulino, 2015.

Canali, Mauro. "The Matteotti Murder and the Origins of Mussolini's Totalitarian Fascist Regime in Italy." *Journal of Modern Italian Studies* 14, no. 2 (2009): 143–67.

Cannistraro, Philip V, Renzo De Felice, Giovanni Ferrara, and Editori Laterza. *La fabbrica del consenso: fascismo e mass media*. Bari: Laterza, 1975.

Cassamagnaghi, Silvia. *Operazione spose di guerra: storie d'amore e di emigrazione*. Milano: Feltrinelli, 2014.

Cavaciocchi, Alberto, and Andrea Ungari. *Gli italiani in guerra*. Milano: Mursia, 2014.

Cave, Laura Delle. *Orme di guerra: lettere e cartoline dal fronte (1912–1919)*. Firenze: Polistampa, 2013.

Cecchinato, Eva. "Sotto l'uniforme: i volontari nella Grande Guerra." *Gli italiani in guerra*, 2008.

Chabod, Federico. *L'Italia Contemporanea (1918–1948)*. Torino: Einaudi, 1961.

Chang, Natasha V. *The Crisis-Woman: Body Politics and the Modern Woman in Fascist Italy*. Toronto: University of Toronto Press, 2015.

Cicchino, Enzo Antonio, and Roberto Olivo. *La grande guerra dei piccoli uomini*. Ancora, 2005.

Corner, Paul. *The Fascist Party and Popular Opinion in Mussolini's Italy*. Oxford: OUP, 2012.

Corti, Paola. *Le donne nelle campagne italiane del Novecento*. Bologna: Il Mulino, 1992.

Curli, Barbara. *Italiane al lavoro: 1914–1920*. Venezia: Marsilio, 1998.

Dagnino, Jorge. *Faith and Fascism: Catholic Intellectuals in Italy, 1925–43*. London: Palgrave Macmillan, 2017.

Davis, John Anthony, and Emiliana Pasca Noether, eds. *Italy and America, 1943–1944: Italian American and Italian American Experiences of the Liberation of the Italian Mezzogiorno*. Napoli: La città del sole, 1997.

De Felice, Renzo. *Interpretations of Fascism*. Cambridge: Harvard University Press, 1977.

De Felice, Renzo. *Mussolini il duce*. Vol. 1. Gli anni del consenso. Torino: Einaudi, 2007.

De Felice, Renzo. *Gli Anni Del Consenso, 1929–1936*. Torino: G. Einaudi, 1974.

De Felice, Renzo. *Storia degli ebrei italiani sotto il fascismo*. Torino: Mondadori Editore, 1977.

De Grazia, Victoria. *The Culture of Consent: Mass Organization of Leisure in Fascist Italy*. Cambridge: Cambridge University Press, 1981.

De Grazia, Victoria. *How Fascism Ruled Women: Italy, 1922–1945*. Berkeley: University of California Press, 1992.

Di Michele, Andrea. *Storia dell'Italia repubblicana: 1948–2008*. Milano: Garzanti, 2008.

Di Nolfo, Ennio, and Maurizio Serra. *La gabbia infranta*. Roma: Laterza, 2010.

Dogliani, Patrizia. *Il fascismo degli italiani: una storia sociale*. Turin: UTET libreria, 2008.

Domenico, Roy Palmer. *Italian Fascists on Trial, 1943–1948*. Chapel Hill: University of North Carolina Press, 2011.

Doumanis, Nicholas. *Myth and Memory in the Mediterranean: Remembering Fascism's Empire*. Basingstoke: Macmillan, 1997.

Duggan, Christopher. *Fascism and the Mafia*. New Haven: Yale University Press, 1989.

Duggan, Christopher. *Fascist Voices: An Intimate History of Mussolini's Italy*. Oxford: Oxford University Press, 2013.

Ebner, Michael R. *Ordinary Violence in Mussolini's Italy*. Cambridge: Cambridge University Press, 2010.

Ermacora, Matteo. "Assistance and Surveillance: War Refugees in Italy, 1914–1918." *Contemporary European History* 16, no. 4 (2007): 445–59.

Fabi, Lucio. *Soldati d'Italia: esperienze, storie, memorie, visioni della Grande Guerra*. Mursia, 2014.

Falasca-Zamponi, Simonetta. *Fascist Spectacle: The Aesthetics of Power in Mussolini's Italy*. Berkeley: University of California Press, 1997.

Fay, Sidney B. "Italy's Entrance into the War." Edited by Antonio Salandra. *Foreign Affairs* 10, no. 1 (1931): 92–103.

Ferris, K. *Everyday Life in Fascist Venice, 1929–40*. London: Palgrave Macmillan, 2012.

Fogu, Claudio. *The Historic Imaginary: Politics of History in Fascist Italy*. Toronto: University of Toronto Press, 2003.

Foot, John. "Via Rasella, 1944: Memory, Truth, and History." *The Historical Journal* 43, no. 4 (2000): 1173–81.

Forgacs, David. *Rethinking Italian Fascism: Capitalism, Populism and Culture*. London: Lawrence and Wishart, 1986.

Forgacs, David. *Rome Open City (Roma Città Aperta)*. London: British Film Institute, 2000.

Forgacs, David. *Italy's Margins: Social Exclusion and Nation Formation since 1861*, Cambridge: Cambridge University Press, 2014.

Gabrielli, Patrizia. *Col freddo nel cuore: uomini e donne nell'emigrazione antifascista*. Donzelli Editore, 2004.

Gabrielli, Patrizia. *Il 1946, le donne, la Repubblica*. Donzelli Editore, 2009.

Gabrielli, Patrizia. *Il primo voto: elettrici ed elette*. Roma: Castelvecchi, 2016.

Gabrielli, Patrizia. *La pace e la mimosa: l'Unione donne italiane e la costruzione politica della memoria (1944–1955)*. Roma: Donzelli, 2005.

Gallo, Patrick J. *For Love and Country: The Italian Resistance*. University Press of America, 2003.

Gentile, Emilio. "Fascism in Italian Historiography: In Search of an Individual Historical Identity." *Journal of Contemporary History* 21, no. 2 (1986): 179–208.

Gentile, Emilio. *Il culto del littorio: la sacralizzazione della politica nell'Italia fascista*. Roma: Laterza, 1993.

Gentile, Emilio. *La Grande Italia: The Myth of the Nation in the Twentieth Century*. Madison: University of Wisconsin Press, 2009.

Gentile, Emilio. *La via italiana al totalitarismo: il partito e lo Stato nel regime fascista*. Roma: NIS, 1994.

Gentile, Emilio. *Politics as Religion*. Princeton, NJ: Princeton University, 2006.

Gentile, Emilio. *Storia del partito fascista*. Roma: Laterza, 1989.

Gerbi, Sandro. *I Cosattini: Una famiglia antifascista di Udine*. Milano: Hoepli, 2016.

Gibelli, Antonio. *Il popolo bambino: infanzia e nazione dalla Grande Guerra a Salò*. Torino: G. Einaudi, 2005.

Gibelli, Antonio. *La guerra grande: Storie di gente comune*. Roma: Laterza, 2016.

Giovacchini, Saverio. "Soccer with the Dead: Mediterraneo and the Myth of Italiani Brava Gente," in *Repicturing the Second World War: Representations in Film and Television*, edited by Michael Paris, 55–69. New York: Palgrave Macmillan, 2007.

Gissi, Alessandra. *Le segrete manovre delle donne levatrici in Italia dall'unità al fascismo*. Roma: Biblink, 2006.

Giuntini, Andrea, and Daniele Pozzi. *Lettere dal fronte: Poste italiane nella grande guerra.* Rizzoli, 2015.

Gobetti, Ada, and Jomarie Alano. *Partisan Diary: A Woman's Life in the Italian Resistance,* Oxford: Oxford University Press, 2014.

Gooch, John. *The Italian Army and the First World War.* Cambridge: Cambridge University Press, 2014.

Gordon, Robert. *The Holocaust in Italian Culture, 1944–2010.* Stanford University Press, 2012.

Gori, Claudia. *Crisalidi. Emancipazioniste liberali in età giolittiana.* Milano: FrancoAngeli, 2003.

Gori, Gigliola. *Italian Fascism and the Female Body: Sport, Submissive Women and Strong Mothers.* London: Routledge, 2004.

Gribaudi, Gabriella. *Combattenti, sbandati, prigionieri: esperienze e memorie di reduci della seconda guerra mondiale.* Roma: Donzelli Editore, 2016.

Gribaudi, Gabriella. *Guerra totale: tra bombe alleate e violenze naziste : Napoli e il fronte meridionale, 1940-44.* Torino: Bollati Boringhieri, 2005.

Gribaudi, Gabriella. *Mediatori: antropologia del potere democristiano nel Mezzogiorno.* Torino: Rosenberg & Sellier, 1991.

Guidi, Laura, ed. *Vivere la guerra: percorsi biografici e ruoli di genere tra Risorgimento e primo conflitto mondiale.* Napoli: Clio Press, 2007.

Gundle, Stephen, Christopher Duggan, and Giuliana Pieri. *The Cult of the Duce: Mussolini and the Italians.* Manchester; New York: Manchester University Press, 2015.

Hametz, Maura Elise. *In the Name of Italy: Nation, Family, and Patriotism in a Fascist Court.* New York: Fordham University Press, 2012.

Helstosky, Carol. *Garlic and Oil: Politics and Food in Italy.* Oxford: Berg, 2006.

Horn, David G. *Social Bodies: Science, Reproduction, and Italian Modernity.* Princeton, NJ: Princeton University Press, 1994.

Iacovetta, Franca, and Lorenza Stradiotti. "Betrayal, Vengeance, and the Anarchist Ideal: Virgilia D'Andrea's Radical Antifascism in (American) Exile, 1928–1933." *Journal of Women's History* 25, no. 1 (2013): 85–110.

Isnenghi, Mario. *La grande guerra.* Giunti Editore, 1993.

Isnenghi, Mario, and Daniele Ceschin. *La Grande guerra: uomini e luoghi del '15–18.* Torino: UTET, 2008.

Isnenghi, Mario, and Giorgio Rochat. *La Grande Guerra: 1914–1918.* Bologna: Il Mulino, 2008.

Kertzer, David I. *The Pope and Mussolini: The Secret History of Pius XI and the Rise of Fascism in Europe.* Oxford: Oxford University Press, 2014.

Koon, Tracy H. *Believe Obey Fight: Political Socialization of Youth in Fascist Italy.* Chapel Hill, NC; London: University of North Carolina Press, 1985.

Laven, David. *Restoration and Risorgimento: Italy 1796-1870.* Oxford: Oxford University Press, 2010.

Ledeen, Michael A. "Renzo de Felice and the Controversy over Italian Fascism." *Journal of Contemporary History* 11, no. 4 (1976): 269–83.

Loparco, Fabiana. *I bambini e la guerra: il Corriere dei piccoli e il primo conflitto mondiale (1915-1918).* Firenze: Nerbini, 2011.

Mafai, Miriam. *Pane nero. Donne e vita quotidiana nella seconda guerra mondiale.* Roma: Ediesse, 2008.

Maiocchi, Roberto. *Scienza italiana e razzismo fascista.* Firenze: La nuova Italia, 1999.

Majanlahti, Anthony, and Amedeo Osti Guerrazzi. *Roma occupata 1943 - 1944: itinerari, storie, immagini.* Milano: Saggiatore, 2010.

Merz, Noemi Crain. *L'illusione della parità. Donne e questione femminile in Giustizia e Libertà e nel Partito d'azione: Donne e questione femminile in Giustizia e Libertà e nel Partito d'azione.* Milano: FrancoAngeli, 2013.

Mignone, Lisa. *The Republican Aventine and Rome's Social Order*. Ann Arbor: University of Michigan Press, 2016.

Mistry, Kaeten. *The United States, Italy and the Origins of Cold War: Waging Political Warfare, 1945-1950*. Cambridge: Cambridge University Press, 2014.

Molinari, Augusta. *Donne e ruoli femminili nell'Italia della Grande Guerra*. Milano: Selene, 2008.

Molinari, Augusta. *Una patria per le donne: la mobilitazione femminile nella Grande Guerra*. Bologna: Il Mulino, 2014.

Montanelli, Indro. *Caporetto, il Piave, la vittoria*. Milano: Rizzoli, 1977.

Monti, Augusto. *Lettere dalla grande guerra*. Boves: Araba Fenice, 2007.

Montroni, Giovanni. *La continuità necessaria: università e professori dal fascismo alla Repubblica*. Firenze: Le Monnier, 2016.

Montroni, Giovanni. "The Professors in and after the Fascist Regime. The Purges in the Universities of Italy (1944-46)." *Journal of Modern Italian Studies* 14, no. 3 (2009): 305-28.

Morgan, Philip. *Italian Fascism, 1919-45*. London: Macmillan, 1995.

Morgan, Philip. *The Fall of Mussolini: Italy, the Italians, and the Second World War*. Oxford: Oxford University Press, 2008.

Musso, Stefano. *Tra fabbrica e società: mondi operai nell'Italia del Novecento*. Feltrinelli Editore, 1999.

Omodeo, Adolfo. *Momenti della vita di guerra: dai diari e dalle lettere dei caduti 1915-1918*. Torino: Einaudi, 1968.

Painter, Borden. *Mussolini's Rome: Rebuilding the Eternal City*. New York: Palgrave Macmillan, 2016.

Passerini, Luisa. *Fascism in Popular Memory: The Cultural Experience of the Turin Working Class*. Cambridge: New York; Paris: Cambridge University Press, 1987.

Passmore, Kevin. *Women, Gender, and Fascism in Europe, 1919-45*. Manchester: Manchester University Press, 2003.

Pavan, Camillo. *In fuga dai tedeschi: l'invasione del 1917 nel racconto dei testimoni; in appendice: preti e vescovi dopo Caporetto*. Treviso: Pavan, 2004.

Pavone, Claudio. *Una guerra civile: saggio storico sulla moralità nella Resistenza*. Torino: Bollati Boringhieri editore, 1991.

Pezzino, Paolo. *Anatomia di un massacro: controversia sopra una strage tedesca*. Bologna: Il Mulino, 1997.

Pezzino, Paolo. "The Italian Resistance between History and Memory." *Journal of Modern Italian Studies* 10, no. 4 (December 1, 2005): 396-412.

Picciotto Fargion, Liliana, and Fondazione Centro di documentazione ebraica contemporanea. *Il libro della memoria: gli ebrei deportati dall'Italia, 1943-1945*. Milano: Mursia, 2011.

Pickering-Iazzi, Robin. *Mothers of Invention: Women, Italian Fascism, and Culture*. Minneapolis: University of Minnesota Press, 1995.

Pojmann, Wendy. *Italian Women and International Cold War Politics, 1944-1968*. New York: Fordham University Press, 2013.

Porciani, Elena. *Le donne nella narrativa della Resistenza: rappresentazioni del femminile e stereotipi di genere*. Catania: Villaggio Maori edizione, 2016.

Portelli, Alessandro. *Biography of an Industrial Town: Terni, Italy, 1831-2014*. Cham: Springer, 2017.

Portelli, Alessandro. *La città dell'acciaio: due secoli di storia operaia*. Roma: Donzelli Editore, 2017.

Portelli, Alessandro. *L'ordine è già stato eseguito: Roma, le Fosse Ardeatine, la memoria*. Milano: Feltrinelli, 2012.

Portelli, Alessandro, and Circolo Gianni Bosio. *Il borgo e la borgata: i ragazzi di don Bosco e l'altra Roma del dopoguerra*. Roma: Donzelli, 2002.

Procacci, Giovanna. "Popular Protest and Labour Conflict in Italy, 1915-18." *Social History* 14, no. 1 (1989): 31-58.

Procacci, Giovanna. *Soldati e prigionieri italiani nella Grande guerra: con una raccolta di lettere inedite*. Roma: Editori Riuniti, 1993.

Pugliese, Stanislao G. *Fascism, Anti-Fascism, and the Resistance in Italy: 1919 to the Present*. Lanham: Rowman & Littlefield, 2004.

Quazza, Guido, Nicola Gallerano, Enzo Forcella. *L'altro dopoguerra: Roma e il Sud 1943–1945*. Milano: FrancoAngeli, 1985.

Rasera, Fabrizio, and Camillo Zadra. *Volontari italiani nella Grande Guerra*. Rovereto: Museo storico italiano della guerra, 2008.

Reich, Jacqueline, and Piero Garofalo. *Re-Viewing Fascism: Italian Cinema, 1922–1943*. Bloomington: Indiana University Press, 2002.

Revelli, Nuto. *Le due guerre: guerra fascista e guerra partigiana*. Torino: Einaudi, 2003.

Revelli, Nuto, and Aldo Garosci. *La guerra dei poveri*. Torino: Einaudi, 1962.

Roberts, David. "Italian Fascism: New Light on the Dark Side." Edited by Davide Rodogno, Adrian Belton, Michele Sarfatti, John Tedeschi, Anne C. Tedeschi, George Talbot, and Manuela A. Williams. *Journal of Contemporary History* 44, no. 3 (2009): 523–33.

Rochat, Giorgio. *Guerre italiane*. Torino: Einaudi, 2005.

Rodogno, Davide. *Fascism's European empire: Italian occupation during the Second World War*. Cambridge; New York: Cambridge University Press, 2008.

Romagnoli, G. Franco. *The Bicycle Runner: A Memoir of Love, Loyalty, and the Italian Resistance*. New York: Thomas Dunne Books, 2009.

Romani, Gabriella. *Postal Culture: Writing and Reading Letters in Post-Unification Italy*. Toronto: University of Toronto Press, 2013.

Rossi-Doria, Anna. *Diventare cittadine: il voto delle donne in Italia*. Firenze: Giunti, 1996.

Row, Thomas. "Mobilizing the Nation: Italian Propaganda in the Great War." *The Journal of Decorative and Propaganda Arts* 24 (2002): 141–69.

Ruth Ben-Ghiat. *Fascist Modernities: Italy, 1922–1945*. Berkeley: University of California Press, 2001.

Saba, Marina Addis. *Partigiane: le donne della Resistenza*. Milano: Mursia, 2007.

Sarfatti, Michele. *Gli ebrei nell'Italia fascista: vicende, identità, persecuzione*. Torino: Einaudi, 2000.

Sarfatti, Michele. *The Jews in Mussolini's Italy: From Equality to Persecution*. Madison: University of Wisconsin Press, 2006.

Scala, Spencer Di. *Italian Socialism: Between Politics and History*. University of Massachusetts Press, 1996.

Serra, Ilaria. "Italy: America's War Bride. How Life Magazine Feminized Italy in the 1950s." *Italica* 86, no. 3 (2009): 452–70.

Sica, Emanuele, and Richard Carrier. *Italy and the Second World War: Alternative Perspectives*. Leiden; Boston: Brill, 2018.

Slaughter, Jane. *Women and the Italian Resistance, 1943–1945*. Denver: Arden Press, 1997.

Smith, Bradley F, and Elena Aga Rossi. *La Resa Tedesca in Italia*. Milano: Feltrinelli, 1979.

Smith, Bradley F, and Elena Aga Rossi. *Operation sunrise*. New York: Basic Books, 1979.

Soddu, Paolo. *La via italiana alla democrazia: Storia della Repubblica 1946–2013*. Bari; Roma: Laterza, 2017.

Spackman, Barbara. *Fascist Virilities: Rhetoric, Ideology, and Social Fantasy in Italy*. University of Minneapolis: Minnesota Press, 1996.

Spitzer, Leo. *Lettere di prigionieri di guerra italiani (1915–1918)*. Bollati Boringhieri, 2014.

Steininger, Rolf. *South Tyrol: A Minority Conflict of the Twentieth Century*. New Brunswick, NJ: Transaction Publishers, 2003.

Stern, Mario Rigoni. *1915–1918: la guerra sugli altipiani: testimonianze di soldati al fronte*. Vicenza: N. Pozza, 2000.

Talamo, Giuseppe. *Da Cavour alla fine della prima guerra mondiale*. Torino: Unione, 1965.

Tambor, Molly. *The Lost Wave: Women and Democracy in Postwar Italy*. Oxford: Oxford University Press, 2014.

Thompson, Mark. *The White War: Life and Death on the Italian Front 1915–1919*. London: Basic Books, 2009.

Tomasoni, Giuseppe, and Carmelo Nuvoli. *La Grande Guerra Raccontata dalle cartoline*. Trento: Arca, 2004.

Torriglia, Anna Maria. *Broken Time, Fragmented Space: A Cultural Map for Postwar Italy*. Toronto: University of Toronto Press, 2002.

Triolo, Nancy Elizabeth. *The Angelmakers: Fascist pro-Natalism and the Normalization of Midwives in Sicily*. PhD Diss, University of California-Berkeley, 1989.

Ungari, Andrea. *The Libyan War 1911–1912*. Newcastle-Upon-Tyne: Cambridge Scholars Publishing, 2014.

Ventresca, Robert. *From Fascism to Democracy: Culture and Politics in the Italian Election of 1948*. Toronto: University of Toronto Press, 2004.

Ventrone, Angelo. *Piccola storia della Grande Guerra*. Roma: Donzelli, 2005.

Villani, Luciano. *Le Borgate del fascismo: Storia urbana, politica e sociale della periferia romana*. Milano: Ledizione, 2012.

Vivarelli, Roberto. *Il fallimento del liberalismo: studi sulle origini del fascismo*. Saggi; 211; Bologna: Il Mulino, 1981.

Wagstaff, Christopher. *Italian Neorealist Cinema: An Aesthetic Approach*. Toronto: University of Toronto Press, 2007.

Wilcox, Vanda. *Morale and the Italian Army during the First World War*. Cambridge: Cambridge University Press, 2016.

Wilcox, Vanda. "'Weeping Tears of Blood': Exploring Italian Soldiers' Emotions in the First World War." *Modern Italy* 17, no. 2 (May 1, 2012): 171–84.

Williams, I. *Allies and Italians under Occupation: Sicily and Southern Italy 1943–45*. Springer, 2013.

Willson, Perry. *Peasant Women and Politics in Fascist Italy: The Massaie Rurali*. New York: Routledge, 2002.

Willson, Perry. *The Clockwork Factory: Women and Work in Fascist Italy*. Oxford; New York: Clarendon Press; Oxford University Press, 1993.

Zamagni, Vera. *Come perdere la guerra e vincere la pace: l'economia italiana tra guerra e dopoguerra: 1938–1947*. Bologna: Il Mulino, 1997.

Zuccotti, Susan. *Italians and The Holocaust*. Lincoln: University of Nebraska Press, 1996.

Zuccotti, Susan. *Under His Very Windows: The Vatican and the Holocaust in Italy*. New Haven; London: Yale University Press, 2002.

Part Four: The Republic

Aga Rossi, Elena, and Victor Zaslavsky. *Togliatti e Stalin: il PCI e la politica estera staliniana negli archivi di Mosca*. Bologna: Il Mulino, 2007.

Aga-Rossi, Elena, and Gaetano Quagliariello. *L'altra faccia della luna: i rapporti tra PCI, PCF e Unione Sovietica*. Bologna: Il Mulino, 2002.

Agnew, John A. *Place and Politics in Modern Italy*. Chicago: University of Chicago Press, 2002.

Al-Azar, Rima. "Italian Immigration Policies - The Metaphor of Water." *The SAIS Europe Journal of Global Affairs*, April 1, 2006.

Amato, Fabio. *Atlante dell'immigrazione in Italia*. Roma: Carocci, 2008.

Amatori, Franco. *Storia dell'IRI. 2*. Roma; Bari: Laterza, 2013.

Amatori, Franco, and Andrea Colli. *Il "miracolo" economico e il ruolo dell'IRI 1949-1972*. Roma: Laterza, 2013.

Andall, Jacqueline, and Derek Duncan. *National Belongings: Hybridity in Italian Colonial and Postcolonial Cultures*. Bern; Oxford: Peter Lang, 2010.

Baumeister, Martin, Bruno Bonomo, and Dieter Schott et. al. *Cities Contested: Urban Politics, Heritage, and Social Movements in Italy and West Germany in the 1970s*. Frankfurt: Campus Verlag, 2017.

Babini, Valeria Paola. *Liberi tutti: manicomi e psichiatri in Italia: una storia del Novecento*. Bologna: Il Mulino, 2011.

Badino, Anna. *Strade in salita: figlie e figli dell'immigrazione meridionale al Nord*. Roma: Carocci, 2012.

Badino, and Inaudi. *Migrazioni femminili attraverso le Alpi. Lavoro, famiglia, trasformazioni culturali nel secondo dopoguerra: Lavoro, famiglia, trasformazioni culturali nel secondo dopoguerra*. Milano: FrancoAngeli, 2013.

Banti, Alberto Mario. *Le questioni dell'età contemporanea*. Roma: Laterza, 2014.

Baratieri, Daniela. *Memories and Silences Haunted by Fascism: Italian Colonialism, MCMXXX-MCMLX*. Bern: Peter Lang, 2010.

Barone, Giuseppe. *Mezzogiorno e modernizzazione elettricità, irrigazione e bonifica nell'Italia contemporanea*. Torino: G. Einaudi, 1986.

Beer, Marina, Anna Benvenuti Papi, Gérard Delille, Maria Pia Di Bella, Lorenzo Fabbri, Ida Fazio, Daniela Lombardi, et al. *Storia Del Matrimonio*. Roma: Laterza, 1996.

Benelli, Elena. "Migration Discourses in Italy." *Conserveries Mémorielles. Revue Transdisciplinaire*, no. #13 (March 10, 2013).

Bernardi, Emanuele, and Paul Ginsborg. *La riforma agraria in Italia e gli Stati Uniti guerra fredda, Piano Marshall e interventi per il Mezzogiorno negli anni del centrismo degasperiano*. Bologna: Il Mulino, 2006.

Bevilacqua, Piero. *Breve storia dell'Italia meridionale: dall'Ottocento a oggi*. Roma: Donzelli, 1993.

Bevilacqua, Piero. *Lezioni sull'Italia repubblicana*. Roma: Donzelli Editore, 1994.

Bevilacqua, Piero, Andreina De Clementi, and Emilio Franzina. *Storia dell'emigrazione italiana*. Roma: Donzelli Editore, 2001.

Bianchi, Ornella. *L'impresa agro-industriale: una economia urbana e rurale tra XIX e XX secolo*. Bari: Edizioni Dedalo, 2000.

Bini, Elisabetta. *La potente benzina italiana: guerra fredda e consumi di massa tra Italia, Stati Uniti e terzo mondo, 1945–1973*. Roma: Carocci editore, 2013.

Boneschi, Marta, and Mondadori. *Senso: i costumi sessuali degli italiani dal 1880 ad oggi*. Milano: Mondadori, 2000.

Bono, Paola, and Sandra Kemp. *Italian Feminist Thought: A Reader*. Oxford; Cambridge, Mass.: Blackwell, 1991.

Bouscaren, A. T. *European Economic Community Migrations*. The Hague: Nijhoff, 1969.

Bracke, Maud Anne. *Women and the Reinvention of the Political: Feminism in Italy, 1968–1983*. New York: Routledge, 2014.

Bravo, Anna. *A colpi di cuore: storie del sessantotto*. Bari: Laterza, 2008.

Bravo, Anna, and Lucetta Scaraffia. *Donne del '900*. Firenze: Liberal Libri, 1999.

Breccia, Alessandro, ed. *Le istituzioni universitarie e il Sessantotto*. Bologna: CLUEB, 2013.

Brogi, Alessandro. *A Question of Self-Esteem: The United States and the Cold War Choices in France and Italy, 1944–1958*. Westport, CT: Praeger, 2001.

Brunetta, Gian Piero. *Il cinema neorealista italiano: Da "Roma città aperta" a "I soliti ignoti."* Roma; Bari: Laterza, 2014.

Brunetta, Gian Piero, Rob Kroes, and David W Ellwood. *Hollywood in Europe: Experience of a Cultural Hegemony*. Amsterdam: VU University Press, 1994.

Brunetta, Renato. "Italy's Other Left." *Daedalus* 130, no. 3 (2001): 25–45.

Bull, A., and M. Gilbert. *The Lega Nord and the Politics of Secession in Italy*. Ebook: Gordonsville: Palgrave Macmillan, 2001.

Bull, Anna Cento. *Social Identities and Political Cultures in Italy: Catholic, Communist, and Leghist Communities Between Civicness and Localism*. New York: Berghahn Books, 2000.

Selected Bibliography and Suggested Readings

Bull, Anna Cento. *Speaking Out and Silencing: Culture, Society and Politics in Italy in the 1970s*. London: Routledge, 2017.

Bull, Martin J., and James L. Newell. *Italian Politics: Adjustment Under Duress*. Cambridge: Polity, 2005.

Burgio, Alberto, ed. *Nel nome della razza: il razzismo nella storia d'Italia, 1870–1945*. Bologna: Il Mulino, 2000.

Calandri, Elena, Daniele Caviglia, and Antonio Varsori. *Détente in Cold War Europe: Politics and Diplomacy in the Mediterranean and the Middle East*. London: I.B.Tauris, 2016.

Canale, Rosaria Rita, and Oreste Napolitano. "National Disparities and Cyclical Dynamics in Italy (1892–2007): Was the Mezzogiorno a Sheltered Economy?" *International Review of Applied Economics* 29, no. 3 (May 2015): 328–48.

Cardini, Antonio. *Il miracolo economico italiano, 1958–1963*. Bologna: Il Mulino, 2006.

Carvalho, Joao. *Impact of Extreme Right Parties on Immigration Policy: Comparing Britain, France and Italy*. London: Routledge, 2013.

Cassamagnaghi, Silvia. *Immagini dall'America: mass media e modelli femminili nell'Italia del secondo dopoguerra, 1945–1960*. Milano: FrancoAngeli, 2007.

Castagnoli, Adriana. *La guerra fredda economica: Italia e Stati Uniti 1947–1989*. Rome: Laterza, 2015.

Castronovo, Valerio. *FIAT: una storia del capitalismo italiano*. Milano: Rizzoli, 2005.

Castronovo, Valerio. *L'Italia del miracolo economico*. Roma: Laterza, 2014.

Castronovo, Valerio. *Storia economica d'Italia: dall'Ottocento ai giorni nostri*. Torino: Einaudi, 2013.

Caviglia, Daniele, and Massimiliano Cricco. *La diplomazia italiana e gli equilibri mediterranei: la politica mediorientale dell'Italia dalla guerra dei sei giorni al conflitto dello Yom Kippur (1967–1973)*. Soveria Mannelli: Rubbettino Editore, 2006.

Cazzullo, Aldo. *I ragazzi che volevano fare la rivoluzione: 1968–1978, storia di Lotta continua*. Milano: A. Mondadori, 2015.

Ceccagno, Antonella. *City Making and Global Labor Regimes: Chinese Immigrants and Italy's Fast Fashion Industry*. Cham: Springer, 2017.

Cento Bull, Anna, and Mark Gilbert. *The Lega Nord and the Northern Question in Italian Politics*. New York: Palgrave, 2001.

Cestaro, Antonio. *"Chiesa e società nel Mezzogiorno moderno e contemporaneo,"* Napoli: Ed. scientifiche italiane, 1995.

Chiarotto, Francesca. *Aspettando il Sessantotto: continuità e fratture nelle culture politiche italiane dal 1956 al 1968*. Torino: Accademia University Press, 2017.

Chiesi, Antonio M., and Deborah De Luca. "Imprenditori immigrati in Italia: il problema della dimensione e dell'efficienza." *Quaderni di Sociologia*, no. 58 (June 1, 2012): 41–65.

Chubb, Judith. *Patronage, Power, and Poverty in Southern Italy: A Tale of Two Cities*. Cambridge: Cambridge University Press, 2009.

Cipolletta, Innocenzo, Paolo Sylos Labini, and Ilvo Diamanti. *Saggio sulle classi sociali*. Roma: Laterza, 2015.

Cohen, Jon, and Giovanni Federico. *The Growth of the Italian Economy, 1820–1960*. Cambridge: Cambridge University Press, 2001.

Colarizi, Simona. *Biografia della Prima Repubblica*. Roma: Laterza, 1996.

Colella, Francesca. *Napoli frontale nel Sessantotto: narrazioni di rivolte e speranze*. Napoli: Libreria Dante & Descartes, 2008.

Colombo, Asher, and Giuseppe Sciortino. *Gli immigrati in Italia*. Bologna: Il Mulino, 2004.

Colombo, E., and P. Rebughini. *Children of Immigrants in a Globalized World: A Generational Experience*. Houndmills, Basingstoke: Palgrave Macmillan, 2012.

Colucci, Michele. *Lavoro in movimento: l'emigrazione italiana in Europa, 1945–57*. Roma: Donzelli, 2008.

Cova, Alberto. *Economia, lavoro e istituzioni nell'Italia del Novecento: scritti di storia economica.* Milano: Vita e Pensiero, 2002.

Crainz, Guido. *Autobiografia di una repubblica: le radici dell'Italia attuale.* Roma: Donzelli Editore, 2009.

Crainz, Guido. *Storia del miracolo italiano: culture, identità, trasformazioni fra anni cinquanta e sessanta.* Roma: Donzelli Editore, 2005.

Craveri, Piero, and Gaetano Quagliariello. *L'antiamericanismo in Italia e in Europa nel secondo dopoguerra.* Soveria Mannelli, Catanzaro: Rubbettino, 2004.

Currie, Samantha. *Gender and Migration in 21st Century Europe.* London: Routledge, 2016.

Dagrada, Elena. *Cinema e Storia 2016: Anni Cinquanta: Il decennio più lungo del secolo breve.* Rubbettino Editore, 2017.

Daniele, Vittorio. *Una modernizzazione difficile: l'economia della Calabria oggi.* Soveria Mannelli: Rubbettino Editore, 2002.

Daniele, Vittorio. *Ritardo e crescita in Calabria: un'analisi economica.* Soveria Mannelli: Rubbettino Editore, 2005.

Daniele, Vittorio, and Paolo Malanima. *Il divario Nord-Sud in Italia, 1861–2011.* Soveria Mannelli: Rubbettino Editore, 2011.

De Grazia, Victoria. *Irresistible Empire: America's Advance through Twentieth-Century Europe.* Cambridge, London: The Belknap Press of Harvard University Press, 2006.

Derossi, Laura, Anna Bravo. *1945, il voto alle donne.* Milano: FrancoAngeli, 1998.

Di Nolfo, Ennio. *La guerra fredda e l'Italia: 1941–1989.* Firenze: Polistampa, 2010.

Diamanti, Ilvo. *La Lega: geografia, storia e sociologia di un nuovo soggetto politico.* Roma: Donzelli, 1993.

Drake, Richard. "Catholics and the Italian Revolutionary Left of the 1960s." *The Catholic Historical Review* 94, no. 3 (2008): 450–75.

Drake, Richard. "Why the Moro Trials Have Not Settled the Moro Murder Case: A Problem in Political and Intellectual History." *The Journal of Modern History* 73, no. 2 (2001): 359–78.

Duggan, Christopher, and Christopher Wagstaff. *Italy in the Cold War: Politics, Culture and Society 1948–1958.* Oxford: Berg Publishers, 1995.

Einaudi, Luca. *Le politiche dell'immigrazione in Italia dall'unità a oggi.* Roma: Laterza, 2007.

Ellwood, David William. *L'alleato nemico: la politica dell'occupazione anglo-americana in Italia: 1943–1946.* Milano: Feltrinelli, 1977.

Fabrizio, De Donno, and Neelam Srivastava. "Colonial and Postcolonial Italy." *Interventions: Journal of Postcolonial Studies* 8, no. 3.

Faenza, Roberto, and Marco Fini. *Gli Americani in Italia.* Milano: Feltrinelli, 1976.

Faggioli, Massimo. "The new elites of Italian Catholicism: 1968 and the New Catholic Movements." *The Catholic Historical Review* 98, no. 1 (2012): 18–40.

Failla, Sergio. *Il Sessantotto dei giovani leoni.* Catania: Zerobook, 2016.

Failla, Sergio, and Pina La Villa. *I Sessantotto di Sicilia.* Ebook: Catania: Zerobook, 2016.

Fantoni, Gianluca. "After the Fall: Politics, the Public Use of History and the Historiography of the Italian Communist Party, 1991–2011." *Journal of Contemporary History* 49, no. 4 (2014): 815–36.

Fasano, Nicoletta, and Mario Renosio. *I giovani e la politica: il lungo '68.* Torino: EGA, 2002.

Fauri, Francesca. *Il Piano Marshall e l'Italia.* Bologna: Il Mulino, 2010.

Favilli, Paolo. *Marxismo e storia: saggio sull'innovazione storiografica in Italia (1945–1970).* Milano: FrancoAngeli, 2006.

Ferrante, Lucia, Maura Palazzi, and Gianna Pomata, eds. *Ragnatele di rapporti patronage e reti di relazione nella storia delle donne.* Torino: Rosenberg & Sellier, 1988.

Fiore, Teresa. *Pre-Occupied Spaces: Remapping Italy's Transnational Migrations and Colonial Legacies.* New York: Fordham University Press, 2017.

Fiume, Giovanna. "Women's History and Gender History: The Italian Experience." *Modern Italy* 10, no. 2 (November 2005): 207.

Flores, Marcello, and Alberto De Bernardi. *Il Sessantotto*. Bologna: Il Mulino, 2003.

Foot, John. *Milan Since the Miracle: City, Culture and Identity*. Oxford; New York: Berg Publishers, 2001.

Forgacs, David. *Italian Culture in the Industrial Era, 1880–1980: Cultural Industries, Politics, and the Public*. Manchester: Manchester University Press, 1990.

Forgacs, David, and Stephen Gundle. *Mass Culture and Italian Society from Fascism to the Cold War*. Bloomington: Indiana University Press, 2007.

Forgacs, David, and Robert Lumley. *Italian Cultural Studies: An Introduction*. Oxford: Oxford University Press, 1996.

Fortunato, Mario, and Salah Methnani. *Immigrato*. Milano: Bompiani, 2012.

Francesco, Antonino De. *The Antiquity of the Italian Nation: The Cultural Origins of a Political Myth in Modern Italy, 1796–1943*. Oxford. Oxford University Press 2013.

Franzosi, Roberto. *The Puzzle of Strikes: Class and State Strategies in Postwar Italy*. Cambridge: Cambridge University Press, 2006.

Gabrielli, Patrizia. *Il 1946, le donne, la Repubblica*. Roma: Donzelli Editore, 2009.

Gabrielli, Patrizia. *La pace e la mimosa: l'Unione donne italiane e la costruzione politica della memoria (1944–1955)*. Roma: Donzelli, 2005.

Galante, Severino. *La politica del PCI Partito Comunista Italiano e il Patto Atlantico*. Padua: Marsilio, 1973.

Galati, Vito G. *Storia della Democrazia cristiana*. Roma: Ed. 5 lune, 1955.

Gallo, Stefano. *Senza attraversare le frontiere: le migrazioni interne dall'unità a oggi*. Roma: Laterza, 2012.

Garelli, Franco. *La Chiesa in Italia*. Bologna: Il Mulino, 2007.

Gattinara, Pietro Castelli. *The Politics of Migration in Italy: Perspectives on Local Debates and Party Competition*. Abingdon; New York: Routledge, 2016.

Gattinara, Pietro Castelli. "The 'Refugee Crisis' in Italy as a Crisis of Legitimacy." *Contemporary Italian Politics* 9, no. 3 (September 2, 2017): 318–31.

Gehler, Michael, and Wolfram Kaiser. *Christian Democracy in Europe Since 1945*. London; New York: Routledge, 2004.

Giachetti, Diego. *Oltre il Sessantotto prima, durante e dopo il movimento*. Pisa: BFS, 1998.

Giarrizzo, Giuseppe. *Mezzogiorno senza meridionalismo: la Sicilia, lo sviluppo, il potere*. Venezia: Marsilio, 1992.

Graziani, Augusto. *L'economia italiana: 1945–1970*. Bologna: Il Mulino, 1972.

Gribaudi, Gabriella. *A Eboli: il mondo meridionale in cent'anni di trasformazioni*. Venezia: Marsilio editori, 1990.

Gribaudi, Gabriella. *Donne, uomini, famiglie: Napoli nel Novecento*. Napoli: L'ancora, 1999.

Gribaudi, Gabriella. "Images of the South: The Mezzogiorno as Seen by Insiders and Outsiders," in *New History of the Italian South: The Mezzogiorno Revisited*, edited by Robert Lumley and Jonathan Morris, 83–113. Exeter, Devon, UK: University of Exeter Press, 1997.

Gualtieri, Roberto. *L'Italia dal 1943 al 1992: DC e PCI nella storia della Repubblica*. Roma: Carocci, 2006.

Gualtieri, Roberto, Carlo Spagnolo, and Ermanno Taviani. *Togliatti nel suo tempo*. Roma: Carocci, 2007.

Gundle, Stephen. *Death and the Dolce Vita: The Dark Side of Rome in the 1950s*. Edinburgh: Canongate Books, 2011.

Gundle, Stephen, and Simon Parker. *The New Italian Republic: From the Fall of the Berlin Wall to Berlusconi*. London: Routledge, 1996.

Henninger, Max. "The Postponed Revolution: Reading Italian Insurrectionary Leftism as Generational Conflict." *Italica* 83, no. 3/4 (2006): 629–48.

Hilwig, Stuart J. *Italy and 1968: Youthful Unrest and Democratic Culture*. Basingstoke: Palgrave Macmillan, 2009.

Jobs, Richard Ivan. *Backpack Ambassadors: How Youth Travel Integrated Europe*. Chicago: University of Chicago Press, 2017.

Jori, Francesco. *Dalla Liga alla Lega: storia, movimenti, protagonisti*. Venezia: Marsilio, 2009.

Krause, Elizabeth L. "Encounters with the 'Peasant': Memory Work, Masculinity, and Low Fertility in Italy." *American Ethnologist* 32, no. 4 (2005): 593–617.

Kuruvilla, Gabriella, Ingy Mubiayi, Igiaba Scego, and Lalia Wadua. *Pecore Nere*. Roma: Laterza, 2011.

La Villa, Pina. "I Sessantotto di Sicilia: linee d'indagine." *Annali Istituto Gramsci. N. 2-3 / 1998-1999, 1998 N. 2-3 / 1998-1999*, no. 2–3 (1998): 1000–1026.

LaPalombara, Joseph. *Democracy, Italian Style*. New Haven: Yale University Press, 1989.

Leonardi, Robert, and Douglas A. Wertman. *Italian Christian Democracy: The Politics of Dominance*. Springer, 1989.

Levy, C., and M. Roseman. *Three Postwar Eras in Comparison: Western Europe 1918–1945–1989*. Basingstoke: Palgrave, 2001.

Lombardi-Diop, Cristina. *Postcolonial Italy: Challenging National Homogeneity*. New York: Palgrave, 2012.

Lumley, Robert. *States of Emergency: Cultures of Revolt in Italy from 1968 to 1978*. New York: Verso, 1989.

Lumley, Robert, and John Foot. *Italian cityscapes: culture and urban change in contemporary Italy*. Exeter, UK: University of Exeter Press, 2004.

Lumley, Robert, and Jonathan Morris. *The New History of the Italian South: The Mezzogiorno Revisited*. Exeter: University of Exeter Press, 1997.

Lupo, Salvatore. *Storia della mafia: dalle origini ai giorni nostri*. Roma: Donzelli Editore, 2004.

Lupo, Salvatore. *Potere criminale: intervista sulla storia della mafia*. Roma: Laterza, 2010.

Lussana, Fiamma. *Il movimento femminista in Italia: esperienze, storie, memorie, 1965–1980*. Roma: Carocci, 2012.

Luzzatto, Sergio. *La crisi dell'antifascismo*. Torino: Einaudi, 2004.

Mammarella, Giuseppe. *L'Italia contemporanea, 1943–2011*. Bologna: Il Mulino, 2012.

Mammone, Andrea. "The Transnational Reaction to 1968: Neo-Fascist Fronts and Political Cultures in France and Italy." *Contemporary European History* 17, no. 2 (2008): 213–36.

Mangiameli, Stelio. *Italian Regionalism: Between Unitary Traditions and Federal Processes: Investigating Italy's Form of State*. Cham: Springer, 2014.

Mateos, Natalia Ribas, and Charito Basa. *How Filipino Immigrants in Italy Send Money Back Home: The Role of Informal Cross-Border Money Remittances in the Global Economy*. Lewiston, NY: Edwin Mellen Press, 2013.

Mellino, Miguel. *Cittadinanze postcoloniali: appartenenze, razza e razzismo in Europa e in Italia*. Roma: Carocci, 2013.

Messeri, Silvia, and Sandro Pintus. *4 novembre 1966: l'alluvione a Firenze*. Empoli: Ibiskos Editrice Risolo, 2006.

Michele, Andrea Di. *Storia dell'Italia repubblicana: 1948–2008*. Milano: Garzanti, 2008.

Mignone, Mario B. *Italy Today: Facing the Challenges of the New Millennium*. New York: Peter Lang, 2008.

Mistry, Kaeten. *The United States, Italy and the Origins of Cold War: Waging Political Warfare, 1945–1950*. Cambridge: Cambridge University Press, 2014.

Morandi, Elia. *Governare l'emigrazione: lavoratori italiani verso la Germania nel secondo dopoguerra*. Torino: Rosenberg & Sellier, 2011.

Morris, Penelope, ed. *Women in Italy, 1945–1960: An Interdisciplinary Study*. New York: Palgrave Macmillan, 2006.

Selected Bibliography and Suggested Readings

Musso, Stefano. *Tra fabbrica e società: mondi operai nell'Italia del Novecento*. Milano: Feltrinelli Editore, 1999.

Nuti, Leopoldo. *Gli Stati Uniti e l'apertura a sinistra: importanza e limiti della presenza americana in Italia*. Roma: Laterza, 1999.

Nuti, Leopoldo. *La sfida nucleare: la politica estera italiana e le armi atomiche, 1945–1991*. Bologna: Il Mulino, 2007.

Oliva, Gianni. *Un secolo d'immigrazione a Torino: storia e storie dall'Ottocento a oggi*, Torino: Edizioni del Capricorno, 2017.

Olivito, Elisa. *Gender and Migration in Italy: A Multilayered Perspective*. London: Routledge, 2017.

Palidda, Salvatore. *Racial Criminalization of Migrants in the 21st Century*. London: Routledge, 2016.

Palumbo, Patrizia. *A Place in the Sun: Africa in Italian Colonial Culture from Post-Unification to the Present*. Berkeley: University of California Press, 2003.

Panebianco, Stefania. *Sulle onde del Mediterraneo: Cambiamenti globali e risposte alle crisi migratorie*. Milano: EGEA spa, 2017.

Panichella, Nazareno. *Meridionali al Nord: migrazioni interne e società italiana dal dopoguerra ad oggi*. Bologna: Il Mulino, 2014.

Paolozzi, Letizia, and Alberto Leiss, eds. *Un paese sottosopra*. Milano: Pratiche editrice, 1999.

of International Migration and Integration, no. 43 (2018).

Parati, Graziella. *Migration Italy: The Art of Talking Back in a Destination Culture*. Toronto: University of Toronto Press, 2013.

Parati, Graziella, and Anthony Julian Tamburri. *The Cultures of Italian Migration*. Lanham Md. Rowman & Littlefield, 2011.

Passerini, Luisa. *Autobiography of a Generation: Italy, 1968*. Hanover, N.H.: University Press of New England, 1996.

Pelaja, Margherita, and Lucetta Scaraffia. *Due in una carne: Chiesa e sessualità nella storia*. Bari; Roma: Laterza, 2014.

Pezzino, Paolo. *Il paradiso abitato dai diavoli: società, élites, istituzioni nel Mezzogiorno contemporaneo*. Milano: FrancoAngeli, 1992.

Pezzino, Paolo. "The Italian Resistance between History and Memory." *Journal of Modern Italian Studies* 10, no. 4 (December 1, 2005): 396–412.

Picchietti, Virginia, and Laura A. Salsini. *Writing and Performing Female Identity in Italian Culture*. Cham: Springer, 2017.

Piccone Stella, Simonetta. *La prima generazione: ragazzi e ragazze nel miracolo economic italiano*. Milano: FrancoAngeli, 1993.

Piccone Stella, Simonetta. *Tra un lavoro e l'altro: vita di coppia nell'Italia postfordista*. Roma: Carocci, 2007.

Pickering-Iazzi, Robin, ed. *The Italian Antimafia, New Media, and the Culture of Legality*. Toronto: University of Toronto Press, 2017.

Pipitone, Daniele. "Settant'anni Dopo. Ripensare La Storia Dell'Italia Repubblicana." *Passaato e Presente*, no. 103 (January 2018): 17–46.

Pojmann, Wendy. "Emancipation or Liberation?: Women's Associations and the Italian Movement." *Historian* 67, no. 1 (Spring 2005): 73–96.

Pojmann, Wendy. *Immigrant Women and Feminism in Italy*. Ebook: Routledge, 2017.

Pojmann, Wendy. *Italian Women and International Cold War Politics, 1944–1968*. New York: Fordham Univ Press, 2013.

Pons, Silvio. *Berlinguer e la fine del comunismo*. Torino: G. Einaudi, 2006.

Pons, Silvio. *L'impossibile egemonia: l'URSS, il PCI e le origini della guerra fredda (1943–1948)*. Roma: Carocci, 1999.

Pons, Silvio, and Federico Romero. *Reinterpreting the End of the Cold War: Issues, Interpretations, Periodizations*. London: F. Cass, 2005.

Prontera, Grazia, and Sandro Rinauro. *Partire, tornare, restare? l'esperienza migratoria dei lavoratori italiani nella Repubblica federale tedesca nel secondo dopoguerra*. Milano: Guerini e associati, 2009.

Reale, Lorella. *Passioni e ragioni nelle voci del femminismo dal dopoguerra a oggi*. Roma: L. Sossella, 2008.

Riccio, Franco, and Salvo Vaccaro. *L'ingranaggio inceppato: il Sessantotto della periferia*. Palermo: ILA palma, 1992.

Ricucci, Roberta. *Second Generations on the Move in Italy: Children of Immigrants Coming of Age*. Lanham, Md: Lexington Books, 2014.

Rinauro, Sandro. *Il cammino della speranza: l'emigrazione clandestina degli Italiani nel secondo dopoguerra*. Torino: Einaudi, 2009.

Rochat, Giorgio. *Guerre italiane*. Torino: Einaudi, 2005.

Romano, Sergio. *L'Italia negli anni della guerra fredda: dal piano Marshall alla caduta del Muro*. Milano: TEA, 2005.

Rossi-Doria, Anna. *Diventare cittadine: il voto delle donne in Italia*. Firenze: Giunti, 1996.

Ruberto, Laura E., and Joseph Sciorra. *New Italian Migrations to the United States: Vols. 1–2: Politics and History Since 1945*. Champaign: University of Illinois Press, 2017.

Sabbatucci, Giovanni. *Storia d'Italia: la repubblica: 1943–1963*. Milano: Mondadori, 2011.

Saresella, Daniela, "Ecclesial Dissent in Italy in the Sixties." *Catholic Historical Review* 102, no. 1 (Winter 2016): 46–68.

Scarpellini, Emanuela. "Shopping American-Style: The Arrival of the Supermarket in Postwar Italy." *Enterprise & Society* 5, no. 4 (November 11, 2004): 625–68.

Schneider, Peter T., and Jane Schneider. *Reversible Destiny: Mafia, Antimafia, and the Struggle for Palermo*. Berkeley: University of California Press, 2003.

Serra, Ilaria. "Italy: America's War Bride. How Life Magazine Feminized Italy in the 1950s." *Italica* 86, no. 3 (2009): 452–70.

Severino, Lina, and Gabriele Licciardi. *Il Sessantotto in periferia: Catania fra il movimento studentesco e la svolta a destra degli anni Settanta: caratteri locali e tendenze nazionali*. Acireale: Bonanno, 2009.

Sigona, Nando. "The Governance of Romani People in Italy: Discourse, Policy and Practice." *Journal of Modern Italian Studies* 16, no. 5 (December 1, 2011): 590–606.

Soddu, Paolo. *La via italiana alla democrazia: Storia della Repubblica 1946–2013*. Bari; Roma: Laterza, 2017.

Sori, Ercole, and Anna Treves. *L'Italia in movimento: due secoli di migrazioni, XIX-XX*. Udine: Forum, 2008.

Spagnolo, Carlo. *La stabilizzazione incompiuta: il piano Marshall in Italia (1947–1952)*. Roma: Carocci, 2001.

Stelliferi, Paola. "Is the Personal Political for Men Too? Encounter and Conflict between 'New Left' Men and Feminist Movements in 1970s Italy." *Gender & History* 27, no. 3 (November 2015): 844–64.

Stille, Alexander. *Excellent Cadavers: The Mafia and the Death of the First Italian Republic*. New York: Pantheon, 1995.

Tambini, Damian. *Nationalism in Italian Politics: The Stories of the Northern League, 1980–2000*. London: Routledge, 2012.

Tambor, Molly. "Red Saints: Gendering the Cold War, Italy 1943–1953." *Cold War History* 10, no. 3 (August 2010): 429–56.

Tambor, Molly. *The Lost Wave: Women and Democracy in Postwar Italy*. Oxford: Oxford University Press, 2014.

Selected Bibliography and Suggested Readings

Tolomelli, Marica. *Il sessantotto: una breve storia*. Roma: Carocci, 2008.

Toniolo, Gianni, ed. *L' Italia e l'economia mondiale: dall'unità a oggi*. Venezia: Marsilio, 2013.

Torriglia, Anna Maria. *Broken Time, Fragmented Space: A Cultural Map for Postwar Italy*. Toronto: University of Toronto Press, 2002.

Tranfaglia, Nicola. "Aldo Moro E Le Culture Politiche Della Repubblica." *Aldo Moro and the Italian Republic's Political Cultures*. 55, no. 2 (April 2014): 481–94.

Turco, Livia, and Paola Tavella. *I nuovi italiani: l'immigrazione, i pregiudizi, la convivenza*. Milano: Mondadori, 2005.

Valli, Vittorio. *L'economia e la politica economica italiana dal 1945 ad oggi*. Milano: Etas libri, 1982.

Varsori, Antonio. "Cold War History in Italy." *Cold War History* 8, no. 2 (May 2008): 157.

Varsori, Antonio. *L'Italia e la fine della guerra fredda: la politica estera dei governi Andreotti (1989–1992)*. Bologna: Il Mulino, 2013.

Vecchio, Giorgio, and Paolo Trionfini. *Storia dell'Italia repubblicana (1946–2014)*. Milano: Monduzzi, 2014.

Venè, Gian Franco. *Vola colomba: vita quotidiana degli italiani negli anni del dopoguerra: 1945–1960*. Milano: Mondadori, 1990.

Ventresca, Robert. *From Fascism to Democracy: Culture and Politics in the Italian Election of 1948*. Toronto: University of Toronto Press, 2004.

Vezzoni, Cristiano, and Ferruccio Biolcati-Rinaldi. "Church Attendance and Religious Change in Italy, 1968–2010: A Multilevel Analysis of Pooled Datasets." *JSSR Journal for the Scientific Study of* Religion 54, no. 1 (2015): 100–118.

Viale, Guido. *Il 68: tra rivoluzione e restaurazione*. Rimini: Nda Press, 2008.

Voli, Stefania. *Quando il privato diventa politico: Lotta continua 1968–1976*. Roma: Edizioni associate, 2006.

Vv, Aa. *Modelli di emigrazione regionale dall'Italia centro-meridionale*. Viterbo: Sette Città, 2006.

Wagstaff, Christopher. *Italian Neorealist Cinema: An Aesthetic Approach*. University of Toronto Press, 2007.

Wanrooij, Bruno. "Youth, Generation Conflict, and Political Struggle in Twentieth-century Italy." *The European Legacy* 4, no. 1 (February 1, 1999): 72–88.

White, Steven F. *Modern Italy's Founding Fathers: The Making of a Postwar Republic*. London: Bloomsbury Academic, 2020.

Willson, Perry. *Women in Twentieth-Century Italy*. Basingstoke: Palgrave Macmillan, 2010.

Woolf, S. J, and Alastair Davidson. *L'Italia repubblicana vista da fuori (1945–2000)*. Bologna: Il Mulino, 2007.

INDEX

Index

Index

Index

Index

Index

race 123–4
   Fascist state and 170–2
   xenophobia and politics 260–3
racial legislation 171
Racketeer Influenced and Corrupt Organizations
   Act (RICO) 239
Radetzky 41, 42, 44–5
Radio Aut 228
RAI (Radiotelevisione Italiana S.p.A) 218
Raphael 7–8
Rattazzi, Urbano 54–5, 62
reconstruction (1943-48) 190–202
   constitution 193–6
   gender 201–2
   making republic 191–201
refugee camps 191
refugees 257–60
Regard, Mary Teresa 171–2
Reggio Emilia 224
regional elections of 1983 237
regionalism 63–6, 206
regional reforms 236–7
Reina, Michele 238
religions 5
   constitution 58, 194–5
   equality 194–5
   expulsion from civil society 58
   political 135
   Scalabrini missions 113
   schools and 166, 220
religious education 168
remittances 104
Renaissance 8
Repubblica Sociale Italiana (Italian Social
   Republic, RSI) 179
Republic. *See* postwar Italy
resistance and civil war (1943-1945)
   186–9
   Ardeatine massacre 189
   partisan groups and activities 187–9
   SS (Nazi police) and 188–9
   women in 186–7
restoration 3, 23–7
   constitution 193–5
revolutionary consequences 44–8
revolutions of 1820 30–1
revolutions of 1848 38–9, 41–4
right-wing violence 233
Riina, Toto 238
Risorgimento (1815-1861) 33–7
   British industrial bourgeoisie 3
   as a cultural revolution 4
   Gramsci's thoughts on 2
   historical studies 1–5
   liberal historians on 2–3
   religiosity of 5

   transnational dimension 4
   women's involvement in 4
Robin Hood mythology 200
Rocchetta, Franco 237
Rocco, Alfredo 161
Rocco e il suo fratello 218–19
Rocco law on labor contracts 161
Rognoni-La-Torre law 239
Roma Città Aperta (Rome Open City) 190
Romagnoli, Gian Franco 168
Romanelli, Raffaele 72
Roman Empire 8, 164
Rome-Berlin Axis treaty of friendship 170
Romeo, Rosario 2
Roosevelt, F. 181
Rosellini, Roberto 190
Rosselli, Carlo 159–60
Rosselli, Nello 159, 160
Rossi, Ernesto 159
Rossi, Luigi 103
Rossi, Paolo 225
Rossi, Pellegrino 43
Rossini, Gioachino 32
Royal Constitutions of 1770 24
Royal Sardinian army 41
Ruffo, Fabrizio 19, 20
rural women 88
Russia, Italian army in 175
Russo, Giovanni 215, 216

Saggio sulla rivoluzione di Napoli del 1799
   (Cuoco) 27–8
St. Peters 8
Salandra, Antonio 141, 142, 144, 146
Salsiccie (Scego) 254
San Carlo Theater 10
San Marino 24, 43
Scalabrini, Giovanni Battista 113
Scalabrini brothers 113
Scalfaro, Oscar 249
scapigliatura 119–20
Scego, Igiabo 254
School of Athens (Raphael) 7–8
schools
   Fascist state and 167–8
   postwar 219
science and society 122–5
second-generation immigrants 256
Second Sex (de Beauvoir) 229
Second World War 173–89
   Allied occupation of South 181–2
   Anglo-Australian forces 182
   Italian Jews 183–6
   Italian participation 174–80
   Nazi-Soviet pact of nonaggression 174
   Pact of Steel 174

Index

Index